SOME PROBABLE EFFECTS OF THE EXEMPTION OF IMPROVEMENTS FROM TAXATION IN THE CITY OF NEW YORK

BY

ROBERT MURRAY HAIG, Ph.D.

NEW YORK
1915

HJ
9289
N7
H2

SOME PROBABLE EFFECTS

OF THE

EXEMPTION OF IMPROVEMENTS FROM TAXATION

IN THE CITY OF NEW YORK

A REPORT
PREPARED FOR
THE COMMITTEE ON TAXATION
OF THE CITY OF NEW YORK

BY

ROBERT MURRAY HAIG, Ph.D.
INSTRUCTOR IN ECONOMICS
COLUMBIA UNIVERSITY

NEW YORK
1915

PRESS OF
CLARENCE S. NATHAN, INC.,
NEW YORK.

COMMITTEE ON TAXATION OF THE CITY OF NEW YORK

Appointed April 10, 1914

BY HONORABLE JOHN PURROY MITCHEL, MAYOR

ALFRED E. MARLING,
    Chairman

FREDERIC C. HOWE,
    Secretary

EDWIN R. A. SELIGMAN,
Chairman, Executive Committee

Robert S. Binkerd
George Cromwell*
Frank Harvey Field
Joseph N. Francolini
John J. Halleran
Hamilton Holt
Jeremiah W. Jenks
Ardolph L. Kline
Frederick C. Leubuscher
Walter Lindner
Cyrus C. Miller

George V. Mullan
Louis Heaton Pink
Lawson Purdy
David Rumsey
Oscar R. Seitz
Frederic B. Shipley
Robert E. Simon
Franklin S. Tomlin
Charles T. White
Delos F. Wilcox
Collin H. Woodward

LAURENCE ARNOLD TANZER,
    Executive Secretary.

* Resigned January 12, 1915.

PREFACE

This study is, in the main, an attempt to secure from an analysis of the assessment rolls for 1914 as much information as possible about the probable effects of the adoption of the plan to reduce the tax rate on buildings. It originated in a request by Professor Edwin R. A. Seligman, Chairman of the Executive Committee of the Committee on Taxation of the City of New York, made to Mr. Lawson Purdy, President of the Commissioners of Taxes and Assessments, for data illustrating the effects of the adoption of such a plan upon the taxes payable by the owners of high buildings, tenements and single-family dwellings. In selecting the samples which should be used for this purpose the advice of Mr. Walter Lindner and Mr. Robert E. Simon, members of the Committee on Taxation, was secured, particularly in regard to the data presented in five of the Manhattan sections (the "Sky-Scraper" Section, the Riverside Drive Section, the Fifth Avenue Section, the Section of Side Streets East of Fifth Avenue and the Mount Morris Park Section). In selecting the samples representative of conditions in the boroughs other than Manhattan, the following method was followed. The relationship of building value to the value of improved land in the given assessment section was ascertained. Then, with the aid of the insurance atlas, a homogeneous group of parcels was sought, whose relationship of building to land value approximated that of the assessment section in which it was located. This group was made the sample from that section. All of the data thus gathered were turned over to the writer for analysis and comment.

During the course of the study it seemed desirable, in order to make the investigation even more representative and to furnish information in regard to the effects in particular sections in which various members of the committee were especially interested, to add several new Manhattan samples—the three tenement sections, the two apartment house sections and four new single-family dwelling sections. As a result, the criticism may be urged that the data presented is not well balanced, too much attention being devoted to the effects upon single-family houses in Manhattan. But this should mislead no one for definite statements are made as to the relative importance of this element.

The writer desires to acknowledge his indebtedness to Mr. Purdy not only for his aid in supervising the preparation of the assessment data but also for his unfailing kindness in answering the numberless queries which inevitably arise in prosecuting an investigation of this type.

Thanks are also due to Mr. Benjamin C. Marsh for exact information furnished in regard to the nature of the proposed plan.

Finally it must be confessed that it is with some trepidation that the study is submitted, because of the lack of the opportunity for adequate checking. The mass of statistics submitted for analysis and the very limited time available made it necessary to delegate a substantial share of the arithmetical calculations. Doubtless errors will be found but the writer bespeaks the indulgence of his critics on the ground of the speed which was demanded both in writing and in printing.

ROBERT MURRAY HAIG.

New York City,
    September 8, 1915.

OUTLINE AND TABLE OF CONTENTS

		PAGE
I.	Introduction..	11
	A. The proposal...	11
	B. Possible effects of the proposed law upon the distribution of tax burdens..	12
	C. Method of ascertaining the redistribution of the tax burdens............	13
	(1) The significance of the ratio between land values and improvement values...	13
	(2) The district for which the standard ratios should be calculated....	14
	D. The standard ratios..	15
II.	Effects in the city as a whole under certain assumed conditions.............	18
	A. Effects upon the tax burdens of the boroughs........................	18
	(1) Increases and decreases..	18
	(2) The assessed values...	20
	(3) The tax rates	20
	(4) The amounts of taxes payable..................................	22
	B. Effects upon the tax burden of various types of property..............	24
	C. Summary...	24
III.	Effects in Manhattan under certain assumed conditions.....................	26
	A. Tax rates...	26
	B. Distribution of burden among the elements of the tax base.............	27
	C. Effects in the various assessment sections of the borough..............	27
	D. Effects in selected sections of the borough...........................	31
	(1) Sky-scraper section..	31
	(2) Tenement sections...	35
	(a) Upper east side section..................................	35
	(b) Rivington Street section.................................	37
	(c) Houston Street section..................................	38
	(3) Apartment sections..	40
	(a) Elevator apartment section..............................	40
	(b) Walk-up apartment section..............................	41
	(4) Sections of single family houses................................	42
	(a) Riverside Drive section..................................	42
	(b) Fifth Avenue section....................................	44
	(c) Section of side streets east of Fifth Avenue................	46
	(d) Section of side streets off Riverside Drive.................	50
	(e) Section of side streets west of Central Park................	53
	(f) Section of side streets east of Lexington Avenue............	54
	(g) Section in Washington Square district.....................	56
	(h) Mount Morris Park section	57
	E. Summary...	60
IV.	Effects in the Bronx under certain assumed conditions......................	61
	A. Tax rates...	61
	B. Distribution of the burden among the elements in the tax base..........	62
	C. Effects in the various assessment sections of the borough..............	62
	D. Effects in selected sections of the borough...........................	66
	(1) Sample district from Assessment Section Nine...................	66
	(2) " " " " " " Ten.....................	68
	(3) " " " " " " Eleven..................	70
	(4) " " " " " " Twelve..................	72
	(5) " " " " " " Fifteen..................	73
	(6) " " " " " " Seventeen...............	75
	E. Summary...	77

			PAGE
V.	Effects in Brooklyn under certain assumed conditions.		78
	A. Tax rates.		78
	B. Distribution of the burden among the elements in the tax base.		79
	C. Effects in the various assessment sections of the borough.		79
	D. Effects in selected sections of the borough.		84
		(1) Sample district from Assessment Section Five.	84
		(2) " " " " " Six.	85
		(3) " " " " " Eight.	87
		(4) " " " " " Twelve.	88
		(5) " " " " " Sixteen.	90
		(6) " " " " " Nineteen.	91
		(7) " " " " " Twenty.	93
		(8) " " " " " Twenty-three.	94
	E. Summary.		96
VI.	Effects in Queens under certain assumed conditions.		97
	A. Tax rates.		97
	B. Distribution of the burden among the elements in the tax base.		98
	C. Effects in the various assessment sections of the borough.		98
	D. Effects in selected sections of the borough.		101
		(1) Sample district from Ward One.	101
		(2) " " " " Two.	102
		(3) " " " " Three.	103
		(4) " " " " Four.	105
		(5) " " " " Five.	106
	E. Summary.		108
VII.	Effects in Richmond under certain assumed conditions.		109
	A. Tax rates.		109
	B. Distribution of the burden among the elements in the tax base.		110
	C. Effects in the various assessment sections of the borough.		110
	D. Effects in selected sections of the borough.		113
		(1) Sample district from Ward One.	113
		(2) " " " " Two.	114
		(3) " " " " Three.	116
		(4) " " " " Four.	117
		(5) " " " " Five.	119
	E. Summary.		120
VIII.	Various disturbing factors taken into account.		121
IX.	The significance of the foregoing data for certain economic classes in the community.		124
	A. Introductory.		124
		(1) The necessity of considering the incidence of the tax.	124
		(2) The incidence of the real estate tax.	124
	B. Significance for real estate owners.		128
		(1) Owners who occupy their own property.	129
		(2) Owners who rent their property.	132
		(3) Owners of vacant land.	132
	C. Significance for renters.		133
	D. Significance for prospective real estate owners.		134

APPENDIX

	PAGE
Detailed information concerning the effects of the proposed plans to untax buildings upon the taxes payable by owners of parcels in the various selected sections....	137

I. Manhattan.. 138
    Sky-scraper section.. 138
    Upper east-side tenement section.. 145
    Rivington Street section... 148
    Houston Street section... 151
    Elevator apartment section... 153
    Walk-up apartment section... 154
    Riverside Drive section.. 155
    Fifth Avenue section... 156
    Section of side streets east of Fifth Avenue............................. 159
    Section of side streets off Riverside Drive............................. 169
    Section of side streets west of Central Park............................. 173
    Section of side streets east of Lexington Avenue......................... 178
    Section in Washington Square district.................................... 181
    Mount Morris Park section.. 183

II. The Bronx... 190
    Sample district from Assessment Section Nine............................. 190
    " " " " " Ten...................................... 194
    " " " " " Eleven................................... 196
    " " " " " Twelve................................... 199
    " " " " " Fifteen.................................. 201
    " " " " " Seventeen................................ 203

III. Brooklyn... 205
    Sample district from Assessment Section Five............................. 205
    " " " " " Six...................................... 208
    " " " " " Eight.................................... 211
    " " " " " Twelve................................... 214
    " " " " " Sixteen.................................. 216
    " " " " " Nineteen................................. 220
    " " " " " Twenty................................... 224
    " " " " " Twenty-three............................. 227

IV. Queens.. 229
    Sample district from Ward One.. 229
    " " " " Two...................................... 231
    " " " " Three.................................... 234
    " " " " " Four..................................... 236
    " " " " Five..................................... 240

V. Richmond... 243
    Sample district from Ward One.. 243
    " " " " Two...................................... 246
    " " " " Three.................................... 248
    " " " " Four..................................... 251
    " " " " Five..................................... 252

I. INTRODUCTION

The proposal to reduce the tax rate on buildings involves a differentiation among the elements of the base upon which the taxes are levied. The adoption of the proposal would increase the taxes of some and decrease those of others. The problem is to determine which sections of the city, which types of property and which economic classes would pay greater taxes and which smaller in consequence of the adoption of the plan.

A. THE PROPOSAL

The manner in which it is proposed to reduce the tax rate on improvements is stated in this language in the bill as introduced in the legislature in 1915:

"The board of aldermen shall, for the year nineteen hundred and sixteen, in fixing the rate of taxation on real estate in the City of New York, exclusive of special franchises, so apportion the rate that the rate on the difference between the value of such real estate, with its improvements, and the value of such real estate wholly unimproved, assessed and provided for in section eight hundred and eighty-nine of this act, shall be ninety per centum of the rate on the value of such real estate wholly unimproved. Every year subsequent to nineteen hundred and sixteen the rate on the difference between the value of such real estate with its improvements and the value of such real estate wholly unimproved shall be still further reduced ten per centum of the rate on the value of such real estate wholly unimproved, for eight consecutive years, and in the ninth year it shall be reduced nine per centum of the rate on the value of such real estate wholly unimproved, until the rate on the difference between the value of such real estate with its improvements, and the value of such real estate wholly unimproved, shall be one per centum of the rate on the value of such real estate wholly unimproved; and thereafter the board of aldermen shall so apportion the rate of taxation that the rate on the difference between the value of such real estate with its improvements and the value of such real estate wholly unimproved, shall be one per centum of the rate on the value of such real estate wholly unimproved."*

It will be noted that this latest proposal practically eliminates the tax on buildings in ten years. The bills introduced in the years prior to 1915 contemplated the decrease of the rate on buildings to one-half that on land by a series of five annual reductions of ten per cent. each.

The proposed law, as interpreted by its sponsors, divides the tax base into three groups: in the first group are personal property and

---

* Senate Bill, No. 1336, introduced by Mr. Heffernan.

special franchises, in the second, improvements (including the improvements of "corporations"*) and in the third, land value (including land value of corporations†). At present the tax base consists of five items: ordinary land value, improvements, personal property, special franchises and real estate of corporations. It is the intent of the bill to increase the tax on group three (land) and decrease the tax on group two (improvements). The tax on group one (personal property and special franchises) is expected to remain constant. Both improvements and land are to be assessed at their full value and the share of the total burden which would fall to group two and group three is to be estimated. Then a calculation is to be made of the rates to be levied against groups two and three in order to produce the apportioned sum, the rate on improvements (group two) becoming progressively less than the rate on group three (land value) until finally eliminated except for a nominal figure. This figure, one per cent., is retained as a part of the tax base in order that the borrowing power of the city may not be affected and in order to avoid constitutional difficulties in the way of the adoption of a plan to exempt improvements entirely.

B. POSSIBLE EFFECTS OF THE PROPOSED LAW UPON THE DISTRIBUTION OF TAX BURDENS

If the tax base were homogeneous, consisting of one kind of property only, or if each element in the base were evenly distributed among all the taxpayers in proportion to each person's total holdings—each person owning part of each item in the tax base in exactly equal proportions—the adoption of the proposed plan would cause no change in the amounts paid as taxes by the individuals. There might be serious effects upon values, it is true, but each person's values would be affected in the same proportion and no discrimination between individuals would result. The principle may be illustrated by an arithmetical example. Suppose there were but three owners of taxable property in the city, A, B and C, and that their holdings were distributed as follows:

	A	B	C
Ordinary land value	$200,000	$1,000,000	$5,000
Improvements	200,000	1,000,000	5,000
Personal property	20,000	100,000	500
Real estate of corporations	20,000	100,000	500
Special franchises	20,000	100,000	500
	$460,000	$2,300,000	$11,500

In this case, in spite of the great differences in the size of the total holdings, the rate on any item in the tax base could be increased or decreased without varying the amount which each individual would be called upon to pay. Even if all the taxes were levied on land, the tax

---
*The "corporations" referred to are for the most part public utility companies, but some miscellaneous property is included.

†This plan, it should be stated, is not considered final and unamendable. There are many among the supporters of the plan who feel that special franchises should be untaxed also and the charges of the public utilities correspondingly reduced.

bill of each individual would remain the same. It is true that the value of the land might be greatly depreciated, in consequence of the heavy levy on the income from that source but each man's land would depreciate in the same proportion so that no inequality would result between individuals.

Such a condition as that described in the illustration is very different from that which actually obtains in the City of New York. Individuals own taxable property in infinitely varying proportions. Complete evenness in the distribution of ownership is almost an impossibility in a growing city. It never existed in any city after the first building was constructed and never can be more than approximated thereafter. It follows, therefore, that the proposed change will result in a redistribution of tax burdens.

C. METHOD OF ASCERTAINING THE REDISTRIBUTION OF THE TAX BURDENS

(1). *The Significance of the Ratio Between Land Values and Improvement Values*

This question then arises: What is the dividing line between the taxpayers whose bills would increase and the taxpayers whose bills would decrease in consequence of the adoption of the proposal?

It has been stated by some that to take the tax off buildings will benefit those individuals whose buildings are worth more than their land and will increase the taxes of those whose land is assessed for more than the buildings. This is evidently based upon the assumption that the relationship of the value of buildings to the value of land is one of equality, lots and houses being approximately equal in value. It is true that this relationship is present in a remarkably large number of cases. It has even been formally stated as a principle that the ideal improvement is one which equals in cost the value of the land on which it stands.* However, this is far from universal and it is not the relationship between the value of land and improvements in the City of New York at present.

Others have said that the ratio between total land values and total improvement values, be the terms equal or unequal, is the ratio which is of significance in this connection.† This is true if land and improvements are the only elements in the tax base. When there are other elements in the tax base, the significant ratio is that between the total value of those elements on which the rate is reduced and the total value of those elements on which the rate is increased. In New York, three other items are present: personal property, real estate of corporations, and special franchises. But according to the terms of the bill as introduced in 1915 and in the preceding years, special franchises

---
* Richard M. Hurd, Principles of City Land Values (N. Y., 1903), p. 97.
† *E. g.,* Edward Polak, Reduction of Tax on Buildings in the City of New York, *Annals of the American Academy,* March, 1915, p. 186, *et seq.*

are grouped with personal property and the rate on these two classes of property is expected neither to increase nor decrease. If the higher rate on land values should result in their depreciation, however, this would mean a smaller total base, and a higher rate of taxation on personal property and special franchises. For the present, nevertheless, let it be assumed that the values of land would not be diminished by virtue of the higher rate of the tax, the stimulating influence upon building and business activity being sufficient to counterbalance the depressing effect of the higher tax rate. In this case these two items, personal property and special franchises, might be eliminated from consideration. They form a separate part of the tax base, unaffected by the manipulations in the rates on the other items. The last element of the base, real estate of corporations, would be divided into its component parts, land and improvements, and added to the items of ordinary land value and improvements. It is evident that the resulting totals should be used in calculating standard relationship.

The first step, then, is to determine the standard ratio. Any piece of property in which the value of the building is greater in proportion to the value of the land than is the case in the general ratio arrived at would pay a smaller tax and any piece of property in which the land was a larger factor than in the general ratio would pay a greater tax than before.

(2). *The District for which the Standard Ratios Should be Calculated*

But the problem is further complicated by the fact that the tax rates finally extended include rates levied for county purposes as well as for general city purposes.* There are five counties within the limits of the city whose expenses are met by a tax on the property which lies in their own boundaries. This results in a variation in the tax rates from county to county. Such being the situation, the question arises as to the jurisdiction for which the standard ratios between land and buildings should be calculated. Is the relation between land and improvements in the entire city the significant relation or is the relation in the county the proper one to be used in the comparisons? This is a matter of some importance for the proportion of land value to building value varies widely among the counties.†

The plan under consideration contemplates no apportionment of general expenses among the counties on the full value basis, but rather a change in the general city rate. This involves a redistribution of the

---

* In those years when there is a direct state tax, the amount apportioned to the city is treated as a general city charge. It is, therefore, unnecessary to treat the state tax separately for the purposes of this study.

† If the general city expenses were to be apportioned among the counties on the basis of assessed valuations, buildings being included at their full value, and the discrimination between land and buildings being made in calculating the rate for each county, the result would be much greater differences between counties in the rates than at present. In this case the general ratios between land and buildings for the counties would be the factors of significance and the standard for comparison in determining whose taxes would be increased and decreased.

burden of general city taxes among the boroughs but it insures that the tax for general city purposes shall be levied on each class of property at a uniform rate over the city. This means that so far as the general city taxes are concerned, the significant relationship is that of land values to building values in the city at large.

The county taxes, being raised from the property within the county, would be redistributed in a different manner. The significant ratio here is that between land and buildings within the county limits.

To determine, therefore, whether the adoption of the proposed plan to untax buildings will increase or decrease the taxes on a particular parcel of real estate, it is necessary to take into account both the county ratio and the general city ratio. For example, assume a piece of property in which the building value is 30 per cent. and the land value 70 per cent. of the total. Assume also that the county relationship is 25 and 75 per cent. This would mean lower county taxes. Assume the general city relationship to be 35 and 65 per cent. This would mean higher city taxes. To determine whether the total tax bill would be increased or decreased it would be necessary to compare the size of the increase with the size of the decrease. Or this may be done by the use of a composite ratio, computed from the general city ratio and the county ratio.*

D. THE STANDARD RATIOS

The following table gives the general percentages from which can be determined the standard relationship of improvement values to building values in 1914 in the various boroughs of the City of New York and in the city at large:†

STANDARD RELATIONSHIPS BETWEEN ASSESSED VALUES OF IMPROVEMENTS AND VALUES OF LAND IN VARIOUS SUBDIVISIONS OF NEW YORK CITY

	Improvements (a)	Land (a)	Percentage of Total	
			Improvements	Land
Manhattan	$1,657,719,056	$3,209,337,610	34.06	65.94
Bronx	274,612,870	357,871,385	43.42	56.58
Brooklyn	795,825,978	797,088,314	49.96	50.04
Queens	179,334,522	293,906,195	37.89	62.11
Richmond	38,087,988	41,655,683	47.76	52.24
Aggregate	$2,945,580,414	$4,699,859,187	38.53	61.47

(a) These amounts include the land and improvements of corporations. The real estate of corporations divided between land and improvements, is as follows:

	Improvements	Land	Total
Manhattan	$45,390,936	$47,387,950	$92,778,886
Bronx	21,331,975	21,755,325	43,087,300
Brooklyn	8,198,205	13,229,155	21,427,360
Queens	13,326,165	13,228,075	26,554,240
Richmond	1,400,615	1,406,575	2,807,190
Aggregate	$89,647,896	$97,007,080	$186,654,976

* Cf. infra, p. 16.
† Unless specifically stated, the assessment values and the tax rates used in this study are for the year 1914. These were the latest available when the data were gathered.

It will be seen from the table that any piece of real estate in Manhattan, for example, will pay greater taxes for general city purposes under the new plan if the building represents less than 38.53 per cent. of the total value of the parcel. The same parcel will pay greater county taxes if the building represents less than 34.06 per cent. of the total value of both land and building.

In cases where county taxes will be increased and general city taxes decreased, the net result may be determined by applying the tax rates and comparing the amounts of the increases and decreases. But this is a slow process. If it is desired to learn merely whether the total taxes are increased or decreased, without reference to the amounts of such increases or decreases, the end can be accomplished by comparing the ratios of the particular parcels with a composite ratio, made up from the general city ratio and the county ratio. The general city taxes are much heavier than the county taxes. Consequently the dividing line between the parcels whose taxes would increase and those whose parcels would decrease lies much nearer the general city ratio than the county ratio. Its exact position is determined by the relative size of the tax levies for city and county purposes.*

The standard composite ratios are as follows:

STANDARD COMPOSITE RATIOS FOR THE VARIOUS SUBDIVISIONS OF NEW YORK CITY (a)

	Improvements	Land
Manhattan	38.34 :	61.66
Bronx	38.71 :	61.29
Brooklyn	39.44 :	60.56
Queens	38.49 :	61.51
Richmond	39.51 :	60.49

(a) These ratios are computed on the assumption that the tax rate on buildings is to be made half of that on land. If the tax rate on buildings were reduced to one per cent., these figures would be altered slightly, in no case so much as to affect unit figures.

These ratios take into consideration all the important peculiarities of the boroughs, their differing tax rates and state of development. To determine, therefore, whether the taxes on a particular parcel of real estate in any borough will be increased or decreased by the adoption of the plan to reduce the tax on buildings† it is only necessary to compare the relationship of assessed building value to assessed land value in that parcel with the standard composite ratio for that borough. Thus, in Manhattan, for example, any parcel in which the land is worth more

---

* The proportion used is as follows: the levy for city purposes in the county is to the levy for county purposes as X is to the difference between the terms of the standard city ratio and the standard county ratio. X in this case represents an amount which may be added to the proper terms in the county or city ratios to form a new composite ratio. The matter is complicated by the fact that the city taxes charged to the property in the various counties vary with the extent to which the tax on buildings is reduced. This factor is of too slight importance, however, to affect the composite ratios seriously.

† To fifty per cent. of that on land, although the ratios are almost identically the same in case the ratio on buildings is reduced to one per cent. of that on land.

than 61.66 per cent. of the total value of the parcel will pay greater taxes and *vice versa*. The variation in the standard composite ratios for the various boroughs is relatively slight. The land factor is most important in Manhattan (61.66 per cent.) and of least importance in Richmond (60.49 per cent.), the difference between the extremes being slightly over one per cent. (1.17 per cent.).

II. EFFECTS IN THE CITY AS A WHOLE UNDER CERTAIN ASSUMED CONDITIONS

Attention may now be turned to a consideration of the effects of transferring the tax to land. What will be the results of the change? Where will the tax bills be greater and where smaller and how great will the changes be? It should be borne in mind that the statements now to be made concerning the effects assume that the additional tax on land values will not have the effect of diminishing the assessed values. Later the probable readjustments in values will be taken into consideration.*

A. EFFECTS UPON THE TAX BURDENS OF THE BOROUGHS

The first point to be determined is the effect of the proposed plan upon the distribution of the taxes among the various boroughs of the city.† The accompanying map shows the boundaries of these subdivisions. Which will pay the greater and which will pay the smaller taxes under the plan?

(1). Increases and Decreases

As has been seen‡, the proposed plan leaves the distribution of county expenses untouched. Presumably they will be neither reduced nor increased. It is only in the distribution of the general city expenses among the boroughs that a change will result. In what direction these changes will occur can be readily determined by a comparison of the standard ratios for the boroughs with that of the city in general. The standard ratios are:

STANDARD RATIOS FOR THE CITY OF NEW YORK AND FOR THE BOROUGHS

	Improvements	:	Land
City of New York	38.5	:	61.5
Manhattan	34.1	:	65.9
Bronx	43.4	:	56.6
Brooklyn	50.0	:	50.0
Queens	37.9	:	62.1
Richmond	47.8	:	52.2

The boroughs which have a larger percentage of land than the city in general (61.5 per cent.) are, strangely enough, Manhattan and Queens.** This indicates that these two boroughs would be charged with a larger share of the city's general expenses than at present. The taxes in the other boroughs would be lightened.

---
* Cf. infra, p. 121 et seq.
† The boroughs and counties are coterminous.
‡ Cf. supra, pp. 14-15.
** Manhattan is the most highly improved of the boroughs in proportion to its area, while Queens, Richmond alone excepted, is the most poorly improved.

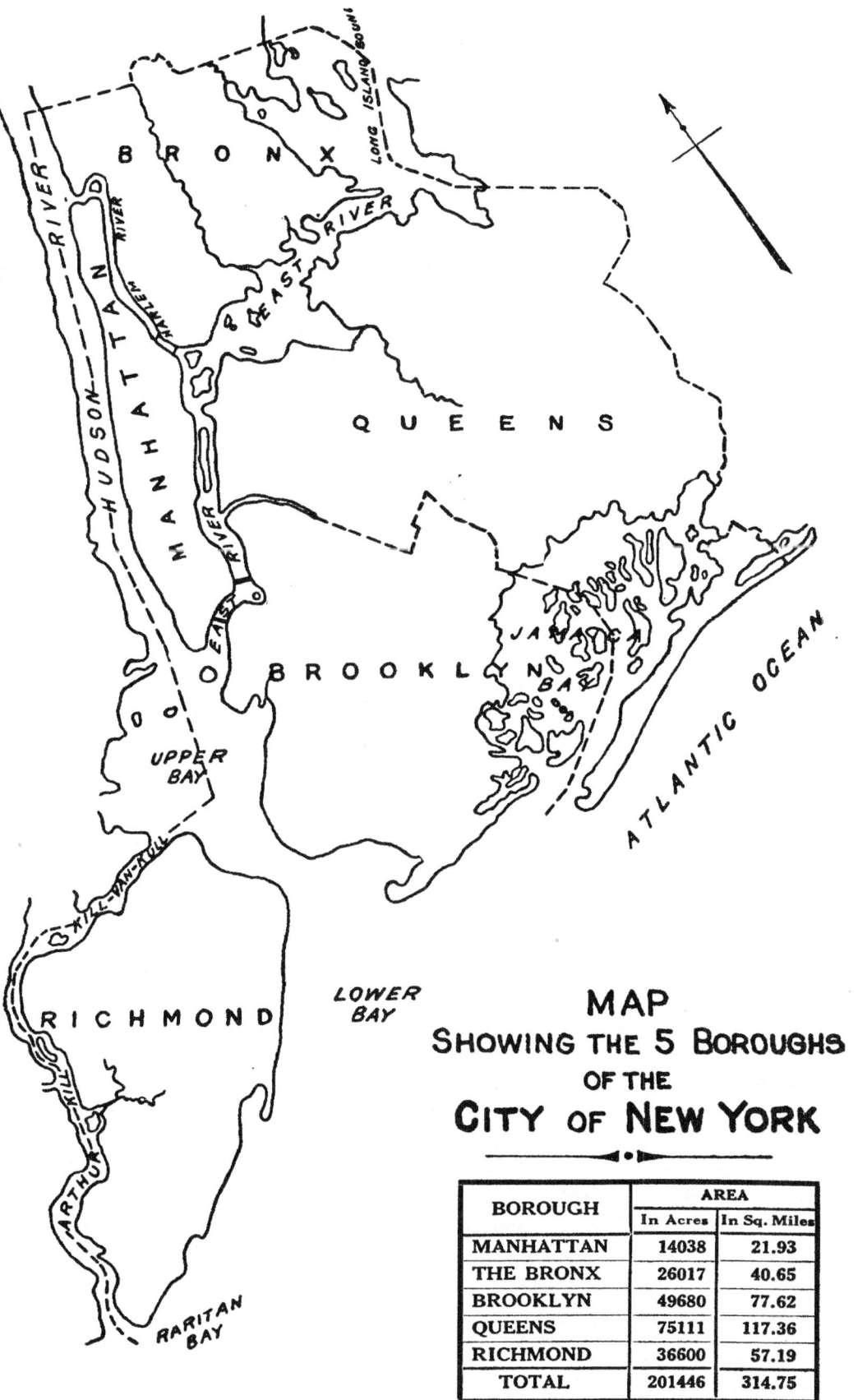

MAP
SHOWING THE 5 BOROUGHS
OF THE
CITY OF NEW YORK

BOROUGH	AREA	
	In Acres	In Sq. Miles
MANHATTAN	14038	21.93
THE BRONX	26017	40.65
BROOKLYN	49680	77.62
QUEENS	75111	117.36
RICHMOND	36600	57.19
TOTAL	201446	314.75

How much the increases and decreases in the various boroughs would be, is a question whose answer involves somewhat elaborate calculations. But since valuable data as to the probable effects upon tax rates and the weight of the burden upon the various classes of property in the tax base are at the same time obtained, the process may be profitably carried through.

(2). *The Assessed Values*

The assessed values of taxable property in the City of New York in 1914, arranged as they would be, were the proposed plan adopted, are presented in the following table:

ASSESSED VALUES OF PROPERTY GROUPED IN ACCORDANCE WITH THE SPECIFICATIONS OF THE PLAN TO UNTAX BUILDINGS

	Group One—Personal Property and Special Franchises	Group Two—Land, including Land of Corporations	Group Three—Improvements, including Improvements of Corporations	Total
Manhattan (New York Co.)	$569,962,364	$3,209,337,610	$1,657,719,056	$5,437,019,030
Bronx	31,908,958	357,871,385	274,612,870	664,393,213
Brooklyn (Kings Co.)	117,557,703	797,088,314	795,825,978	1,710,471,995
Queens	21,361,189	293,906,195	179,334,522	494,601,906
Richmond	3,925,657	41,655,683	38,087,988	83,669,328
Aggregate	$744,715,871	$4,699,859,187	$2,945,580,414	$8,390,155,472

(3). *The Tax Rates*

The tax rates would be more complicated than at present. The tax payer to-day is quoted a single figure for each borough—a rate secured by adding the county rate for that borough to the general city rate. Under the proposed plan there would be three tax rates for each borough: (1) one for personal property, which, presumably, would be the same as the rate under the present system; (2) a rate on land, higher than the first; and (3) a rate on buildings lower than the first and one-half or one one-hundredth of the second, depending upon which plan was in force. The tax rates which would result from adoption of the plans under the assumed conditions* are set forth in the accompanying table.† The rate on personal property would remain everywhere the same as at present. If the tax rate on buildings were halved, the rate on land in Manhattan would increase approximately twenty-three per cent. (to 2.20) and if the tax on buildings were reduced to one one-hundredth, the rate on land would increase sixty-one per cent. (to 2.86). The rate on land in the Bronx would be less than the Manhattan rate. The rates in the other three boroughs would be higher, the

---

* *Cf. supra*, p. 18.

† From the total levy in each case was subtracted the amount charged against Group One. The remainder was made one term of an equation, the other of which was the assessed value of land (Group One) multiplied by X plus the assessed value of buildings multiplied by one-half X or one one-hundredth X (as the case might be). The result was the rate on land. The rate on buildings was one-half or one one-hundredth of this amount.

The Rates Under the Present System and Under the Proposed Plans to Untax Buildings

		Manhattan (New York County)	Bronx	Brooklyn (Kings County)	Queens	Richmond
Group One: Personal Property and Special Franchises	General City Purposes { Present System	1.69972	1.69972	1.69972	1.69972	1.69972
	Rate on Improvements, ½	Do.	Do.	Do.	Do.	Do.
	Rate on Improvements, 1/100	Do.	Do.	Do.	Do.	Do.
	County Purposes { Present System	.07612	.06215	.13724	.09687	.19067
	Rate on Improvements, ½	Do.	Do.	Do.	Do.	Do.
	Rate on Improvements, 1/100	Do.	Do.	Do.	Do.	Do.
	Total { Present System	1.77584	1.76187	1.83696	1.79659	1.89039
	Rate on Improvements, ½	Do.	Do.	Do.	Do.	Do.
	Rate on Improvements, 1/100	Do.	Do.	Do.	Do.	Do.
Group Two: Land, including Land of Corporations	General City Purposes { Present System	1.69972	1.69972	1.69972	1.69972	1.69972
	Rate on Improvements, ½	2.10527	2.10527	2.10527	2.10527	2.10527
	Rate on Improvements, 1/100	2.74777	2.74777	2.74777	2.74777	2.74777
	County Purposes { Present System	.07612	.06215	.13724	.09687	.19067
	Rate on Improvements, ½	.09174	.07938	.18294	.11952	.25049
	Rate on Improvements, 1/100	.11485	.10900	.27155	.15503	.36170
	Total { Present System	1.77584	1.76187	1.83696	1.79659	1.89039
	Rate on Improvements, ½	2.19701	2.18465	2.28974	2.22510	2.35576
	Rate on Improvements, 1/100	2.86262	2.85677	3.01932	2.90280	3.10947
Group Three: Improvements, including Improvements of Corporations	General City Purposes { Present System	1.69972	1.69972	1.69972	1.69972	1.69972
	Rate on Improvements, ½ (a)	1.05263	1.05263	1.05263	1.05263	1.05263
	Rate on Improvements, 1/100 (b)	.02747	.02747	.02747	.02747	.02747
	County Purposes { Present System	.07612	.06215	.13724	.09687	.19067
	Rate on Improvements, ½ (a)	.04587	.03969	.09147	.05976	.12524
	Rate on Improvements, 1/100 (b)	.00114	.00109	.00271	.00155	.00361
	Total { Present System	1.77584	1.76187	1.83696	1.79659	1.89039
	Rate on Improvements, ½ (a)	1.09850	1.09232	1.14487	1.11255	1.17788
	Rate on Improvements, 1/100 (b)	.02862	.02856	.03019	.02902	.03109

(a) These rates were carried to six decimal places. The figures given are exactly one-half the rates on Group Two.
(b) These rates were carried to seven decimal places. The figures given are exactly one one-hundredth of the rates of Group Two.

highest rate being in Richmond (3.11 assuming the more drastic plan in force). The rates on improvements in Manhattan would drop to 1.05, with the tax rate halved, and to practically nothing with the full plan in force.

(4). *The Amounts of Taxes Payable*

The changes in the rates are much more violent than the changes in the weight of the burden borne by the various boroughs. As will be observed from the table on page 23, the amount of taxes payable would not be seriously affected in three of the boroughs. The Bronx and Richmond would be called upon to pay slightly smaller sums for general city purposes and Queens a slightly larger sum. Brooklyn and Manhattan are the only boroughs where material changes of this type would result. If the full plan were put in force Manhattan's share of the general expenses of the city would increase approximately six million dollars while Brooklyn's share would decrease by almost the same amount. These facts are more plainly set forth in the graph.

GENERAL CITY TAXES PAID BY THE VARIOUS BOROUGHS OF THE CITY UNDER THE PRESENT SYSTEM AND UNDER THE PROPOSED PLANS TO UNTAX BUILDINGS

PRESENT SYSTEM
(a)

| MANHATTAN 92.4 MILLIONS | BRONX 11.3 MILLIONS | BROOKLYN 29 MILLIONS | QUEENS 8.4 MILLIONS |

RATE ON IMPROVEMENTS ONE HALF RATE ON LAND
(b)

| 94.7 MILLIONS | 10.9 MILLIONS | 27.2 MILLIONS | 8.4 MILLIONS |

RATE ON IMPROVEMENTS ONE-ONE-HUNDREDTH RATE ON LAND

| 98.3 MILLIONS | 10.5 MILLIONS | 24.1 MILLIONS | 8.5 MILLIONS |

(c)

RICHMOND
(a) 1.4 MILLIONS
(b) 1.3 MILLIONS
(c) 1.2 MILLIONS

Distribution of Taxes Among Boroughs of the City and Classes of Property Under the Present System and Under the Proposed Plans to Untax Buildings (a)

		Manhattan (New York County)	Bronx	Brooklyn (Kings County)	Queens	Richmond	Entire City
Group One: Personal Property and Special Franchises	General City Purposes { Present System Rate on Improvements, ½/100. Rate on Improvements, 1/100.	$9,687,764.29 Do. Do.	$542,362.94 Do. Do.	$1,998,151.79 Do. Do.	$363,080.40 Do. Do.	$66,725.18 Do. Do.	$12,658,084.60 Do. Do.
	County Purposes { Present System Rate on Improvements, ½/100. Rate on Improvements, 1/100.	433,855.35 Do. Do.	19,831.42 Do. Do.	161,336.19 Do. Do.	20,692.58 Do. Do.	7,485.05 Do. Do.	643,200.59 Do. Do.
	Total { Present System Rate on Improvements, ½/100. Rate on Improvements, 1/190.	10,121,619.64 Do. Do.	562,194.36 Do. Do.	2,159,487.98 Do. Do.	383,772.98 Do. Do.	74,210.23 Do. Do.	13,301,285.19 Do. Do.
Group Two: Land, including Improvements of Corporations	General City Purposes { Present System Rate on Improvements, ½/100. Rate on Improvements, 1/100.	54,549,753.22 67,565,221.90 88,185,216.04	6,082,814.51 7,534,158.91 9,833,482.56	3,548,269.49 6,780,861.15 21,902,153.56	4,995,582.38 6,187,518.95 8,075,866.25	708,029.98 876,964.60 1,144,602.36	79,884,446.58 98,944,725.51 129,141,320.77
	County Purposes { Present System Rate on Improvements, ½/100. Rate on Improvements, 1/100.	2,442,947.79 2,944,246.32 3,685,924.25	222,417.07 284,078.31 390,079.81	1,093,924.00 1,458,193.36 2,164,493.32	284,706.93 351,276.68 455,642.77	79,424.89 104,343.32 150,668.61	4,123,420.68 5,122,137.99 6,846,808.76
	Total { Present System Rate on Improvements, ½/100. Rate on Improvements, 1/100.	56,992,701.01 70,509,468.22 91,871,140.29	6,305,228.58 7,818,237.22 10,223,552.37	14,642,193.49 18,239,054.51 24,066,646.88	5,280,289.31 6,538,795.63 8,531,509.02	787,454.87 981,307.92 1,295,270.97	84,007,867.26 104,086,863.50 135,988,129.53
Group Three: Improvements, including Improvements of Corporations	General City Purposes { Present System Rate on Improvements, ½/100. Rate on Improvements, 1/100.	28,176,582.34 17,449,730.99 455,503.07	4,667,649.87 2,890,671.18 75,457.30	13,526,813.31 8,377,142.78 218,674.68	3,048,184.74 1,887,737.95 49,277.00	647,389.15 400,927.49 10,465.70	50,066,619.41 31,006,210.39 809,377.75
	County Purposes { Present System Rate on Improvements, ½/100. Rate on Improvements, 1/100.	1,261,855.75 760,428.89 19,038.90	170,671.90 108,996.59 2,993.28	1,092,191.57 727,942.02 21,610.65	173,721.35 107,170.31 2,780.22	72,622.37 47,703.30 1,377.64	2,771,062.94 1,752,241.11 47,800.69
	Total { Present System Rate on Improvements, ½/100. Rate on Improvements, 1/100.	29,438,438.09 18,210,159.88 474,541.97	4,838,321.77 2,999,667.77 78,450.58	14,619,004.88 9,105,084.80 240,285.33	3,221,906.09 1,994,908.26 52,057.22	720,011.52 448,630.79 11,843.34	52,837,682.35 32,758,451.50 857,178.44
Total Taxable Property	General City Purposes { Present System Rate on Improvements, ½/100. Rate on Improvements, 1/100.	92,414,099.86 94,702,717.18 98,328,483.40	11,292,824.32 10,967,193.03 10,451,302.80	29,073,234.59 27,156,155.72 24,118,980.03	8,406,847.52 8,438,337.30 8,488,223.65	1,422,144.30 1,344,617.27 1,221,793.24	142,609,150.59 142,609,020.50 142,608,783.12
	County Purposes { Present System Rate on Improvements, ½/100. Rate on Improvements, 1/100.	4,138,658.89 4,138,530.56 4,138,818.50	412,920.38 412,906.32 412,904.51	2,347,451.77 2,347,471.57 2,347,440.16	479,120.87 479,139.57 479,115.57	159,532.31 159,531.67 159,531.30	7,537,684.22 7,537,579.69 7,537,810.04
	Total { Present System Rate on Improvements, ½/100. Rate on Improvements, 1/100.	96,552,758.75 98,841,247.74 102,467,301.90	11,705,744.70 11,380,099.35 10,864,207.31	31,420,686.36 29,503,627.29 26,466,420.19	8,885,968.39 8,917,476.87 8,967,339.22	1,581,676.61 1,504,148.94 1,381,324.54	150,146,834.81 150,146,600.19 150,146,593.16

(a) The tax rates were carried only to five decimal points. As a consequence there are slight discrepancies in the totals. No one of these amounts to more than $1,000.

B. EFFECTS UPON THE TAX BURDEN OF VARIOUS TYPES OF PROPERTY

One more point calls for consideration at this place: *viz.*, the effect of the proposed changes upon the amounts of taxes charged to the various types of property which enter into the composition of the tax base. With the aid of the graph these effects become apparent.

PORTION OF TOTAL TAXES CARRIED BY VARIOUS ELEMENTS OF THE TAX BASE UNDER THE PRESENT SYSTEM AND UNDER THE PROPOSED PLANS TO UNTAX IMPROVEMENTS

Personal property would, under the assumed conditions, continue to pay the same amount as before. The share of land would increase from 84 to 104 millions, if the rate on buildings were halved, and to 136 millions, if the full plan were adopted. These increases, of course, are accompanied by exactly corresponding decreases in the share of general city taxes payable by buildings.

C. SUMMARY

It is seen, then, that, under the assumed conditions of unvarying values in the tax base, the adoption of the plan to untax buildings would result in a redistribution of general city expenses among the boroughs.

The taxes of Manhattan would be considerably increased and those of Brooklyn considerably decreased. Taxes in Queens would be very slightly increased and in the Bronx and in Richmond, slightly decreased. Tax rates on land would, under the plan to halve the rate on improvements, increase by amounts ranging from 42 points (Manhattan and the Bronx) to 47 points (Richmond). Under the plan to reduce the tax on buildings to one one-hundredth of the rate on land, the land rate would increase 109 points in Manhattan and the Bronx, 111 points in Queens, 118 points in Brooklyn and 122 points in Richmond. The rates on improvements in the case of the first plan would be approximately two-thirds of the present rates and under the full plan would be negligible.

In the city at large, the adoption of the first plan* would increase the amount now paid by land owners as taxes from 84 millions to 104 millions. The adoption of the full plan† means the increase of this sum to 136 millions.

---

* By this is meant the plan to reduce the tax on buildings to one-half the tax on land.
† This is the reduction of the tax on buildings to one one-hundredth the tax on land.

III. THE EFFECTS IN MANHATTAN UNDER CERTAIN ASSUMED CONDITIONS*

The increase in general city taxes which would fall to the share of Manhattan has already been discussed.† The effects within the borough will next be traced.

A. TAX RATES

The following graph‡ presents the results which may be anticipated upon the Manhattan tax rates in case the proposed plans to untax buildings are adopted.

MANHATTAN

RATES UPON THE VARIOUS CLASSES OF PROPERTY UNDER THE PRESENT SYSTEM AND UNDER THE PROPOSED PLANS TO UNTAX BUILDINGS

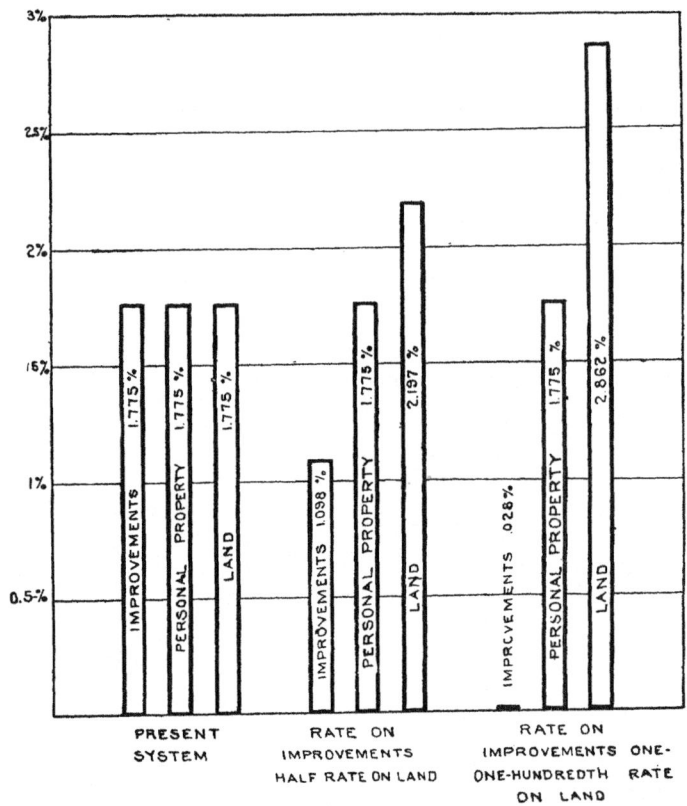

---

* The most important condition assumed is that the assessed values will not be disturbed. *Cf. supra*, p. 18.

† *Cf. supra*, pp. 22-23.

‡ The statistics upon which this graph is based are presented in detail in the table on p. 21.

B. DISTRIBUTION OF BURDEN AMONG THE ELEMENTS IN THE TAX BASE

The share of the tax burden in Manhattan which is carried by personal property, land and improvements under the present system and the changes that will be wrought by the adoption of proposed plans are set forth in the following graph:

MANHATTAN

DISTRIBUTION OF TAXES AMONG THE ELEMENTS OF THE TAX BASE UNDER THE PRESENT SYSTEM AND UNDER THE PROPOSED PLANS TO UNTAX BUILDINGS

PRESENT SYSTEM

| PERSONAL PROPERTY 10.1 MILLIONS | LAND 57 MILLIONS | IMPROVEMENTS 29.4 MILLIONS |

RATE ON IMPROVEMENTS ONE-HALF RATE ON LAND

| PERSONAL PROPERTY 10.1 MILLIONS | LAND 70.5 MILLIONS | IMPROVEMENTS 18.2 MILLIONS |

RATE ON IMPROVEMENTS ONE-ONE-HUNDREDTH RATE ON LAND (a)

| PERSONAL PROPERTY 10.1 MILLIONS | LAND 91.9 MILLIONS | IMPROVEMENTS |

(a) $474,541.97

C. EFFECTS IN THE VARIOUS ASSESSMENT SECTIONS OF THE BOROUGH

For the purposes of assessment the Borough of Manhattan is divided into eight sections, whose boundaries are traced on the map on page 28.

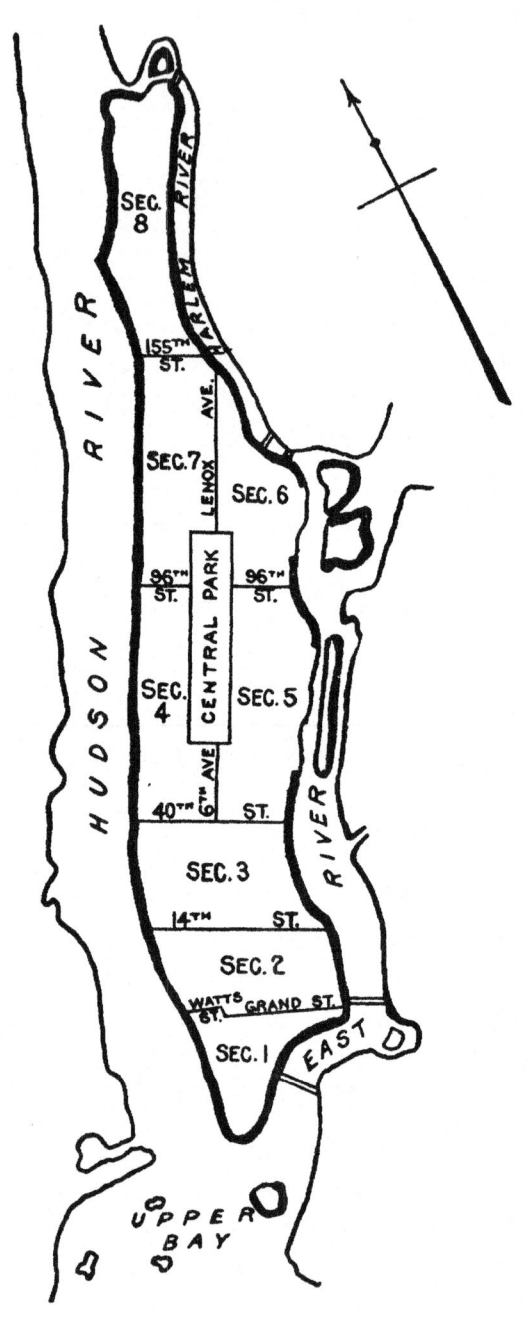

BOROUGH OF MANHATTAN

TAX LEVIES UPON THE REAL ESTATE (a) IN THE VARIOUS ASSESSMENT SECTIONS OF MANHATTAN UNDER THE PRESENT SYSTEM, AND UNDER THE PROPOSED PLANS TO UNTAX BUILDINGS

	Levies			Increases and Decreases	
	Present System	Rate on Improvements, One-Half	Rate on Improvements, One One-Hundredth	Rate on Improvements, One-Half	Rate on Improvements, One One-Hundredth
SECTION 1:					
Land.............	$9,771,736.30	$12,089,266.12	$15,751,851.38		
Improvements......	4,368,995.27	2,702,575.29	70,412.11		
	$14,140,731.57	$14,791,841.41	$15,822,263.49	+$651,109.84	+$1,681,531.92
SECTION 2:					
Land.............	$5,969,478.52	$7,385,239.67	$9,622,684.82		
Improvements......	3,152,794.37	1,950,257.13	50,811.43		
	$9,122,272.89	$9,335,496.80	$9,673,496.25	+213,223.91	+551,223.36
SECTION 3:					
Land.............	$12,921,181.26	$15,985,654.35	$20,828,696.21		
Improvements......	5,457,975.16	3,376,197.02	87,962.46		
	$18,379,156.42	$19,361,851.37	$20,916,658.67	+982,694.95	+2,537,502.25
SECTION 4:					
Land.............	$7,623,248.70	$9,431,228.96	$12,288,530.61		
Improvements......	4,163,987.86	2,575,761.70	67,108.15		
	$11,787,236.56	$12,006,990.66	$12,355,638.76	+219,754.10	+568,402.20
SECTION 5:					
Land.............	$11,087,941.49	$13,717,631.28	$17,873,548.89		
Improvements......	5,191,772.13	3,211,529.01	83,672.24		
	$16,279,713.62	$16,929,160.29	$17,957,221.13	+649,446.67	+1,677,507.51
SECTION 6:					
Land.............	$2,610,385.35	$3,229,481.67	$4,207,891.09		
Improvements......	1,748,392.79	1,081,521.69	28,177.65		
	$4,358,778.14	$4,311,003.36	$4,236,068.74	−47,774.78	−122,709.40
SECTION 7:					
Land.............	$4,511,848.63	$5,581,908.59	$7,273,013.40		
Improvements......	3,545,599.52	2,193,238.74	57,142.01		
	$8,057,448.15	$7,775,147.33	$7,330,155.41	−282,300.82	−727,292.74
SECTION 8:					
Land.............	$1,655,346.59	$2,047,939.58	$2,668,386.94		
Improvements......	1,002,850.59	620,343.82	16,162.26		
	$2,658,197.18	$2,668,283.40	$2,684,549.20	+10,086.22	+26,352.02
TOTAL					
Land.............	$56,151,166.84	$69,468,350.23	$90,514,603.36		
Improvements......	28,632,367.69	17,711,424.40	461,448.31		
	$84,783,534.53	$87,179,774.63	$90,976,051.67	+2,396,240.10	+6,192,517.14

(a) Not including the "Real Estate of Corporations."

The largest increase in taxes would result in Section Three between 14th and 40th streets. The net increase for the real estate of the island under the plan to halve the tax rate on buildings would be $2,936,240.10 and under the full plan, $6,192,517.14.

In which of these sections taxes on real estate would increase and in which they would decrease may be ascertained from the data presented in the following table:

ASSESSED VALUES AND RATIOS IN THE VARIOUS ASSESSMENT SECTIONS OF MANHATTAN

(*Standard Composite Ratio, 38.34: 61.66*)

	Assessed Values			Taxes Payable
	Improvements	Land	Ratios	
Section 1............	$246,024,150	$550,259,950	30.9 : 69.1	Increased
Section 2............	177,538,200	336,149,570	34.6 : 65.4	"
Section 3............	307,346,110	727,609,540	29.7 : 70.3	"
Section 4............	234,479,900	429,275,650	35.3 : 64.7	"
Section 5............	292,355,850	624,377,280	31.9 : 68.1	"
Section 6............	98,454,410	146,994,400	40.1 : 59.9	Decreased
Section 7............	199,657,600	254,068,420	44.0 : 56.0	"
Section 8............	56,471,900	93,214,850	37.7 : 62.3	Increased

It appears from this table that the only sections in Manhattan where real estate as a whole (land and improvements) will pay smaller taxes under the new plan than at present are sections six and seven, comprising a belt of territory from 96th Street to 155th Street entirely across the island.

The amounts of the increases and decreases in the levies on real estate in the various assessment sections are shown in the table on page 29.

D. EFFECTS IN SELECTED SECTIONS OF THE BOROUGH

(1). *The "Sky Scraper" Section*

Increased	65
Decreased	99
	164

South of Chambers Street in 1914 there were 164 buildings ten stories or more in height. The ratio of improvement value to land value was obtained for each of these parcels. By comparing with the standard composite ratio for Manhattan (38.34:61.66) it became evident that the adoption of the plan to untax buildings would mean reduced taxes for the great majority. Only a few more than one-third (65 as compared with 164) of these buildings would have their taxes increased. Moreover, as is shown by the following table the increased taxes will fall chiefly upon the smaller buildings.

BUILDINGS WHOSE TAXES WILL BE INCREASED OR DECREASED GROUPED ACCORDING TO HEIGHT

Number of Stories	Number of Parcels Whose Taxes Would be Increased	Number of Parcels Whose Taxes Would be Decreased	Total
10	17	11	28
11	5	8	13
12	14	24	38
13	6	5	11
14	2	3	5
15	3	6	9
16	6	8	14
17	1	2	3
18	4	3	7
19	1	3	4
20	2	4	6
21	2	5	7
22	1	1	2
23	..	3	3
25	1	3	4
26	..	2	2
30	..	2	2
32	..	3	3
33	..	1	1
40	..	1	1
54	..	1	1
	65	99	164

It will be observed that every building in the district over twenty-five stories in height (ten) would pay smaller taxes. If the tax on buildings were halved, the Woolworth building, with its 54 stories, would receive a decrease in annual taxes of $28,847.64; the 40 story Singer building would receive one of $3,473.40; and the 33 story City Investment building one of $12,742.36. If the full plan were adopted, the Woolworth building, instead of paying $156,273.92 annually, as at present, would pay but $81,870.56 and the other buildings would receive corresponding decreases not so great.

The simple arithmetic average of the assessed values of all ten-story buildings was calculated and the ratio between the land value and building value of this "type" was determined. The result showed the average ten-story building in this district stood on a plot whose value was three times that of the building. This relationship (25:75) is above the standard composite ratio for Manhattan (38.34:61.66), which indicates that the taxes on the typical ten-story building would increase were the proposed plan adopted. The same calculations were made for buildings of every height and it was found that this was true also of the average eleven, thirteen and eighteen story building. Average buildings of every other height would be taxed less heavily. In some cases the number of buildings of a particular height is so small as to make the type identical with a single building. This is, of course, unsatisfactory, and leads to a table whose items are of uneven merit. But from the table as it stands, some conclusions may be drawn. As will be seen, there is considerable unevenness in the average values and some unevenness, although considerably less, in the ratios.

ARITHMETIC AVERAGE OF THE ASSESSED VALUES OF BUILDINGS OF VARIOUS HEIGHTS AND THE RELATIONSHIP BETWEEN THE VALUE OF LAND AND BUILDING

(Standard Composite Ratio, 38.34:61.66)

Number of Stories	Number of Buildings	Assessed Values—Average Parcel		Ratio
		Value of Building	Value of Land	
10	28	$256,071.43	$758,928.57	25:75
11	13	377,307.69	698,461.54	35:65
12	38	280,263.16	419,207.89	40:60
13	11	341,363.64	562,727.27	38:62
14	5	296,000.00	459,000.00	39:61
15	9	866,666.67	1,313,888.89	40:60
16	14	735,357.14	936,071.43	44:56
17	3	496,666.67	775,000.00	39:61
18	7	617,285.71	1,098,357.14	36:64
19	4	950,000.00	1,206,250.00	44:56
20	6	715,833.34	1,011,666.67	41:59
21	7	1,550,000.00	2,296,428.57	40:60
22	2	1,425,000.00	1,725,000.00	45:55
23	3	1,328,333.33	1,105,000.00	55:45
25	4	997,500.00	1,091,250.00	48:52
26	2	1,737,500.00	1,062,500.00	62:38
30	2	1,775,000.00	2,100,000.00	46:54
32	3	1,841,666.67	2,458,333.33	43:57
33	1	3,700,000.00	2,925,000.00	56:44
40	1	3,000,000.00	4,000,000.00	43:57
54	1	6,000,000.00	2,800,000.00	68:32

This latter fact is brought out more clearly in the accompanying graph which presents the same facts concerning the ratios as are given in the table. It will be seen that the curve representing the relationship of land value to building value is somewhat irregular, particularly in the part dealing with the higher buildings where the number of buildings in each class is smaller. The general direction of the curve is, however, very clear. If "smoothed" by grouping a number of the types together, it would show a fairly steady progress downward. Stated in general terms, the analysis of the facts shows that the higher the building,

RELATIONSHIP OF IMPROVEMENT VALUE TO LAND VALUE IN THE CASE OF AVERAGE BUILDINGS OF VARIOUS HEIGHTS IN NEW YORK CITY

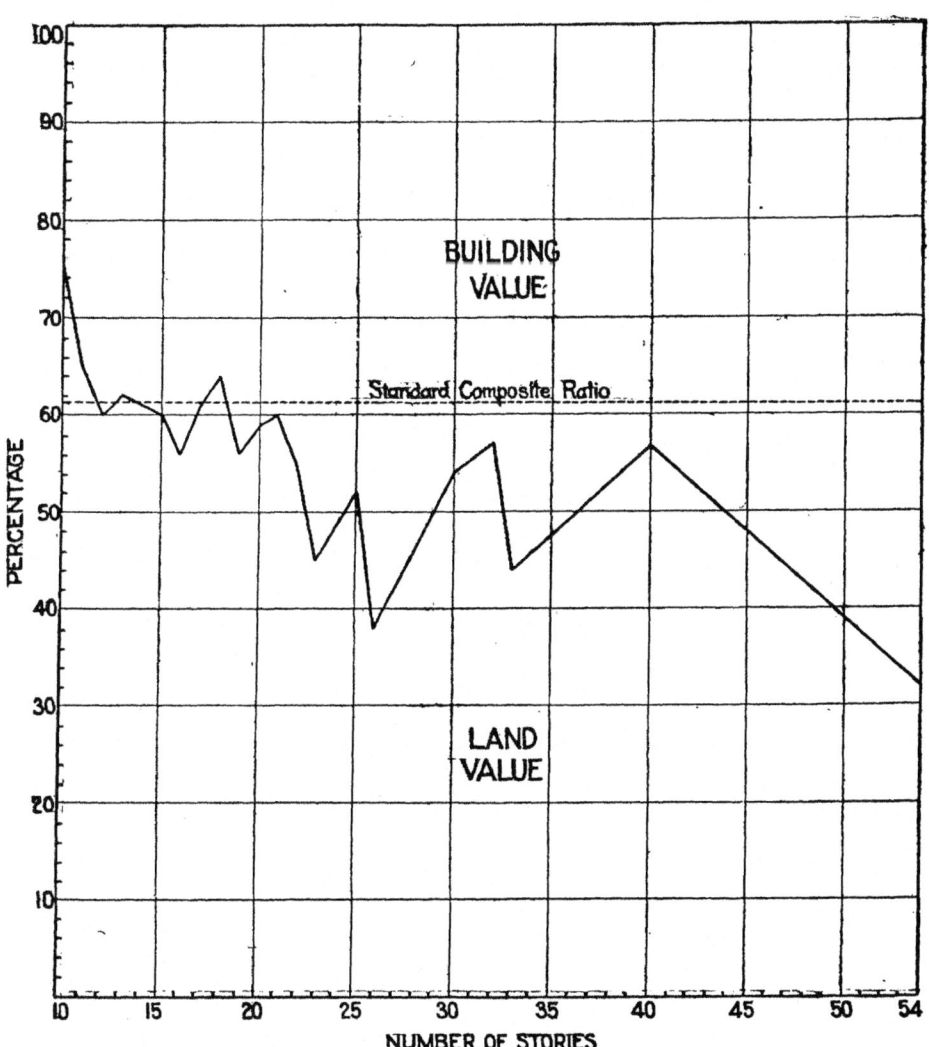

the larger the value of the building as compared with the value of the land. The deduction is that the higher the building, the greater will be the reduction in the tax on that parcel. In other words, in the situation actually present, the taller the building the greater the reduction in taxes, not merely absolutely but proportionally. To the extent that the buildings are owned by individuals, the change in the system would amount to the application of the principle of regressivity among the owners of buildings over ten stories in height.

In the detailed data which are presented in an appendix* the buildings are classified according to height, and are then subdivided into groups, Group A, consisting of those parcels whose taxes would be increased, and, Group B, of those whose taxes would be decreased. The assessed values falling within each group and class are presented herewith.

ASSESSED VALUES OF BUILDINGS TEN STORIES HIGH AND OVER SOUTH OF CHAMBERS STREET GROUPED ACCORDING TO HEIGHT AND THE EFFECT UPON TAXES PAYABLE UNDER THE PROPOSED PLAN TO UNTAX BUILDINGS

GROUP A: Parcels whose Taxes would be Increased

Number of Stories	Assessed Values		
	Improvements	Land	Total
10	$4,960,000	$19,565,000	$24,525,000
11	1,955,000	5,940,000	7,895,000
12	3,800,000	9,970,000	13,770,000
13	1,555,000	3,655,000	5,210,000
14	650,000	1,750,000	2,400,000
15	5,065,000	9,200,000	14,265,000
16	3,320,000	6,305,000	9,625,000
17	425,000	1,375,000	1,800,000
18	3,350,000	7,175,000	10,525,000
19	1,100,000	1,850,000	2,950,000
20	1,355,000	2,925,000	4,280,000
21	1,850,000	3,575,000	5,425,000
22	1,100,000	2,900,000	4,000,000
25	550,000	950,000	1,500,000
	$31,035,000	$77,135,000	$108,170,000

GROUP B: Parcels whose Taxes would be Decreased

Number of Stories	Assessed Values		
	Improvements	Land	Total
10	$2,210,000	$1,685,000	$3,895,000
11	2,950,000	3,140,000	6,090,000
12	6,850,000	5,959,900	12,809,900
13	2,200,000	2,535,000	4,735,000
14	830,000	545,000	1,375,000
15	2,735,000	2,625,000	5,360,000
16	6,975,000	6,800,000	13,775,000
17	1,065,000	950,000	2,015,000
18	971,500	513,500	1,485,000
19	2,700,000	2,975,000	5,675,000
20	2,940,000	3,145,000	6,085,000
21	9,000,000	12,500,000	21,500,000
22	1,750,000	550,000	2,300,000
23	3,985,000	3,315,000	7,300,000
25	3,440,000	3,415,000	6,855,000
26	3,475,000	2,125,000	5,600,000
30	3,550,000	4,200,000	7,750,000
32	5,525,000	7,375,000	12,900,000
33	3,700,000	2,925,000	6,625,000
40	3,000,000	4,000,000	7,000,000
54	6,000,000	2,800,000	8,800,000
	$75,851,500	$74,078,400	$149,929,900

* *Infra*, pp. 138-144.

By extending the tax rates against the total values thus determined the results presented in the accompanying table are obtained.

TAX LEVIES ON SKYSCRAPERS (a) SOUTH OF CHAMBERS STREET UNDER THE PRESENT SYSTEM AND UNDER THE PROPOSED PLANS TO UNTAX BUILDINGS

	Present System	Rate on Improvements One-Half		Rate on Improvements One One-Hundredth	
	Levy	Levy	Increase or Decrease	Levy	Increase or Decrease
GROUP A: Parcels whose taxes would be increased:					
Improvements.........	$551,131.94	$340,919.48	—$210,212.46	$8,882.22	—$542,249.72
Land.................	1,369,794.18	1,694,663.66	+324,869.48	2,208,081.94	+838,287.76
	$1,920,926.12	$2,035,583.14	+$114,657.02	$2,216,964.16	+$296,038.04
GROUP B: Parcels whose taxes would be decreased:					
Improvements.........	$1,347,001.28	$833,228.73	—$513,772.55	$21,708.70	—$1,325,292.58
Land.................	1,315,513.86	1,627,509.86	+311,996.00	2,120,583.09	+805,069.23
	$2,662,515.14	$2,460,738.59	—$201,776.55	$2,142,291.79	—$520,223.35
TOTAL:					
Improvements.........	$1,898,133.22	$1,174,148.21	—$723,985.01	$30,590.92	—$1,867,542.30
Land.................	2,685,308.04	3,322,173.52	+636,865.48	4,328,665.03	+1,643,356.99
	$4,583,441.26	$4,496,321.73	—$87,119.53	$4,359,255.95	—$224,185.31

(a) All buildings over ten stories are included.

The imposition of the plan to halve the rate on buildings would increase the taxes of certain of the smaller buildings by $114,657.02 and decrease the taxes of the other parcels $201,776.55. The annual revenue to the city from this class of property would be diminished $87,119.53. If the full plan were adopted, the increases to the smaller buildings would amount to $296,038.04 and the total decreases to $520,223.35, a net reduction in taxes on buildings of this type of $224,185.31.

If the entire decrease in the tax on buildings were passed on to the tenants, rents might be expected to decrease in these buildings $723,-985.01 under the half-rate plan and $1,867,542.30 under the full plan. The other side of the shield is shown when it is stated that the owners of the plots on which these buildings stand would suffer, under the assumed conditions* a diminution in their net annual return from their land of $636,865.48 under the half-rate plan and of $1,643,356.99 under the full plan. Capitalized at five per cent. this would mean a depreciation of $12,737,309.60 or approximately eight and one-half per cent. under the half-rate plan and of $32,867,139.80 or nearly twenty-two per cent. in case the full plan were adopted.

(2). *Tenement Sections*

(a). Upper East Side Section

Increased 2
Decreased....................... 120
                                            122

---

* The asssumptions here are that the reduction of the tax on buildings will not release forces which will increase land values and that the change will be made suddenly without an opportunity for it to be discounted beforehand.

Between First and Second avenues and between 99th and 103rd streets lies a district almost solidly built up with tenements.* Practically all of the buildings are of five or six stories. Some were built before the new tenement law went into effect in 1901, 43 of the 55 buildings which are five stories in height and twelve of the 67 six-story buildings being of this class.† It will be seen that more than half, however, are of the variety commonly known as "new-law" tenements.

The effects of removing the tax on buildings in this section are practically all in one direction. On only two of the 122 parcels would taxes be increased. Both of these are old, five-story tenements. Most of the buildings bear a very high proportion to the value of the land on which they stand.

The assessed values, grouped according to the effects of the plans, are:

ASSESSED VALUES OF PARCELS IN THE UPTOWN TENEMENT HOUSE SECTION

	Improvements	Land	Total
GROUP A: Parcels whose taxes would be increased......	$14,500	$24,000	$38,500
GROUP B: Parcels whose taxes would be decreased......	2,521,000	1,315,500	3,836,500
Total...............................	$2,535,500	$1,339,500	$3,875,000

Applying the tax rates, the following results are obtained:

TAXES PAYABLE BY THE OWNERS OF PARCELS IN THE UPTOWN TENEMENT SECTION UNDER THE PRESENT SYSTEM AND UNDER THE PROPOSED PLANS TO UNTAX BUILDINGS.

	Present System	Rate on Improvements One-Half		Rate on Improvements One One-Hundredth	
	Levy	Levy	Increase or Decrease	Levy	Increase or Decrease
GROUP A: Parcels whose taxes would be increased:					
Improvements.........	$257.50	$159.28	—$98.22	$4.15	—$253.35
Land...............	426.20	527.28	+101.08	687.03	+260.83
	$683.70	$686.56	+$2.86	$691.18	+$7.48
GROUP B: Parcels whose taxes would be decreased:					
Improvements.........	$44,768.93	$27,693.18	—$17,075.75	$721.51	—$44,047.42
Land...............	23,361.18	28,906.67	+5,545.49	37,657.77	+14,296.59
	$68,130.11	$56,599.85	—$11,530.26	$38,379.28	—$29,750.83
TOTAL:					
Improvements.........	$45,026.43	$27,852.46	—$17,173.97	$725.66	—$44,300.77
Land...............	23,787.38	29,433.95	+5,646.57	38,334.80	+14,547.42
	$68,813.81	$57,286.41	—$11,527.40	$39,060.46	—$29,753.35

* This district includes assessment blocks 1671, 1672, 1673 and 1674.
† The insurance atlas was used to secure this information and there is a possibility of slight inaccuracies.

If the full plan were put into effect, the total taxes on the 122 tenements would be almost cut in half. Instead of paying $68,813.81 they would pay $39,060.46. If the rate on buildings were halved there would be a net reduction in the taxes of $11,527.40, or approximately seventeen per cent. The movement is practically all in one direction, the increase on the two tenements which would pay heavier taxes being almost negligible.

The average parcel in this section consists of a building worth $20,783 and a plot worth $10,979. The taxes at present on such a parcel amount to $564.04. If the rate on buildings were halved they would be seventeen per cent. less, or $469.51. If the full plan were adopted the decrease would amount to $243.80, or 43%. The amount payable then would be but $320.24.

The decrease in the annual taxes on buildings alone in this section under the half-rate plan amounts to the considerable sum of $17,173.97. Under the assumed conditions this is the maximum sum available for lowering rents. Under the same set of assumptions the net revenue to the land owners would be decreased $5,646.57. Capitalized at a rate of five per cent., the decrease in the selling value of the land amounts to $112,931.40, or 8.4 per cent. The reduction in the average plot would be $926—from $10,979 to $10,053.*

(b). Rivington Street Section

Increased 114
Decreased 59
                                        ———
                                        173

The sample of 173 parcels from the Rivington Street section is selected from one of the most congested districts in the city. It extends from Stanton to Rivington streets and from Eldridge to Suffolk streets.† Most of the parcels are old-law tenements. The average parcel is assessed at $36,856. In about two-thirds of the cases (114 as compared with 173) the imposition of the plan to reduce the tax on buildings would mean heavier taxes for these parcels.

The assessed values of the parcels, arranged according to the effect following table are obtained:

ASSESSED VALUES OF PARCELS IN THE SAMPLE FROM THE RIVINGTON STREET SECTION

	Improvements	Land	Total
GROUP A: Parcels whose taxes would be increased......	$1,020,000	$2,729,500	$3,749,500
GROUP B: Parcels whose taxes would be decreased......	1,123,500	1,540,000	2,663,500
Total................................	$2,143,500	$4,269,500	$6,413,000

* The detailed statistics for this section are given in an appendix. *Cf. infra.*, pp. 145-147.
† This district consists of assessment blocks, 354, 411 and 416.

Applying the tax rates to these values the figures presented in the following table are obtained:

TAXES PAYABLE BY OWNERS OF PARCELS FROM THE RIVINGTON STREET SECTION UNDER THE PRESENT SYSTEM AND UNDER THE PROPOSED PLANS TO UNTAX BUILDINGS

	Present System	Rate on Improvements One-Half		Rate on Improvements One One-Hundredth	
	Levy	Levy	Increase or Decrease	Levy	Increase or Decrease
GROUP A: Parcels whose taxes would be increased:					
Improvements..........	$18,113.57	$11,204.70	—$6,908.87	$291.92	—$17,821.65
Land.................	48,471.55	59,967.39	+11,495.84	78,135.21	+29,663.66
	$66,585.12	$71,172.09	+$4,586.97	$78,427.13	+$11,842.01
GROUP B: Parcels whose taxes would be decreased:					
Improvements..........	$19,951.56	$12,341.65	—$7,609.91	$321.55	—$19,630.01
Land.................	27,347.94	33,833.95	+6,486.01	+44,084.35	+16,736.41
	$47,299.50	$46,175.60	—$1,123.90	$44,405.90	—$2,893.60
TOTAL:					
Improvements..........	$38,065.13	$23,546.35	—$14,518.78	$613.47	—$37,451.66
Land.................	75,819.49	93,801.34	+17,981.85	122,219.56	+46,400.07
	$113,884.62	$117,347.69	+$3,463.07	$122,833.03	+$8,948.41

It will be noticed that the net increase in taxes under the plan to halve the rate on buildings is $3,463.07, or $19.90 per parcel. The maximum available for decreases in rents is $14,518.78, or $83.44 per building. The net annual returns to the owners of the plots on which the tenements stand would be lessened $17,981.85, or $103.34 per plot. Capitalized,* this means a possible decrease in land values of $359,637, or $2,067 per plot. The average plot would thus decrease in selling value from $24,537 to $22,470.†

(c). Houston Street Section

Increased 70
Decreased 30
                                    ———
                                    100

The one hundred parcels lying in the district between Avenue A and First Avenue, Houston and 3rd streets, are, again, tenements in an extremely congested quarter of the lower east side.‡ The average parcel is assessed at $32,625 (improvements, $12,443, and land, $20,182). In more than two-thirds of the cases (70 as compared with 100), the adoption of the plan to untax buildings would mean greater taxes for these tenements.

---
* Interest rate, five per cent.
† For details of this sample, cf. *infra*, pp. 148-150.
‡ The district consists of assessment blocks 428, 429 and 430.

The table which follows gives the assessed values, grouped in the usual fashion:

Assessed Values of Parcels in Sample from Rivington Street Section

	Improvements	Land	Total
Group A: Parcels whose taxes would be increased......	$463,800	$1,151,700	$1,615,500
Group B: Parcels whose taxes would be decreased......	780,500	866,500	1,647,000
Total.............................	$1,244,300	$2,018,200	$3,262,500

When the tax rates are extended against these values the following results are obtained:

Taxes Payable by Owners of Parcels in the Sample of Houston Street Section Under the Present System and Under the Proposed Plans to Untax Buildings

	Present System	Rate on Improvements One-Half		Rate on Improvements One One-Hundredth	
	Levy	Levy	Increase or Decrease	Levy	Increase or Decrease
Group A: Parcels whose taxes would be increased:					
Improvements..........	$8,236.40	$5,094.88	—$3,141.52	$132.74	—$8,103.66
Land.................	20,452.34	25,302.96	+4,850.62	32,968.79	+12,516.45
	$28,688.74	$30,397.84	+$1,709.10	$33,101.53	+$4,412.79
Group B: Parcels whose taxes would be decreased:					
Improvements..........	$13,860.43	$8,573.79	—$5,286.64	$223.38	—$13,637.05
Land.................	15,387.65	19,037.09	+3,649.44	24,804.60	+9,416.95
	$29,248.08	$27,610.88	—$1,637.20	$25,027.98	—$4,220.10
Total:					
Improvements..........	$22,096.83	$13,668.67	—$8,428.16	$356.12	—$21,740.71
Land.................	35,839.99	44,340.05	+8,500.06	57,773.39	+21,933.40
	$57,936.82	$58,008.72	+$71.90	$58,129.51	+$192.69

The net increase in taxes under the half-rate plan would be only $71.90. This is because the decrease upon the thirty buildings whose taxes would be made heavier ($1,637.20) is so great as practically to cancel the increase on the other group ($1,709.10). The reduction in the taxes on buildings, the maximum available for the reduction of rents, would be $8,428.16, or $84.28 per building. The increase in land tax would be $8,500.06, a diminution in the annual rent return to the owner of the average plot of $85.00. Capitalized,* the prospective loss in land value would be $170,001.20, or $1,700.01 per plot.†

(*) Interest rate, five per cent.
(†) For details of this sample, cf. infra, pp. 151–153.

(3). *Apartment Sections*

(a). Elevator Apartment Section

Increased 0
Decreased.......................... 35
                                        ―――
                                         35

A section of Washington Heights lying between Broadway and the Hudson River and between 177th Street and 181st Street was selected as the field for investigating the probable effects of the plan upon high-class elevator apartment property.* In this district there are thirty-five six-story elevator apartment buildings, all of which have been built fairly recently. The apartments, which are of various sizes, rent for approximately ten dollars per room per month.

If the plan to untax the buildings were adopted, the taxes on every one of these pieces of property would be materially reduced. Not one has a high enough percentage of land value to bring the parcel ratio near the standard composite ratio.

The assessed valuation of the land on which these apartments stand is $2,213,000. The buildings are assessed for $5,165,000. Applying the rates, the amounts given in the following table are obtained. They represent the total taxes payable under the present system and under the proposed plans.

TAXES PAYABLE BY OWNERS OF ELEVATOR APARTMENTS IN WASHINGTON HEIGHTS SECTION

	Improvements	Land	Total
Present system—Levy	$91,722.14	$39,299.34	$131,021.48
Rate on improvements one-half—Levy	56,737.55	48,619.83	105,357.38
Increase or decrease	—34,984.59	+9,320.49	—25,664.10
Rate on improvements one one-hundredth Levy	1,478.22	63,349.78	64,828.00
Increase or decrease	—90,243.92	+24,050.44	—66,193.48

The decreases here would be very great. If the full plan were adopted the taxes on these parcels would be reduced by more than one-half. If the rate on buildings were halved it would mean a decrease of twenty per cent.

The average apartment in this sample section is assessed at $147,571 and the average value of the plot at $63,229. The taxes at present on this parcel amount to $3,743.47. If the rate on buildings were halved, the parcel would be charged with $3,010.21 and if the full plan were adopted, with only $1,852.24. The decrease in the first case would be $733.26 and in the second, $1,891.23.

If the rate on buildings were halved, there would be a reduction of $34,984.59 in the tax on buildings, which under certain conditions might be available for the reduction of rents. This means a thousand dollars

―――――――――
* The district consists of assessment blocks 2176 and 2177.

($999.84) per apartment per year. At the same time the owners of the plots would suffer a reduction in their income from the land of $9,320.49. Assuming an interest rate of five per cent. and capitalizing this amount, $186,409.80 is obtained as representing the probable depreciation in the selling value of the plots. If this be true the average plot would decrease $5,325.97 in value—from $63,229 to $57,903. This decrease amounts to 8.4 per cent.*

(b). "Walk-up" Apartment Section

Increased 0
Decreased.......................... 44
                                     ——
                                     44

The district bounded by Broadway, 178th Street, Amsterdam Avenue and 174th Street contains forty-four five-story "walk-up" apartment buildings.† An examination of the ratios of buildings and land values shows that here, as in the case of the elevator apartments, reductions would be made in the taxes of every apartment house. The proportion of building value to total value is not as great as is the case in the typical elevator apartment and the advantages which would accrue if buildings were untaxed would therefore not be so great either absolutely or proportionally.

The total assessed value of the 44 buildings is $1,632,000 and of the plots on which they stand, $1,034,000. The taxes paid at present by these parcels, and the changes which would result were the proposed plans adopted are shown in the following statement:

Taxes Payable by Owners of "Walk-up" Apartments in Washington Heights Section

	Improvements	Land	Total
Present system—Levy	$28,981.71	$18,362.19	$47,343.90
Rate on improvements one-half—Levy ...	17,927.52	22,717.08	40,644.60
Increase or decrease	—11,054.19	+4,354.89	—6,699.30
Rate on improvements one one-hundredth Levy..........................	467.08	29,599.49	30,066.57
Increase or decrease	—28,514.63	+11,237.30	—17,277.33

The adoption of the full plan would mean that taxes on these apartments would be reduced approximately one-third. Making the rate on buildings one-half the rate on land would mean a reduction of nearly seven thousand dollars or approximately fourteen per cent.

The average "walk-up" apartment building in this section is assessed at $37,091, and it stands on a plot assessed at $23,500. Taxes at present

---

* Detailed information in regard to this section may be found in an appendix. *Cf. infra,* p. 153.

† This territory consists of assessment blocks 2131, 2132 and 2133.

on such a parcel are $1,076. With the rate on buildings halved, they would be $923.74, a reduction of $152.26. The adoption of the full plan would increase the reduction to $392.67. The amount payable would then be only $683.33.

It will be noticed that in halving the rate on improvements the taxes on the structures would be decreased $11,054.19 and this represents the amount available under certain circumstances for reductions in rents. At the same time the net annual return to the owners of the land on which the apartments are built would be diminished $4,354.89. With the interest rate at five per cent. the depreciation in the selling value would be $87,097.80. The average parcel might be expected under the assumptions to decrease $1,979.50 from $23,500 to $21,521.*

(4). *Sections of Single Family Houses*

(a). Riverside Drive Section

Increased	9
Decreased	42
	51

The section of Riverside Drive included in the half-mile between 72nd and 82nd streets is one of the choicest residential districts in the city. With the exception of one apartment house, the entire stretch is used for single family dwellings. Among them is one of the show places of the city, the magnificent residence of Charles M. Schwab. In all there are fifty-one houses on this section of the drive. The adoption of the proposed plan would reduce the taxes on all except nine parcels. Among the nine is the Schwab property, which it will be recalled, stands in a park approximately two hundred by four hundred feet in size. Even when this large amount of land is used the increase in taxes amounts only to $17.58, under the plan to halve the rate on buildings and to $54.26, under the plan to reduce the rate on buildings to one per cent. of that on land. In other words, the Schwab property almost coincides with the hypothetical type of the standard composite ratio. Parcels, therefore, whose taxes would be increased contain a larger share of land value than is the case with the Schwab property.

In order to determine the magnitude of the readjustments which would be caused by the adoption of the proposed plans, the assessed values of the property have been separated into two groups, Group A consisting of the parcels whose taxes would be increased, and Group B of those whose taxes would be decreased. The assessed values thus arranged are as follows:

---

* The details for this section are given in an appendix. *Cf. infra*, p. 154.

ASSESSED VALUES OF REAL ESTATE IN RIVERSIDE DRIVE SECTION

	Improvements	Land	Total
GROUP A: Parcels whose taxes would be increased......	$769,000	$1,250,000	$2,019,000
GROUP B: Parcels whose taxes would be decreased......	1,061,000	1,202,500	2,263,500
Total..........................	$1,830,000	$2,452,500	$4,282,500

Applying the tax rates the following results are obtained:

TAXES PAYABLE BY OWNERS IN RIVERSIDE DRIVE SECTION UNDER THE PRESENT SYSTEM AND UNDER THE PROPOSED PLANS TO UNTAX BUILDINGS

	Present System	Rate on Improvements One-Half		Rate on Improvements One One-Hundredth	
	Levy	Levy	Increase or Decrease	Levy	Increase or Decrease
GROUP A: Parcels whose taxes would be increased.............	$35,854.21	$35,910.09	+$55.88	$36,002.84	+$148.62
GROUP B: Parcels whose taxes would be decreased.............	40,196.14	38,074.13	−2,122.01	34,726.66	−5,469.48
Total...............	$76,050.35	$73,984.22	−$2,066.13	$70,729.50	−$5,320.86

To halve the tax rate on buildings would increase the taxes of a few owners the slight amount of $55.88 while it would decrease the taxes of other owners by $2,122.01, the net reduction in taxes amounting to $2,066.13 annually. The adoption of the full plan would involve a decrease in the contribution from this section of $5,320.86.

In the table which follows the parcels are classified according to value and according to the effects of the proposed plans:

PARCELS IN THE RIVERSIDE DRIVE SECTION CLASSIFIED ACCORDING TO VALUE AND THE EFFECT UPON THEM OF THE PLANS TO UNTAX BUILDINGS

Value of Parcels	Number of Parcels	
	Increased	Decreased
Less than $40,000............................	4	4
$40,000 to $49,999...........................	3	19
$50,000 to $59,999...........................	1	7
$60,000 to $69,999...........................	0	4
$70,000 to $79,999...........................	0	4
Over $80,000................................	1	4
	9	42

It will be noticed that the median in the case of the parcels whose taxes would be increased is decidedly lower than that among the parcels whose taxes would be decreased.* That is, the parcels in this section whose taxes would be raised are in general not the more expensive but rather the less expensive ones. This is a phenomenon which is found to recur often in the Manhattan samples.†

(b). Fifth Avenue Section

Increased	95
Decreased	32
	127

The effects of the partial exemption of improvements in the Fifth Avenue district would be almost exactly the reverse of the effects in the Riverside Drive section just examined. Curiously enough along Fifth Avenue most of the single family residences would pay greater, not smaller, taxes, as was the case along the drive. In 1914 there were 127 parcels of this character on the Avenue between 60th and 93rd Streets, facing the park. This is probably the choicest residential section in the city. Here are the town houses of Carnegie, ex-Senator Clark, Astor and J. B. Duke. Ninety-five of the 146 parcels would be charged with higher taxes, if the plan to untax buildings were adopted. Thirty-two would pay smaller taxes.

The explanation of this situation is not difficult to discover. The building value in the great majority of cases is a much smaller part of the total value of the parcel than is the case in the standard composite ratio for Manhattan (38.34:61.66) because of the limitation on the type of building which may be placed upon this land. The enormous land values in this section are due to its desirability as sites for the private residences of the very wealthy. Great emphasis is placed upon being located in this particular section. To place an improvement on the land which would bear the ordinary relationship to the value of the land is a difficult task, if the improvement is to be a single-family residence and not a tall building of some sort. Only by covering the entire plot and by using the most expensive building materials can enough building value be secured to bring it above the typical proportion.

The most expensive house on Fifth Avenue is that of ex-Senator Clark. It was assessed in 1914 at three millions. The land was assessed at one million. This is an extreme case, for more building value has been put upon this plot than upon any plot of like value in the section. The taxes on this parcel would be reduced $16,108.50, if the rate on buildings were halved. If the rate were reduced to one one-hundredth of the rate on land, the Clark property would pay only $29,484.80 in annual taxes.

---

*The presence of one parcel, the Schwab property, with an assessed value many times that of any other parcel, unfits the material for the use of the simple arithmetic average in this case.
† The detailed data for the section is given in an appendix. *Cf. infra,* p. 155.

As the parcel now pays $71,033.60 this would mean a reduction of $41,548.80, more than one-half.

Other parcels on which taxes would be reduced include the residences of J. B. Duke and E. H. Gary.

On the other hand the taxes would be increased considerably on several parcels. The Carnegie property shows the most important changes in this direction. The taxes would increase $4,679.57 under the plan to halve the rate on buildings, and $12,077.83 under the plan to eliminate all except one per cent. The taxes at present on this parcel are $41,732.24.

The average value of the parcels whose taxes would be increased is $436,895 and that of those whose taxes would be decreased is $469,344. The figures are very close but it will be noted that the average is a little higher in the case of the parcels whose taxes would be decreased. The table which follows classifies the parcels according to value and according to the effects of the proposed plans.

CLASSIFICATION OF PARCELS IN THE FIFTH AVENUE SECTION ACCORDING TO VALUE AND ACCORDING TO THE EFFECTS OF THE ADOPTION OF THE PLAN TO UNTAX BUILDINGS

Value of Parcel	Number of Parcels	
	Increased	Decreased
$100,000 to $199,999	13	3
$200,000 to $299,999	34	12
$300,000 to $399,999	10	9
$400,000 to $499,999	13	4
$500,000 to $599,999	9	1
$600,000 to $699,999	3	1
$700,000 to $799,999	4	0
$800,000 to $899,999	2	0
More than $900,000	7	2
	95	32

From these figures it is evident that in this section the median, both for the parcels whose taxes will be increased and those whose taxes will be decreased is at about the same value.

The assessed values of the real estate in the Fifth Avenue section, grouped according to the effects of the proposed change, are as follows:

ASSESSED VALUES OF PARCELS IN FIFTH AVENUE SECTION

	Improvements	Land	Total
GROUP A:			
Parcels whose taxes would be increased	$10,088,000	$31,417,000	$41,505,000
GROUP B:			
Parcels whose taxes would be decreased	7,873,000	7,146,000	15,019,000
Total	$17,961,000	$38,563,000	$56,524,000

Applying the tax rates to these values the following results are obtained:

TAXES PAYABLE BY OWNERS IN THE FIFTH AVENUE SECTION UNDER THE PRESENT SYSTEM AND UNDER THE PROPOSED PLANS TO UNTAX BUILDINGS

	Present System	Rate on Improvements One-Half		Rate on Improvements One One-Hundredth	
	Levy	Levy	Increase or Decrease	Levy	Increase or Decrease
GROUP A: Parcels whose taxes would be increased............	$737,062.39	$801,051.31	+$63,988.92	$902,236.51	+$165,174.12
GROUP B: Parcels whose taxes would be decreased............	266,713.41	243,483.24	—23,230.17	206,816.07	—59,897.34
Total...............	$1,003,775.80	$1,044,534.55	+$40,758.75	$1,109,052.58	+$105,276.78

It appears that if the rate on buildings were halved, the taxes on certain parcels would increase $63,988.92, while those on other parcels would decrease $23,230.17, making the net increase for the district $40,-758.75. In case the full plan were adopted the net increase would be $105,276.76.*

(c). Section of Side Streets East of Fifth Avenue

Increased 471
Decreased........................ 113
                                   ———
                                   584

Along the side streets east of Fifth Avenue between 60th and 93rd streets are located a large number of single-family dwellings of a very high type. This is the region where a person who desires a residence in Manhattan which would cost, for land and house, approximately one hundred thousand dollars is likely to locate. Although most of the houses are far from new, the region as a whole cannot be said to be far advanced in the transition stage toward another use, such as for business or apartment purposes. This statement does not hold true for the margin along Madison Avenue. Almost all of the streets in the district, however, are considered proper sites for the construction of new residences.

In this selected section there were at the time of assessment in 1914, 584 parcels, improved by one-family houses. An examination of the relative value of building to land in these parcels reveals the fact that approximately four-fifths of the parcels (471) would be charged with heavier taxes under the plan to untax buildings.

---

* The detailed information for the Fifth Avenue section is given in an appendix. *Cf. infra*, pp. 156-158.

The following table classifies the parcels by streets:

NUMBER OF PARCELS (a) IN THE SIDE STREETS OFF FIFTH AVENUE WHOSE TAXES WOULD BE INCREASED AND DECREASED IN CONSEQUENCE OF THE ADOPTION OF THE PROPOSAL TO UNTAX BUILDINGS

	Increased	Decreased
60th Street between Fifth Avenue and Madison Avenue	7	0
61st " " " " " " "	16	3
62d " " " " " " "	17	5
63d " " " " " " "	18	3
64th " " " " " " "	19	3
65th " " " " " " "	16	4
66th " " " " " " "	17	2
67th " " " " " " "	18	4
68th " " " " " " "	11	2
69th " " " " " " "	14	1
70th " " " " " " "	11	6
71st " " " " " " "	9	5
72d " " " " " " "	16	1
73d " " " " " " "	16	6
74th " " " " " " "	27	0
75th " " " " " " "	20	1
76th " " " " " " "	21	6
77th " " " " " " "	21	1
78th " " " " " " "	15	3
79th " " " " " " "	13	9
80th " " " " " " "	17	6
81st " " " " " " "	17	6
82d " " " " " " "	7	13
83d " " " " " " "	18	3
84th " " " " " " "	12	4
85th " " " " " " "	11	0
86th " " " " " " "	9	4
87th " " " " " " "	0	2
88th " " " " " " "	1	3
89th " " " " " " "	0	5
90th " " " " " " "	2	2
91st " " " " " " "	2	0
92d " " " " " " "	26	0
93d " " " " " " "	27	0
	471	113

(a) Single-family dwellings only.

The results are on the whole fairly regular. The parcels whose taxes would be decreased are scattered evenly through the section. The assessment rolls show that in the few blocks where the number of decreases is large, such as 82nd, 87th, 88th, 89th and 90th streets, apartment houses are also present. These are for the most part old buildings.

An interesting point becomes evident when the parcels are grouped according to their value. By referring to the table, it will be seen that, as the value of the properties increases, there is a regular progression in the percentage of parcels whose taxes would be decreased.

INCREASES AND DECREASES IN TAXES AMONG THE SINGLE-FAMILY DWELLINGS IN THE SECTION OF SIDE STREETS EAST OF FIFTH AVENUE GROUPED ACCORDING TO THE VALUE OF PROPERTIES

Value of Parcels	Number of Parcels		Percentage	
	Increased	Decreased	Increased	Decreased
Less than $50,000	65	0	100	0
$50,000 to $99,999	246	15	94	6
$100,000 to $149,999	109	39	74	26
$150,000 to $199,999	31	27	53	47
More than $200,000	20	32	38	62

In other words the situation here is similar to that in the sky-scraper section: the more expensive the parcel the larger the proportion of building value. The two graphs which follow may aid in making this plan:

PARCELS WHOSE TAXES WOULD BE INCREASED AND DECREASED AMONG THE SINGLE-FAMILY DWELLINGS IN THE SECTION OF SIDE STREETS EAST OF FIFTH AVENUE GROUPED ACCORDING TO THE VALUE OF THE PROPERTY

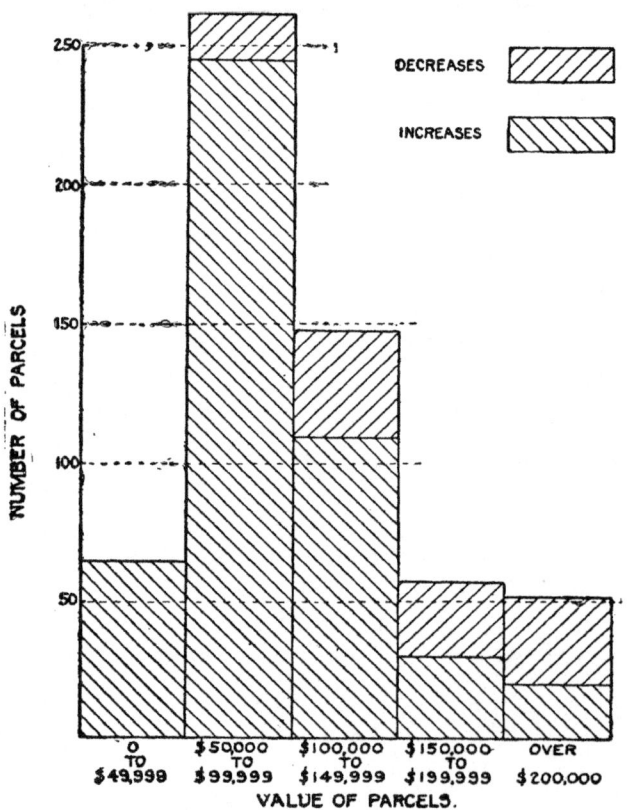

PERCENTAGES OF PARCELS WHOSE TAXES WOULD BE INCREASED AND DECREASED AMONG THE SINGLE-FAMILY DWELLINGS IN THE SECTION OF SIDE STREETS EAST OF FIFTH AVENUE, GROUPED ACCORDING TO THE VALUE OF THE PROPERTY

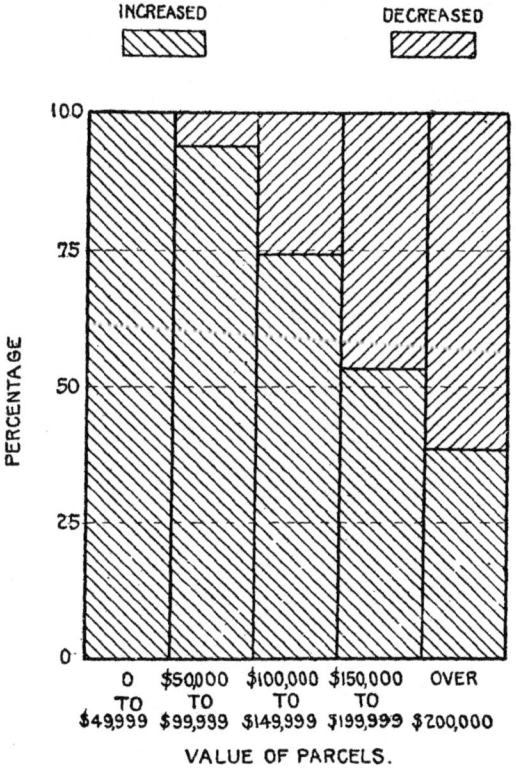

The first shows the number of parcels. It will be noted that by far the greater number of the parcels on which the taxes will be increased fall in the lower two classes, viz., below $100,000, whereas almost all of the parcels whose taxes will be increased are assessed for more than that sum.

In order to determine amounts involved in the readjustments in taxes among the owners in this section the assessed values of the parcels whose taxes would be increased were separated from those of the parcels whose taxes would be decreased with the following results:

ASSESSED VALUES OF PARCELS IN THE SECTION OF SIDE STREETS EAST OF FIFTH AVENUE

	Improvements	Land	Total
GROUP A:			
Parcels whose taxes would be increased...	$9,430,500	$34,575,000	$44,005,500
GROUP B:			
Parcels whose taxes would be decreased...	8,902,500	10,067,500	18,970,000
Total..............................	$18,333,000	$44,642,500	$62,975,500

It will be noticed that these figures confirm the point already made that on the whole the decreases are among the more valuable parcels. Whereas the number of parcels whose taxes would be decreased constitute but one-fifth of the total number, they make nearly one-third of the total value.

Extending the rates against these values, the taxes payable by the two groups under the proposed plans are obtained:

TAXES PAYABLE BY OWNERS IN SECTION OF SIDE STREETS EAST OF FIFTH AVENUE UNDER THE PRESENT SYSTEM AND UNDER THE PROPOSED PLANS TO UNTAX BUILDINGS

	Present System	Rate on Improvements One-Half		Rate on Improvements One One-Hundredth	
	Levy	Levy	Increase or Decrease	Levy	Increase or Decrease
Group A: Parcels whose taxes would be increased............	$781,467.27	$863,210.25	+$81,742.98	$992,449.87	+$210,982.60
GROUP B: Parcels whose taxes would be decreased............	336,876.85	318,977.94	—17,898.91	290,742.18	—46,134.67
Total...............	$1,118,344.12	$1,182,188.19	+$63,844.07	$1,283,192.05	+$164,847.93

The foregoing table indicates that the houses in this section as a group would pay approximately six per cent. greater taxes if the rate on buildings were halved and approximately fifteen per cent. higher taxes if the rate on improvements were made one one-hundredth of that on land. The decreases in the taxes upon certain parcels amount in both cases to roughly one-fifth of the increases upon certain other parcels.

The average of the assessed values of the parcels in this section is $107,835 (land $76,443 and building $31,392). The taxes at present on a parcel of this type are $1,914.98. If the rate on buildings were halved the taxes would be $2,024.30, or $109.32 greater than before. If the full plan were adopted the taxes would be increased $282.28 (to $2,197.26.)*

    (d). Section of Side Streets off Riverside Drive

    1914 Increased 71
            Decreased 150

                                         221

    1915 Increased 159
            Decreased 58

                                         217

The side streets off Riverside Drive between 82nd and 88th streets, and between the drive and West End Avenue form a sample of a

---

* The detailed data for this section will be found in an appendix. *Cf. infra*, pp. 159-168.

district which until fairly recently has been a stronghold of the single family dwelling of high type. The parcels in this region are assessed for the most part at figures between twenty and thirty thousand dollars. Lately apartments have begun to crowd rapidly into the district until in 1915 there were not less than forty-three buildings of this type on these streets.* Such a movement has the effect of detracting from the desirability of the region as sites for private residences and as a consequence most of the owners are in full retreat, the region being thickly strewn with signs advertising the property for sale.

The assessment data for the two years, 1914 and 1915, when compared, show very plainly the nature of the change which is taking place. In 1914 the ratio of building to land value in the various plots was such that, had the plan to untax buildings been adopted then, approximately two-thirds of the parcels would have received lower taxes. But in 1915, conditions had so changed, land values having increased as compared with building values, that the situation is exactly reversed. If the plan had been imposed in 1915, two-thirds of the parcels would have paid greater instead of lower taxes.

The assessed values for the two years, grouped in the usual manner, are:

ASSESSED VALUES OF PARCELS IN THE SAMPLE FROM SECTION OF SIDE STREETS OFF RIVERSIDE DRIVE (a)

	Improvements	Land	Total
GROUP A:			
Parcels whose taxes would be increased:			
1914	$578,800	$1,350,000	$1,928,800
1915	1,106,300	3,250,700	4,357,000
GROUP B:			
Parcels whose taxes would be decreased:			
1914	2,289,500	2,419,500	4,709,000
1915	799,200	107,090	906,290
Total, 1914	$2,868,300	$3,769,500	$6,637,800
Total, 1915	1,905,500	3,357,790	5,263,290

(a) The number of parcels is not the same in the two years, several houses having been torn down during the intervening period, and therefore the amounts are not strictly comparable.

Applying the tax rates, the results given in the table on page 52 are obtained.

It will be noted that under the half-tax plan and on the basis of the 1914 valuations, the total net taxes in this section would decrease slightly ($3,552.13), whereas on the basis of the 1915 valuation the net

---

*This number includes the buildings situated on the corners even when facing on the drive or West End Avenue.

TAXES PAYABLE BY OWNERS OF PARCELS IN THE SAMPLE FROM SECTION OF SIDE STREETS OFF RIVERSIDE DRIVE UNDER THE PRESENT SYSTEM AND UNDER THE PROPOSED PLANS TO UNTAX BUILDINGS

On the Basis of the 1914 and 1915 Assessed Values (a)

	Present System Levy		Rate on Improvements One-Half				Rate on Improvements One One-Hundredth			
			Levy		Increase or Decrease		Levy		Increase or Decrease	
	1914	1915	1914	1915	1914	1915	1914	1915	1914	1915
GROUP A: Parcels whose taxes would be increased:										
Improvements....	$10,278.56	$19,646.12	$6,358.12	$12,152.71	−$3,920.44	−$7,493.41	$165.65	$316.62	−$10,112.91	−$19,329.50
Land............	23,973.84	57,727.23	29,659.64	71,418.20	+5,685.80	+13,690.97	38,645.37	93,055.19	+14,671.53	+35,327.96
	$34,252.40	$77,373.35	$36,017.76	$83,570.91	+$1,765.36	+$6,197.56	$38,811.02	$93,371.81	+$4,558.62	+$15,998.46
GROUP B: Parcels whose taxes would be decreased:										
Improvements....	$40,657.86	$14,192.51	$25,150.16	$8,779.21	−$15,507.70	−$5,413.30	$655.25	$228.73	−$40,002.61	−$13,963.78
Land............	42,966.45	1,901.75	53,156.66	2,352.78	+10,190.21	+451.03	69,261.09	3,065.58	+26,294.64	+1,163.83
	$83,624.31	$16,094.26	$78,306.82	$11,131.99	−$5,317.49	−$4,962.27	$69,916.34	$3,294.31	−$13,707.97	−$12,799.95
TOTAL:										
Improvements....	$50,936.42	$33,838.63	$31,508.28	$20,931.92	−$19,428.14	−$12,906.71	$820.90	$545.35	−$50,115.52	−$33,293.28
Land............	66,940.29	59,628.98	82,816.30	73,770.98	+15,876.01	+14,142.00	107,906.46	96,120.77	+40,966.17	+36,491.79
	$117,876.71	$93,467.61	$114,324.58	$94,702.90	−$3,552.13	+$1,235.29	$108,727.36	$96,666.12	−$9,149.35	+$3,198.51

(a) The number of parcels is not the same in the two years and the results are therefore not strictly comparable. Also it must be understood that the amounts given for 1915 are arrived at by the use of the same tax rates as in the case of the 1914 figures.

taxes would be increased somewhat, ($1,235.29). According to the 1914 figures the increase in the land tax would amount to $15,876.01. Capitalized,* this amounts to $317,520.20, which represents the probable depreciation in land values due to the adoption of the plan.†

(e). Section of Side Streets West of Central Park

```
1914   Increased ...................... 165
       Decreased ...................... 129
                                        ───
                                        294
1915   Increased ...................... 283
       Decreased ......................  11
                                        ───
                                        294
```

This sample consists of 294 single-family houses situated between Central Park West and Columbus Avenue, 90th and 95th streets. Here, as in the side streets east of Riverside Drive, apartments are pushing in with the result that land values are rising while building values of the single-family houses are falling. In 1914, when the average parcel in the sample was assessed at $20,861, the imposition of the plan to untax buildings would have increased the taxes of 165 parcels and decreased those of 129 parcels. The parcels whose taxes would be increased average 18,685 in value, while those whose taxes would be decreased average $23,628, another example of the tendency often noted in the Manhattan sections. So rapidly are changes taking place in the district, however, that by 1915 the number of parcels whose taxes would be increased had swollen from 165 to 283, while those in the other group had shrunk from 129 to eleven.

By referring to the table of assessed values for 1914 which follows, it will be seen that, despite the disparity in numbers between the two groups, the assessed values are approximately the same.

Assessed Values of Parcels in Sample from Section of Side Streets West of Central Park

	Improvements	Land	Total
Group A: Parcels whose taxes would be increased...	$950,500	$2,133,500	$3,084,000
Group B: Parcels whose taxes would be decreased...	1,322,500	1,726,500	3,049,000
Total..........................	$2,273,000	$3,860,000	$6,133,000

* Interest rate, five per cent.
† The details for this section are given in an appendix. Cf. *infra*, pp. 169-172.

Applying the tax rates to the assessed values the results given in the following table are obtained:

TAXES PAYABLE BY OWNERS OF PARCELS IN THE SAMPLE FROM SECTION OF SIDE STREETS WEST OF CENTRAL PARK UNDER THE PRESENT SYSTEM, AND UNDER THE PROPOSED PLANS TO UNTAX BUILDINGS

	Present System	Rate on Improvements One-Half		Rate on Improvements One One-Hundredth	
	Levy	Levy	Increase or Decrease	Levy	Increase or Decrease
GROUP A: Parcels whose taxes would be increased:					
Improvements	$16,879.36	$10,441.24	—$6,438.12	$273.03	—$16,606.33
Land	37,887.55	46,873.21	+8,985.66	61,074.00	+23,186.45
	$54,766.91	$57,314.45	+$2,547.54	$61,347.03	+$6,580.12
GROUP B: Parcels whose taxes would be decreased:					
Improvements	$23,485.48	$14,527.66	—$8,957.82	$378.50	—$23,106.98
Land	30,659.88	37,931.38	+7,271.50	49,423.13	+18,763.25
	$54,145.36	$52,459.04	—$1,686.32	$49,801.63	—$4,343.73
TOTAL:					
Improvements	$40,364.84	$24,968.90	—$15,395.94	$651.53	—$39,713.31
Land	68,547.43	84,804.59	+16,257.16	110,497.13	+41,949.70
	$108,912.27	$109,773.49	+$861.22	$111,148.66	+$2,236.39

The increase in the taxes upon the larger number of the parcels is almost balanced by the decreases on the smaller number of more valuable parcels. Thus if the rate on buildings were halved the taxes on one group of parcels would be increased $2,547,54, while those upon another group would be decreased $1,686.32.*

(f). Section of Side Streets East of Lexington Avenue

Increased 107
Decreased.......................... 47
—
154

This section consists of 154 houses located between Lexington and Third avenues on the following streets: 70th, 71st, 72nd, 73rd, 74th, 78th and 79th. In some of the streets in this section there is considerable grouping of ownership, indicating the change which is going on from the use of the land for residences to its use for apartment purposes. Already a number of apartments have been built and some of the old residences converted into apartments, but all these have been eliminated from the sample. Certainly a few and probably a considerable number of the houses in the sample are used as rooming and boarding houses.

---
* The details of this sample are given in an appendix. *Cf. infra,* pp. 173-177.

The average parcel in the section is assessed at $25,305. In the case of 107 of the 154 parcels the tax would increase under the proposed plans to untax buildings. The average value of these buildings is $20,178, while that of the 47 parcels whose taxes would be decreased is $36,979. This shows that the same situation is here present as that which was found in so many other Manhattan sections, *viz.*, that the more valuable parcels in the group would receive decreases which are larger both absolutely and proportionally as compared with the less expensive parcels.

The assessed values, arranged in the usual fashion, are as follows:

Assessed Values of Parcels in Section of Selected Side Streets East of Lexington Avenue

	Improvements	Land	Total
Group A: Parcels whose taxes would be increased...	$578,500	$1,570,000	$2,148,500
Group B: Parcels whose taxes would be decreased...	872,000	866,000	1,738,000
Total	$1,450,500	$2,436,000	$3,886,500

The larger value per parcel among the houses in Class B once more becomes apparent.

Extending the tax rates against the values in the table given above, the following results are obtained:

Taxes Payable by Owners of Parcels in Section of Selected Side Streets East of Lexington Avenue Under the Present System and Under the Proposed Plans to Untax Buildings

	Present System Levy	Rate on Improvements One-Half Levy	Rate on Improvements One-Half Increase or Decrease	Rate on Improvements One One-Hundredth Levy	Rate on Improvements One One-Hundredth Increase or Decrease
Group A: Parcels whose taxes would be increased:					
Improvements	$10,273.23	$6,354.82	—$3,918.41	$165.57	—$10,107.66
Land	27,880.69	34,493.06	+6,612.37	44,943.13	+17,062.44
	$38,153.92	$40,847.88	+$2,693.96	$45,108.70	+$6,954.78
Group B: Parcels whose taxes would be decreased:					
Improvements	$15,485.32	$9,578.92	—$5,906.40	$249.57	—$15,235.75
Land	15,378.77	19,026.11	+3,647.34	24,790.29	+9,411.52
	$30,864.09	$28,605.03	—$2,259.06	$25,039.86	—$5,824.23
Total:					
Improvements	$25,758.55	$15,933.74	—$9,824.81	$415.14	—$25,343.41
Land	43,259.46	53,519.17	+10,259.71	69,733.42	+26,473.96
	$69,018.01	$69,452.91	+$434.90	$70,148.56	+$1,130.55

It will be noted that the net change would be very slight, there being only an increase of $434.90 under the plan to halve the rate on buildings. This amounts to $2.82 per parcel. The decreases on the fewer more expensive parcels (Group B) almost counterbalances the increases on the many less expensive parcels (Group A).*

(g). Section in Washington Square District

Increased 126
Decreased 0
                                        ———
                                        126

This section consists of 126 single family dwellings situated on 9th, 10th and 11th streets between Fifth and Sixth avenues. Most of the houses are old and not less than fifteen of the number are used as rooming houses. The assessed value of the average parcel is $25,218. Every parcel of the 126 would pay higher taxes if the plan to untax buildings were adopted.

The assessed values for the group of parcels are improvements $518,300, land $2,660,800 and total $3,179.100. Applying the tax rates, the figures presented in the following table are obtained:

TAXES PAYABLE BY OWNERS OF PARCELS IN THE SAMPLE FROM THE WASHINGTON SQUARE DISTRICT, UNDER THE PRESENT SYSTEM, AND UNDER THE PROPOSED PLANS TO UNTAX BUILDINGS

	Present System	Rate on Improvements One-Half		Rate on Improvements One One-Hundredth	
	Levy	Levy	Increase or Decrease	Levy	Increase or Decrease
GROUP A: Parcels whose taxes would be increased:					
Improvements..........	$9,204.18	$5,693.53	—$3,510.65	$148.34	—$9,055.84
Land.................	47,251.55	58,458.04	+11,206.49	76,168.59	+28,917.04
	$56,455.73	$64,151.57	+$7,695.84	$76,316.93	+$19,861.20

It will be seen that, under the plan to halve the tax rate, there would be a net increase in taxes on these parcels of $7,695.84 or $61.08 per parcel. There would be a decrease in the net annual return to the owners of the land of $11,206,49 or $88.94 per lot. Capitalized,† this sum amounts to $1,778.80 which represents the probable decrease in the selling value of the average plot, which is now assessed at $21,117.‡

---
* The details for the sample are given in an appendix. *Cf. infra*, pp. 178-180.
† Interest rate, five per cent.
‡ The details of this sample are given in an appendix. *Cf. infra*, pp. 181-182.

(h). Mount Morris Park Section

Increased 204
Decreased 191
_____
395

The single-family dwellings in the somewhat irregular district bounded roughly by 118th Street, Seventh Avenue, 124th Street and Mount Morris Avenue, are of an unpretentious type. Practically all of the parcels are assessed at sums between ten and thirty thousand dollars. That the property in this region is about to be diverted to a different use is evident from the following statement of Tax Commissioner Purdy:

"An inspection of the names of the owners shows that the gathering of plottage is going on in this section, and in view of the building of tenement houses immediately south of Mount Morris Park it seems clear that tenement houses will at no distant day intrude into these residential blocks. With the building of the first tenement house on a block, the value of the remaining houses declines greatly."

The one-family houses situated on twenty-two blocks front were selected for analysis. In all there were 395 residences. It was found that in almost all of these parcels the ratio of building to land value was very close to the standard composite ratio for Manhattan. In approximately one-half of the cases the ratio was above the standard and in the other cases it was below. The table which follows shows the number of parcels whose taxes would be increased and decreased, grouped by streets:

NUMBER OF PARCELS (a) IN THE SELECTED BLOCKS OF THE MOUNT MORRIS PARK SECTION WHOSE TAXES WOULD INCREASE AND DECREASE IN CONSEQUENCE OF THE ADOPTION OF THE PROPOSAL TO UNTAX BUILDINGS

	Increased	Decreased
118th Street, north side, Seventh to Lenox Avenues	0	24
119th Street, Seventh to Lenox Avenues	22	33
120th Street, Seventh to Lenox Avenues	21	36
121st Street, Seventh to Lenox Avenues	13	48
122d Street, Seventh to Lenox Avenues	37	26
123d Street, south side, Seventh to Lenox Avenues	34	0
120th Street, north side, Lenox to Mt. Morris Avenues	12	0
121st Street, Lenox to Mt. Morris Avenues	6	16
122d Street, Lenox to Mt. Morris Avenues	14	2
123d Street, Lenox to Mt. Morris Avenues	22	2
124th Street, south side, Lenox to Mt. Morris Avenues	5	0
Mt. Morris Avenue, 120th to 121st Streets	6	4
Mt. Morris Avenue, 121st to 122d Streets	4	0
Mt. Morris Avenue, 122d to 123d Streets	5	0
Mt. Morris Avenue, 123d to 124th Streets	3	0
	204	191

(a) Single-family dwellings only.

Here, it will be seen, is considerable irregularity. In general the bulk of the decreases would occur in the southern portion of the section, *viz.*, south of 120th Street, while most of the increases would occur north of that street. The lots in this section are very narrow, most of them being eighteen to twenty feet in width. A considerable number have even less frontage than this.

Interesting results are secured when the parcels are grouped according to value. As is shown by the accompanying table and graphs the same condition here prevails as in the side streets east of Fifth Avenue. It is among the parcels of lower value that the bulk of the increases occur. The higher the value of the property, the greater is the decrease in taxes both absolutely and proportionally.

INCREASES AND DECREASES IN TAXES AMONG THE SINGLE-FAMILY DWELLINGS IN THE MOUNT MORRIS PARK SECTION GROUPED ACCORDING TO VALUE

	Number of Parcels		Percentage	
	Increased	Decreased	Increased	Decreased
$5,000 to $9,999	15	0	100	0
$10,000 to $14,999	64	4	94	6
$15,000 to $19,999	100	113	47	53
Over $20,000	25	74	25	75
	204	191	...	...

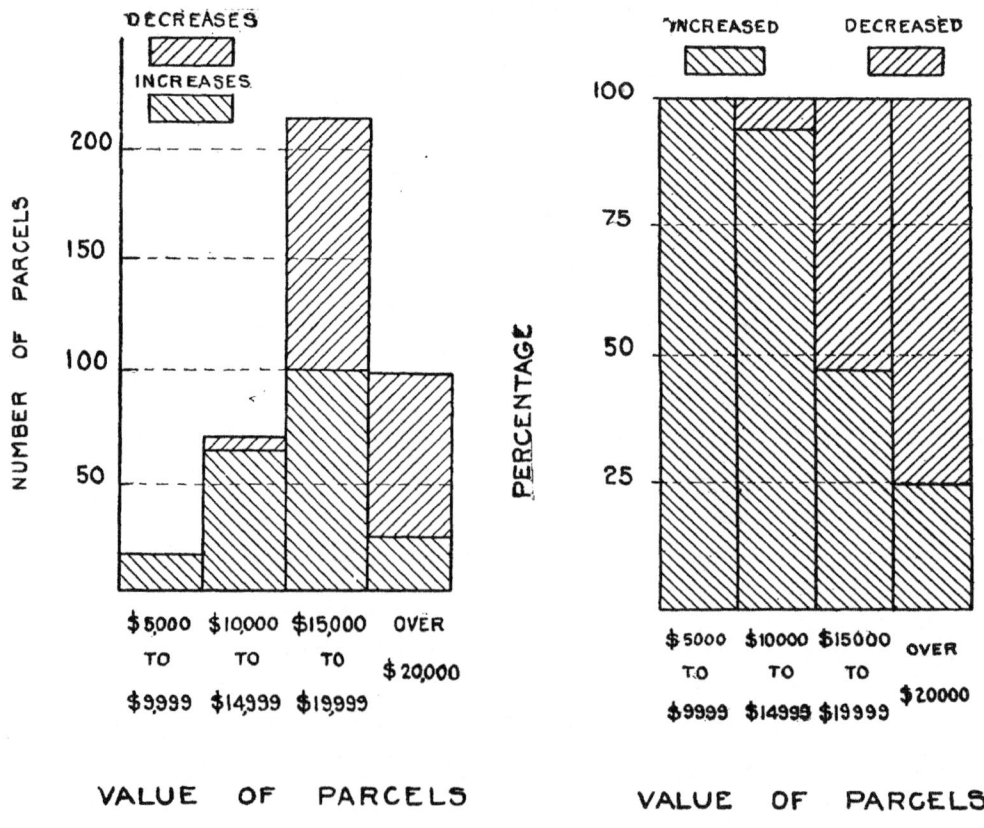

The assessed values of the parcels whose taxes would be increased or decreased may be grouped as follows:

ASSESSED VALUES OF SINGLE-FAMILY DWELLINGS IN MOUNT MORRIS PARK SECTION

	Improvements	Land	Total
GROUP A: Parcels whose taxes would be increased....	$1,015,200	$2,237,200	$3,252,400
GROUP B: Parcels whose taxes would be decreased....	1,579,300	1,963,900	3,543,200
Total.........................	$2,594,500	$4,201,100	$6,795,600

Applying the tax rates the following results are obtained:

TAXES PAYABLE BY OWNERS OF SINGLE-FAMILY DWELLINGS IN THE MOUNT MORRIS PARK SECTION UNDER THE PRESENT SYSTEM AND UNDER THE PROPOSED PLANS TO UNTAX BUILDINGS

	Present System	Rate on Improvements One-Half		Rate on Improvements One One-Hundredth	
	Levy	Levy	Increase or Decrease	Levy	Increase or Decrease
GROUP A: Parcels whose taxes would be increased.............	$57,757.42	$60,303.48	+$2,546.06	$64,333.08	+$6,575.66
GROUP B: Parcels whose taxes would be decreased.............	62,921.56	60,495.69	−2,425.87	56,670.99	−6,250.57
Total...............	$120,678.98	$120,799.17	+$120.19	$121,004.07	+$325.09

It will be seen that the net change in this district is almost negligible. If the full plan were put in effect the parcels in this district would yield only $325.09 more in taxes. Certain parcels would pay $6,575.66 more in taxes, while the other group would pay $6,250.57 less, the two figures almost offsetting each other.

The average house in this group is assessed at $6,568 and the land on which it stands at $10,636. The taxes on this property under the present system are $305.52. So near are the values in this parcel to the standard composite ratio for Manhattan that the adoption of the proposed changes would make almost no difference in the taxes charged against the parcel. Even if the full plan were put into operation the annual tax bill would increase only sixty-three cents (to $306.26).*

E. SUMMARY

It appears that in general the tax burden of Manhattan would be increased by the adoption of the proposed plan to untax buildings. The tax rate on land under the partial reduction plan would increase to 2.20

---

* The full data for this section is given in an appendix. *Cf. infra*, pp. 183-189.

and under the full plan to 2.86. Most of the sky-scrapers below Chambers Street would receive a decrease in taxes. Downtown tenements would pay higher and uptown tenements would pay lower taxes. Uptown apartment houses of good type, both elevator and walk-up types, would receive substantial reductions. Upon single-family houses the plan would have a variety of effects. On Fifth Avenue the typical house would pay higher taxes. On Riverside Drive it would pay lower taxes. In the case of the more modest houses in the side streets the typical parcel in almost every section would pay heavier taxes as a result of the adoption of the plan.

IV. EFFECTS IN THE BRONX UNDER CERTAIN ASSUMED CONDITIONS *

It has already been shown that in the redistribution of the general city taxes among the boroughs,† consequent to the adoption of the plan to untax buildings, the taxes for the Borough of the Bronx would be slightly reduced. It remains to discuss the effects within the borough.

A. TAX RATES

The effects upon the tax rates are shown in detail by the following graph :‡

THE BRONX

RATES UPON THE VARIOUS CLASSES OF PROPERTY UNDER THE PRESENT SYSTEM AND UNDER THE PROPOSED PLANS TO UNTAX BUILDINGS

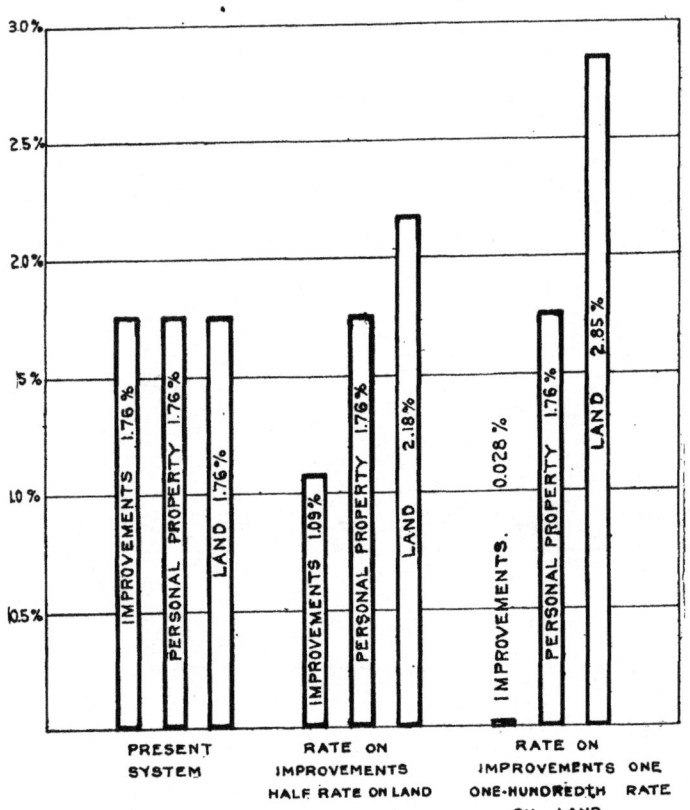

---

* The most important condition assumed is that the assessed values will not be disturbed. Cf. supra, p. 18.

† Cf. supra, pp. 22-23.

‡ The statistics upon which this graph is based are presented in the table on p. 21.

61

Under the assumptions, the increase in the rate on land would be to 2.18 if half the tax on buildings were removed and to 2.85 if the full plan were adopted.

B. DISTRIBUTION OF THE BURDEN AMONG THE ELEMENTS IN THE TAX BASE

How the present burden carried by the three elements in the tax base would be affected by the proposed changes is set forth in the accompanying graph.

THE BRONX
DISTRIBUTION OF TAXES AMONG THE ELEMENTS OF THE TAX BASE UNDER THE PRESENT SYSTEM AND UNDER THE PROPOSED PLANS TO UNTAX BUILDINGS

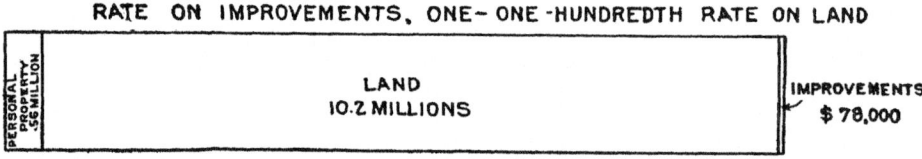

C. EFFECTS IN THE VARIOUS ASSESSMENT SECTIONS OF THE BOROUGH

The Borough of the Bronx is divided into ten assessment sections, whose boundaries are indicated in the map on page 63.

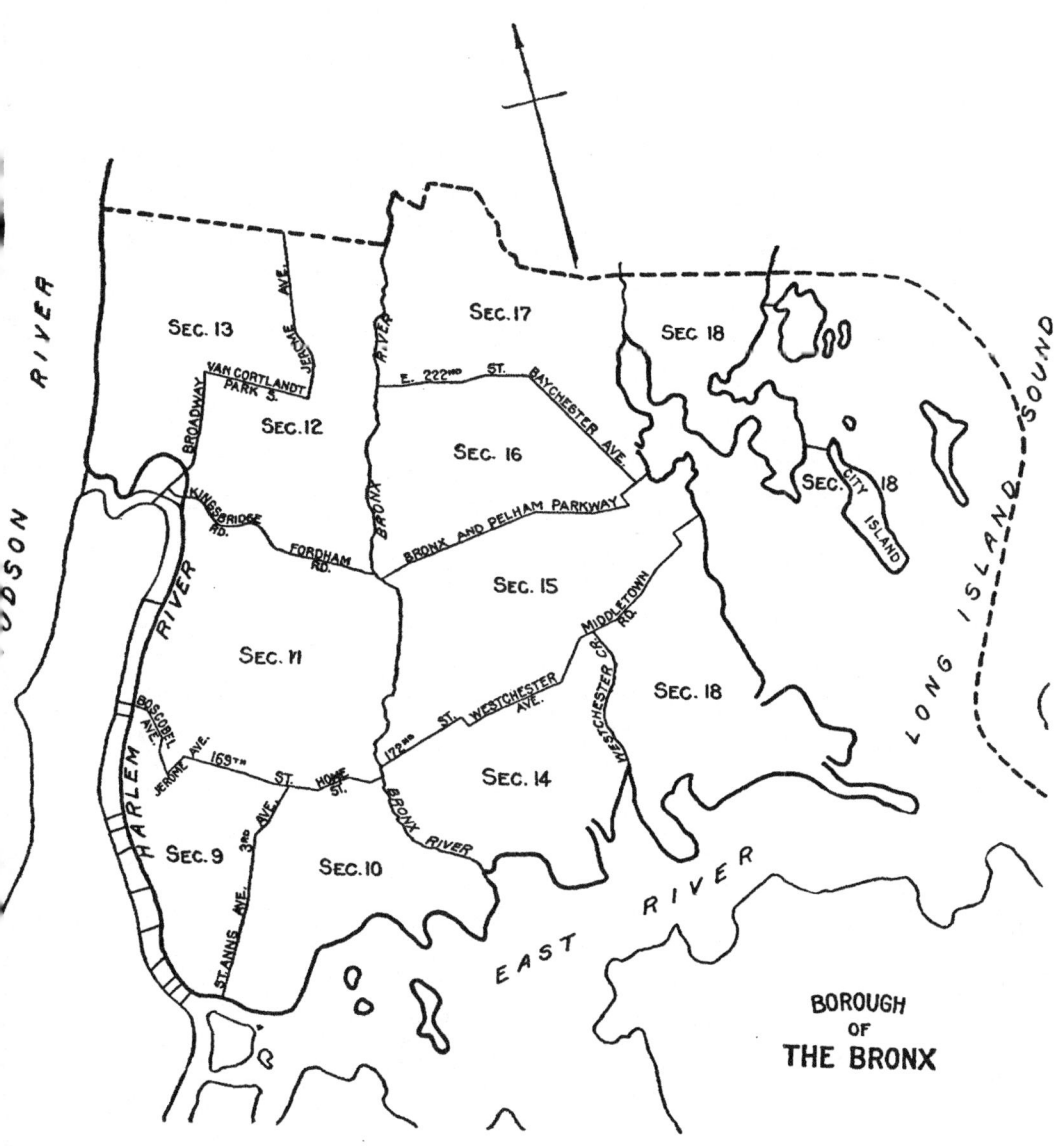

Tax Levies Upon the Real Estate (a) in the Various Assessment Sections of the Borough of The Bronx Under the Present System, and Under the Proposed Plan to Untax Buildings

	Levies			Increases and Decreases	
	Present System	Rate on Improvements One-Half	Rate on Improvements One One-Hundredth	Rate on Improvements One-Half	Rate on Improvements One One-Hundredth
Section 9:					
Land	$1,243,152.85	$1,541,460.99	$2,015,700.23		
Improvements	1,104,663.24	684,866.51	17,906.65		
	$2,347,816.09	$2,226,327.50	$2,033,606.88	—$121,488.59	—$314,209.21
Section 10:					
Land	$1,062,546.00	$1,317,515.55	$1,722,856.71		
Improvements	1,267,855.75	786,042.21	20,552.00		
	$2,330,401.75	$2,103,557.76	$1,743,408.71	—226,843.99	—586,993.04
Section 11:					
Land	$1,627,077.45	$2,017,512.50	$2,638,211.70		
Improvements	1,413,438.62	876,300.34	22,911.91		
	$3,040,516.07	$2,893,812.84	$2,661,123.61	—146,703.23	—379,392.46
Section 12:					
Land	$436,732.53	$541,531.28	$708,136.46		
Improvements	230,002.97	142,596.70	3,728.36		
	$666,735.50	$684,127.98	$711,864.82	+17,392.48	+45,129.32
Section 13:					
Land	$270,678.64	$335,630.95	$438,889.72		
Improvements	55,350.29	34,315.94	897.23		
	$326,028.93	$369,946.89	$439,786.95	+43,917.96	+113,758.02
Section 14:					
Land	$225,943.00	$280,160.50	$366,353.47		
Improvements	74,821.33	46,387.55	1,212.86		
	$300,764.33	$326,548.05	$367,566.33	+25,783.72	+66,802.00
Section 15:					
Land	$347,724.00	$431,164.18	$563,814.30		
Improvements	142,989.23	88,650.12	2,317.86		
	$490,713.23	$519,814.30	$566,132.16	+29,101.07	+75,418.93
Section 16:					
Land	$244,922.50	$303,694.34	$397,127.63		
Improvements	65,076.34	40,345.88	1,054.89		
	$309,998.84	$344,040.22	$398,182.52	+34,041.38	+88,183.68
Section 17:					
Land	$231,746.34	$287,356.41	$375,763.24		
Improvements	70,340.46	43,609.51	1,140.22		
	$302,086.80	$330,965.92	$376,903.46	+28,879.12	+74,816.66
Section 18:					
Land	$231,404.71	$286,932.80	$375,209.31		
Improvements	37,941.87	23,523.11	615.04		
	$269,346.58	$310,455.91	$375,824.35	+41,109.33	+106,477.77
Total:					
Land	$5,921,928.03	$7,342,959.50	$9,602,062.77		
Improvements	4,462,480.10	2,766,637.87	72,337.02		
	$10,384,408.13	$10,109,597.37	$9,674,399.79	—274,810.76	—710,008.34

(a) Not including the "Real Estate of Corporations."

The assessed values of land and improvements in these sections together with their ratios are as follows:

ASSESSED VALUES AND RATIOS IN THE VARIOUS ASSESSMENT SECTIONS OF THE BRONX

(Standard Composite Ratio: 38.71:61.29)

	Assessed Values			Taxes Payable
	Improvements	Land	Ratios	
Section 9	$62,698,340	$70,558,716	47.1:52.9	Decreased
" 10	71,960,800	60,307,855	54.5:45.5	"
" 11	80,223,775	92,349,461	46.5:53.5	"
" 12	13,054,480	24,788,011	34.5:65.5	Increased
" 13	3,141,565	15,363,145	17.0:83.0	"
" 14	4,246,700	12,824,045	24.9:75.1	"
" 15	8,115,765	19,736,076	29.2:70.8	"
" 16	3,693,595	13,901,281	21.0:79.0	"
" 17	3,992,375	13,153,430	23.9:76.7	"
" 18	2,153,500	13,134,040	14.1:85.9	"

An inspection of the ratios reveals the fact that the real estate in three sections (nine, ten and eleven) will pay smaller taxes while that in the other seven sections will pay greater. Sections nine, ten and eleven comprise the southwest portion of the borough—that which lies nearest the center of the city.

The amounts of the increases and decreases in the levies in real estate in the various assessment sections are shown in the table on page 64. It will be noticed that the net reduction upon the land and improvements in the borough would be $274,810.76 under the plan to halve the rate on buildings and $710,008.34 under the full plan. The increases, in those sections where the taxes would be raised, are relatively slight in amount.

D. EFFECTS IN SELECTED SECTIONS OF THE BOROUGH

(1). *Sample District from Assessment Section Nine*

Increased	11
Decreased	196
	207

Section Nine is one of the three Bronx sections whose taxes would be decreased. If the rate on buildings were halved the real estate in this section would pay smaller taxes by $121,488.59. If the full plan were adopted its tax bill would be decreased $314,209.21. This is in spite of the fact that approximately one-fourth of the land value of the section is made up of vacant lots ($18,663,715 as compared with $70,558,716). The taxes on this land would be increased from $328,830.40 to $407,736.85 under the plan to halve the building rate and to $533,179.41 under the full plan, but the decrease in the taxes on buildings would more than counterbalance this.

The character of the improvements in the section can be judged from the following data:

CLASSIFICATION OF BUILDINGS IN ASSESSMENT SECTION NINE, BOROUGH OF THE BRONX

	Number	Percentage
Single-family houses	2,334	34
Two-family houses	987	14
Tenements	2,969	43
Miscellaneous buildings	633	9
Total	6,923	100

Tenements and small houses of the one and two-family type constitute the bulk of improvements. The average of the value of the buildings is $9,056 and that of the improved plots is $7,496. It will be seen that there would be a considerable decrease in the taxes on the parcels in this section.

The sample selected consists of two assessment blocks (2284 and 2286) lying between Willis and Brook avenues. One block is that between 139th and 140th streets and the other by 141st and 142nd streets. In these two blocks, the vacant lots and exempt property being disregarded, there are 207 parcels, almost all of them small two-story houses. The average house is assessed for $2,924 and the average lot for $3,372. Of these 207 parcels all except eleven would receive decreases in taxes. All except one of these eleven are on Willis Avenue, and they comprise the more expensive parcels in the group.

The assessed values of the parcels in the sample grouped in the usual fashion are:

ASSESSED VALUES OF PARCELS IN THE SAMPLE FROM ASSESSMENT SECTION NINE, BOROUGH OF THE BRONX

	Improvements	Land	Total
GROUP A: Parcels whose taxes would be increased.......	$41,700	$88,500	$130,200
GROUP B: Parcels whose taxes would be decreased......	563,600	609,500	1,173,100
Total..............................	$605,300	$698,000	$1,303,300

The amounts by which the taxes in the parcels will be increased and decreased are shown in the following table:

TAXES PAYABLE BY OWNERS OF PARCELS IN THE SAMPLE FROM ASSESSMENT SECTION NINE, BOROUGH OF THE BRONX

	Present System	Rate on Improvements One-Half		Rate on Improvements One One-Hundredth	
	Levy	Levy	Increase or Decrease	Levy	Increase or Decrease
GROUP A: Parcels whose taxes would be increased:					
Improvements.........	$734.70	$455.50	—$279.20	$11.91	—$722.79
Land................	1,559.25	1,933.41	+374.16	2,528.24	+968.99
	$2,293.95	$2,388.91	+$94.96	$2,540.15	+$246.20
GROUP B: Parcels whose taxes would be decreased:					
Improvements.........	$9,929.90	$6,156.31	—$3,773.59	$160.96	—$9,768.94
Land................	10,738.60	13,315.44	+2,576.84	17,412.02	+6,673.42
	$20,668.50	$19,471.75	—$1,196.75	$17,572.98	—$3,095.52
TOTAL:					
Improvements.........	$10,664.60	$6,611.81	—$4,052.79	$172.87	—$10,491.73
Land................	12,297.85	15,248.85	+2,951.00	19,940.26	+7,642.41
	$22,962.45	$21,860.66	—$1,101.79	$20,113.13	—$2,849.32

If the half rate on buildings were adopted the taxes on the eleven parcels would increase $94.96 while the taxes on 196 parcels would decrease $1,196.75. In case the full rate were adopted the increase would be $246.20 and the decrease $3,095.52.

The average parcel at present pays $110.93 in taxes. This charge would be $105.61, or $5.32 less, under the half-rate plan and would be $97.16, or $13.77 less, under the full plan. The reduction, it will be seen, is not great, being in the first case less than five per cent. and under the full plan approximately twelve and one-half per cent.

Practically all of the houses included in this sample are rented. According to the assessment roll one man owns 94 of the 207 parcels. If the rate on buildings were halved and the entire reduction in the house-tax passed on to the tenants the annual rents paid by the occupants of these houses might be reduced at the most $3,052.79, or $14.75 on each parcel. The same action which would deprive the landlords of this sum would also decrease their total tax bill $1,101.79, but would increase the tax on their land $2,951.00. Assuming an interest rate of five per cent., the selling value of the land might be expected to depreciate $59,020 or approximately eight and one-half per cent.*

(2). *Sample District from Assessment Section Ten*

Increased 12
Decreased 87
                                         ———
                                          99

In Section Ten, it will be recalled, taxes upon real estate in general would be decreased even more than in Section Nine, just discussed.† This is in spite of the fact that there is greater percentage of vacant lots, almost one-third of the total land value of the section consisting of such property ($19,243,190 as compared with $60,307,855). Under the plan to halve the rate on buildings, this vacant land would pay $420,396.35 instead of $339,039.99. Under the full plan it would pay $549,733.68, an increase of $210,693.68. The total value of the improvements is very high compared with the value of the land on which they stand, the ratio being improvements, 63.7, to land, 36.3. The standard composite ratio is 38.71 (improvements) to 61.28 (land).

The character of the improvements is shown by the following summary:

CLASSIFICATION OF BUILDINGS IN ASSESSMENT SECTION TEN, BOROUGH OF THE BRONX

	Number	Percentage
Single-family houses	1,472	24
Two-family houses	1,264	21
Tenements	2,905	47
Miscellaneous buildings	495	8
Total	6,136	100

One and two-family houses and approximately the same number of tenements make up the bulk of the buildings. The average of the building values is $11,728 and of the improved plots $6,692. The decreases upon the parcels is so considerable, the values being as they are, that they counterbalance the great increase in the taxes on vacant land.

The sample district of this section consists of twelve blocks front as follows:—those included in the square bounded by 168th and 169th streets, and Union and Prospect avenues; those on both sides of Beck

---

* These statements assume, of course, that the change is made suddenly and that there is no opportunity for the effects to be discounted beforehand. Detailed data for this section is given in an appendix. *Cf. infra*, pp. 190-193.

† The reduction would be $226,843.99 under the half-rate plan and $586,993.04 under the full plan.

Street and the east side of Kelly Street between Longwood and Leggett avenues and those on both sides of 156th Street between Kelly and Beck streets. In these blocks there are ninety-nine houses. In the case of twelve parcels taxes would be increased by the adoption of the plan to untax buildings. For the other eighty-seven there would be a decrease. The parcels where taxes would be increased average $7,900 in value while those whose taxes would be decreased average $8,753.

The assessed values grouped according to the effect of the tax stand as follows:

ASSESSED VALUES OF PARCELS IN THE SAMPLE FROM ASSESSMENT SECTION TEN, BOROUGH OF THE BRONX

	Improvements	Land	Total
GROUP A:			
Parcels whose taxes would be increased..........	$30,300	$55,600	$85,900
GROUP B:			
Parcels whose taxes would be decreased..........	426,000	335,500	761,500
Total..................................	$456,300	$391,100	$847,400

The increases and decreases in the taxes on these parcels are shown in the accompanying table:

TAXES PAYABLE BY OWNERS OF PARCELS IN THE SAMPLE OF ASSESSMENT SECTION TEN, BOROUGH OF THE BRONX

	Present System	Rate on Improvements One-Half		Rate on Improvements One One-Hundredth	
	Levy	Levy	Increase or Decrease	Levy	Increase or Decrease
GROUP A:					
Parcels whose taxes would be increased:					
Improvements.........	$533.85	$330.97	—$202.88	$8.65	—$525.20
Land................	979.60	1,214.67	+235.07	1,588.36	+608.76
	$1,513.45	$1,545.64	+$32.19	$1,597.01	+$83.56
GROUP B:					
Parcels whose taxes would be decreased:					
Improvements.........	$7,505.57	$4,653.28	—$2,852.29	$121.67	—$7,383.90
Land................	5,911.07	7,329.50	+1,418.43	9,584.46	+3,673.39
	$13,416.64	$11,982.78	—$1,433.86	$9,706.13	—$3,710.51
TOTAL:					
Improvements.........	$8,039.42	$4,984.25	—$3,055.17	$130.32	—$7,909.10
Land................	6,890.67	8,544.17	+1,653.50	11,172.82	+4,282.15
	$14,930.09	$13,528.42	—$1,401.67	$11,303.14	—$3,626.95

An inspection of the names of the owners in this section reveals very few duplications, indicating a larger degree of home ownership by occupiers than in the previous sample. It appears from the table that, if the rate on improvements were halved, there would be a diminution in the taxes on the structures of $3,055.17. This means a potential reduction in annual rents, under certain assumed conditions, of $30.86 for each house in the sample district. The increase in the tax on land, on the other hand, would diminish the income of the owners $1,653.50. If this be capitalized (interest rate, five per cent), it appears that a depreciation of $33,070 in the selling value of the land is in prospect. The average parcel, under the assumed conditions, would decrease $334.04—from $3,950.56 to $3,616.52.*

(3). *Sample District From Assessment Section Eleven*

Increased............................	20
Decreased............................	138
	158

Section Eleven, the third Bronx section whose taxes would be decreased by the adoption of the proposed plan,† contains much vacant land, ($37,123,496 as compared with a total land value of $92,349,461), but, again, the improvements form so high a percentage of the value of the improved parcels that the decrease on such parcels more than counterbalances the increases on the vacant lots.

The character of the buildings in the section is shown by the following table:

CLASSIFICATION OF BUILDINGS IN ASSESSMENT SECTION ELEVEN, BOROUGH OF THE BRONX

	Number	Percentage
Single-family houses	4,045	42
Two-family houses	1,992	21
Tenements	2,974	31
Miscellaneous	550	6
Total	9,561	100

It will be noted that the one and two-family houses constitute nearly two-thirds of the total buildings.

The sample from this section consists of six blocks-front as follows: East 169th and 170th streets between Findlay and Teller avenues, East 170th Street, Teller to Clay avenues, and between East 169th and 170th streets on Findlay Avenue (east side), on Teller Avenue (both sides) and Clay Avenue (west side). In this sample there are 158 houses. The average parcel is assessed at $6,320 (house, $3,372 and land, $2,948). In the case of only twenty of these parcels would taxes be increased. All the remainder, 138 parcels, would pay lower taxes. The average value of the parcels whose taxes would be increased is considerably above the average of all, being $7,065 as compared with $6,320.

The assessed values, classified in the usual fashion, follow:

---

* Detailed information in regard to this sample may be found in an appendix. *Cf. infra,* pp. 194-195.
† *Cf. supra,* p. 64-65.

ASSESSED VALUES OF PARCELS IN THE SAMPLE FROM ASSESSMENT SECTION ELEVEN, BOROUGH OF THE BRONX

	Improvements	Land	Total
GROUP A: Parcels whose taxes would be increased	$46,200	$95,100	$141,300
GROUP B: Parcels whose taxes would be decreased	486,600	370,700	857,300
Total	$532,800	$465,800	$998,600

Applying the tax rates, the results shown in the following table are obtained:

TAXES PAYABLE BY OWNERS OF PARCELS IN ASSESSMENT SECTION ELEVEN, BOROUGH OF THE BRONX, UNDER THE PRESENT SYSTEM AND UNDER THE PROPOSED PLANS TO UNTAX BUILDINGS

	Present System	Rate on Improvements One-Half		Rate on Improvements One One-Hundredth	
	Levy	Levy	Increase or Decrease	Levy	Increase or Decrease
GROUP A: Parcels whose taxes would be increased:					
Improvements	$813.98	$504.65	—$309.33	$13.19	—$800.79
Land	1,675.54	2,077.60	+402.06	2,716.79	+1,041.25
	$2,489.52	$2,582.25	+$92.73	$2,729.98	+$240.46
GROUP B: Parcels whose taxes would be decreased:					
Improvements	$8,573.26	$5,315.23	—$3,258.03	$138.97	—$8,434.29
Land	6,531.25	8,098.50	+1,567.25	10,590.05	+4,058.80
	$15,104.51	$13,413.73	—$1,690.78	$10,729.02	—$4,375.49
TOTAL:					
Improvements	$9,387.24	$5,819.88	—$3,567.36	$152.16	—$9,235.08
Land	8,206.79	10,176.10	+1,969.31	13,306.84	+5,100.05
	$17,594.03	$15,995.98	—$1,598.05	$13,459.00	—$4,135.03

The net decrease in taxes under the half-rate plan would be $1,598.05 or $10.11 per parcel. The movement is nearly all in one direction, the increases on the few parcels in Group A amount to only $92.73, while the decreases in Group B are $1,690.78.

Altogether there would be, under the assumed conditions, a decrease of $3,567.36 in the tax on buildings if the rate levied on them were halved. This means a possible decrease in rent of $22.58 per house per year. There is little grouping of ownership in the section, indicating some degree of home ownership. The same action which would tend to reduce rents in this fashion would decrease net land revenue $1,969.31 and, at an assumed interest rate of five per cent., depreciate the selling value of the land $39,386.20. The average plot might be expected to decrease in value $249—from $2,948 to $2,699.*

---

* The details for this sample are given in an appendix. *Cf. infra*, pp. 196-198.

(4). *Sample District from Assessment Section Twelve*

Increased	4
Decreased	79
	83

Assessment Section Twelve lies south and east of Van Cortlandt Park. The untaxing of buildings would, it will be recalled,* increase the taxes on the real estate of this district. This is because of the very large proportion of vacant land, the vacant lots of this section being assessed at $15,131,761, and the improved lots at only $9,656,250, the vacant lots thus constituting three-fifths of the total land value. In the case of the improved parcels alone, however, the building value constitutes a high percentage of the total value (57.4 per cent.).

As will appear from an inspection of the following table, the single-family dwelling is the predominant type of improvement.

CLASSIFICATION OF BUILDINGS IN ASSESSMENT SECTION TWELVE, BOROUGH OF THE BRONX

	Number	Percentage
Single-family houses	1,454	47.9
Two-family houses	842	27.8
Tenements	335	11.1
Miscellaneous	397	13.2
Total	3,028	100.0

The sample selected consists of the following blocks front: Briggs Avenue, (east side), 194th to 196th streets and Bedford Park Boulevard to 201st Street; Bainbridge Avenue, (west side) 194th to 196th streets and Bedford Park Boulevard to 201st Street; Bedford Park Boulevard, (north side), from Briggs to Bainbridge avenues; 201st Street (south side), Briggs to Bainbridge avenues; and the four sides of the block bounded by 201st Street, Bainbridge Avenue, Perry Avenue and Mosholu Park Boulevard. In this sample there are eighty-three parcels. In only four cases would the taxes be increased. The average value of these four parcels is $10,800, while that of the 79 parcels would be decreased is only $8,849.

The assessed values grouped in the usual fashion are:

ASSESSED VALUES OF PARCELS IN THE SAMPLE FROM ASSESSMENT SECTION TWELVE, BOROUGH OF THE BRONX

	Improvements	Land	Total
GROUP A: Parcels whose taxes would be increased	$15,300	$27,900	$43,200
GROUP B: Parcels whose taxes would be decreased	403,000	296,100	699,100
Total	$418,300	$324,000	$742,300

* *Cf. supra,* pp. 64-65.

By applying the tax rates, the following results are obtained:

TAXES PAYABLE BY OWNERS OF PARCELS IN THE SAMPLE OF ASSESSMENT SECTION TWELVE, BOROUGH OF THE BRONX, UNDER THE PRESENT SYSTEM AND UNDER THE PROPOSED PLANS TO UNTAX BUILDINGS

	Present System	Rate on Improvements One-Half		Rate on Improvements One One-Hundredth	
	Levy	Levy	Increase or Decrease	Levy	Increase or Decrease
GROUP A: Parcels whose taxes would be increased:					
Improvements..........	$269.57	$167.12	—$102.45	$4.37	—$265.20
Land.................	491.56	609.52	+117.96	797.04	+305.48
	$761.13	$776.64	+$15.51	$801.41	+$40.28
GROUP B: Parcels whose taxes would be decreased:					
Improvements..........	$7,100.34	$4,402.05	—$2,698.29	$115.10	—$6,985.24
Land.................	5,216.90	6,468.75	+1,251.85	8,458.90	+3,242.00
	$12,317.24	$10,870.80	—$1,446.44	$8,574.00	—$3,743.24
TOTAL:					
Improvements..........	$7,369.91	$4,569.17	—$2,800.74	$119.47	—$7,250.44
Land.................	5,708.46	7,078.27	+1,369.81	9,255.94	+3,547.48
	$13,078.37	$11,647.44	—$1,430.93	$9,375.41	—$3,702.96

If the rate on buildings be halved, it appears that the net taxes on these 83 parcels will be decreased $1,430.93 or $17.23 per parcel. There is little grouping of ownership but if the houses were all rented there would be the sum of $2,800.74, decreased taxes on houses, which under certain conditions might be available for lowered rents. This would mean a reduction of $33.74 per parcel. At the same time the net annual income to the owners of the plots would diminish $1,369.81. Capitalized (interest rate, five per cent.) this sum would be $27,396.20. The owner of the average plot could then anticipate a reduction in the selling value of his plot of $330—from $3,904 to $3,574.*

(5). *Sample District from Assessment Section Fifteen*

Increased...................... 0
Decreased...................... 117
                               ———
                               117

The great bulk of the land in Section Fifteen, Borough of the Bronx, is vacant, $15,881,191 as compared with $19,736,076. This section extends from the Sound to Bronx River, between Bronx and Pelham parkways and Westchester Avenue and Middletown Road. Where the parcels are improved, the building values bear a high proportion to the value of the land (68 per cent.). The real estate in the section as a whole, it will be recalled,† would pay heavier taxes under the plan to untax buildings, but the taxes on typical improved plots would be decreased.

* Detailed statistics for the section are given in an appendix. *Cf. infra*, pp. 199-200.
† *Cf. supra*, pp. 64-65.

The character of the improvements in the section is shown in the following tabulation:

CLASSIFICATION OF BUILDINGS IN ASSESSMENT SECTION FIFTEEN, BOROUGH OF THE BRONX

	Number	Percentage
Single-family houses	1,073	37
Two-family houses	1,386	48
Tenements	205	07
Miscellaneous buildings	247	08
Total	2,911	100

Here the tenements are a small factor, the one and two-family houses constituting 85 per cent. of the total number of buildings.

The sample selected consists of the fronts of eight blocks as follows: Morris Park Avenue, (north side), between Amethyst Avenue and Victor Street and between Cruger and Holland avenues; Rhinelander Avenue, (south side), Unionport Road to Victor Street; and the following blocks between Rhinelander and Morris Park avenues, Amethyst Avenue and Unionport Road, (east side), Victor Street, (west side), Cruger Avenue (east side), and Holland Avenue (west side). In the district thus described there are 117 houses. The total assessed values of these parcels are improvements, $369,100, and land, $162,550. The average house is assessed for $3,155 and the plot on which it stands for $1,389; total, $4,544. In every case the taxes on these parcels would be decreased by the adoption of the plan to untax buildings. The following table shows the amounts of the decreases:

TAXES PAYABLE BY OWNERS OF PARCELS IN ASSESSMENT SECTION FIFTEEN, BOROUGH OF THE BRONX

	Present System	Rate on Improvements One-Half		Rate on Improvements One One-Hundredth	
	Levy	Levy	Increase or Decrease	Levy	Increase or Decrease
GROUP B: Parcels whose taxes would be decreased:					
Improvements	$6,503.06	$4,031.75	—$2,471.31	$105.41	—$6,397.65
Land	2,863.92	3,551.15	+687.23	6,643.68	+1,779.76
	$9,366.98	$7,582.90	—$1,784.08	$4,749.09	—$4,617.89

The net decrease in taxes on the average parcel under the plan to halve the rate on buildings is $15.25. The gross decrease in the tax on buildings would be $2,471.31. There is considerable grouping of ownership indicating that many of these houses are rented. If the entire decrease in the tax on buildings were passed on to the tenants, rents would be decreased $21.12 per parcel per year. At the same time the owners of the plots would receive $687.28 less each year. As a consequence their land might be expected to depreciate in price (interest rate five per cent.) $13,745.60. Each plot would under these conditions sell for $117 less, for $1,272 instead of $1,389.*

(6). *Sample District from Assessment Section Seventeen*

Increased 8
Decreased............................. 79
                                        ———
                                        87

Assessment Section Seventeen, Borough of the Bronx, which lies to the extreme north, is in all essentials similar to the section just discussed. With a total land value of $13,153,430, its vacant lots alone are assessed at $10,185,855. This predominance of vacant land is the cause for the increased taxes which real estate as a whole in this section would be called upon to bear,† were the rate on buildings decreased.

Of the parcels which are improved, the buildings form a high percentage of the total value (57 per cent.). The character of the improvements is shown in the following statement:

CLASSIFICATION OF BUILDINGS IN ASSESSMENT SECTION SEVENTEEN, BOROUGH OF THE BRONX

	Number	Percentage
Single-family houses..	816	55
Two-family houses...	528	35
Tenements...	38	3
Miscellaneous..	109	7
Total...	1,491	100

In this case ninety per cent. of the structures are small houses.

The sample selected consists of eleven fronts of blocks as follows: 222nd Street (north side), Barnes to Bronxwood avenues; 223rd Street (both sides), between the same avenues; 224th Street (south side), between the same avenues and on both sides between the White Plains Road and Barnes Avenue; 225th Street (south side), between the road and Barnes Avenue; the White Plains Road (east side), 224th to 225th streets; and Barnes Avenue (east side), 222nd Street to 223rd Street and (both sides) 223rd to 224th streets.

In the sample are 87 houses. Their average value is $4,809. In the case of only eight of these parcels would the taxes be increased if the rate on buildings were lowered. Moreover, the average value of the parcels whose taxes would be increased is greater than that of those whose taxes would be decreased.

---
* The details for this sample are given in an appendix. *Cf. infra,* pp. 201-202.
† *Cf. supra,* pp. 64-65.

The assessed values, grouped according to effect of the imposition of the plan, are as follows:

ASSESSED VALUES OF PARCELS IN THE SAMPLE FROM ASSESSMENT SECTION SEVENTEEN, BOROUGH OF THE BRONX

	Improvements	Land	Total
GROUP A: Parcels whose taxes would be increased..........	$13,500	$31,600	$45,100
GROUP B: Parcels whose taxes would be decreased..........	263,600	109,700	373,300
Total..................................	$277,100	$141,300	$418,400

By applying the tax rates the following figures, showing the amounts of the increases and decreases, are obtained:

TAXES PAYABLE BY OWNERS OF PARCELS IN ASSESSMENT SECTION SEVENTEEN, BOROUGH OF THE BRONX

	Present System	Rate on Improvements One-Half		Rate on Improvements One One-Hundredth	
	Levy	Levy	Increase or Decrease	Levy	Increase or Decrease
GROUP A: Parcels whose taxes would be increased:					
Improvements..........	$237.85	$147.46	−$90.39	$3.86	−$233.99
Land.................	556.75	690.35	+133.60	902.74	+345.99
	$794.60	$837.81	+$43.21	$906.60	+$112.00
GROUP B: Parcels whose taxes would be decreased:					
Improvements..........	$4,644.29	$2,879.36	−$1,764.93	$75.28	−$4,569.01
Land.................	1,932.77	2,396.56	+463.79	3,133.88	+1,201.11
	$6,577.06	$5,275.92	−$1,301.14	$3,209.16	−$3,367.90
TOTAL:					
Improvements..........	$4,882.14	$3,026.82	−$1,855.32	$79.14	−$4,803.00
Land.................	2,489.52	3,086.91	+597.39	4,036.62	+1,547.10
	$7,371.66	$6,113.73	−$1,257.93	$4,115.76	−$3,255.90

To halve the tax rate on buildings would be to diminish the net taxes on the average parcel $14.46. The reduction in the tax on buildings alone amounts to $1,855.32 or $21.33 per parcel. These are the sums, which under certain circumstances would be available for lowering rents. The net return to the owners of plots would at the same time be diminished $597.39, or $6.87 per parcel. Such a decrease, capitalized at an assumed interest rate of five per cent., would mean a diminution in the selling value of $11,947.80, or $137.32 per parcel.*

---

* For the detailed statistics for the sample, cf. infra, pp. 203-204.

E. SUMMARY

The presence of the large quantity of vacant land in the Bronx is all that prevents a very large decrease of taxes in this borough under the proposed plans to untax buildings. Vacant lots constitute more than half of the number of parcels and almost half of the land values in the borough.* If the vacant land were disregarded there would be a very considerable decrease in the taxes upon the remaining real estate.† In the samples selected from the various assessment sections it was only an exceptional parcel whose taxes would be increased by the proposed change. In almost every case a substantial net reduction appeared to be involved. Finally, contrary to the situation in Manhattan, those parcels whose taxes would be increased were not, on the average the less valuable parcels in each group but rather the more valuable ones. This indicates that in the Bronx the expenditure for houses by the more well-to-do in the various sections tends to turn toward a larger relative use of land than of buildings.

---

*The exact figures are:
Assessed Values of Land:
    Vacant.. $153,089,599
    Total... 336,116,060
Number of Parcels:
    Vacant.. 34,337
    Total... 66,598

†This is indicated by the following figures:
Improved Parcels:
    Land.. $183,026,461
    Improvements... 253,280,895

V. EFFECTS IN BROOKLYN UNDER CERTAIN ASSUMED CONDITIONS *

It has already been pointed out that the adoption of the proposed plan to untax buildings would mean decreased taxes for real estate in the Borough of Brooklyn as a whole.† The effects within the borough will now be examined in some detail.

A. TAX RATES

The accompanying graph illustrated the probable effects of the adoption of the proposed plans to untax buildings upon the tax rates levied on various types of property within the borough.‡

BROOKLYN
RATES UPON THE VARIOUS CLASSES OF PROPERTY UNDER THE PRESENT SYSTEM AND UNDER THE PROPOSED PLANS TO UNTAX BUILDINGS

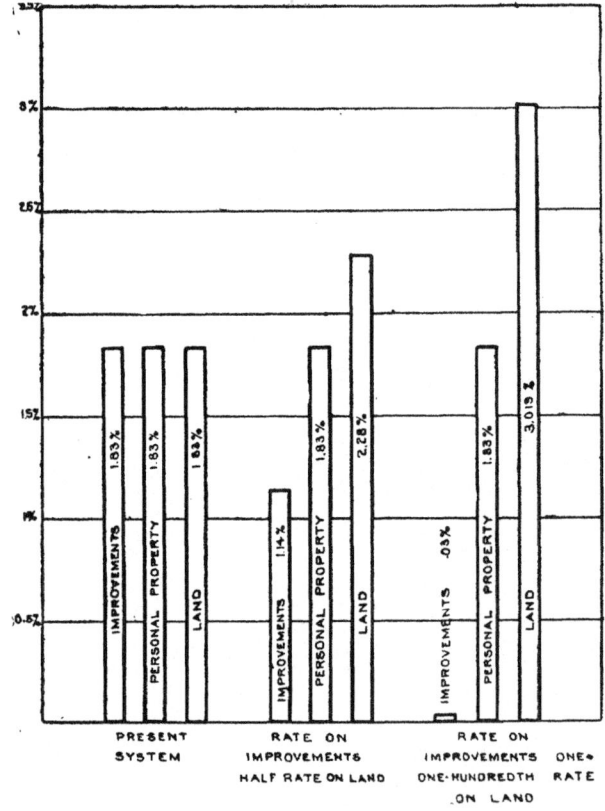

---

* The most important assumption is that the assessed values will not be disturbed. *Cf. supra*, p. 18.
† *Cf. supra*, pp. 22-23.
‡ The statistics upon which this graph is based are given in more detail in the table on p. 21.

B. DISTRIBUTION OF THE BURDEN AMONG THE ELEMENTS IN THE TAX BASE

The portions of the tax burden borne at present by the various types of property subjected to taxation, together with the probable changes that would result from the adoption of the plan to tax buildings at a lower rate, are shown in the graph which follows:

BROOKLYN

DISTRIBUTION OF TAXES AMONG THE ELEMENTS OF THE TAX BASE UNDER THE PRESENT SYSTEM AND UNDER THE PROPOSED PLANS TO UNTAX BUILDINGS

C. EFFECTS IN THE VARIOUS ASSESSMENT SECTIONS OF THE BOROUGH

Brooklyn is divided into twenty-five assessment sections, whose boundaries are traced on the map on page 80.

The assessed values in these sections together with the ratios comparable with the standard composite ratio for Brooklyn are given in the table on page 81.

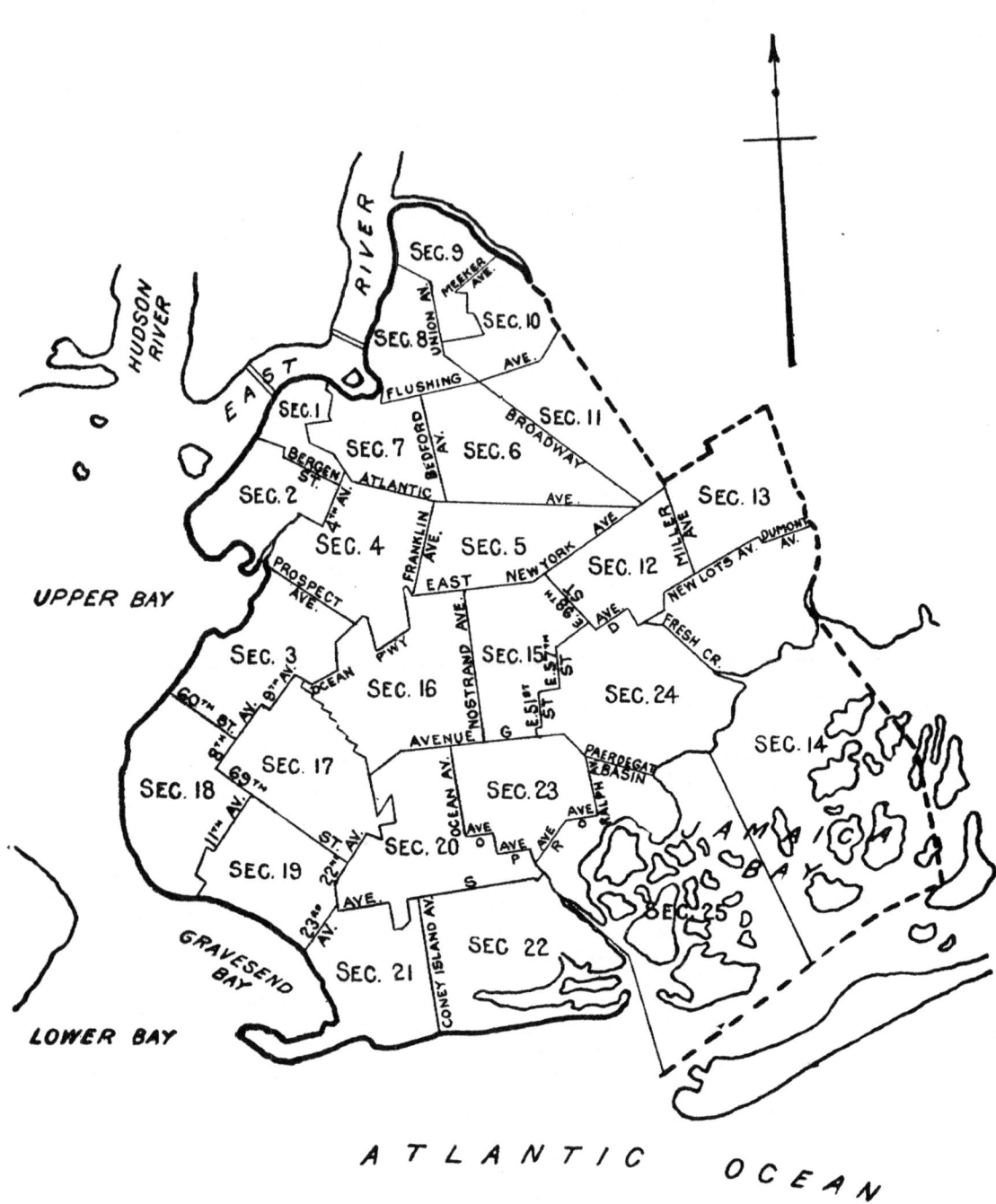

BOROUGH
OF
BROOKLYN

ASSESSED VALUES AND RATIOS IN THE VARIOUS ASSESSMENT SECTIONS OF BROOKLYN

(*Standard Composite Ratio: 39.44:60.56*)

	Assessed Values			Taxes Payable
	Improvements	Land	Ratio	
Section 1	$59,074,520	$82,879,500	41.6:58.4	Decreased
" 2	41,630,640	43,627,860	48.9:51.1	"
" 3	50,792,815	42,620,745	54.4:45.6	"
" 4	73,479,520	54,778,685	57.3:42.7	"
" 5	50,245,035	36,054,290	58.3:41.7	"
" 6	93,405,022	69,526,513	57.4:42.6	"
" 7	52,054,901	50,907,754	50.5:49.5	"
" 8	54,035,205	44,436,235	54.9:45.1	"
" 9	29,819,285	33,171,985	47.3:52.7	"
" 10	22,550,160	22,480,315	50.1:49.9	"
" 11	50,906,645	42,707,090	54.4:45.6	"
" 12	28,959,505	20,937,985	58.1:41.9	"
" 13	26,496,910	18,517,280	58.9:41.1	"
" 14	2,021,745	4,361,255	31.7:68.3	Increased
" 15	9,030,880	12,456,020	42.0:58.0	Decreased
" 16	50,658,780	46,196,160	52.3:47.7	"
" 17	19,491,380	20,039,475	49.3:50.7	"
" 18	18,828,220	32,393,205	36.8:63.2	Increased
" 19	15,399,305	20,022,900	43.5:56.5	Decreased
" 20	15,620,575	22,147,580	42.4:58.6	"
" 21	10,941,400	26,094,955	29.5:70.5	Increased
" 22	3,866,890	13,476,290	22.3:77.7	"
" 23	5,621,455	13,035,505	30.1:69.9	"
" 24	1,874,900	7,207,150	20.6:79.4	"
" 25	822,080	3,782,427	17.9:82.1	"

It will be noted that in the case of seven sections out of the twenty-five the taxes will be increased, while in the other eighteen sections they will be decreased. By referring to the map it can be seen that the sections whose taxes would be increased (14, 18, 21, 22, 23, 24 and 25) are in the extreme south-east portion of Brooklyn and in the extreme south-west portion. In all of these sections the vacant land is a very important factor.

The amounts of the increases and decreases in the levies on land and improvements in the various assessment sections are shown in the table on pages 82 and 83. The net decrease for the borough would be very considerable—$1,901,935.56 under the half-rate plan and $4,962,585.17 under the full plan.

TAX LEVIES UPON THE REAL ESTATE (a) IN THE VARIOUS ASSESSMENT SECTIONS OF PROPOSED PLANS TO

	Levies			Increases and Decreases	
	Present System	Rate on Improvements One-Half	Rate on Improvements One One-Hundredth	Rate on Improvements One-Half	Rate on Improvements One One-Hundredth
SECTION 1:					
Land.............	$1,522,463.26	$1,897,725.06	$2,502,397.32		
Improvements......	1,085,175.30	676,326.46	17,834.60		
	$2,607,638.56	$2,574,051.52	$2,520,231.92	—$33,587.04	—$87,406.64
SECTION 2:					
Land.............	$801,426.34	$998,964.56	$1,317,264.70		
Improvements......	764,738.20	476,616.71	12,568.29		
	$1,566,164.54	$1,475,581.27	$1,329,832.99	—90,583.27	—236,331.55
SECTION 3:					
Land.............	$782,926.04	$975,904.25	$1,286,856.68		
Improvements......	933,043.69	581,511.70	15,334.35		
	$1,715,969.73	$1,557,415.95	$1,302,191.03	—158,553.78	—413,778.70
SECTION 4:					
Land.............	$1,006,262.53	$1,254,289.46	$1,653,943.79		
Improvements......	1,349,789.39	841,244.98	22,183.47		
	$2,356,051.92	$2,095,534.44	$1,676,127.26	—260,517.48	—679,924.66
SECTION 5:					
Land.............	$662,302.89	$825,549.50	$1,088,594.39		
Improvements......	922,981.19	575,240.33	15,168.98		
	$1,585,284.08	$1,400,789.83	$1,103,763.37	—184,494.25	—481,520.71
SECTION 6:					
Land.............	$1,277,174.23	$1,591,976.38	$2,099,227.91		
Improvements......	1,715,812.89	1,069,366.08	28,198.98		
	$2,992,987.12	$2,661,342.46	$2,127,426.89	—331,644.66	—865,560.23
SECTION 7:					
Land.............	$935,155.08	$1,165,655.21	$1,537,068.00		
Improvements......	956,227.71	595,960.95	15,715.37		
	$1,891,382.79	$1,761,616.16	$1,552,783.37	—129,766.63	—338,599.42
SECTION 8:					
Land.............	$816,275.86	$1,017,474.25	$1,341,672.13		
Improvements......	992,605.10	618,632.85	16,313.23		
	$1,808,880.96	$1,636,107.10	$1,357,985.36	—172,773.86	—450,895.60
SECTION 9:					
Land.............	$609,356.10	$759,552.21	$1,001,568.38		
Improvements......	547,768.34	341,392.05	9,002.44		
	$1,157,124.44	$1,100,944.26	$1,010,570.82	—56,180.18	—146,553.62
SECTION 10:					
Land.............	$412,954.39	$514,740.76	$678,752.65		
Improvements......	414,237.42	258,170.02	6,807.89		
	$827,191.81	$772,910.78	$685,560.54	—54,281.03	—141,631.27
SECTION 11:					
Land.............	$784,512.16	$977,881.32	$1,289,463.71		
Improvements......	935,134.71	582,814.91	15,368.72		
	$1,719,646.87	$1,560,696.23	$1,304,832.43	—158,950.64	—414,814.44
SECTION 12:					
Land.............	$384,622.41	$479,425.42	$632,184.77		
Improvements......	531,974.52	331,548.68	8,742.87		
	$916,596.93	$810,974.10	$640,927.64	—105,622.83	—275,669.29
SECTION 13:					
Land.............	$340,155.03	$423,997.57	$559,095.94		
Improvements......	486,737.64	303,355.17	7,999.42		
	$826,892.67	$727,352.74	$567,095.36	—99,539.93	—259,797.31

(a) Not including the "Real Estate of Corporations."

THE BOROUGH OF BROOKLYN, UNDER THE PRESENT SYSTEM, AND UNDER THE UNTAX BUILDINGS

	Levies			Increases and Decreases	
	Present System	Rate on Improvements, One-Half	Rate on Improvements One One-Hundredth	Rate on Improvements One-Half	Rate on Improvements One One-Hundredth
SECTION 14:					
Land...............	$80,114.51	$99,861.40	$131,680.24		
Improvements.......	37,138.65	23,146.35	610.36		
	$117,253.16	$123,007.75	$132,290.60	+5,754.59	+15,037.44
SECTION 15:					
Land...............	$228,812.10	$285,210.47	$376,087.10		
Improvements.......	165,893.65	103,391.84	2,726.42		
	$394,705.75	$388,602.31	$378,813.52	—6,103.44	—15,892.23
SECTION 16:					
Land...............	$848,604.98	$1,057,771.95	$1,394,809.90		
Improvements.......	930,581.53	579,977.17	15,293.89		
	$1,779,186.51	$1,637,749.12	$1,410,103.79	—141,437.39	—369,082.72
SECTION 17:					
Land...............	$368,117.14	$458,851.87	$605,055.88		
Improvements.......	358,048.85	223,150.96	5,884.45		
	$726,165.99	$682,002.83	$610,940.33	—44,163.16	—115,225.66
SECTION 18:					
Land...............	$595,050.22	$741,720.17	$978,054.52		
Improvements.......	345,866.87	215,558.64	5,684.24		
	$940,917.09	$957,278.81	$983,738.76	+16,361.72	+42,821.67
SECTION 19:					
Land...............	$367,812.66	$458,472.35	$604,555.42		
Improvements.......	282,879.07	176,302.02	4,649.05		
	$650,691.73	$634,774.37	$609,204.47	—15,917.36	—41,487.26
SECTION 20:					
Land...............	$406,842.19	$507,122.00	$668,706.31		
Improvements.......	286,943.71	178,835.28	4,715.85		
	$693,785.90	$685,957.28	$673,422.16	—7,828.62	—20,363.74
SECTION 21:					
Land...............	$479,353.88	$597,506.62	$787,890.20		
Improvements.......	200,989.14	125,264.81	3,303.21		
	$680,343.02	$722,771.43	$791,193.41	+42,428.41	+110,850.39
SECTION 22:					
Land...............	$247,554.06	$308,572.00	$406,892.32		
Improvements.......	71,033.22	44,270.86	1,167.41		
	$318,587.28	$352,842.86	$408,059.73	+34,255.58	+89,472.45
SECTION 23:					
Land...............	$239,457.01	$298,479.17	$393,583.61		
Improvements.......	103,263.88	64,358.35	1,697.12		
	$342,720.89	$362,837.52	$395,280.73	+20,116.63	+52,559.84
SECTION 24:					
Land...............	$132,392.46	$165,025.00	$217,606.92		
Improvements.......	34,441.16	21,465.17	566.03		
	$166,833.62	$186,490.17	$218,172.95	+19,656.55	+51,339.33
SECTION 25:					
Land...............	$69,481.67	$86,607.74	$114,203.57		
Improvements.......	15,101.28	9,411.75	248.19		
	$84,582.95	$96,019.49	$114,451.76	+11,436.54	+29,868.81
ALL SECTIONS:					
Land...............	$14,399,179.21	$17,948,336.71	$23,667,216.36		
Improvements.......	14,468,407.14	9,017,314.08	237,784.82		
	$28,867,586.35	$26,965,650.79	$23,905,001.18	—1,901,935.56	—4,962,585.17

D. EFFECTS IN SELECTED SECTIONS OF THE BOROUGH

(1). *Sample District from Assessment Section Five*

Increased	4
Decreased	148
	152

Vacant land accounts for less than one-fourth of the total land value of Assessment Section Five, Borough of Brooklyn ($8,999,460 as compared with $36,054,290). At the same time the value of the buildings makes up a very large share of the total value of improved real estate ($50,245,035 as compared with $77,299,865). It is readily seen that the adoption of the plan would mean much decreased taxes for this section.*

The following table reveals the type of the improvements:

CLASSIFICATION OF BUILDINGS IN ASSESSMENT SECTION FIVE, BOROUGH OF BROOKLYN

	Number	Percentage
Single-family houses	2,879	32
Two-family houses	3,519	40
Tenements	2,148	24
Miscellaneous	321	4
Total	8,867	100

Small houses comprise 72 per cent. of the total number of structures.

The sample selected from this section consists of the block bounded by Albany Avenue, Park Place, Troy Avenue, and Sterling Place, and of three fronts of the block bounded by Troy Avenue, Park Place, Sterling Place and Schenectady Avenue. There are 152 small houses in this sample and in the case of only four would the taxes be increased. The four parcels whose taxes would be increased in this case average much less in value than those whose taxes would be decreased ($3,000 as compared with $5,018).

The assessed values arranged according to the effect of the proposed plan are as follows:

ASSESSED VALUES OF REAL ESTATE IN SECTION FIVE, BOROUGH OF BROOKLYN

	Improvements	Land	Total
GROUP A:			
Parcels whose taxes would be increased	$3,375	$8,625	$12,000
GROUP B:			
Parcels whose taxes would be decreased	471,555	271,025	742,580
Total	$474,930	$279,650	$754,580

By applying the tax rates the figures given in the following table are obtained:

---

* *Cf. supra*, pp. 81-83.

TAXES PAYABLE BY OWNERS OF PARCELS IN SECTION FIVE, BOROUGH OF BROOKLYN, UNDER THE PRESENT SYSTEM AND UNDER THE PROPOSED PLANS TO UNTAX BUILDINGS

	Present System	Rate on Improvements One-Half		Rate on Improvements One One-Hundredth	
	Levy	Levy	Increase or Decrease	Levy	Increase or Decrease
GROUP A: Parcels whose taxes would be increased:					
Improvements	$62.00	$38.64	—$23.36	$1.02	—$60.98
Land	158.44	197.49	+39.05	260.42	+101.98
	$220.44	$236.13	+$15.69	$261.44	+$41.00
GROUP B: Parcels whose taxes would be decreased:					
Improvements	$8,662.28	$5,398.69	—$3,263.59	$142.36	—$8,519.92
Land	4,978.62	6,205.77	+1,227.15	8,183.11	+3,204.49
	$13,640.90	$11,604.46	—$2,036.44	$8,325.47	—$5,315.43
TOTAL:					
Improvements	$8,724.28	$5,437.33	—$3,286.95	$143.38	—$8,580.90
Land	5,137.06	6,403.26	+1,266.20	8,443.53	+3,306.47
	$13,861.34	$11,840.59	—$2,020.75	$8,586.91	—$5,274.43

It appears that to halve the tax rate on buildings would result in a decrease in the net taxes on this group of 152 parcels of $2,020.75 or $13.30 per parcel. The reduction in the tax on buildings alone would be $3,286.95, and if this were passed on as lower rents to the tenants it would mean $21.62 less in the annual rent on the average house. The owners of the plots would suffer a diminution of $1,266.20 in the net annual return from the land. Capitalized at five per cent. this amounts to $25,324.00, or a depreciation in the selling price of each parcel of land equal to $166.61.*

(2). *Sample District from Assessment Section Six*

Increased 7
Decreased 123
                                    ———
                                    130

In Section Six vacant land is of still less importance than it was shown to be in the section just discussed. Out of a total assessed land value of $69,526,513, only $2,358,280 is credited to vacant lots. Here again the buildings are responsible for the bulk of the value of improved real estate (improvements $93,405,022; total, $160,573,255). This explains the decrease in the taxes on the real estate of the section in general,† a decrease greater than that of any other section in Brooklyn.

The buildings in the section may be grouped as follows:

CLASSIFICATION OF BUILDINGS IN ASSESSMENT SECTION SIX, BOROUGH OF BROOKLYN

	Number	Percentage
Single-family houses	11,879	54
Two-family houses	4,313	20
Tenements	4,941	22
Miscellaneous	941	4
Total	22,074	100

* The details of the sample are given in an appendix. Cf. *infra*, pp. 205-207.
† Cf. *supra*, pp. 79-83.

Small houses, it will be noticed, constitute 74 per cent. of the total number.

The sample selected, which contains 130 small houses, consists of one side each of Decatur and McDonough streets between Lewis and Reid avenues and one side of Reid Avenue between McDonald and Decatur streets. The average parcel is assessed at $8,061 (building, $5,320, and land $2,741). In the cases of only seven out of the 130 parcels would the taxes be increased by the adoption of the plan to untax buildings. These parcels, as in the previous section, average lower in value than the parcels whose taxes would be decreased.

The assessed values, grouped in the usual manner are:

ASSESSED VALUES OF PARCELS IN SAMPLE FROM SECTION SIX, BOROUGH OF BROOKLYN

	Improvements	Land	Total
GROUP A: Parcels whose taxes would be increased........	$14,125	$33,075	$47,200
GROUP B: Parcels whose taxes would be decreased........	677,415	323,275	1,000,690
Total.................................	$691,540	$356,350	$1,047,890

The tax levies arrived at by applying the tax rates to the foregoing valuations are:

TAXES PAYABLE BY OWNERS OF PARCELS IN SAMPLE FROM SECTION SIX, BOROUGH OF BROOKLYN, UNDER THE PRESENT SYSTEM AND UNDER THE PROPOSED PLANS TO UNTAX BUILDINGS

	Present System	Rate on Improvements One-Half		Rate on Improvements One One-Hundredth	
	Levy	Levy	Increase or Decrease	Levy	Increase or Decrease
GROUP A: Parcels whose taxes would be increased:					
Improvements..........	$259.47	$161.71	—$97.76	$4.26	—$255.21
Land................	607.57	757.33	+149.76	998.64	+391.07
	$867.04	$919.04	+$52.00	$1,002.90	+$135.86
GROUP B: Parcels whose taxes would be decreased:					
Improvements..........	$12,443.84	$7,755.52	—$4,688.32	$204.51	—$12,239.33
Land................	5,938.43	7,402.16	+1,463.73	9,760.71	+3,822.28
	$18,382.27	$15,157.68	—$3,224.59	$9,965.22	—$8,417.05
TOTAL:					
Improvements..........	$12,703.31	$7,917.23	—$4,786.08	$208.77	—$12,494.54
Land................	6,546.00	8,159.49	+1,613.49	10,759.35	+4,213.35
	$19,249.31	$16,076.72	—$3,172.59	$10,968.12	—$8,281.19

The adoption of the half-rate plan, it will be seen, would mean a net reduction for these 130 parcels of $3,172.59, or $24.40 per parcel. The maximum reduction in rent is represented by the decrease in building taxes which is $4,786.08, or $36.82 per parcel. Net annual revenues to the owners of the plots would be diminished $1,613.49, or $12.41 per plot. Capitalized* this would mean a possible diminution in the value of the average plot of $248.20.†

(3). *Sample District from Assessment Section Eight*

Increased 1
Decreased 161
                                    ———
                                    162

Assessment Section Eight has the same characteristics as the two preceding ones—a small proportion of vacant land ($2,079,290 as compared with a total land value of $44,436,235), and a high proportion of building value to land value in the improved parcels ($54,035,205, buildings, as compared with $42,356,945, land). Taxes on real estate as a whole in this section would decrease considerably by the adoption of the proposed plan.‡

The typical improvement in this section is the tenement. This is apparent from the following data:

CLASSIFICATION OF BUILDINGS IN ASSESSMENT SECTION EIGHT, BOROUGH OF BROOKLYN

	Number	Percentage
Single-family houses	445	5
Two-family houses	2,289	28
Tenements	4,473	55
Miscellaneous	953	12
Total	8,160	100

The sample selected consist of 162 parcels from assessment blocks 2,199, 2,200, and 2,201, extending between Bedford and Division avenues and Keap and Hooper streets. The parcels average $6,926 in value. If the plan to untax buildings were adopted, only one parcel out of the 162 would pay increased taxes. This parcel is more valuable than the average, being assessed at $10,500.

The assessed values of the parcels in the sample, grouped according to the effect of the proposed plan, are as follows:

---

* Interest rate, five per cent.
† For details of the parcels in this sample, *cf. infra*, pp. 208-210.
‡ *Cf. supra*, pp. 79-83.

ASSESSED VALUES OF REAL ESTATE IN SAMPLE FROM SECTION EIGHT, BOROUGH OF BROOKLYN

	Improvements	Land	Total
GROUP A: Parcels whose taxes would be increased	$2,900	$7,600	$10,500
GROUP B: Parcels whose taxes would be decreased	584,800	526,650	1,111,450
Total	$587,700	$534,250	$1,121,950

The following table shows the result of extending the tax rates against the preceding values:

TAXES PAYABLE BY OWNERS OF PARCELS IN SAMPLE SECTION EIGHT, BOROUGH OF BROOKLYN, UNDER THE PRESENT SYSTEM AND UNDER THE PROPOSED PLANS TO UNTAX BUILDINGS

	Present System	Rate on Improvements One-Half		Rate on Improvements One One-Hundredth	
	Levy	Levy	Increase or Decrease	Levy	Increase or Decrease
GROUP A: Parcels whose taxes would be increased:					
Improvements	$53.27	$33.20	−$20.07	$0.88	−$52.39
Land	139.61	174.02	+34.41	229.47	+89.86
	$192.88	$207.22	+$14.34	$230.35	+$37.47
GROUP B: Parcels whose taxes would be decreased:					
Improvements	$10,742.54	$6,695.20	−$4,047.34	$176.55	−$10,565.99
Land	9,674.35	12,058.92	+2,384.57	15,901.25	+6,226.90
	$20,416.89	$18,754.12	−$1,662.77	$16,077.80	−$4,339.09
TOTAL:					
Improvements	$10,795.81	$6,728.40	−$4,067.41	$177.43	−$10,618.38
Land	9,813.96	12,232.94	+2,418.98	16,130.72	+6,316.76
	$20,609.77	$18,961.34	−$1,648.43	$16,308.15	−$4,301.62

Under the plan to halve the rate on buildings, there would be a net reduction on the parcels in the sample of $1,648.43, or $10.18 per parcel. The maximum reduction in rents would correspond with the amount of the decrease in the tax on buildings, which is $4,067.41, or $25.11 per parcel. On the other hand, the same action would diminish the net annual revenue of the owners of the plots $2,418.98, or $14.93 per plot. Capitalized* this means a possible decrease in selling value of $298.60 per plot.†

(4). *Sample District from Assessment Section Twelve*

Increased	0
Decreased	98
	98

Assessment Section Twelve contains relatively more vacant land than the preceding sections ($6,281,550 as compared with a total land

---

* Interest rate, five per cent.
† For the detailed statistics for the sample, *cf. infra*, pp. 211-213.

value of $20,937,985). However, the value of buildings is so great as compared with the value of the plots on which they stand (improvements, $28,959,505; improved land $14,656,435), as to counterbalance the influence of the vacant lands and the taxes for the section as a whole show a decrease.*

In this section, again, tenements form the bulk of the improvements. This is made plain by the following table:

CLASSIFICATION OF BUILDINGS IN ASSESSMENT SECTION TWELVE, BOROUGH OF BROOKLYN

	Number	Percentage
Single-family houses	1,386	21
Two-family houses	1,526	23
Tenements	3,436	51
Miscellaneous	314	5
Total	6,662	100

The sample from this section consists of the eight blocks-front in the district stretching from New Jersey Avenue to Bradford Street and from Belmont to Sutter avenues. Every one of the ninety-eight parcels in this section would receive a decrease in taxes.

The assessed values of the parcels in the sample section are, improvements $318,600 and land $106,100. The average parcel is assessed, then, at $4,333.67.

The levies against this property are shown in the following table:

TAXES PAYABLE BY OWNERS OF PARCELS IN SAMPLE FROM AS   MENT SECTION TWELVE BOROUGH OF BROOKLYN, UNDER THE PRESENT SYSTEM AND UNDER THE PROPOSED PLANS TO UNTAX BUILDINGS

	Present System	Rate on Improvements One-Half		Rate on Improvements One One-Hundredth	
	Levy	Levy	Increase or Decrease	Levy	Increase or Decrease
GROUP B: Parcels whose taxes would be decreased:					
Improvements	$5,852.55	$3,647.56	—$2,204.99	$91.18	—$5,761.37
Land	1,949.01	2,429.41	+480.40	3,203.50	+1,254.49
	$7,801.56	$6,076.97	—$1,724.59	$3,294.68	—$4,506.88

The adoption of the half rate would reduce the net taxes of the owners of these 98 parcels $1,724.59, or $17.60 per parcel. The maximum available for lowered rents would be $2,204.99, or $22.50 per parcel per year. The decrease in net annual return to the owners of the plots would be $480.40, or $4.90 per year per parcel.†

* Cf. supra, p. 79-83.
† The details for the parcels in the sample are given in an appendix. Cf. infra, pp. 212-213.

(5). *Sample District from Assessment Section Sixteen*

> Increased 4
> Decreased 238
> ———
> 242

Assessment Section Sixteen (located in Flatbush), Borough of Brooklyn, contains considerable vacant land ($9,789,375 as compared with a total land value of $46,196,160), but here again the building value is great enough ($50,658,780; improved land, $36,406,785) to counterbalance, so that there would be a net decrease in taxes for the real estate of the entire section.*

The single-family houses outnumber all other types of building in this section. The details are as follows:

CLASSIFICATION OF BUILDINGS IN SAMPLE FROM ASSESSMENT SECTION SIXTEEN
BOROUGH OF BROOKLYN

	Number	Percentage
Single-family houses	6,303	57
Two-family houses	3,381	31
Tenements	836	8
Miscellaneous	441	4
Total	10,961	100

The sample from this section consists of thirty-two blocks-front selected from the following districts: Dorchester Road to Ditmas Avenue; Stratford to Marlborough roads; Ditmas to Newkirk avenues, 16th to 19th streets; Foster Avenue to Avenue G, 17th to 19th streets, In these blocks there are 242 houses. The average parcel is assessed at $10,481.20. Every parcel of the 242, except four, would pay lower taxes were the plans to untax buildings adopted. The four parcels whose taxes would be increased are among the most expensive in the entire sample, averaging $22,325 a piece.

The assessed values grouped in the usual fashion are:

ASSESSED VALUES OF PARCELS IN SAMPLE FROM ASSESSMENT SECTION SIXTEEN,
BOROUGH OF BROOKLYN

	Improvements	Land	Total
GROUP A:			
Parcels whose taxes would be increased	$33,700	$55,600	$89,300
GROUP B:			
Parcels whose taxes would be decreased	1,396,600	1,050,550	2,447,150
Total	$1,430,300	$1,106,150	$2,536,450

Extending the tax rates against these values, the following results are obtained:

———
* *Cf. supra*, pp. 79-83.

Taxes Payable by Owners of Parcels in Sample from Assessment Section Sixteen, Borough of Brooklyn, Under the Present System and Under the Proposed Plans to Untax Buildings

	Present System	Rate on Improvements One-Half		Rate on Improvements One One-Hundredth	
	Levy	Levy	Increase or Decrease	Levy	Increase or Decrease
GROUP A: Parcels whose taxes would be increased:					
Improvements	$619.06	$385.82	—$233.24	$10.17	—$608.89
Land	1,021.35	1,273.09	+251.74	1,678.74	+657.39
	$1,640.41	$1,658.91	+$18.50	$1,688.91	+$48.50
GROUP B: Parcels whose taxes would be decreased:					
Improvements	$25,654.98	$12,027.43	—$13,627.55	$317.16	—$25,337.82
Land	19,298.18	24,054.86	+4,756.68	31,719.47	+12,421.29
	$44,953.16	$36,082.29	—$8,870.87	$32,036.63	—$12,916.53
TOTAL:					
Improvements	$26,274.04	$12,413.25	—$13,860.79	$327.33	—$25,946.71
Land	20,319.53	25,327.95	+5,008.42	33,398.21	+13,078.68
	$46,593.57	$37,741.20	—$8,852.37	$33,725.54	—$12,868.03

To halve the tax rate on buildings would be to decrease the net taxes on these parcels $8,852.37, or $36.58 per parcel. The maximum available for reduced rents would be $13,860.79, or $57.28 per house each year. The diminution in the net annual return to the owners of the plots would be $5,008.42, or $20.70 per lot. Capitalized* this amounts to $414, which may be accepted as the possible depreciation in the selling value of the average plot.†

(6). *Sample District from Assessment Section Nineteen*

Increased	1
Decreased	209
	210

Assessment Section Nineteen, Borough of Brooklyn, which fronts on Gravesend Bay, contains a relatively large amount of vacant land ($8,601,325 as compared with a total land value of $20,022,900), but here again the improvements are of sufficient value to turn the tide in favor of a general reduction for the section.‡

Single-family houses predominate in Section Nineteen, as is shown by the following table:

Classification of Buildings in Assessment Section Nineteen, Borough of Brooklyn

	Number	Percentage
Single-family houses	2,559	61
Two-family houses	1,425	34
Tenements	92	2
Miscellaneous	145	3
Total	4,221	100

* Interest rate, five per cent.
† For the details of the parcels in this sample, *cf. infra*, pp. 216-219.
‡ The improvements are assessed at $15,399,305 and the improved land for $11,421,575. *Cf. supra*, pp. 79-83.

The sample consists of seventeen blocks-front selected from the following districts: 18th to 19th avenues, 70th to 71st streets; 13th to 14th avenues, 71st to 72nd streets, 73rd to 74th streets and 75th to 77th streets. The 210 parcels are assessed at $4,919.76 per parcel. Every parcel except one would pay lower taxes as a result of the adoption of the plan to untax buildings. This piece of property is assessed at $7,000, considerably more than the average parcel.

The assessed values grouped according to the effect of the proposed plan are given in the following table:

Assessed Values of Parcels in Sample from Section Nineteen, Borough of Brooklyn

	Improvements	Land	Total
Group A: Parcels whose taxes would be increased........	$2.500	$4,500	$7,000
Group B: Parcels whose taxes would be decreased........	728,550	297,600	1,026,150
Total................................	$731,050	$302,100	$1,033,150

Applying the tax rates the following levies are determined:

Taxes Payable by Owners of Parcels in Sample from Assessment Section Nineteen, Borough of Brooklyn, Under the Present System and Under the Proposed Plans to Untax Buildings

	Present System	Rate on Improvements One-Half		Rate on Improvements One One-Hundredth	
	Levy	Levy	Increase or Decrease	Levy	Increase or Decrease
Group A: Parcels whose taxes would be increased:					
Improvements..........	$45.92	$28.62	—$17.30	$0.75	—$45.17
Land................	82.66	103.04	+20.38	135.87	+53.21
	$128.58	$131.66	+$3.08	$136.62	+$8.04
Group B: Parcels whose taxes would be decreased:					
Improvements..........	$13,383.17	$8,340.95	—$5,042.22	$219.95	—$13,163.22
Land................	5,466.79	6,814.27	+1,347.48	8,985.50	+3,518.71
	$18,849.96	$15,155.22	—$3,694.74	$9,205.45	—$9,644.51
Total:					
Improvements..........	$13,429.09	$8,369.57	—$5,059.52	$220.70	—$13,208.39
Land................	5,549.45	6,917.31	+1,367.86	9,121.37	+3,571.92
	$18,978.54	$15,286.88	—$3,691.66	$9,342.07	—$9,636.47

Under the plan to halve the tax rate, the net decrease in taxes on the parcels in the sample is seen to be $3,691.66 or $17.56 on each parcel. The maximum sum available for rent reductions is $5,059.52, or $24.09 per building annually. The prospective decrease in the annual net return

to the owners of plots is $1,367.86, or $6.52 per plot. By capitalizing*
this sum the probable depreciation in the selling value of the average
plot is found to be $130.40.†

(7). *Sample District from Assessment Section Twenty*

Increased	1
Decreased	132
	133

In Assessment Section Twenty, located in Flatbush, over one-half of
the land is vacant ($12,604,240 as compared with $22,147,580), and yet
the taxes for the real estate of the entire section would be decreased by
the adoption of the plan to lower the tax on buildings.‡ This is because
of the very high value of the improvements as compared with the value
of the plots on which they stand ($15,620,575 as compared with
$9,543,340).

The table which follows shows that single-family houses are by far
the most important type of improvement.

CLASSIFICATION OF BUILDINGS IN ASSESSMENT SECTION TWENTY, BOROUGH OF BROOKLYN

	Number	Percentage
Single-family houses	2,607	70
Two-family houses	941	25
Miscellaneous	184	5
Total	3,732	100

The sample consists of 133 parcels of an average value of $9,170.
The parcels are situated in thirteen blocks-front, selected from these
two districts: Avenue G to Avenue H, Westminster to Argyle roads;
and Avenue G to Wellington Courts, Rugby Road to 17th Street. In
only one parcel out of the entire 133 would taxes be increased and this
parcel is clearly an abnormal one, being assessed at $19,000, more than
twice as much as the average parcel in the sample.

The assessed values, grouped in the usual fashion are:

ASSESSED VALUES OF PARCELS IN SAMPLE FROM ASSESSMENT SECTION TWENTY, BOROUGH OF BROOKLYN

	Improvements	Land	Total
GROUP A:			
Parcels whose taxes would be increased	$6,400	$12,600	$19,000
GROUP B:			
Parcels whose taxes would be decreased	707,930	492,710	1,200,640
Total	$714,330	$505,310	$1,219,640

* Interest rate, five per cent.
† For details of this sample, *cf. infra*, pp. 220-223.
‡ *Cf. supra*, pp. 79-83.

By extending the tax rates against these values the following results are secured:

TAXES PAYABLE BY OWNERS OF PARCELS IN SAMPLE FROM ASSESSMENT SECTION TWENTY, BOROUGH OF BROOKLYN, UNDER THE PRESENT SYSTEM AND UNDER THE PROPOSED PLANS TO UNTAX BUILDINGS

	Present System	Rate on Improvements One-Half		Rate on Improvements One One-Hundredth	
	Levy	Levy	Increase or Decrease	Levy	Increase or Decrease
GROUP A: Parcels whose taxes would be increased:					
Improvements..........	$117.57	$73.27	—$44.30	$1.93	—$115.64
Land.................	231.46	288.51	+57.05	380.43	+148.97
	$349.03	$361.78	+$12.75	$382.36	+$33.33
GROUP B: Parcels whose taxes would be decreased:					
Improvements..........	$13,004.39	$8,104.88	—$4,899.51	$213.72	—$12,790.67
Land.................	9,050.89	11,281.78	+2,230.89	14,876.49	+5,825.60
	$22,055.28	$19,386.66	—$2,668.62	$15,090.21	—$6,965.07
TOTAL:					
Improvements..........	$13,121.96	$8,178.15	—$4,943.81	$215.65	—$12,906.31
Land.................	9,282.35	11,570.29	+2,287.94	15,256.92	+5,974.57
	$22,404.31	$19,748.44	—$2,655.87	$15,472.57	—$6,931.74

The adoption of the plan to halve the tax rate on buildings would result in a net decrease in the taxes on these parcels of $2,655.87, or $19.97 per parcel. The maximum amount available for reductions in rents is $4,943.81, or $37.17 per parcel. The net annual return to the owners of the plots would be diminished $2,287.94, or $17.20 per parcel. Capitalizing this,* the amount of $344 is obtained as the probable depreciation in the selling value of the average plot.†

(8). *Sample District from Assessment Section Twenty-Three*

Increased........................... 0
Decreased........................... 96
                                    ———
                                     96

The real estate in Section Twenty-Three, one of the Jamaica Bay sections, would bear heavier taxes if the buildings were untaxed. The cause is readily understood when the amount of vacant land is determined. Out of a total land value of $13,035,505 not less than $10,156,010 is represented by vacant lots. Such improvements as there are ($5,621,455) bear a high relationship to the value of the land on which they stand ($2,879,495).

---

* Interest rate, five per cent.
† For details of this section, cf. *infra*, pp. 224-226.

The table which follows shows that single-family houses are here once more the most important type:

CLASSIFICATION OF BUILDINGS IN ASSESSMENT SECTION TWENTY-THREE, BOROUGH OF BROOKLYN

	Number	Percentage
Single-family houses	1,095	75
Two-family houses	319	22
Miscellaneous	47	3
Total	1,461	100

The sample consists of 96 parcels with a total assessed value of $554,000 (improvements $345,550, land $208,450). The average parcel, therefore, is assessed at $5,771. The parcels are from the district bounded by Avenue G, 35th Street, Avenue H and 32nd Street. Every parcel of the 96 would pay lower taxes, were the proposal to untax buildings adopted.

The changes in the levies which would result are shown in the following table:

TAXES PAYABLE BY OWNERS OF PARCELS IN SAMPLE DISTRICT FROM ASSESSMENT SECTION TWENTY-THREE, BOROUGH OF BROOKLYN, UNDER THE PRESENT SYSTEM AND UNDER THE PROPOSED PLANS TO UNTAX BUILDINGS

	Present System	Rate on Improvements One-Half		Rate on Improvements One One-Hundredth	
	Levy	Levy	Increase or Decrease	Levy	Increase or Decrease
GROUP B: Parcels whose taxes would be decreased:					
Improvements	$6,347.62	$3,956.10	—$2,391.52	$104.32	—$6,243.30
Land	3,829.14	4,772.96	+943.82	6,293.77	+2,464.63
	$10,176.76	$8,729.06	—$1,447.70	$6,398.09	—$3,778.67

Under the plan to halve the tax rate on buildings the net decrease in the taxes on the parcels would be $1,447.70, or $15.08 per parcel. The maximum available for an increase in rents would be $2,391.52, or $24.50 per house. The increase in the total tax on land would be but $943.82, or $9.83 per lot. Capitalizing this sum*, $196.60 is obtained as the probable depreciation in the selling value of the average parcel.†

---

* Interest rate, five per cent.
† For details of parcels in this sample, cf. *infra*, pp. 227-228.

F. SUMMARY

Vacant land in Brooklyn is not a factor of sufficient importance to affect the situation to anything approaching the degree that it affects conditions in the Bronx.* Indeed in only seven sections would there be actual increases in the total taxes on real estate. The value of the improvements in the borough as a whole exceeds the total land value, even including the vacant land (improvements, $787,627,773, and land, $783,859,159). It is clear that with a standard composite ratio of 39.44 (improvements) to 60.56 (land) the average improved parcel in Brooklyn would receive a substantial decrease in taxes under the proposed plans. Finally, the tendency apparent in Manhattan, to decrease the tax burden of the more expensive parcels of each group of houses, reappears in three samples of Brooklyn houses. But on the other hand the opposite tendency is present in five samples, the result being not so clear cut as in the case of the other two boroughs.

---

*The figures for vacant lots in Brooklyn:
  Assessed Values of Land:
    Vacant.................................... $153,123,447
    Total..................................... 783,859,159
  Number of Parcels:
    Vacant....................................   50,381
    Total.....................................   214,211

VI. EFFECTS IN QUEENS UNDER CERTAIN ASSUMED CONDITIONS*

The slight increase which would be the result in Queens if the tax on buildings were lowered has already been commented upon.† An attempt will now be made to form an estimate of the probable effects within the borough.

A. TAX RATES

The graph which follows makes plain the probable effects upon tax rates in Queens of the proposed plans to untax buildings.‡

QUEENS

RATES UPON THE VARIOUS CLASSES OF PROPERTY UNDER THE PRESENT SYSTEM AND UNDER THE PROPOSED PLANS TO UNTAX BUILDINGS

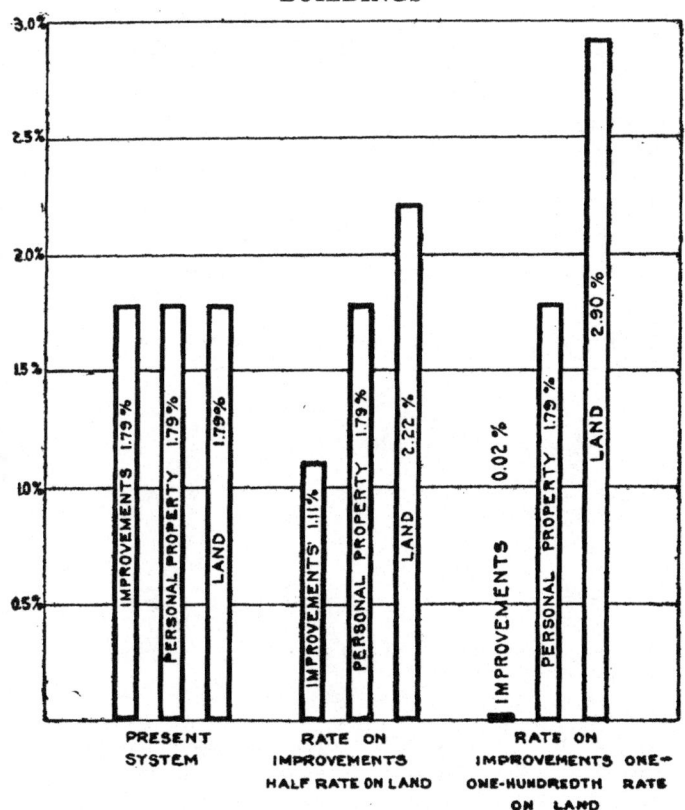

---

* The most important condition is that assessed values will not be changed. *Cf. supra*, p. 18.
† *Cf. supra*, pp. 22-23.
‡ The statistics upon which this graph is based are given in more detail on p. 21.

B. DISTRIBUTION OF BURDEN AMONG THE ELEMENTS IN THE TAX BASE

How the burden now borne by land, improvements and personal property would be affected by the proposed plans is shown by accompanying graph:

QUEENS

DISTRIBUTION OF TAXES AMONG THE ELEMENTS OF THE TAX BASE UNDER THE PRESENT SYSTEM AND UNDER THE PROPOSED PLANS TO UNTAX BUILDINGS

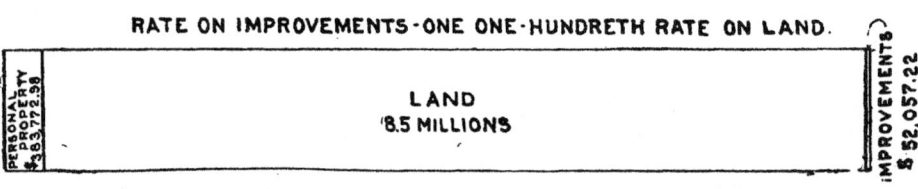

C. EFFECTS IN THE VARIOUS ASSESSMENT SECTIONS OF THE BOROUGH

The division lines of the borough utilized for assessment purposes are those of the wards and they are traced on the accompanying map.

By an inspection of the following table, which shows the assessed values of improvements and land for each ward, and the ratio between the two, it is possible to determine which wards will pay greater and which smaller taxes under the proposed plans.

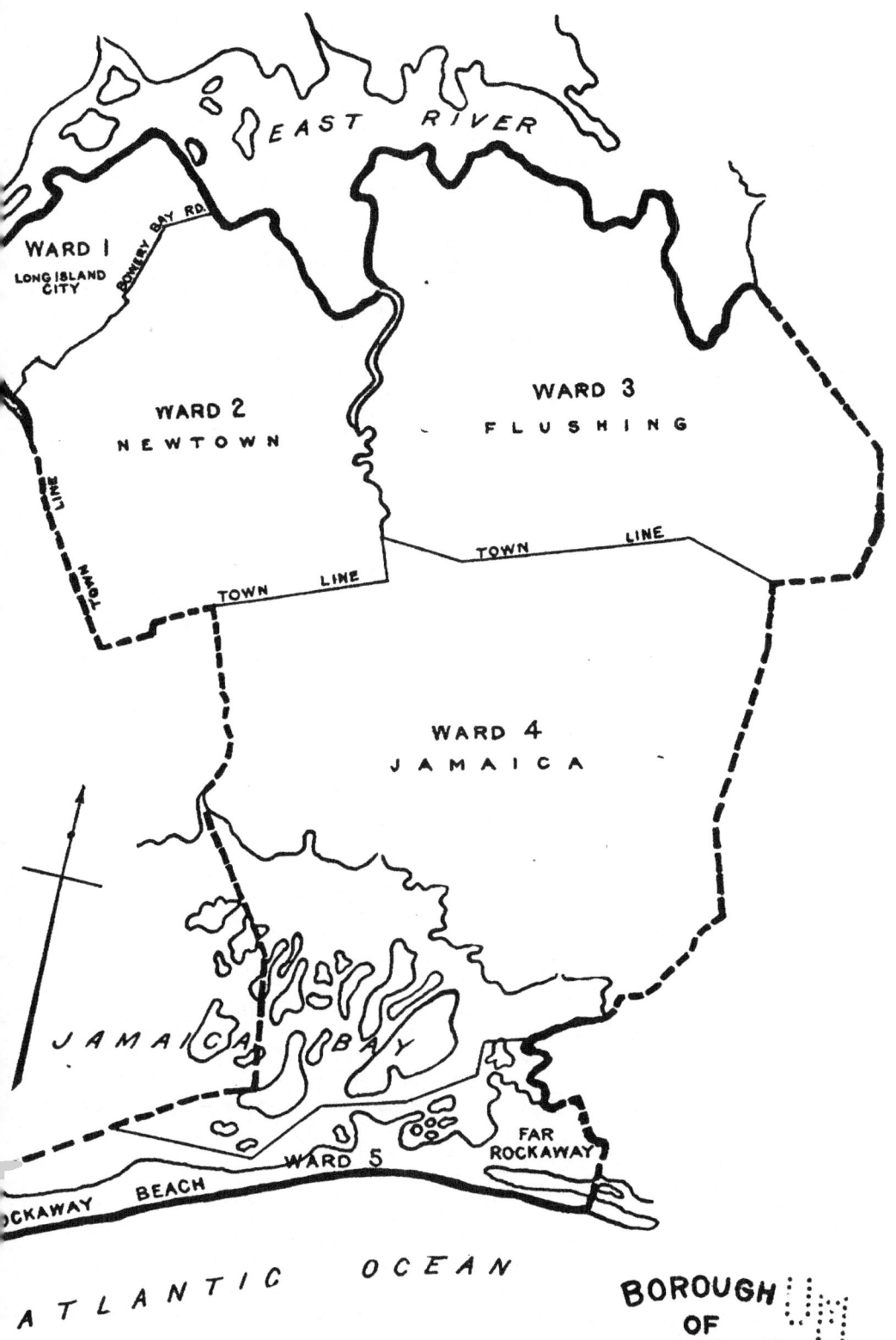

ASSESSED VALUES AND RATIOS IN THE VARIOUS WARDS OF THE BOROUGH OF QUEENS
(*Standard Composite Ratio: 38.49:61.51*)

	Assessed Values		Ratios	Taxes Payable
	Improvements	Land		
Ward 1	$35,069,580	$62,322,945	36:64	Increased
Ward 2	48,707,490	63,655,920	43.3:56.7	Decreased
Ward 2	21,331,680	49,024,620	30.3:69.7	Increased
Ward 4	43,392,677	75,820,135	36.4:63.6	Increased
Ward 5	17,506,930	29,854,500	37:63	Increased

It appears that the only ward in which the real estate will pay lower taxes because of the adoption of the proposed plans is Ward Two (Newtown). The amounts of the increases and decreases are shown in the following table:

TAX LEVIES UPON THE REAL ESTATE (a) IN THE VARIOUS ASSESSMENT SECTIONS OF BOROUGH OF QUEENS, UNDER THE PRESENT SYSTEM, AND UNDER THE PROPOSED PLANS TO UNTAX BUILDINGS

	Levies			Increases and Decreases	
	Present System	Rate on Improvements, One-Half	Rate on Improvements, One One-Hundredth	Rate on Improvements, One-Half	Rate on Improvements One One-Hundredth
WARD 1:					
Land............	$1,119,687.80	$1,386,747.85	$1,809,110.45		
Improvements......	630,056.57	390,166.61	10,177.19		
	$1,749,744.37	$1,776,914.46	$1,819,287.64	+$27,170.09	+$69,543.27
WARD 2:					
Land............	$1,143,635.89	$1,416,407.88	$1,847,804.05		
Improvements......	875,073.89	541,895.18	14,134.91		
	$2,018,709.78	$1,958,303.06	$1,861,938.96	—60,406.72	—156,770.82
WARD 3:					
Land............	$880,771.42	$1,090,846.82	$1,423,086.67		
Improvements......	383,242.83	237,325.61	6,190.45		
	$1,264,014.25	$1,328,172.43	$1,429,277.12	+64,158.18	+165,262.87
WARD 4:					
Land............	$1,362,176.96	$1,687,073.82	$2,200,906.88		
Improvements......	779,588.50	482,765.23	12,592.55		
	$2,141,765.46	$2,169,839.05	$2,213,499.43	+28,073.59	+71,733.97
WARD 5:					
Land............	$536,362.96	$664,292.48	$866,616.43		
Improvements......	314,527.75	194,773.35	5,080.51		
	$850,890.71	$859,065.83	$871,696.94	+8,175.12	+20,806.23
ALL WARDS:					
Land............	$5,042,635.04	$6,245,368.85	$8,147,524.47		
Improvements......	2,982,489.54	1,846,925.98	48,175.62		
	$8,025,124.58	$8,092,294.83	$8,195,700.09	+$67,170.25	+$170,575.51

(a) This does not include the "Real Estate of Corporations."

It will be noticed that the changes involved—both increases and decreases—are relatively slight and unimportant. If the tax rate were halved the real estate of the whole of the Borough of Queens would pay only $67,170.25 more taxes than at present.

D. EFFECTS IN SELECTED SECTIONS OF THE BOROUGH.

(1). *Sample District from Ward One*

Increased	8
Decreased	61
	69

The taxes on the real estate in Ward One would be increased.* As usual, this is because of the large amount of vacant land, which is responsible for more than half of the total land value in the ward ($32,347,495 as compared with $62,322,945). Indeed the value of the buildings in the ward greatly exceeds the value of the land on which they stand ($35,069,580 as compared with $29,975,450).

One and two-family houses are the most common types of improvements, as the following table shows:

CLASSIFICATION OF BUILDINGS IN WARD ONE, BOROUGH OF QUEENS

	Number	Percentage
Single-family houses	3,100	38
Two-family houses	2,849	35
Tenements	1,314	16
Miscellaneous	931	11
Total	8,194	100

The sample consists of 69 parcels taken from the two blocks bounded as follows: Crescent, Jamaica, and Ely avenues and Elm Street; and Trowbridge and Woolsey streets, Hoyt Avenue and Willow Street. The average value of these parcels is $4,151. If the plan to untax buildings were adopted eight of these parcels would pay higher and 61 would pay lower taxes. The average value of the eight parcels is $3,938, somewhat less than that of the parcels whose taxes would be decreased.

The assessed values, arranged according to the effect of the adoption of the plan upon the taxes payable by the parcels, are presented in the following table:

ASSESSED VALUE OF PARCELS IN SAMPLE FROM WARD ONE, BOROUGH OF QUEENS

	Improvements	Land	Total
GROUP A: Parcels whose taxes would be increased	$10,700	$20,800	$31,500
GROUP B: Parcels whose taxes would be decreased	143,050	111,850	254,900
Total	$153,750	$132,650	$286,400

* *Cf. supra*, p. 100.

By applying the rates of taxation to these values the following results are obtained:

TAXES PAYABLE BY OWNERS OF PARCELS IN SAMPLE DISTRICT FROM WARD ONE, BOROUGH OF QUEENS, UNDER THE PRESENT SYSTEM AND UNDER THE PROPOSED PLANS TO UNTAX BUILDINGS

	Present System Levy	Rate on Improvements One-Half Levy	Rate on Improvements One-Half Increase or Decrease	Rate on Improvements One One-Hundredth Levy	Rate on Improvements One One-Hundredth Increase or Decrease
GROUP A: Parcels whose taxes would be increased:					
Improvements..........	$192.24	$119.04	—$73.20	$3.11	—$189.13
Land.................	373.69	462.82	+89.13	603.78	+230.09
	$565.93	$581.86	+$15.93	$606.89	+$40.96
GROUP B: Parcels whose taxes would be decreased:					
Improvements..........	$2,570.02	$1,591.50	—$978.52	$41.51	—$2,528.51
Land.................	2,009.49	2,488.77	+479.28	3,246.78	+1,237.29
	$4,579.51	$4,080.27	—$499.24	$3,288.29	—$1,291.22
TOTAL:					
Improvements..........	$2,762.26	$1,710.54	—$1,051.72	$44.62	—$2,717.64
Land.................	2,383.18	2,951.59	+568.41	3,850.56	+1,467.38
	$5,145.44	$4,662.13	—$483.31	$3,895.18	—$1,250.26

Under the plan to halve the tax rate on buildings, the net taxes payable by the owners of these sample parcels would be decreased $483.31 or seven dollars per parcel. The maximum available for the reduction of rents is $1,051.72, or $15.24 per house. Net annual returns to the owners of lands would be diminished $568.41, or $8.24 per lot. Capitalized,* this means a probable depreciation in the value of each plot of $164.80.†

(2). *Sample District from Ward Two*

Increased 0
Decreased........................... 110
                                        ———
                                        110

Ward Two is the only ward in the Borough of Queens where the taxes on real estate would be decreased by the adoption of the plan to untax buildings.‡ Even here the vacant land is a very prominent factor, slightly exceeding the improved land in amount ($33,526,160, vacant, and $30,129,760 improved). The value of improvements is relatively very large, however ($48,707,490).

That one and two-family houses are the most common type of improvement is shown by the following table:

---
* Interest rate assumed to be five per cent.
† For details of this sample, cf. *infra*, pp. 229-230.
‡ Cf. *supra*, p. 100.

CLASSIFICATION OF BUILDINGS IN WARD TWO, BOROUGH OF QUEENS

	Number	Percentage
Single-family houses	7,145	39
Two-family houses	5,665	31
Tenements	2,733	15
Miscellaneous	2,689	15
Total	18,232	100

One hundred and ten houses were selected as samples.* The average value of the parcels is $4,233. The total assessed value of the buildings is $349,250, and of the land $118,350. If the rate on buildings were reduced, the taxes on every one of these parcels would be reduced. The amounts of the reductions are shown in the following table:

TAXES PAYABLE BY OWNERS OF PARCELS IN SAMPLE SECTION FROM WARD TWO, BOROUGH OF QUEENS, UNDER THE PRESENT SYSTEM AND UNDER THE PROPOSED PLANS TO UNTAX BUILDINGS

	Present System	Rate on Improvements One-Half		Rate on Improvements One One-Hundredth	
	Levy	Levy	Increase or Decrease	Levy	Increase or Decrease
GROUP B: Parcels whose taxes would be decreased:					
Improvements	$6,274.59	$3,885.58	—$2,389.01	$101.35	—$6,173.24
Land	2,126.26	2,633.41	+507.15	3,435.46	+1,309.20
	$8,400.85	$6,518.99	—$1,881.86	$3,536.81	—$4,864.04

The net reduction in taxes, if the rate on buildings were halved, would be $1,881.86 or $17.11 per parcel. The maximum which would be available for lowering rents would be $2,389.01, or $21.72 per house. The net annual returns to the owners of the land would be less by $507.15, or $4.63 per lot. Capitalizing this figure,† the sum of $92.60 is obtained as the probable depreciation of the average plot.‡

(3). *Sample District from Ward Three*

Increased 4
Decreased 80
                                       ———
                                        84

Ward Three presents an unusual situation. It is one of the wards where taxes would be increased by the plan to untax buildings, if adopted.** Here the vacant land constitutes considerably less than half of the total land value, ($21,802,040 as compared with $49,024,620). The peculiarity of this ward is the relatively low value of the improvements when compared with the land on which they stand ($21,331,680 as compared with $27,222,580).

Single-family houses are shown once more by the classification table to be the predominant type of improvement.

---
* The selections are from assessment blocks 55, 65, 175 and 176.
† Interest rate, five per cent.
‡ For the details of this sample, *cf. infra*, pp. 231-233.
** *Cf. supra*, p. 100.

CLASSIFICATION OF BUILDINGS IN WARD THREE, BOROUGH OF QUEENS

	Number	Percentage
Single-family houses	6,971	68
Two-family houses	721	7
Miscellaneous	2,576	25
	10,268	100

The sample consists of 84 parcels from the district bounded by Lincoln Street, Parsons Avenue, Madison Avenue and Percy Street, and that bounded by Amity Street, Bowne Avenue, Barclay Street and Parsons Avenue. The average value of these parcels is $7,251. Only four of the parcels would be charged with heavier taxes under the proposed plan to untax buildings. The average assessed value of these four parcels is $9,133, a figure considerably higher than the general average.

The assessed values of the parcels in the sample grouped in the usual fashion are presented in the following table:

ASSESSED VALUES OF PARCELS IN SAMPLE FROM WARD THREE, BOROUGH OF QUEENS

	Improvements	Land	Total
GROUP A:			
Parcels whose taxes would be increased	$11,800	$25,400	$37,200
GROUP B:			
Parcels whose taxes would be decreased	274,100	297,800	571,900
Total	$285,900	$323,200	$609,100

The changes in the levies involved in the proposed plans are set forth in the table which follows:

TAXES PAYABLE BY OWNERS OF PARCELS IN SAMPLE SECTION FROM WARD THREE, BOROUGH OF QUEENS, UNDER THE PRESENT SYSTEM AND UNDER THE PROPOSED PLANS TO UNTAX BUILDINGS

	Present System	Rate on Improvements One-Half		Rate on Improvements One One-Hundredth	
	Levy	Levy	Increase or Decrease	Levy	Increase or Decrease
GROUP A:					
Parcels whose taxes would be increased:					
Improvements	$212.00	$131.28	—$80.72	$3.42	—$208.58
Land	456.33	565.18	+108.85	737.31	+280.98
	$668.33	$696.46	+$28.13	$740.73	+$72.40
GROUP B:					
Parcels whose taxes would be decreased:					
Improvements	$4,924.45	$3,049.50	—$1,874.95	$79.54	—$4,844.91
Land	5,350.24	6,626.35	+1,276.11	8,644.54	+3,294.30
	$10,274.69	$9,675.85	—$598.84	$8,724.08	—$1,550.61
TOTAL:					
Improvements	$5,136.45	$3,180.78	—$1,955.67	$82.96	—$5,053.49
Land	5,806.57	7,191.53	+1,384.96	9,381.85	+3,575.28
	$10,943.02	$10,372.31	+$570.71	$9,464.81	—$1,478.21

To halve the rate on buildings would mean a net reduction in taxes to the owners of the 84 parcels of $570.71, or $6.79 per parcel. The maximum sum available from this source for lowering rents would be $1,955.67, or $23.28 per house. The owners of the plots would receive $1,384.96 less each year as the net annual return from their land. This would be a reduction on each lot of $16.49. Capitalized* this would mean a depreciation in the selling value of each lot of $329.80.†

(4). *Sample District from Ward Four*

Increased 21
Decreased 137
                                          ———
                                          158

In Ward Four, where taxes would be slightly increased by the adoption of the proposed plans to untax buildings,‡ the vacant land is of greater value than the improved ($41,770,445 as compared with $34,049,690). The value of improvements ($43,392,677), however, is considerably greater than the value of the plots on which they stand.

The classification of buildings given below shows the single-family house to be the typical improvement.

CLASSIFICATION OF BUILDINGS IN WARD FOUR, BOROUGH OF QUEENS

	Number	Percentage
Single-family houses	13,838	68
Two-family houses	4,021	19
Miscellaneous	2,630	13
Total	20,489	100

The sample consists of 158 parcels of an average value of $6,233. Twenty-one of these parcels would have increased taxes, while in 137 cases the taxes would be decreased. The average value of the parcels whose taxes would be increased ($6,900) is slightly greater than the average of the other group.

The assessed values, arranged in the usual manner, are:

ASSESSED VALUES OF PARCELS IN WARD FOUR, BOROUGH OF QUEENS

	Improvements	Land	Total
GROUP A:			
Parcels whose taxes would be increased	$50,300	$94,600	$144,900
GROUP B:			
Parcels whose taxes would be decreased	477,755	370,505	$848,260
Total	$528,055	$465,105	993,160

* Interest rate, five per cent.
† Detailed statistics for this sample are given on pages 234 and 235.
‡ *Cf. supra*, p. 100.

The increases and decreases in the levies presented herewith are obtained by extending the tax rates against the preceding values:

TAXES PAYABLE BY OWNERS OF PARCELS IN SAMPLE FROM WARD FOUR, BOROUGH OF QUEENS, UNDER THE PRESENT SYSTEM AND UNDER THE PROPOSED PLANS TO UNTAX BUILDINGS

	Present System	Rate on Improvements One-Half		Rate on Improvements One One-Hundredth	
	Levy	Levy	Increase or Decrease	Levy	Increase or Decrease
GROUP A: Parcels whose taxes would be increased:					
Improvements	$903.68	$559.61	—$344.07	$8.79	—$894.89
Land	1,699.57	2,104.94	+405.37	2,746.05	+1,046.48
	$2,603.25	$2,664.55	+$61.30	$2,754.84	+$151.59
GROUP B: Parcels whose taxes would be decreased:					
Improvements	$8,583.30	$5,315.26	—$3,268.04	$138.64	—$8,444.66
Land	6,656.46	8,244.11	+1,587.65	10,755.02	+4,098.56
	$15,239.76	$13,559.37	—$1,680.39	$10,893.66	—$4,346.10
TOTAL:					
Improvements	$9,486.98	$5,874.87	—$3,612.11	$147.43	—$9,339.55
Land	8,356.03	10,349.05	+1,993.02	13,501.07	+5,145.04
	$17,843.01	$16,223.92	—$1,619.09	$13,648.50	—$4,194.51

If the rate on buildings is halved the net taxes of the owners of the parcels in the sample section would decrease $1,619,09, or $10.25 per parcel. The maximum available from this source for the reduction of rents would be $3,612.11, or $22.22 per house. Net annual returns to land-owners would be diminished $1,993.02, or $12.61 per lot. Capitalized,* this amounts to $252.20, which represents the prospective depreciation in the selling value of each lot in the sample.†

(5). *Sample District from Ward Five*

Increased	19
Decreased	82
	101

In Ward Five, also, taxes would be increased.‡ Here it is not the preponderance of vacant land which is of greatest importance, for only about one-third of the land is unimproved ($9,966,360, as compared with $29,854,500). It is rather the low percentage of building value to land value in the case of the lands which are improved ($17,506,930, improvements, to $19,888,140, lands).

Almost all the buildings in the ward are shown by the table which follows, to be one-family houses:

---
* Interest rate, five per cent.
† For details of this sample, *cf. infra,* pp. 236-239.
‡ *Cf. supra,* p. 100.

CLASSIFICATION OF BUILDINGS IN WARD FIVE, BOROUGH OF QUEENS

	Number	Percentage
One-family houses	4,609	86
Two-family houses	80	2
Tenements	266	5
Miscellaneous	377	7
Total	5,332	100

The sample consists of 101 parcels of an average value of $6,728. Nineteen of the 101 parcels would pay heavier taxes under the proposed plans to untax buildings, while 82 would pay lighter taxes. The parcels whose taxes would be increased average $7,321 apiece, somewhat higher than the average in the other group.

The assessed values, arranged in the usual fashion, are given in the following table:

ASSESSED VALUES OF PARCELS IN SAMPLE FROM WARD FIVE, BOROUGH OF QUEENS

	Improvements	Land	Total
GROUP A:			
Parcels whose taxes would be increased	$37,600	$101,500	$139,100
GROUP B:			
Parcels whose taxes would be decreased	313,775	226,625	540,400
Total	$351,375	$328,125	$679,500

The detailed changes which would result in the tax levies, arrived at by extending the tax rates against the preceding values, are given in the following statement:

TAXES PAYABLE BY OWNERS OF PARCELS IN SAMPLE SECTION FROM WARD FIVE, BOROUGH OF QUEENS, UNDER THE PRESENT SYSTEM AND UNDER THE PROPOSED PLANS TO UNTAX BUILDINGS

	Present System	Rate on Improvements One-Half		Rate on Improvements One One-Hundredth	
	Levy	Levy	Increase or Decrease	Levy	Increase or Decrease
GROUP A:					
Parcels whose taxes would be increased:					
Improvements	$675.52	$418.32	—$257.20	$10.91	—$664.61
Land	1,823.54	2,258.48	+434.94	2,946.34	+1,122.80
	$2,499.06	$2,676.80	+$177.74	$2,957.25	+$458.19
GROUP B:					
Parcels whose taxes would be decreased:					
Improvements	$5,637.25	$3,490.90	—$2,146.35	$91.06	—$5,546.19
Land	4,071.52	5,042.63	+971.11	6,578.47	+2,506.95
	$9,708.77	$8,533.53	—$1,175.24	$6,669.53	—$3,039.24
TOTAL:					
Improvements	$6,312.77	$3,909.22	—$2,403.55	$101.97	—$6,210.80
Land	5,895.06	7,301.11	+1,406.05	9,524.81	+3,629.75
	$12,207.83	$11,210.33	—$997.50	$9,626.78	—$2,581.05

The adoption of the plan to tax buildings at one-half the rate used in the case of land would mean $997.50 lower taxes for the owners of the 101 parcels in the sample section. This is $9.88 per parcel. The maximum amount available for decreasing rents would be $2,403.55, or $23.80 per house. Net annual returns to land owners would be diminished $1,406.05, or $13.92 per lot. Capitalized,* this sum becomes $278.40, which represents the probable depreciation in the selling value of each parcel in the sample.†

F. SUMMARY

Large quantities of vacant land‡ combine with a fairly low ratio of building to land value in the improved parcels** to cause a slight increase in the total taxes charged to the real estate of Queens under the plan to exempt improvements. If the vacant land be eliminated from consideration, the values of the improved parcels are found to form a ratio well within the standard composite ratio for the borough. An overwhelming majority of the individual parcels included within the samples taken in the various wards show decreases in taxes as the probable results of the proposed changes. The parcels whose taxes would be increased were in three wards out of four, the more expensive parcels in the group.

---

* Interest rate, five per cent.
† For the details of this sample, *cf. infra*, pp. 240-242.
‡ The exact figures are:
  Assessed values of land:
    Vacant..................................... $139,412,500
    Total...................................... 280,678,120
  Number of Parcels:
    Vacant..................................... 82,065
    Total...................................... 134,987
** This is indicated by the following figures:
  Improved Parcels:
    Land....................................... $141,265,620
    Improvements............................... 166,008,357

VII. EFFECTS IN RICHMOND UNDER CERTAIN ASSUMED CONDITIONS*

Note has already been made† of the decrease in general city taxes which would result in the Borough of Richmond in case the project to reduce the tax rate on buildings were adopted. It remains, however, to examine the probable effects of that step within the limits of the borough.

A. TAX RATES

The effects of the proposed plan upon the tax rates in the Borough of Richmond is illustrated by the following graph.‡

RICHMOND

RATES UPON THE VARIOUS CLASSES OF PROPERTY UNDER THE PRESENT SYSTEM AND UNDER THE PROPOSED PLANS TO UNTAX BUILDINGS

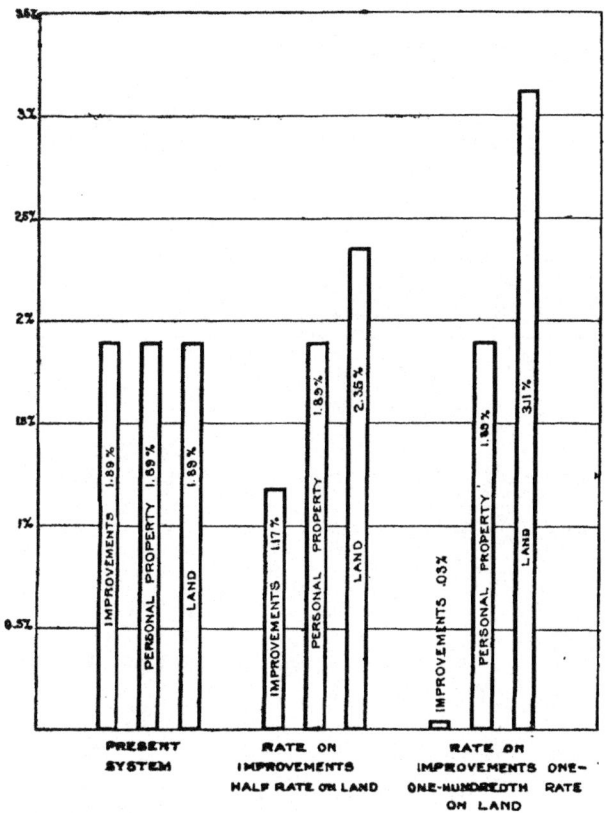

---

* The most important condition is that assessed values would remain constant. *Cf. supra*, p. 18.
† *Supra*, pp. 22-23.
‡ The statistics upon which this graph is based are presented in detail in the table on p. 21.

B. DISTRIBUTION OF THE BURDEN AMONG THE ELEMENTS IN THE TAX BASE.

The effects which may be expected upon the burdens of taxation thrown upon the various elements in the tax base, in case the proposed plans to untax buildings were adopted, are made clear by the accompanying graph:

RICHMOND
DISTRIBUTION OF TAXES AMONG THE ELEMENTS OF THE TAX BASE UNDER THE PRESENT SYSTEM AND UNDER THE PROPOSED PLANS TO UNTAX BUILDINGS

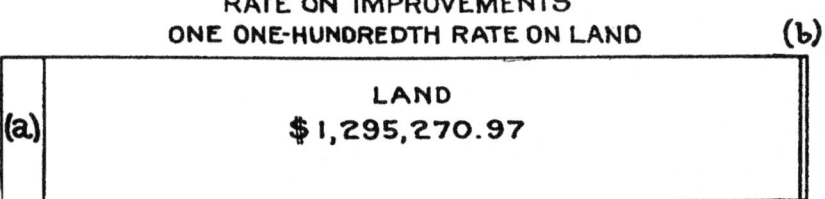

PRESENT SYSTEM

| (a) | LAND $787,454.87 | IMPROVEMENTS $720,011.52 |

RATE ON IMPROVEMENTS ONE-HALF RATE ON LAND

| (a) | LAND $981,307.92 | IMPROVEMENTS $448,630.79 |

RATE ON IMPROVEMENTS ONE ONE-HUNDREDTH RATE ON LAND (b)

| (a) | LAND $1,295,270.97 |

(a) PERSONAL PROPERTY $74,210.23
(b) IMPROVEMENTS $11,843.34

C. EFFECTS IN THE VARIOUS ASSESSMENT SECTIONS OF THE BOROUGH

The wards are used in Richmond as sub-divisions for assessment purposes. Their boundaries are shown on the accompanying map.

The effects of the proposed plans to untax buildings upon the amounts payable as taxes in the various wards may be ascertained from an inspection of the ratios given in the following table:

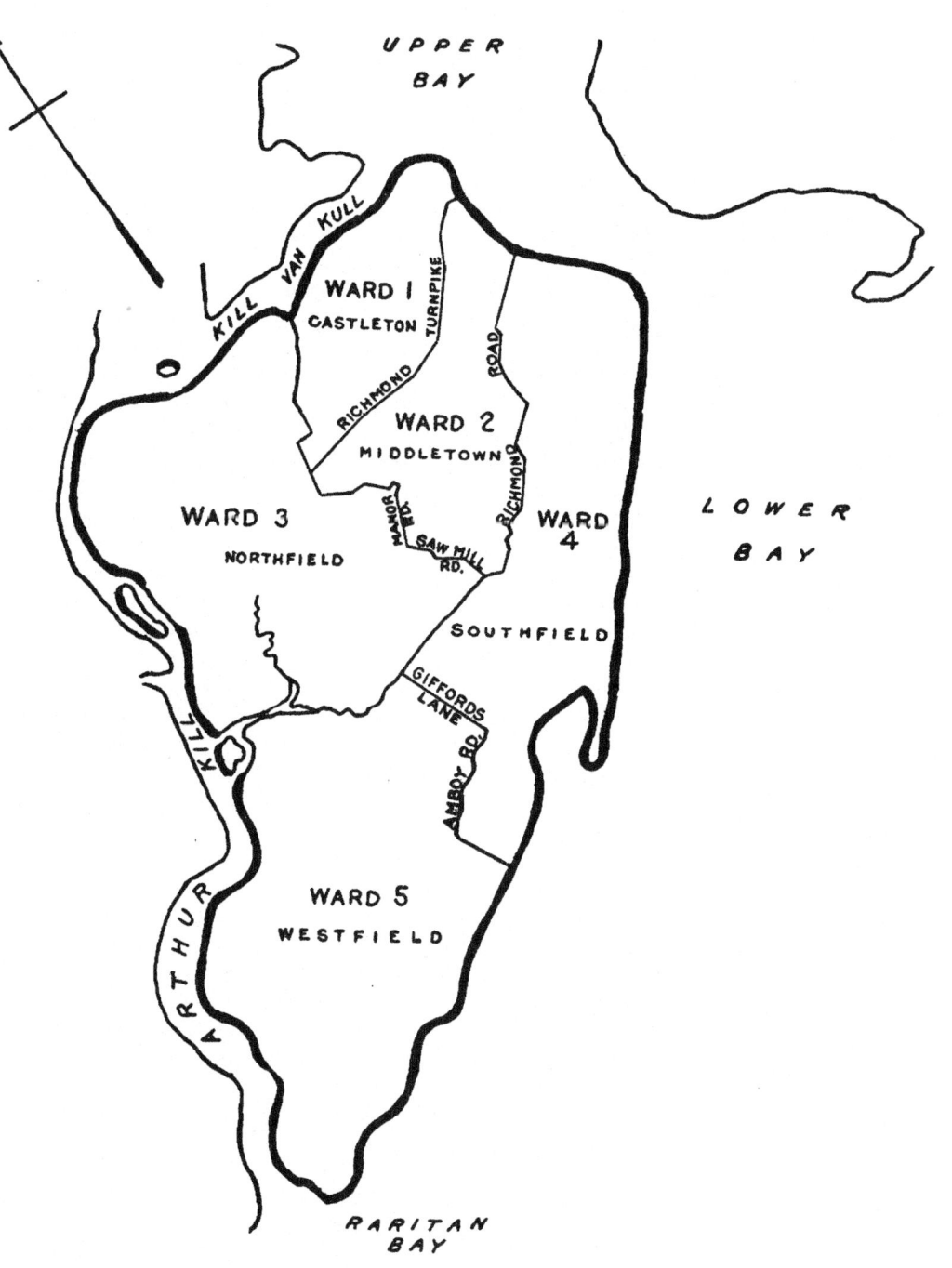

BOROUGH OF RICHMOND

ASSESSED VALUES AND RATIOS IN THE VARIOUS ASSESSMENT SECTIONS OF THE BOROUGH OF RICHMOND

(*Standard Composite Ratio: 39.51:60.49*)

	Assessed Values			Taxes Payable
	Improvements	Land	Ratios	
Ward 1	$12,415,460	$11,459,630	52.1:47.9	Decreased
Ward 2	7,049,440	8,819,005	44.4:55.6	Decreased
Ward 3	8,251,483	7,895,842	51.1:48.9	Decreased
Ward 4	5,106,155	7,815,680	39.5:60.5	Stationary
Ward 5	3,864,835	4,258,951	47.8:52.2	Decreased

It will be seen that the proportion of building value is greater than that in the standard composite ratio in all cases except that of Ward Four, where it is substantially identical with it. This means a decrease in taxes for all the wards except Ward Four, where they will remain stationary.

The amounts of the increases and decreases in the levies on the real estate of the various wards are shown in the following table:

TAX LEVIES UPON THE REAL ESTATE (a) IN THE VARIOUS ASSESSMENT SECTIONS OF THE BOROUGH OF RICHMOND, UNDER THE PRESENT SYSTEM AND UNDER THE PROPOSED PLANS TO UNTAX BUILDINGS

	Levies			Increases and Decreases	
	Present System	Rate on Improvements One-Half	Rate on Improvements One One-Hundredth	Rate on Improvements One-Half	Rate on Improvements One One-Hundredth
WARD 1:					
Land	$216,631.70	$269,961.38	$356,333.76		
Improvements	234,700.61	146,239.22	3,859.97		
	$451,332.31	$416,200.60	$360,193.73	—$35,131.71	—$91,138.58
WARD 2:					
Land	$166,713.59	$207,754.59	$274,224.31		
Improvements	133,261.91	83,033.94	2,191.67		
	$299,975.50	$290,788.53	$276,415.98	—9,186.97	—23,559.52
WARD 3:					
Land	$149,262.21	$186,007.09	$245,518.84		
Improvements	155,985.21	97,192.57	2,565.39		
	$305,247.42	$283,199.66	$248,084.23	—22,047.76	—57,163.19
WARD 4:					
Land	$147,746.83	$184,118.66	$243,026.22		
Improvements	96,526.24	60,144.38	1,587.50		
	$244,273.07	$244,263.04	$244,613.72	—10.03	(b) +340.65
WARD 5:					
Land	$80,510.78	$100,330.66	$132,430.80		
Improvements	73,060.45	45,523.12	1,201.58		
	$153,571.23	$145,853.78	$133,632.38	—7,717.45	—19,938.85
ALL WARDS:					
Land	$760,865.11	$948,172.39	$1,251,533.94		
Improvements	693,534.43	432,133.23	11,406.10		
	$1,454,399.54	$1,380,305.62	$1,262,940.04	—74,093.92	—191,459.50

(a) Not including the "Real Estate of Corporations."
(b) The relationship between building and land in Ward Four (39.516:60.484) is almost identical with the standard composite ratio (39.51:60.49). Owing to the fact that the tax rates are carried out only to the fifth decimal point the irregularity develops of a decrease in case the rate on improvements is halved and an increase in case the rate is made one one-hundredth of the rate on buildings. The amounts are negligible, however.

It will be seen that the decreases which occur so regularly are relatively slight in amount, the largest, under the plan to halve the tax rate on buildings, being $35,131.71 in Ward One.

D. EFFECTS IN SELECTED SECTIONS OF THE BOROUGH

(1). *Sample District from Ward One*

Increased 3
Decreased 112
                                           ———
                                           115

In Ward One of the Borough of Richmond the value of the vacant lands is less than one-third of the total land value ($3,352,543 as compared with $1,459,630). The value of the improvements, however, is about one-third greater than the value of the lots on which they stand, (improvements, $12,415,460, improved land, $8,107,087). It will be readily seen that the typical parcel in this ward would receive a substantial reduction under the proposed plans to untax buildings.

Single-family houses are the predominant type of improvement, constituting, as is shown by the following table, nearly sixty per cent. of the total value:

CLASSIFICATION OF BUILDINGS IN WARD ONE, BOROUGH OF RICHMOND

	Number	Percentage
Single-family houses	3,095	59
Two-family houses	914	17
Tenements	448	9
Miscellaneous buildings	810	15
	5,267	100

The sample from this ward consists of 115 parcels of an average value of $3,140. In every case except three the adoption of the plan to untax buildings would cause a decrease in taxes. The average value of the three parcels whose taxes would be increased is $2,033, which is considerably below the value of the average of all the parcels.

The assessed value of the parcels in the sample arranged according to the effect of the adoption of the plan to untax buildings are given in the following table:

ASSESSED VALUES OF PARCELS IN SAMPLE DISTRICT FROM WARD ONE, BOROUGH OF RICHMOND

	Improvements	Land	Total
GROUP A: Parcels whose taxes would be increased	$1,950	$4,150	$6,100
GROUP B: Parcels whose taxes would be decreased	254,850	100,145	354,995
Total	$256,800	$104,295	$361,095

By applying the tax rates to the foregoing values the results presented in the following table are obtained:

TAXES PAYABLE BY OWNERS OF PARCELS IN SAMPLE DISTRICT FROM WARD ONE, BOROUGH OF RICHMOND, UNDER THE PRESENT SYSTEM AND UNDER THE PROPOSED PLANS TO UNTAX BUILDINGS

	Present System	Rate on Improvements One-Half		Rate on Improvements One One-Hundredth	
	Levy	Levy	Increase or Decrease	Levy	Increase or Decrease
GROUP A: Parcels whose taxes would be increased:					
Improvements	$36.86	$22.97	—$13.89	$0.61	—$36.25
Land	78.45	97.76	+19.31	129.04	+50.59
	$115.31	$120.73	+$5.42	$129.65	+$14.34
GROUP B: Parcels whose taxes would be decreased:					
Improvements	$4,817.66	$3,001.83	—$1,815.83	$79.23	—$4,738.43
Land	1,893.13	2,359.18	+466.05	3,113.98	+1,220.85
	$6,710.79	$5,361.01	—$1,349.78	$3,193.21	—$3,517.58
TOTAL:					
Improvements	$4,854.52	$3,024.80	—$1,829.72	$79.84	—$4,774.68
Land	1,971.58	2,456.94	+485.36	3,243.02	+1,271.44
	$6,826.10	$5,481.74	—$1,344.36	$3,322.86	—$3,503.24

The adoption of the half-rate plan would mean a net reduction in the taxes on these parcels of $1,344.36, or $11.69 per parcel. The total reduction in the taxes on the houses is $1,829.72. This represents the maximum available from this source for the reduction of rents. It amounts to $15.91 per parcel.

The increase in the tax on land would be $485.36. Capitalized* this increase amounts to $9,707.20, which may be accepted as the probable depreciation in selling value. This would mean a depreciation of $84.41 per parcel.†

(2). *Sample District from Ward Two*

Increase 2
Decrease 103
                                       ———
                                       105

In Ward Two, Borough of Richmond, as in Ward One, the vacant land does not form a particularly large share of the total land value, being less than one-third ($2,545,005 as compared with $8,819,005). Here also the improvements are valued at a considerably larger sum than the plots on which they stand, (improvements, $7,049,440, improved land, $6,274,000).

---

* Interest rate, five per cent.
† The details for this section are given in an appendix. *Cf. infra*, pp. 243-245.

Almost all the buildings in this ward are single-family houses. The classification follows:

CLASSIFICATION OF BUILDINGS IN WARD TWO, BOROUGH OF RICHMOND

	Number	Percentage
Single-family houses	2,245	77
Two-family houses	346	12
Miscellaneous buildings	337	11
	2,928	100

The sample from Ward Two consists of 105 parcels, with an average value of $4,461. In the case of every one of these parcels except two the adoption of the plans to untax buildings would cause a decrease in taxes. These two parcels have an average value of $8,000.

The assessed values, arranged in the usual fashion, are as follows:

ASSESSED VALUES OF PARCELS IN SAMPLE FROM WARD TWO, BOROUGH OF RICHMOND

	Improvements	Land	Total
GROUP A:			
Parcels whose taxes would be increased	$5,300	$10,700	$16,000
GROUP B:			
Parcels whose taxes would be decreased	296,850	155,550	452,400
Total	$302,150	$166,250	$468,400

Applying the tax rates to the foregoing values the results presented in the following table are obtained:

TAXES PAYABLE BY OWNERS OF PARCELS IN SAMPLE FROM WARD TWO, BOROUGH OF RICHMOND, UNDER THE PRESENT SYSTEM AND UNDER THE PROPOSED PLANS TO UNTAX BUILDINGS

	Present System	Rate on Improvements One-Half		Rate on Improvements One One-Hundredth	
	Levy	Levy	Increase or Decrease	Levy	Increase or Decrease
GROUP A: Parcels whose taxes would be increased:					
Improvements	$100.19	$62.43	—$37.76	$1.65	—$98.54
Land	202.27	252.07	+49.80	332.71	+130.44
	$302.46	$314.50	+$12.04	$334.36	+$31.90
GROUP B: Parcels whose taxes would be decreased:					
Improvements	$5,611.62	$3,496.54	—$2,115.08	$92.29	—$5,519.33
Land	2,940.50	3,664.38	+723.88	4,836.78	+1,896.28
	$8,552.12	$7,160.92	—$1,391.20	$4,929.07	—$3,623.05
TOTAL:					
Improvements	$5,711.81	$3,558.97	—$2,152.84	$93.94	—$5,617.87
Land	3,142.77	3,916.45	+773.68	5,169.49	+2,026.72
	$8,854.58	$7,475.42	—$1,379.16	$5,263.43	—$3,591.15

The net reduction in taxes under the plan to halve the tax rates on buildings would be $1,379.16, or $13.13 per parcel. The reduction in taxes on buildings alone would be $2,152.84. This represents the maximum available from this source for the reduction of rents. It amounts to $20.50 per parcel. The increase in the tax on land would be $773.68. Since the net annual returns to the owners of this land would be decreased by this amount the selling value of the land might be expected to decrease. Capitalizing this decrease* the sum of $15,473.60 is obtained as the decrease in the selling value of the parcels. This amounts to $147.37 per parcel.†

(3). *Sample District from Ward Three*

```
Increase  ..............................   3
Decrease  ..............................  102
                                          ―――
                                          105
```

Ward Three, Borough of Richmond is in all essentials similar to the two wards just described. The value of the vacant lots is approximately one-third of the total land value ($2,378,320 as compared with $7,895,842). The value of improvements again exceeds the value of the plots on which they stand by a considerable margin ($8,251,483 as compared with $5,517,552).

Here again single-family houses predominate. The classification of the buildings follows:

CLASSIFICATION OF BUILDINGS IN WARD THREE, BOROUGH OF RICHMOND

	Number	Percentage
Single-family houses	3,542	77
Two-family houses	169	4
Miscellaneous	899	19
	4,610	100

The sample consists of 105 parcels, the average value of which is $3,380. In only three cases out of the 105 would taxes be increased under the plan to untax buildings. The average value of these three parcels is $4,066, which is somewhat above the average value of all the parcels.

The assessed values, grouped in the usual fashion, are as follows:

ASSESSED VALUES OF PARCELS IN SAMPLE FROM WARD THREE, BOROUGH OF RICHMOND

	Improvements	Land	Total
GROUP A: Parcels whose taxes would be increased	$3,800	$8,400	$12,200
GROUP B: Parcels whose taxes would be decreased	231,855	110,800	342,655
Total	$235,655	$119,200	$354,855

* Interest rate, five per cent.
† The details for this parcel are given in an appendix. *Cf. infra*, pp. 246–247.

When the tax rates are applied to these values the results presented in the following table are obtained:

TAXES PAYABLE BY OWNERS OF PARCELS IN SAMPLE FROM WARD THREE, BOROUGH OF RICHMOND, UNDER THE PRESENT SYSTEM AND UNDER THE PROPOSED PLANS TO UNTAX BUILDINGS

	Present System	Rate on Improvements One-Half		Rate on Improvements One One-Hundredth	
	Levy	Levy	Increase or Decrease	Levy	Increase or Decrease
GROUP A: Parcels whose taxes would be increased:					
Improvements	$71.83	$44.76	—$27.07	$1.18	—$70.65
Land	158.79	197.88	+39.09	261.20	+102.41
	$230.62	$242.64	+$12.02	$262.38	+$31.76
GROUP B: Parcels whose taxes would be decreased:					
Improvements	$4,382.96	$2,730.97	—$1,651.99	$72.08	—$4,310.88
Land	2,094.55	2,610.18	+515.63	3,445.29	+1,350.74
	$6,477.51	$5,341.15	—$1,136.36	$3,517.37	—$2,960.14
TOTAL:					
Improvements	$4,454.79	$2,775.73	—$1,679.06	$73.26	—$4,381.53
Land	2,253.34	2,808.06	+554.72	3,706.49	+1,453.15
	$6,708.13	$5,583.79	—$1,124.34	$3,779.75	—$2,928.38

The adoption of the plan to halve the taxes on buildings would result in a net decrease in the tax on parcels in the sample of $1,124.34, or $10.71 per parcel. The decrease in the tax on buildings alone would be $1,679.06, or $15.99 per house, which figures represent the largest amounts available for reductions in rents from this source. The increase in the tax on land amounts to $554.72. Capitalized this sum gives $11,094.40, or $105.66 per plot. These amounts represent the probable decrease in the selling value of the plots.†

(4). *Sample District from Ward Four*

Increase 2
Decrease 39
                                        ――
                                        41

In Ward Four vacant land forms a somewhat higher percentage of the total land value than was the case in the wards thus far considered. Here nearly fifty per cent of the total land value consists of vacant lands, ($3,722,170 as compared with $7,815,680). Here again, however, improvements exceed in value the plots on which they stand, ($5,106,155 as compared with $4,093,510).

The buildings in this ward are almost entirely single-family houses. the classification follows:

---

* Interest rate, five per cent.
† Details for this property are given in an appendix. *Cf. infra*, pp. 248-250.

CLASSIFICATION OF BUILDINGS IN WARD FOUR, BOROUGH OF RICHMOND

	Number	Percentage
Single-family houses	3,011	78
Tenements	128	3
Miscellaneous buildings	749	19
	3,888	100

The sample from this ward consists of 41 parcels whose average value is 3657. In case of 39 out of the 41 parcels the tax would be decreased by the adoption of the plan to untax buildings. The average value of the two parcels whose taxes would be increased is $5,750, which is considerably above the value of the average of all.

The assessed values of the parcels in the sample section arranged in the usual fashion, are as follows:

ASSESSED VALUES OF PARCELS IN SAMPLE FROM WARD FOUR, BOROUGH OF RICHMOND

	Improvements	Land	Total
GROUP A:			
Parcels whose taxes would be increased	$4,000	$7,500	$11,500
GROUP B:			
Parcels whose taxes would be decreased	100,000	38,450	138,450
Total	$104,000	$45,950	$149,950

Applying the tax rates to the above values, the results presented in the following table are obtained:

TAXES PAYABLE BY OWNERS OF PARCELS IN SAMPLE FROM WARD FOUR, BOROUGH OF RICHMOND, UNDER THE PRESENT SYSTEM AND UNDER THE PROPOSED PLANS TO UNTAX BUILDINGS

	Present System	Rate on Improvements One-Half		Rate on Improvements One One-Hundredth	
	Levy	Levy	Increase or Decrease	Levy	Increase or Decrease
GROUP A:					
Parcels whose taxes would be increased:					
Improvements	$75.62	$47.12	—$28.50	$1.24	—$74.38
Land	141.78	176.68	+34.90	233.21	+91.43
	$217.40	$223.80	+$6.40	$234.45	+$17.05
GROUP B:					
Parcels whose taxes would be decreased:					
Improvements	$1,890.39	$1,177.88	—$712.51	$31.09	—$1,859.30
Land	726.85	905.79	+178.94	1,195.59	+468.74
	$2,617.24	$2,083.67	—$533.57	$1,226.68	—$1,390.56
TOTAL:					
Improvements	$1,966.01	$1,225.00	—$741.01	$32.33	—$1,933.68
Land	868.63	1,082.47	+213.84	1,428.80	+560.17
	$2,834.64	$2,307.47	—$527.17	$1,461.13	—$1,373.51

It will be noted that the net reduction in taxes on the parcels in the sample, upon the adoption of the half-rate plan, would be $527.17, or $12.86 per parcel. The reduction in the taxes on buildings alone would be $741.01, or $18.08 per house. These figures represent the greatest reductions in rents which can be hoped for from this direction. The increase in the tax on land amounts to $213.84. Capitalized,* this amounts to $4,276.80, which is the probable reduction in the selling value of the land. The probable reduction per lot is $104.31.†

(5). *Sample District from Ward Five*

Increase 3
Decrease 119
                                        ———
                                        122

The situation in Ward Five is in no respect unusual when compared with that in other Richmond wards. Considerably less than one-half the total land value is made up of vacant lots ($1,735,886 as compared with $4,258,951). The value of the improvements once more exceeds by a substantial amount the value of the plots on which the buildings stand ($3,864,835 as compared with $2,523,065).

Single-family dwellings form the chief type of building. The table classifying the buildings follows:

CLASSIFICATION OF BUILDINGS IN WARD FIVE, BOROUGH OF RICHMOND

	Number	Percentage
Single-family houses	2,326	68
Miscellaneous	1,101	32
	3,427	100

The sample from Ward Five consists of 122 parcels, whose average value is $2,950. In only three cases would taxes be increased under the proposed plan to untax buildings. The average value of these three parcels is $2,233, which, as was the case in Ward One, is somewhat lower than the value of the average parcel.

The assessed values, arranged in the usual fashion, are as follows:

ASSESSED VALUES OF PARCELS IN SAMPLE FROM WARD FIVE, BOROUGH OF RICHMOND

	Improvements	Land	Total
GROUP A: Parcels whose taxes would be increased	$2,175	$3,525	$5,700
GROUP B: Parcels whose taxes would be decreased	241,600	111,650	353,250
Total	$243,775	$115,175	$358,950

Applying the tax rates to the preceding values, the following results are obtained:

---
* Interest rate, five per cent.
† Details for this sample are given in an appendix. *Cf. infra,* p. 251.

Taxes Payable by Owners of Parcels in Sample from Ward Five, Borough of Richmond, Under the Present System and Under the Proposed Plans to Untax Buildings

	Present System	Rate on Improvements One-Half		Rate on Improvements One One-Hundredth	
	Levy	Levy	Increase or Decrease	Levy	Increase or Decrease
GROUP A: Parcels whose taxes would be increased:					
Improvements	$41.12	$25.62	−$15.50	$0.68	−$40.44
Land	66.64	83.04	+16.40	109.61	+42.97
	$107.76	$108.66	+$0.90	$110.29	+$2.53
GROUP B: Parcels whose taxes would be decreased:					
Improvements	$4,567.18	$2,845.76	−$1,721.42	$75.11	−$4,492.07
Land	2,210.62	2,630.21	+519.59	3,471.72	+1,361.10
	$6,677.80	$5,475.97	−$1,201.83	$3,546.83	−$3,130.97
TOTAL:					
Improvements	$4,608.30	$2,871.38	−$1,736.92	$75.79	−$4,532.51
Land	2,177.26	2,713.25	+535.99	3,581.33	+1,404.07
	$6,785.56	$5,584.63	−$1,200.93	$3,657.12	−$3,128.44

The total net reduction in the taxes on the parcels in this sample, under the plan to halve the tax rate on buildings would be $1,200.93, or $9.84 per parcel. The total reduction on buildings alone amounts to $1,736.92, or $14.24 per house. The increased burden of the owners of lots would be $535.99 annually, or $4.39 per plot. Capitalized* this would mean a decrease of $87.80 in the selling value of the average lot.†

E. SUMMARY

It is in spite of the presence of a large quantity of vacant land‡ that the Borough of Richmond as a whole would receive a reduction in taxes under the plan to reduce the tax rate on buildings. With the vacant land eliminated the land value of the borough would be $26,515,184. The value of the improvements in the borough is $36,687,373. This sum forms a very high ratio with the assessed value of improved lands —approximately 58:42. When it is recalled that the standard composite ratio for Richmond is 39.51:60.49, there is no cause for wonder over the predominance of decreases among the parcels in the various sample sections. In two of the wards of Richmond the samples show that the parcels whose taxes would be increased by the adoption of the plan are less valuable than the average while the samples from the remaining three wards show the opposite condition.

* Interest rate, five per cent.
† Details for this sample are given in an appendix. Cf. infra, pp. 252-254.
‡ The exact figures for 1914 are:
    Assessed values of Land:
        Vacant... $13,733,924
        Total... 40,249,108
    Number of Parcels:
        Vacant... 19,092
        Total... 34,245

VIII. VARIOUS DISTURBING FACTORS TAKEN INTO ACCOUNT

The foregoing analysis has been made under certain very definite pre-suppositions. Conditions have been assumed to be static where they are undoubtedly dynamic. Shrewd guesses as to the degree and direction of the changes which are to be expected may be made by those familiar with real estate conditions in the city, but after all they would be merely guesses. It was thought best to present the material under the given assumptions and to allow each individual to modify it in accordance with his own opinions as to what may be expected to happen. However, it is possible to outline how various kinds of changes which may occur would modify the forecasts of probable effects set forth in detail in the preceding pages and in this section an attempt will be made to do this briefly.

It will be recalled, in the first place, that the tax rates were calculated on the assumption that the assessed values would remain constant. Even though the tax rate on land would be increased considerably, the assessed values of the land, according to the calculations, would remain exactly the same. Yet, if the selling price of land, which is the standard for assessments, rests upon the annual net return from the land and if the tax on land cannot be shifted* to the tenant, the reduced net annual return due to the increased taxes will certainly be reflected in a diminished selling value of the land and, consequently, in a smaller assessed value. It is seen, therefore, that in the attempt to make the problem simple, an increase in land values has in reality been already assumed—an increase equal in amount to the capitalization of the new burden on land. This element must now be taken into account. In Manhattan this new burden, if the half-rate plan is adopted, is calculated at $13,516,767.21.† To raise the given amounts at the given rates, taking into account the depreciation in values under the heavier rate, assumes that in Manhattan land values must increase enough to counterbalance a depreciation of $270,335,344‡ or nearly eight and one-half per cent. In other words, if the statements made in the preceding sections are to hold strictly true, the income from the land on Manhattan must increase by a sum large enough when capitalized to equal $270,335,344. What the

---
* *Cf. infra*, p. 124 *et seq.*
† This is under the assumption that the tax is imposed suddenly and that land value is not given an opportunity to slip from the rolls through a process of discounting the anticipated burden.
‡ $13,516,767.21, capitalized. Interest rate, five per cent.

prospects are for such an increase in Manhattan land values must be left to those who are familiar with the local situation.

Another assumption involved has been that the change itself would not set loose forces which would increase land values. But some of the supporters of the plan find in it a cause for increased values which, they believe, would be of considerable importance. If the tax on buildings were reduced, they argue, building activity and general economic prosperity would be so stimulated that an increase in land values would result which would probably equal any depreciation which might be expected because of the increased burden on the land. Since there is no way of measuring the stimulus referred to, or its effect upon land values, little can be said of the degree of importance which the argument deserves. It may be remarked, however, that the remission of certain charges which have formerly been paid by buildings, may under certain conditions be expected to stimulate the production of those articles for which the sums, thus released, would be spent. One of these articles for which the demand would be stimulated from this source would doubtless be buildings. But there would also be others and what they would be depends upon the desires and spending habits of the various individuals whose taxes would be decreased. On the other hand there must be taken into account a possible reduction in the purchasing power* of those who are called upon to pay higher taxes on the land. On the whole it would seem very rash to assume that all which might be taken from the land owner in increased taxes would return to him in increased net returns from his lands. Probably the stimulus would return to him only a small fraction of the amount by which his taxes would be increased.

If for any reason there is not an improvement in the real estate situation at least equal in degree to that specified above, there will be a variety of interesting effects. In the first place diminished land values, due to the discounting of the heavier rate on land, would decrease the size of the total tax base. Under the provisions of the proposed bill, if the budget is not to be decreased, the effect of this would be to raise the rates of taxation on all the elements in the tax base. Land would be taxed at a slightly heavier rate but because of the discounting process would pay a somewhat smaller amount as taxes than under the conditions assumed in the early sections. Whatever is cut from the burden on land would fall to the share of the other elements in the tax base. The rate on buildings would be greater, and the prospective benefits in the way of lower rents and decreased carrying charges thereby diminished. The rate on personal property and special franchises would also be increased with results which can be only a matter for conjecture.

Finally, the calculations have been made as though no changes were to take place during the period in which the plan was being put

---

* At least a temporary reduction.

into operation. The proposed reduction would be made gradually, ten per cent. per year, and this must be kept in mind in considering the possibilities in regard both to the discounting of the changes and to the increases in land values.

To summarize, the effects as outlined in detail in this report presuppose a moderate increase in the yield from land. If this improvement does not materialize, the new burden upon real estate will be somewhat less than indicated while the reductions in the taxes on buildings and the prospective decreases in rents will also be slightly less. That is, whatever less of evil may accrue to the landowner, that much more of good will be kept from the tenant. If there should be a greater improvement in the land values than that indicated, the transition would be made correspondingly easier for the land owners. And, last of all, proper allowance must be made in interpreting the data for the fact that the plan proposes a gradual reduction stretching over a period of years, rather than a sudden one, as is assumed in the analysis.

IX. THE SIGNIFICANCE OF THE FOREGOING DATA FOR CERTAIN ECONOMIC CLASSES IN THE COMMUNITY

A. INTRODUCTORY

(1). *The Necessity of Considering the Incidence of the Tax*

Most of the statements which have been made thus far in regard to increased or decreased taxes have referred only to the amounts which the owners of the properties in question would be called upon to pay in taxes under the proposed plans. They have been of interest directly to the owners of real estate. They shed light on the question of the effects of the proposed plan upon the tax bills of the owners of real property. But as is often the case, the less immediate effects are here the more important ones and none of these has thus far been taken into account. That one individual pays a greater or smaller tax bill to the city than he did before may or may not be of significance. Everything depends on whether or not the tax is shifted. The importance of the change cannot be measured unless it is known whether the payer of the tax is the bearer also. If the bearer is some other person than the payer, he must be found, and the amount of his new burden calculated if the truly important effects of the change are to be grasped. It means little to the landlord to have his taxes increased if he can pass the increase along to the tenant in higher rents, but the change in this case would mean as much to the tenant as though he paid the tax directly. It is evident that there can be no intelligent discussion of the effects of the change which does not take into consideration the incidence of the tax.

(2). *The Incidence of the Real Estate Tax*

There is perhaps no principle of economics upon which there is more unanimous agreement than that which governs the return to land. It is generally recognized that of the amount which can be "made" through the utilization of a piece of improved real estate, there is a part which is properly a return on that portion of the property which can be removed and replaced, sold off and restored. In the second place there is part which is properly a return upon the advantage which that particular plot has for the economic purposes of the community as compared with other plots under the general economic conditions then prevailing.

This second part of the income from real estate is capitalized into what is known as site value and comprises almost the sole element in the value of city land.*

The supply of sites available for utilization is relatively much more determined and fixed than the supply of capital to construct the improvements which is the source of the first part of the income from real estate. The number of available sites will certainly not be decreased if the financial return is diminished.† The supply of capital to construct buildings or other such improvements upon the sites is quickly affected in case a diminution in the return below that which can be obtained if the capital is invested in some other direction. Buildings wear out and must be constantly repaired and replaced. Nothing is more simple than to refrain from re-investing in an unprofitable venture. To secure the houses and improvements the community must, in the long run, pay those who are in a position to supply the capital needed for building houses the same return on their funds as they could obtain elsewhere. In the case of the owner of land the situation is different. His property consists of the right to collect periodically for the use of his site a sum which represents the advantage which his site has over other available sites. Out of this sum he must pay expenses, chiefly taxes. The remainder, capitalized, constitutes the selling value of the land.‡

The dividing line between the two kinds of real-estate income is not commonly observed in the accounts of real estate men and the importance of the distribution is often underrated. It is, of course, true that most buildings possess considerable permanency and that their selling value once built, depends upon a capitalization of their expected yields. But, nevertheless, the permanency of a building and the permanency of a site are enough different to justify the use of two categories. The distinction is one which can be made without great difficulty, as is shown by the fact that it is considered of prime importance in determining values for assessment purposes.

In consequence of the differences between sites and improvements outlined above, important conclusions are drawn in regard to the incidence of taxes upon them. It is generally agreed that a charge which is levied upon city land values must be deducted by the land owner from the sum he already receives from his site. He is already, theoretically,

---

*In order to make the site value of the land available for use, the expenditure of capital is ofttimes necessary, as when lots are graded or filled. The return upon a graded or filled lot is determined by the same forces, however, as would be the case if the grading or filling had been unnecessary. The capitalization of that return, therefore, may justly be termed site value.

† The capital expended for the purpose of making sites available when the improvements are permanent, such as grading, usually cannot be withdrawn from the land. The normal situation is that the person who makes such an improvement expects it to be of permanent value and makes the expenditure as soon as the project promises a return merely on the outlay with no allowance for replacements. On the other hand, that a decreased return on sites to the individuals owning them would act as a deterrent to the expenditure of capital for the purpose of making available new sites by grading, blasting, *etc.*, is entirely probable.

‡ This is true only in case the present conditions are expected to continue indefinitely. The capitalized amount is, of course, the sum of the expected annual yields, discounted at the current rate of interest.

collecting all he can collect from the tenant—the equivalent of the advantages his site possesses over others under the conditions obtaining. The heavier tax apportioned according to land values, it may be claimed, would affect these conditions. It certainly will not decrease the number of sites. If it has any effect in this direction it will be probably that of increasing the number, through forcing lands into use. The possible relief afforded other subjects of taxation by virtue of the adoption of this land tax, might stimulate to some degree the demand for sites and thus, indirectly, increase ground rents. There is no way of measuring the importance of this element. It is true, of course, that the relief afforded to all the other objects which might otherwise be taxed is exactly equal to the burden put upon land values alone.

It follows that land taxes tend to be borne by the payer. There is no shifting. The resting place is with the owner.

The incidence of the tax on buildings is different. The new tax is a charge connected with supplying improvements on land to those who desire them. The person who supplies the improvements is the capitalist. He can place his capital here or place it elsewhere. To place it here he must be given the same return which he should receive elsewhere. Placing his capital here involves the payment of a tax charge which can usually be avoided if he places it elsewhere. The person, therefore, who wishes the improvement on land here must meet this charge in order that this option to the capitalist may be as attractive as the other. Taxes on buildings and other improvements which wear out, tend, therefore, to be shifted to the tenant.

But, it may be said, the capitalist has already committed himself. He has built houses and agreed to certain terms of payment. The reply to this is that the terms of the agreement are temporary and the improvements themselves are temporary. In the case of agreements that a fixed rental be paid for a given period, the tenant will escape the tax during the life of the agreement. Such are merely instances of incidental friction.

A more important element of friction is the other case mentioned. The capitalist has invested his funds in houses. He certainly will attempt to raise rents. But can he increase them, under actual conditions? The answer must be indefinite. The weapon of the capitalist is the refusal to reinvest in the same direction. Rarely can he withdraw his capital when in the form of a building.

If the members of the community cannot or will not pay larger sums for rent, there will be no general immediate increase in rents equal in amount to the added tax. Some landlords will get higher rents. Perhaps all will get somewhat higher ones. The man who pays $40 for a four room apartment, may refuse to pay $50 for the same accommodations. He may move to a three room apartment and continue to pay $40. Perhaps some other individual who before rented a five room apartment will now occupy the four rooms. But in this movement into smaller apartments there would be a decrease in the demand for the larger ones which would result in a reaction. Owners of such apartments might reason that part of a loaf were better than none and rent their rooms at a price which would not bring a fair return on their investment. This could not be a permanent situation, however, for the weapon of the landlord presently becomes effective. Under those circumstances he will not reinvest his money in the same direction. Enough has been said to show that the answer to this question depends upon what is known as the "elasticity of demand" for accommodations, *viz.,* the variation in the demand in response to the changes in price. In a city where a large proportion of the accommodations are rented, this elasticity might be expected to be greater than where the houses are owned by the occupants. People would more readily move when the rents were increased or decreased. This results in throwing a larger share of the burden upon the shoulders of the landlord. Suppose a case where, because of an increase in the tax on buildings, the landlords attempt to increase the rent. In a city of tenants this question presents itself: Shall a smaller apartment be taken or shall a larger part of the income be spent for house room? The tenant considers this question without reference to the interests of the landlord. His answer will not be influenced by the fact that to take the smaller apartment may leave the larger one vacant with a resulting loss. On the other hand, in the city of home-owners, the occupier is also the landlord. The increased tax presents to him a different problem. If he is not to pay a larger amount of his income for hiring accommodations he must negotiate a trade or sale. His interest as a landlord may affect his action as a tenant. It would seem that in the city of owners many more individuals would decide to pay more for their living accommodations than in the city of tenants. That is, the variation in price would result in less change in demand. In the city of tenants, there would be more elasticity. A similar situation develops in the case of a decrease in the tax on buildings. The renter in the city of tenants would be relatively quick to move into a larger apartment. The owner of a home would take action more slowly. He might add a room to his home, sell it or trade it for another, but this would probably be done much less often than the corresponding action in the city of tenants.

It is perhaps sufficiently evident that a decrease in the tax on buildings will tend to be passed along to the tenants and that an increase will have the same tendency. That is, whereas the tax on land tended to remain where placed and be borne by the payer, the tax on buildings tends to be shifted and be borne by the tenant in the form of a part of the rental charge. There are various disturbing elements in the situation which obstruct the operation of these principles. One of the most important of these is the investments in buildings already erected. The more elastic the demand for building accommodations in a given city, the more disadvantageous to the owners of real estate is a change in the tax on buildings likely to be. In a city where the percentage of tenants is large, the elasticity of this demand will be relatively large. But in spite of the elements of friction in the situation, the general principle still holds that a tax on land is ordinarily borne by the owner and a tax on improvements by the tenant.

B. SIGNIFICANCE FOR REAL ESTATE OWNERS

Before proceeding further it may be well to present such statistics as are available concerning the relative importance of the classes whose interests are to be discussed. Both the tenement house department and the tax department gather statistics which are of interest in this connection. The data from the report of the latter is more comprehensive, including in its classification all the buildings in the city. A summary from the 1914 report is presented herewith:

CLASSIFICATION OF BUILDINGS IN THE BOROUGHS OF THE CITY OF NEW YORK

	Manhattan	The Bronx	Brooklyn	Queens	Richmond	Total
CLASS 1: One-family dwellings	25,212	13,549	62,080	35,663	14,219	150,723
CLASS 2: Two-family dwellings	2,681	8,154	49,505	13,336	1,519	75,195
CLASS 3: Tenements without elevators	39,421	9,617	45,956	4,876	634	100,504
CLASS 4: Hotels and elevator apartment houses	2,155	70	209	231	82	2,747
CLASS 5: Miscellaneous buildings	15,380	3,773	14,630	8,419	3,666	45,868
Total	84,849	35,163	172,380	62,525	20,120	375,037

The information given in the above table is well supplemented by the following data from the records of the tenement house department:

APARTMENTS AND APARTMENT BUILDINGS IN THE BOROUGHS OF THE CITY OF NEW YORK (a)

	Buildings	Apartments
Manhattan	40,905	532,509
Bronx	9,873	122,243
Brooklyn	46,669	259,521
Queens	5,256	25,375
Richmond	411	1,661
Total	103,114	941,309

(a) Data for June 30, 1915.

It will be noted that the sum of classes three and four of the first table is approximately equal to the total number of apartment buildings as given in second table*. Many houses as well as many apartments accommodate more than one family, but no information is available as to the comparative extent of this condition. Practically all of the apartments are, of course, rented, while a large number of the houses are occupied by the owners. Here again exact information is lacking. An inspection of the figures, incomplete as they are, shows very clearly, however, that the class of persons who own the premises which they occupy is very small indeed as compared with those who rent. The total number of single-family houses is 150,723 and of two-family houses 75,195. Multiplying the latter figure by two and adding it to the former, 301,113 is obtained. Assuming that every house or part of a house is owned by the occupier, which is of course not true, the figures indicate that still over three-fourths of the families of the city live in apartments. In Manhattan, by this test, less than six per cent. of the families live in their own houses.

(1). *Owners who Occupy their own Property*

The case of the owners of real estate who occupy their own property will first be discussed. Although statistics indicate that the number in this class is relatively small, particularly in Manhattan, it is nevertheless a class of considerable importance and one which from a social point of view it seems desirable to encourage. What does the foregoing analysis mean for the home-owner? The answer cannot be given in a word, for the effects vary in the different sections of the city. Some of the finest residence parcels in Manhattan would receive decreases in taxes, but the owner of the average single-family house would be called upon to pay a larger amount under the plan. On the other hand, the home-owners in the outlying boroughs would very generally receive considerable decreases. An explanation which may be made of this is that the single family dwelling is an improper improvement in Manhattan; that the land in general is suited to a more intensive use and that the man who builds a single family dwelling on the Island must be prepared to assume the responsibilities and penalties connected with using a plot for a lower purpose than that for which it is adapted. But a number of things may be said in reply to such a contention. First, it is a question whether a policy should be adopted which places a heavier burden upon those who, even though the expense for land is greater, still find a residence in Manhattan desirable. In the next place, in many cases the high proportion of land value is due to shifts in the suitable use to which the land may be put. Many sections are filled with old houses which it would be foolish to replace with new because business buildings and apartments are creeping in and reduce the attractiveness

---

* The definition of "tenement" followed by the tenement house department is that of a structure accommodating three families or more, who live independently of one another, and whose cooking is done on the premises. This, of course, excludes hotels.

of the sites for single-family dwellings. But, it may be said, this new use is a higher use bringing with it higher land values. Although the statement may be true in general, nevertheless the entire areas of these districts cannot be sold at any one time for this new use, the owners sometimes finding it necessary to carry the plots a long time, and, the change and its consequent increase in selling value may have been expected and paid for beforehand, when the land was bought.

But whatever may be thought of the desirability of the effects there is no doubt as to what they will be upon the magnitude of the taxes payable by the owners of the single-family dwellings in Manhattan. Their net burden will in general be substantially increased.

Another point of interest developed in the course of the investigation into the effects upon the owners of residence parcels in Manhattan. In this borough it was very generally the case that, while the bulk of the houses would be charged with heavier taxes, there would be within each group a number which would receive reductions. An examination of these parcels showed that in practically every case they were the more expensive parcels of the sample. That is, in Manhattan, the adoption of the plan would mean virtually a regressive tax among the home owners. In the other boroughs, strangely enough, this condition either does not obtain at all or only to a very limited extent.

The discussion thus far has dealt with the net taxes payable. Of more significance is the question of the increases and decreases upon the two elements in the value of the parcel—land and buildings. The net taxes might remain exactly the same and the adoption of the plan still have grave effects upon the interests of the owners of property. Thus the mere fact that their net taxes would be reduced does not necessarily mean that the owners of residences in the outlying boroughs would receive a net benefit through the adoption of the plan. The plan proposes to take the tax off buildings and put it on the land. If the shifting takes place in the manner indicated above* the owner will find that his house will not sell for more because of its lowered tax while his land will sell for less because of its increased tax. Whether he will benefit in the end depends upon the relative importance of his gain as a tax-payer and his loss as a land-owner. Of course, if the adoption of the plan should itself raise land values, his loss as an owner of land would be diminished. The owner of a Manhattan residence would lose in both directions, both as a tax-payer and as a land-owner.

The approximate importance of the plan to untax buildings as a depressing influence upon land values may be judged from the following figures. The table shows the value of improved real estate in the various boroughs, the present taxes chargeable to this part of the tax base and the increased burden which the land would be called upon to carry if the half-rate plan were adopted all at once:

Supra, p. 124, *et seq.*

LEVIES UPON IMPROVED LAND IN THE VARIOUS BOROUGHS UNDER THE PRESENT SYSTEM AND UNDER THE PROPOSED PLANS TO HALVE THE RATE ON BUILDINGS

Boroughs	Assessed Value of Improved Lands	Levy		Increase	
		Present Plan	Rate on Improvements One-Half	Amount	Percentage
Manhattan	$3,003,267,830	$53,333,231	$65,982,098	$12,648,867	24
Bronx	183,026,461	3,224,688	3,998,488	773,800	24
Brooklyn	630,735,712	11,586,364	14,442,208	2,855,844	25
Queens	141,265,565	2,537,963	3,143,300	605,337	24
Richmond	26,515,184	501,240	624,634	123,394	25

It appears that every owner of an improved parcel in Manhattan, for example, must face the prospect, upon the adoption of the half-rate plan, of a diminution in the value of his plot equal to the capitalization of a twenty-four per cent. increase in the tax on his plot. However, this percentage, of course, may be lowered somewhat by a process of discounting during the five-year period over which the change would be spread and by forces increasing land values which may be set in motion by the adoption of the plan itself. Assuming an interest rate of five per cent., the prospective depreciation in the value of the improved lots in Manhattan would amount to $252,977,340, approximately eight and one-half per cent. Under the assumption of a six per cent. rate the prospective decrease would be $210,813,607, or approximately seven per cent.

It is seen, then, that under the proposed plans owners of property which they themselves occupy would in most of the boroughs pay lower net taxes than at present. This, however, is not true of Manhattan. But as the owners of land these individuals have cause for apprehension in the adoption of the plan which threatens a depreciation in the selling value of the land. If they attempted to sell their land they would probably find the market price lower by a considerable amount than it otherwise would have been. It will be noted that the gain in lowered taxes accrues to the owners in their capacity as users of the property, rather than in their capacity as the owners of the property. That is, as owners of property they, with all other owners, would lose. As users of property they, together with all other users would gain. The reduced tax on buildings could not usually be expected to be capitalized and added to the market value of the parcel. Its benefit would accrue to the user. On the other hand the heavier tax on land would be capitalized and substracted from the selling value of the land. The benefit would accrue to the public treasury and the injury to the owner. The gain or loss of the individual who occupies his own property would, therefore, depend upon whether he gained more in reduced net taxes than he would lose through reduced selling value of his property. Viewed from this standpoint the owner of the single-family dwelling on Manhattan would be particularly hard hit by the adoption of the plan to lower the rate on buildings.

(2). *Owners who Rent their Property*

The effect of the adoption of the proposed plans to untax buildings upon the owners of rented property may be quickly disposed of. In so far as their interest as land owners is concerned, they are at one with the class of owners just discussed, who occupy their own property. But the owner who rents would have finally no compensating factor in the way of a smaller burden of taxation on his building. For, if the analysis is correct, the decreased tax on the buildings will not, in the long run, accrue to the advantage of the owner but rather to the advantage of the tenant. Friction will develop, no doubt, in transmitting the decrease in building taxes to the tenant. In the long run, however, the owner who rents his property may compute as his probable loss merely the capitalization of his increased land tax, modified by several factors. Among these are the amount of the decrease in building taxes which he can hold back from his tenants and whatever amount his larger land tax may be diminished either by the discounting process or by the stimulation to land values traceable to the operation of the plan itself.

Some light may here be thrown upon the question as to whether the degree of shrinkage in land values would be great enough to endanger real estate as security for mortgage loans. It will be seen from the table presented above* what the probable decreases in land values from this source would be. It would seem that unless the adoption of the plan would so shock the faith of the community in the desirability of real estate investments as to cause a real estate panic, little need be feared by the holders of mortgages which are protected by a margin of value which is at all conservative. It must be remembered that the figures are based upon the 1914 assessments and tax rates. The 1915 rates are considerably higher than those of 1914 and this, of course, increases the prospective depreciation in land values.

(3). *Owners of Vacant Land*

The owners of vacant land would be in the worst position of all if the plan to untax buildings were adopted. The table which follows shows the value of the vacant lots and the increases in the burdens which would be put upon their owners under the proposed plan.

LEVIES UPON VACANT LOTS IN THE VARIOUS BOROUGHS UNDER THE PRESENT SYSTEM, AND UNDER THE PROPOSED PLAN TO HALVE THE RATE ON BUILDINGS

Boroughs	Assessed Values	Present System Levy	Rate on Improvements One-Half Levy	Increase Amount	Percentage
Manhattan	$158,681,830	$2,817,935	$3,486,255	$668,320	24
Bronx	153,089,599	2,697,240	3,344,472	647,232	24
Brooklyn	153,123,447	2,812,816	3,506,128	693,312	25
Queens	139,412,555	2,504,672	3,102,069	597,397	24
Richmond	13,733,924	2,596,247	3,235,382	639,135	24
				$3,245,396	

Supra, p. 131.

It is seen that the decrease in the selling value of vacant lands, under the assumption of a five per cent. interest rate, might be as much as $64,907,920. If the tax rate be increased, as it has been in 1915, this decrease would be still greater. On the other hand, the process of discounting and any increase in land values due to the operation of the plan would be available for reducing the burden.

(C). SIGNIFICANCE FOR RENTERS

The total decrease in the taxes on rented buildings might be supposed to be available for lower rents if the process of shifting worked perfectly. That this amount is very substantial can be seen by referring back to the table of tax levies.* But several important factors must be taken into account at this point. The first is the amount of friction which must be expected in transferring the decrease in the tax on buildings to the tenants. It will be accepted as true that in general the tenants are less well informed and less fully alive to their interests than the landlords. They would not be conversant with the details of the operation of the new plan and would have no exact knowledge of the reduction which had been made on the parcels or fractions of a parcel they occupied. Moreover, there would be the usual reluctance to change the *status quo* and the difficulties attendant upon a change involving odd sums. Finally, the weapon of the tenant in forcing the landlord to give lower rents, that of moving to some other man's house, is not entirely in his own hands. If rents were reduced there would be some who would prefer to take the reduction in the form of larger and better quarters. This means that some of the tenants who desired to force lower terms from their landlords would have to wait for new capital to enter the field. While the new buildings were being constructed the landlords could continue to collect a considerable portion at least of the sum which theoretically belongs to the tenant. This friction would be a force which would operate only temporarily but it would doubtless operate as a very important check upon the immediate benefits to the tenants under the proposed plan.

The second factor is of perhaps even greater importance. It is urged by some that building takes place in the City of New York in anticipation of demand and before a full return can be secured on the investment; that this building is due, indirectly, to the lure of the unearned increment because owners of vacant land, in order to preserve titles to increments, are willing to sacrifice a part of it by building before suitable rents can be asked for the building. It is notorious that depreciation funds are seldom provided for the buildings in New York, dependence being placed upon the increase in land values to counterbalance the decrease in building values through wear and tear. The

---

*Suprp, p. 23.

question then arises: Would not a tax which increases the burden of land so much as to decrease materially its selling value, operate to discourage early building and the dependence upon increasing land values to cover depreciation charges? Would it not make higher rents necessary to care for these demands? Thus it is seen that the operation of the plan may set in motion forces which would mean an increase in rents and this increase must be compared with the decreases in the tax on buildings before an answer can be given as to the exact effect on rents, of the plan to untax buildings.

(D). SIGNIFICANCE FOR PROSPECTIVE REAL ESTATE OWNERS

The prospective real estate owner may expect little benefit from the proposed plan. It is true that any building he might erect would be taxed at a smaller rate than before but in case he proposes to build for his own use this benefit could be secured by him without himself building, for it is a benefit which ultimately accrues to the user rather than to the owner. If he plans to build in order to rent, the decreased taxes must ultimately be passed on to the tenant. It is true also that he would probably be able to buy his plot at a lower price, but after he has bought it he will have to part with this supposed advantage through the increased annual charges to which he will be liable because of the higher tax rate. The adoption of the plan, therefore, would seem to involve making the proposition to the prospective buyer apparently more attractive without adding anything to its real attractiveness after all.

Except in a few directions the foregoing analysis does not lend itself readily to brief and accurate generalization. The adoption of the proposed plan to untax buildings is seen to promise a great variety of results. In almost every borough there are conditions present which make the effects very different from those in every other borough. In Manhattan, the best developed, and Queens, almost the worst developed of all the boroughs, taxes would be increased by the adoption of the proposed plan. In Manhattan it is the inordinately high value of the improved land and in Queens the vast number of vacant lots which is responsible for the situation. The predominance of well-improved parcels, mostly single-family dwellings, would win for Brooklyn a very large decrease in taxes. Houses in Manhattan would usually pay higher taxes while those in other boroughs would pay lower ones. In Manhattan the more expensive parcels in the samples would receive decreases; in the Bronx, the less expensive ones. Tenements in one portion of Manhattan would pay greater taxes while those in other sections would pay smaller.

Two conclusions, however, stand forth very prominently. In the first place, the change promises ultimate benefits of considerable importance to all tenants and to many of the home-owners in the out-lying boroughs. These benefits, however, may be very slow of realization. Secondly, the owners of land would be charged with the cost of these benefits. The cost, in turn, would also be considerable. Its amount, as well as the modifying factors have been set forth in some detail.

What has been presented determines only a few of the variables which should be taken into consideration in reaching a truly scientific decision as to the desirability of the plan. Many of them, unfortunately can be determined only by actually trying the experiment under the conditions here existing.

APPENDIX

DETAILED INFORMATION CONCERNING THE
EFFECTS OF THE PROPOSED PLANS TO UNTAX
BUILDINGS UPON THE TAXES PAYABLE
BY OWNERS OF PARCELS IN THE
VARIOUS SELECTED SECTIONS

I. MANHATTAN

SKY-SCRAPER SECTION

(The district consists of all the buildings south of Chambers Street, ten stories high or more.)

(Standard Composite Ratio: 38.34:61.66)

BUILDINGS TEN STORIES IN HEIGHT

Group A: Parcels Whose Taxes Would Be Increased

Address	Assessed Values		Ratio
	Improvements	Land	
15-21 Wall St.	$175,000	$2,200,000	7:93
8-16 Broad St.	1,110,000	4,200,000	21:79
11-23 Broad St.	675,000	3,500,000	16:84
64-68 Broad St.	170,000	575,000	23:77
16-22 William St.	275,000	600,000	31:69
26-28 William St.	175,000	400,000	30:70
45-49 William St.	125,000	725,000	15:85
7 Pine St.	60,000	210,000	22:78
25 Pine St.	75,000	225,000	25:75
14 Maiden Lane	65,000	130,000	33:67
93-109 Broadway	825,000	2,575,000	24:76
176-178 Broadway	375,000	1,200,000	24:76
203 Broadway	190,000	810,000	19:81
65-69 Nassau St.	100,000	460,000	18:82
93-99 Nassau St.	275,000	775,000	26:74
3-9 Beekman St.	200,000	750,000	21:79
119-123 Beekman St.	90,000	230,000	28:72
	$4,960,000	$19,565,000	

Group B: Parcels Whose Taxes Would Be Decreased

Address	Assessed Values		Ratio
	Improvements	Land	
41-45 Broadway	$625,000	$750,000	45:55
125-131 Broadway	225,000	150,000	60:40
34-40 Fletcher St.	70,000	30,000	70:30
182-184 Front St.	85,000	65,000	57:43
11-13 Cliff St.	125,000	55,000	70:30
61-65 Cliff St.	195,000	80,000	71:29
69-71 Cliff St.	250,000	150,000	63:37
192-194 Greenwich St.	85,000	85,000	50:50
165-167 William St.	75,000	100,000	43:57
88-90 Gold St.	225,000	100,000	69:31
34-40 Rose St.	250,000	120,000	68:32
	$2,210,000	$1,685,000	

BUILDINGS ELEVEN STORIES IN HEIGHT

Group A: Parcels Whose Taxes Would Be Increased

Address	Assessed Values		Ratio
	Improvements	Land	
45-49 Cedar St.	$335,000	$565,000	37:63
80 Broadway	400,000	2,200,000	15:85
40-42 Wall St.	825,000	1,875,000	31:69
46 Pine St.	45,000	150,000	23:77
36-38 Park Row	350,000	1,150,000	23:77
	$1,955,000	$5,940,000	

GROUP B: PARCELS WHOSE TAXES WOULD BE DECREASED

Address	Assessed Values		Ratio
	Improvements	Land	
13-18 State St.	$375,000	$450,000	46:54
13-17 Pearl St.	475,000	425,000	53:47
N. & S. E. Cor. State and Pearl Sts.	525,000	675,000	44:56
1-9 William St.	450,000	420,000	52:48
64-66 Wall St.	275,000	425,000	39:61
114-118 Liberty St.	365,000	235,000	61:39
35-39 Maiden Lane	245,000	325,000	43:57
18-20 Frankfort St.	240,000	185,000	57:43
	$2,950,000	$3,140,000	

BUILDINGS TWELVE STORIES IN HEIGHT

GROUP A: PARCELS WHOSE TAXES WOULD BE INCREASED

Address	Assessed Values		Ratio
	Improvements	Land	
52-54 Maiden Lane	$225,000	$375,000	38:62
63 Maiden Lane	110,000	190,000	37:63
1 Broadway	700,000	1,300,000	35:65
10-12 Broadway	200,000	450,000	31:69
52-56 Broadway	800,000	2,050,000	28:72
84 Broadway	275,000	1,700,000	14:86
174 Broadway	60,000	365,000	14:86
180 Broadway	100,000	360,000	22:78
198 Broadway	100,000	325,000	24:76
261-264 Broadway	450,000	1,050,000	30:70
271 Broadway	105,000	360,000	23:77
74-78 William St.	400,000	700,000	36:64
30-32 Pine St.	210,000	520,000	28:72
68-70 Nassau St.	65,000	225,000	22:78
	$3,800,000	$9,970,000	

GROUP B: PARCELS WHOSE TAXES WOULD BE DECREASED

Address	Assessed Values		Ratio
	Improvements	Land	
47 West St.	$140,000	$85,000	62:38
23-25 South St.	400,000	150,000	73:27
78-80 Wall St.	200,000	300,000	40:60
82-88 Wall St.	260,000	340,000	43:57
50-52 Pine St.	200,000	210,000	49:51
95-97 Liberty St.	165,000	235,000	41:59
120-122 Liberty St.	265,000	179,900	60:40
137-139 Liberty St.	940,000	625,000	60:40
122-144 Greenwich St.	295,000	125,000	70:30
276 Greenwich St.	65,000	60,000	52:48
39-41 Cortlandt St.	275,000	300,000	48:52
12-16 John St.	150,000	200,000	43:57
49 John St.	300,000	350,000	46:54
47-49 Maiden Lane	200,000	300,000	40:60
51-53 Maiden Lane	250,000	280,000	47:53
56 Maiden Lane	150,000	225,000	40:60
92 William St.	225,000	275,000	45:55
123-133 William St.	515,000	435,000	54:46
236-242 William St.	300,000	150,000	67:33
110-116 Nassau St.	400,000	450,000	47:53
81-83 Fulton St.	250,000	180,000	58:42
409 Pearl St.	360,000	90,000	80:20
9-15 Murray St.	360,000	350,000	51:49
71-73 Murray St.	185,000	65,000	74:26
	$6,850,000	$5,959,900	

BUILDINGS THIRTEEN STORIES IN HEIGHT

Group A: Parcels Whose Taxes Would Be Increased

Address	Assessed Values		Ratio
	Improvements	Land	
63-65 Wall St.	$225,000	$400,000	36:64
27-29 Pine St.	225,000	550,000	29:71
34-36 Pine St.	300,000	525,000	36:64
66 Maiden Lane	95,000	180,000	34:66
10-14 Beekman St.	260,000	500,000	34:66
53-65 Park Row	450,000	1,500,000	23:77
	$1,555,000	$3,655,000	

Group B: Parcels Whose Taxes Would Be Decreased

Address	Assessed Values		Ratio
	Improvements	Land	
79-85 Wall St.	$225,000	$350,000	39:61
56-58 Pine St.	390,000	310,000	56:44
44½-46 Maiden Lane	310,000	475,000	40:60
20-24 Vesey St.	375,000	375,000	50:50
253 Broadway	900,000	1,025,000	47:53
	$2,200,000	$2,535,000	

BUILDINGS FOURTEEN STORIES IN HEIGHT

Group A: Parcels Whose Taxes Would Be Increased

Address	Assessed Values		Ratio
	Improvements	Land	
44-48 Cedar St.	$300,000	$500,000	38:62
135-137 Broadway	350,000	1,250,000	22:78
	$650,000	$1,750,000	

Group B: Parcels Whose Taxes Would Be Decreased

Address	Assessed Values		Ratio
	Improvements	Land	
15-17 Beekman St.	$235,000	$200,000	54:46
Frankfort St. (N. Y. Press)	395,000	245,000	62:38
90-92 W. Broadway	200,000	100,000	67:33
	$830,000	$545,000	

BUILDINGS FIFTEEN STORIES IN HEIGHT

Group A: Parcels Whose Taxes Would Be Increased

Address	Assessed Values		Ratio
	Improvements	Land	
28-30 Nassau St.	$3,700,000	$6,300,000	37:63
35-39 Nassau St.	775,000	1,575,000	33:67
24-26 Cortlandt St.	590,000	1,325,000	31:69
	$5,065,000	$9,200,000	

GROUP B: PARCELS WHOSE TAXES WOULD BE DECREASED

Address	Assessed Values		Ratio
	Improvements	Land	
82-92 Beaver St.	$500,000	$400,000	56:44
68-70 William St.	460,000	600,000	43:57
216-218 William St.	390,000	110,000	78:22
9-17 Dey St.	800,000	875,000	48:52
9-13 Maiden Lane	340,000	435,000	44:56
106-108 Fulton St.	245,000	205,000	55:45
	$2,735,000	$2,625,000	

BUILDINGS SIXTEEN STORIES IN HEIGHT

GROUP A: PARCELS WHOSE TAXES WOULD BE INCREASED

Address	Assessed Values		Ratio
	Improvements	Land	
24-28 Broad St.	$600,000	$1,250,000	22:68
32-36 Broad St.	950,000	1,550,000	38:62
32-34 Broadway	350,000	600,000	37:63
160-164 Broadway	600,000	1,125,000	35:65
39-42 Park Row	400,000	1,100,000	27:73
71-73 Nassau St.	420,000	680,000	38.18:61.8
	$3,320,000	$6,305,000	

GROUP B: PARCELS WHOSE TAXES WOULD BE DECREASED

Address	Assessed Values		Ratio
	Improvements	Land	
5-11 Broadway	$1,750,000	$1,500,000	54:46
22-30 Broadway	1,550,000	1,700,000	48:52
256-257 Broadway	375,000	550,000	41:49
63-65 Beaver St.	450,000	425,000	52:48
14-22 Cortlandt St.	1,175,000	1,225,000	48:52
98-105 William St.	960,000	940,000	51:49
135-141 William St.	300,000	200,000	60:40
57-61 John St.	415,000	260,000	62:38
	$6,975,000	$6,800,000	

BUILDINGS SEVENTEEN STORIES IN HEIGHT

GROUP A: PARCELS WHOSE TAXES WOULD BE INCREASED

Address	Assessed Values		Ratio
	Improvements	Land	
126-128 Broadway	$425,000	$1,375,000	24:76

GROUP B: PARCELS WHOSE TAXES WOULD BE DECREASED

Address	Assessed Values		Ratio
	Improvements	Land	
67-69 William St.	$390,000	$425,000	48:52
84-88 William St.	675,000	525,000	56:44
	$1,065,000	$950,000	

BUILDINGS EIGHTEEN STORIES IN HEIGHT

Group A: Parcels Whose Taxes Would Be Increased

Address	Assessed Values		Ratio
	Improvements	Land	
49-51 Broadway	$950,000	$1,900,000	33:67
66-70 Broadway	1,400,000	2,650,000	35:65
86 Broadway	150,000	650,000	19:81
166-172 Broadway	850,000	1,975,000	30:70
	$3,350,000	$7,175,000	

Group B: Parcels Whose Taxes Would Be Decreased

Address	Assessed Values		Ratio
	Improvements	Land	
26-28 Beaver St	$250,000	$150,000	63:37
28-30 Beaver St	355,000	270,000	57:43
59-61 Pearl St	366,500	93,500	80:20
	$971,500	$513,500	

BUILDINGS NINETEEN STORIES IN HEIGHT

Group A: Parcels Whose Taxes Would Be Increased

Address	Assessed Values		Ratio
	Improvements	Land	
141-147 Broadway	$1,100,000	$1,850,000	37:63

Group B: Parcels Whose Taxes Would Be Decreased

Address	Assessed Values		Ratio
	Improvements	Land	
11-13 William St	$800,000	$875,000	48:52
27 William St	1,150,000	1,150,000	50:50
154-162 Nassau St	750,000	950,000	44:56
	$2,700,000	$2,975,000	

BUILDINGS TWENTY STORIES IN HEIGHT

Group A: Parcels Whose Taxes Would Be Increased

Address	Assessed Values		Ratio
	Improvements	Land	
72-74 Broadway	$355,900	$1,125,000	24:76
27-33 Nassau St	1,000,000	1,800,000	36:64
	$1,355,000	$2,925,000	

Group B: Parcels Whose Taxes Would Be Decreased

Address	Assessed Values		Ratio
	Improvements	Land	
46-52 Broad St	$1,150,000	$1,100,000	51:49
50-54 William St	640,000	810,000	44:56
15-19 Maiden Lane	600,000	735,000	45:55
68-76 Maiden Lane	550,000	500,000	52:48
	$2,940,000	$3,145,000	

BUILDINGS TWENTY-ONE STORIES IN HEIGHT

Group A: Parcels Whose Taxes Would Be Increased

Address	Assessed Values		Ratio
	Improvements	Land	
100-106 Broadway	$700,000	$1,725,000	29:71
20 Broad St.	1,150,000	1,850,000	38.33:61.67
	$1,850,000	$3,575,000	

Group B: Parcels Whose Taxes Would Be Decreased

Address	Assessed Values		Ratio
	Improvements	Land	
36-42 Broadway	$2,200,000	$2,100,000	51:49
67-73 Broadway	1,600,000	2,500,000	39:61
111 Broadway	2,500,000	4,000,000	38.4:61.6
113-119 Broadway	2,200,000	3,200,000	41:59
92-94 Liberty St.	500,000	700,000	41:59
	$9,000,000	$12,500,000	

BUILDINGS TWENTY-TWO STORIES IN HEIGHT

Group A: Parcels Whose Taxes Would Be Increased

Address	Assessed Values		Ratio
	Improvements	Land	
5-11 Nassau St.	$1,100,000	$2,900,000	28:72

Group B: Parcels Whose Taxes Should Be Decreased

Address	Assessed Values		Ratio
	Improvements	Land	
87-93 West St.	$1,750,000	$550,000	76:24

BUILDINGS TWENTY-THREE STORIES IN HEIGHT

Group B: Parcels Whose Taxes Would Be Decreased

Address	Assessed Values		Ratio
	Improvements	Land	
58-60 Broadway	$1,350,000	$1,650,000	45:55
8 Rector St.	2,050,000	900,000	69:31
2-6 Spruce St.	585,000	765,000	43:57
	$3,985,000	$3,315,000	

BUILDINGS TWENTY-FIVE STORIES IN HEIGHT

Group A: Parcels Whose Taxes Would Be Increased

Address	Assessed Values		Ratio
	Improvements	Land	
218-222 Broadway	$550,000	$950,000	37:63

GROUP B: PARCELS WHOSE TAXES WOULD BE DECREASED.

Address	Assessed Values		Ratio
	Improvements	Land	
37-43 Wall St.	$1,025,000	$1,300,000	44:56
43-49 Exchange Pl.	1,150,000	750,000	61:39
13-21 Park Row	1,265,000	1,365,000	48:52
	$3,440,000	$3,415,000	

BUILDINGS TWENTY-SIX STORIES IN HEIGHT

GROUP B: PARCELS WHOSE TAXES WOULD BE DECREASED

Address	Assessed Values		Ratio
	Improvements	Land	
60-62 Wall St.	$1,175,000	$925,000	56:44
80 Maiden Lane	2,300,000	1,200,000	66:34
	$3,475,000	$2,125,000	

BUILDINGS THIRTY STORIES IN HEIGHT

GROUP B: PARCELS WHOSE TAXES WOULD BE DECREASED

Address	Assessed Values		Ratio
	Improvements	Land	
1 Nassau St.	$2,600,000	$3,200,000	45:55
53-57 Liberty St.	950,000	1,000,000	49:51
	$3,550,000	$4,200,000	

BUILDINGS THIRTY-TWO STORIES IN HEIGHT

GROUP B: PARCELS WHOSE TAXES WOULD BE DECREASED

Address	Assessed Values		Ratio
	Improvements	Land	
9 Battery Place	$1,725,000	$1,575,000	52:48
27-31 Broadway	1,900,000	2,900,000	40:60
57-61 Broadway	1,900,000	2,900,000	40:60
	$5,525,000	$7,375,000	

BUILDINGS THIRTY-THREE STORIES IN HEIGHT

GROUP B: PARCELS WHOSE TAXES WOULD BE DECREASED

Address	Assessed Values		Ratio
	Improvements	Land	
165-167 Broadway	$3,700,000	$2,925,000	59:41

BUILDINGS FORTY STORIES IN HEIGHT

GROUP B: PARCELS WHOSE TAXES WOULD BE DECREASED

Address	Assessed Values		Ratio
	Improvements	Land	
149-163 Broadway	$3,000,000	$4,000,000	43:57

BUILDINGS FIFTY-FOUR STORIES IN HEIGHT

GROUP B: PARCELS WHOSE TAXES WOULD BE DECREASED

Address	Assessed Values		Ratio
	Improvements	Land	
227-237 Broadway	$6,000,000	$2,800,000	68:32

UPPER EAST SIDE TENEMENT SECTION

(Standard Composite Ratio: 38.34:61.66)

GROUP A: PARCELS WHOSE TAXES WOULD BE INCREASED

Address	Assessed Values		Ratio
	Improvements	Land	
1968 Second Ave.	$8,500	$14,000	38:62
1990 Second Ave.	6,000	10,000	37:63
	$14,500	$24,000	

GROUP B: PARCELS WHOSE TAXES WOULD BE DECREASED

Address	Assessed Values		Ratio
	Improvements	Land	
1933-35 First Ave.	$29,500	$22,500	57:43
1937-39 First Ave.	21,500	16,000	57:43
1941-43 First Ave.	21,500	16,000	57:43
1945-47 First Ave.	21,500	16,000	57:43
1949-51 First Ave.	29,500	22,500	57:43
1953 First Ave.	52,500	37,500	63:37
1957-9 First Ave.	27,000	18,000	59:41
1961 First Ave.	27,000	18,000	59:41
1963 First Ave.	35,000	25,000	58:42
1969 First Ave.	37,000	33,000	59:41
1922 Second Ave.	42,000	26,500	61.3:38.7
1924-6 Second Ave.	33,500	17,500	66:34
1928-30 Second Ave.	33,500	17,500	66:34
1932-4 Second Ave.	33,500	17,500	66:34
1936-8 Second Ave.	42,000	26,500	61.3:38.7
1946 Second Ave.	13,500	16,500	45:55
1948 Second Ave.	8,000	10,000	44:56
1950 Second Ave.	8,000	10,000	44:56
1952 Second Ave.	10,000	10,000	50:50
1954 Second Ave.	10,000	10,000	50:50
1956 Second Ave.	8,000	10,000	44:56
1958 Second Ave.	8,000	10,000	44:56
1960 Second Ave.	13,500	16,500	45:55
1970 Second Ave.	7,500	8,500	47:53
1972 Second Ave.	7,500	8,500	47:53
1974 Second Ave.	7,500	8,500	47:53
1976 Second Ave.	10,000	10,000	50:50
1978 Second Ave.	10,000	10,000	50:50
1980 Second Ave.	10,000	10,000	50:50
1982 Second Ave.	13,500	16,500	45:55
1984 Second Ave.	10,500	14,000	40:60
1986 Second Ave.	7,500	8,500	47:53
1988 Second Ave.	7,500	8,500	47:53
1992 Second Ave.	10,000	10,000	50:50
1994 Second Ave.	10,000	10,000	50:50
1996 Second Ave.	10,000	10,000	50:50
1998 Second Ave.	13,500	16,500	45:55
303 East 99th St.	26,000	7,500	78:22
305-7 East 99th St.	26,000	7,500	78:22
309 East 99th St.	26,000	7,500	78:22
311-13 East 99th St.	26,000	7,500	78:22
305 East 100th St.	27,500	9,500	64:36
306-8 East 100th St.	33,000	12,000	73:27
307-9 East 100th St.	27,500	9,500	64:36
310-12 East 100th St.	33,000	12,000	73:27
311 East 100th St.	27,500	9,500	64:36
313-15 East 100th St.	27,500	9,500	64:36
314-16 East 100th St.	33,000	12,000	73:27
317 East 100th St.	27,500	9,500	64:36

UPPER EAST SIDE TENEMENT SECTION—*Continued*
GROUP B: PARCELS WHOSE TAXES WOULD BE DECREASED

Address	Assessed Values		Ratio
	Improvements	Land	
318-20 East 100th St.	$33,000	$12,000	73:27
319 East 100th St.	14,000	6,000	70:30
321 East 100th St.	14,000	6,000	70:30
322-24 East 100th St.	33,000	12,000	73:27
323 East 100th St.	14,000	6,000	70:30
325 East 100th St.	14,000	6,000	70:30
326-28 East 100th St.	33,000	12,000	73:27
327 East 100th St.	21,000	9,000	70:30
329 East 100th St.	21,000	9,000	70:30
330-32 East 100th St.	33,000	12,000	73:27
331 East 100th St.	21,000	9,000	70:30
333 East 100th St.	21,000	9,000	70:30
334-36 East 100th St.	33,000	12,000	73:27
338-340 East 100th St.	33,000	12,000	73:27
302 East 101st St.	27,000	11,000	71:29
303 East 101st St.	9,000	7,000	56:44
304 East 101st St.	15,000	7,000	68:32
305 East 101st St.	8,000	7,000	53:47
306 East 101st St.	15,000	7,000	68:32
307 East 101st St.	8,000	7,000	53:47
308 East 101st St.	15,000	7,000	68:32
309 East 101st St.	8,000	7,000	53:47
310-12 East 101st St.	15,000	7,000	68:32
311 East 101st St.	8,000	7,000	53:47
313 East 101st St.	8,000	7,000	53:47
314-16 East 101st St.	25,500	9,500	74:26
315 East 101st St.	16,000	7,000	70:30
317 East 101st St.	20,000	8,000	71:29
318-20 East 101st St.	25,500	9,500	74:26
319 East 101st St.	19,500	8,000	71:29
321 East 101st St.	19,500	8,000	71:29
322-24 East 101st St.	25,500	9,500	74:26
323 East 101st St.	19,500	8,000	71:29
325 East 101st St.	19,500	8,000	71:29
326-28 East 101st St.	25,500	9,500	74:26
327 East 101st St.	19,500	8,000	71:29
329 East 101st St.	19,500	8,000	71:29
330 East 101st St.	25,500	9,500	74:26
331-33 East 101st St.	27,500	9,500	74:26
332 East 101st St.	25,500	9,500	74:26
334 East 101st St.	25,500	9,500	74:26
335-37 East 101st St.	27,500	9,500	74:26
336 East 101st St.	25,500	9,500	74:26
338-40 East 101st St.	25,500	9,500	74:26
339-41 East 101st St.	27,500	9,500	74:26
343-45 East 101st St.	27,500	9,500	74:26
302 East 102nd St.	11,000	7,000	61:39
303 East 102nd St.	10,000	6,000	62:38
304 East 102nd St.	11,000	7,000	61:39
305 East 102nd St.	26,000	10,500	71:29
306 East 102nd St.	13,000	7,000	65:35
307-9 East 102nd St.	26,000	10,500	71:29
308 East 102nd St.	11,000	7,000	61:39
310 East 102nd St.	11,000	7,000	61:39
311 East 102nd St.	26,000	10,500	71:29
313-15 East 102nd St.	26,000	10,500	71:29
317 East 102nd St.	26,000	10,500	71:29
319 East 102nd St.	26,000	10,500	71:29
320 East 102nd St.	11,500	7,000	62:38
322 East 102nd St.	10,500	7,000	60:40
324 East 102nd St.	10,500	7,000	60:40
326-28 East 102nd St.	25,500	10,500	71:29
330 East 102nd St.	25,500	10,500	71:29

UPPER EAST SIDE TENEMENT SECTION—*Concluded*

GROUP B: PARCELS WHOSE TAXES WOULD BE DECREASED

Address	Assessed Values		Ratio
	Improvements	Land	
332-34 East 102nd St.	$25,500	$10,500	71:29
336 East 102nd St.	25,500	10,500	71:29
304 East 103rd St.	26,000	10,500	71:29
306-08 East 103rd St.	26,000	10,500	71:29
310 East 103rd St.	26,000	10,500	71:29
312-14 East 103rd St.	26,000	10,500	71:29
316-18 East 103rd St.	26,000	10,500	71:29
320 East 103rd St.	26,000	10,500	71:29
	$2,521,000	$1,315,500	

RIVINGTON STREET SECTION

(Standard Composite Ratio: 38.34 : 61.66)

Group A: Parcels Whose Taxes Would Be Increased

Address	Assessed Values		Ratio
	Improvements	Land	
54 Rivington Street	$14,000	$31,000	31:69
56 Rivington Street	2,000	16,000	11:89
62 Rivington Street	4,000	16,000	20:80
64 Rivington Street	9,000	16,000	36:64
70 Rivington Street	8,000	30,000	21:79
72 Rivington Street	4,000	16,000	20:80
74 Rivington Street	4,000	16,000	20:80
76 Rivington Street	5,000	16,000	24:76
88 Rivington Street	9,000	16,000	31:69
90 Rivington Street	9,000	20,000	31:69
92 Rivington Street	10,000	19,000	34:66
98 Rivington Street	13,000	26,000	33:67
112 Rivington Street	7,000	18,000	28:72
126 Rivington Street	3,000	16,000	16:84
130-38 Rivington Street	30,000	58,000	34:66
134 Rivington Street	4,000	18,000	18:82
144 Rivington Street	12,000	18,000	31:69
167 Stanton Street	2,000	11,000	15:85
97 Stanton Street	6,000	18,000	25:75
99 Stanton Street	5,000	17,000	23:77
113 Stanton Street	7,000	20,000	26:74
123 Stanton Street	9,000	19,000	32:68
125 Stanton Street	9,000	19,000	32:68
127 Stanton Street	7,000	19,000	27:73
129-31 Stanton Street	10,000	20,000	33:67
143 Stanton Street	1,500	14,000	10:90
145 Stanton Street	1,000	12,000	8:92
196 Eldridge Street	10,000	20,000	33:67
198 Eldridge Street	10,000	20,000	33:67
202 Eldridge Street	12,000	20,000	37:63
208 Eldridge Street	11,500	20,500	34:66
210 Elddrige Street	4,000	23,000	38:62
218 Eldridge Street	9,500	20,500	32:68
220 Eldridge Street	9,500	20,500	32:68
152 Allen Street	10,000	19,000	34:66
154 Allen Street	10,000	19,000	34:66
165 Allen Street	3,000	17,000	15:85
167 Allen Street	6,000	17,000	26:74
170 Allen Street	10,000	19,000	34:66
172 Allen Street	10,000	19,000	34:66
173 Allen Street	3,000	17,000	15:85
175 Allen Street	1,000	14,000	7:93
177 Allen Street	8,000	21,000	28:72
146 Orchard Street	7,000	22,500	24:76
148 Orchard Street	6,000	22,000	21:79
150 Orchard Street	6,000	22,000	21:79
152 Orchard Street	6,000	22,000	21:79
154 Orchard Street	6,000	22,000	21:79
156 Orchard Street	6,500	22,000	23:77
158 Orchard Street	6,500	22,500	22:78
160 Orchard Street	6,500	21,500	23:77
162 Orchard Street	6,500	22,000	23:77
168-70 Orchard Street	25,000	45,000	36:64
135 Ludlow Street	500	3,500	12:88
136 Ludlow Street	5,000	19,000	21:79
137 Ludlow Street	12,000	23,000	34:66
144 Ludlow Street	12,000	23,000	34:66
145 Ludlow Street	4,000	15,000	21:79
146 Ludlow Street	12,000	23,000	34:66
147 Ludlow Street	4,000	15,000	21:79

RIVINGTON STREET SECTION—*Continued*

GROUP A: PARCELS WHOSE TAXES WOULD BE INCREASED.

Address	Assessed Values		Ratio
	Improvements	Land	
148 Ludlow St.	$10,000	$23,000	30:70
149 Ludlow St.	15,000	23,000	18:82
150 Ludlow St.	10,000	23,000	30:70
151 Ludlow St.	15,000	23,000	18:82
152 Ludlow St.	7,000	23,000	23:77
154 Ludlow St.	7,000	23,000	23:77
155 Ludlow St.	14,000	23,000	38:62
156 Ludlow St.	7,000	23,000	23:77
157 Ludlow St.	14,000	23,000	38:62
158 Ludlow St.	7,000	23,000	23:77
159 Ludlow St.	5,000	12,000	29:71
160 Ludlow St.	20,000	35,000	36:64
139-41 Ludlow St.	5,000	46,000	10:90
132 Essex St.	30,000	60,000	33:67
136 Essex St.	10,000	25,000	29:71
137 Essex St.	8,500	22,500	27:73
138 Essex St.	10,000	25,000	29:71
139 Essex St.	13,500	22,500	37:63
140 Essex St.	10,000	25,000	29:71
141 Essex St.	13,500	22,500	37:63
142 Essex St.	9,000	25,000	26:74
143 Essex St.	13,500	22,500	37:63
144 Essex St.	9,000	25,000	26:74
145 Essex St.	13,500	22,500	36:64
146 Essex St.	9,500	25,000	28:72
147 Essex St.	12,500	22,500	36:64
148 Essex St.	11,500	25,000	32:68
150 Essex St.	7,000	25,000	22:78
152 Essex St.	5,000	25,000	17:83
153 Essex St.	8,000	18,000	31:69
155 Essex St.	7,000	18,000	28:72
157 Essex St.	10,000	27,000	27:73
135 Norfolk St.	13,500	24,000	36:64
136 Norfolk St.	10,000	24,000	29:71
137 Norfolk St.	13,500	24,000	36:64
138 Norfolk St.	10,000	24,000	29:71
139 Norfolk St.	13,500	24,000	36:64
140 Norfolk St.	7,000	24,000	23:77
141 Norfolk St.	13,500	23,500	36:64
142 Norfolk St.	10,500	23,500	31:69
143 Norfolk St.	13,500	23,500	36:64
144 Norfolk St.	7,500	23,500	24:76
145 Norfolk St.	7,500	23,500	24:76
146 Norfolk St.	7,500	23,500	24:76
148 Norfolk St.	8,500	23,500	27:73
150 Norfolk St.	8,500	23,500	27:73
157 Norfolk St.	5,500	21,500	20:80
159 Norfolk St.	6,500	15,500	30:70
25 Suffolk St.	8,000	24,000	25:75
27 Suffolk St.	8,000	24,000	25:75
29 Suffolk St.	8,000	24,000	25:75
31 Suffolk St.	9,000	24,000	27:73
33 Suffolk St.	10,000	24,000	29:71
35 Suffolk St.	10,000	24,000	29:71
	$1,020,000	$2,729,500	

RIVINGTON STREET SECTION—*Concluded*
GROUP B: PARCELS WHOSE TAXES WOULD BE DECREASED

Address	Assessed Values		Ratio
	Improvements	Land	
66-68 Rivington St.	$39,000	$43,000	48:52
86 Rivington St.	21,000	32,000	40:60
94-96 Rivington St.	31,000	42,000	42:58
100 Rivington St.	40,000	50,000	44:56
132 Rivington St.	31,000	42,000	42:58
136-38 Rivington St.	32,000	40,000	44:56
146 Rivington St.	28,000	42,000	40:60
79 Stanton St.	13,000	19,000	41:59
81 Stanton St.	13,000	19,000	41:59
83 Stanton St.	13,000	19,000	41:59
85 Stanton St.	13,000	19,000	41:59
87 Stanton St.	20,000	32,000	38.46:61.54
101-3 Stanton St.	20,000	33,000	48:62
121 Stanton St.	20,000	28,500	41:59
147 Stanton St.	17,000	23,000	42.5:57.5
200 Eldridge St.	13,000	20,000	40:60
204-6 Eldridge St.	29,000	41,000	41:59
212 Eldridge St.	7,000	11,000	38.9:61.1
214-16 Eldridge St.	24,000	26,000	48:52
151-3 Allen St.	27,000	27,000	50:50
156 Allen St.	13,000	16,000	45:55
158 Allen St.	13,000	16,000	45:55
157-9 Allen St.	30,000	28,000	52:48
160 Allen St.	13,000	16,000	45:55
161 Allen St.	20,000	17,000	54:46
162 Allen St.	13,000	16,000	45:55
163 Allen St.	13,000	17,000	43:57
164 Allen St.	13,000	16,000	45:55
166 Allen St.	13,000	16,000	45:55
169 Allen St.	14,000	17,000	45:55
171 Allen St.	14,000	17,000	45:55
141-43 Orchard St.	40,000	50,000	44:56
145 Orchard St.	13,500	21,500	38.6:61.4
147 Orchard St.	13,500	21,500	38.6:61.4
149 Orchard St.	13,500	21,500	38.6:61.4
151 Orchard St.	13,500	21,500	38.6:61.4
153 Orchard St.	13,500	21,500	38.6:61.4
155 Orchard St.	13,500	21,500	38.6:61.4
157 Orchard St.	13,500	21,500	38.6:61.4
159 Orchard St.	17,000	26,000	40:60
161 Orchard St.	17,000	26,000	40:60
163 Orchard St.	14,500	22,500	39:61
164 Orchard St.	17,000	22,000	44:56
165 Orchard St.	14,500	22,500	39:61
166 Orchard St.	17,000	22,000	44:56
138-40 Orchard St.	30,000	45,000	40:60
142 Orchard St.	15,000	23,000	40:60
143 Orchard St.	24,000	33,000	42:58
147 Orchard St.	16,500	23,500	43:57
149 Orchard St.	16,500	23,500	43:57
151 Orchard St.	16,500	23,500	43:57
152 Orchard St.	15,500	23,500	40:60
153 Orchard St.	16,500	23,500	43:57
154 Orchard St.	15,500	23,500	40:60
156-58 Orchard St.	28,000	43,000	39:61
123 Suffolk St.	13,500	20,000	40:60
137 Suffolk St.	17,000	24,000	41:59
139 Suffolk St.	16,500	24,000	41:59
147-49 Suffolk St.	31,000	45,000	41:59
	$1,123,500	$1,540,000	

HOUSTON STREET SECTION

(Standard Composite Ratio: 38.34:61.66)

GROUP A: PARCELS WHOSE TAXES WOULD BE INCREASED

Address	Assessed Values		Ratio
	Improvements	Land	
4 First Ave.	$8,000	$20,000	29:71
6 First Ave.	8,000	20,000	29:71
12 First Ave.	10,000	31,000	24:76
14 First Ave.	12,000	26,000	32:68
16 First Ave.	7,000	20,000	26:74
22 First Ave.	4,000	20,000	17:83
32 First Ave.	16,000	27,000	37:63
34 First Ave.	8,000	17,000	32:68
36 First Ave.	9,000	23,000	28:72
38 First Ave.	10,000	22,000	31:69
40 First Ave.	5,000	14,000	26:74
42 First Ave.	8,000	19,000	30:70
44 First Ave.	8,000	19,000	30:70
46 First Ave.	12,000	30,000	29:71
1-3 Avenue A	15,000	30,000	33:67
5 Avenue A	15,000	35,000	31:69
9 Avenue A	7,500	14,500	27:73
13 Avenue A	5,500	13,500	22:78
15 Avenue A	4,000	14,000	29:71
17 Avenue A	4,000	11,000	34:66
23 Avenue A	4,000	11,000	30:70
29 Avenue A	8,000	21,000	20:80
33 Avenue A	9,000	21,000	25:75
35 Avenue A	9,000	21,000	25:75
37 Avenue A	7,000	21,000	30:70
39 Avenue A	7,000	21,000	30:70
41 Avenue A	15,000	20,000	28:72
194 East Houston St.	5,000	10,000	33:67
208 East Houston St.	10,000	17,000	37:63
222 East Houston St.	5,000	10,000	33:67
224 East Houston St.	5,000	9,500	34:66
226 East Houston St.	4,800	9,200	34:66
228 East Houston St.	5,000	9,000	35:64
78 East 1st St.	7,000	17,000	29:71
81 East 1st St.	1,000	7,000	13:87
83 East 1st St.	1,000	7,000	13:87
89 East 1st St.	3,000	6,000	33:67
91 East 1st St.	3,000	6,000	33:67
98½ East 1st St.	3,000	15,000	17:83
100 East 1st St.	6,000	15,000	29:71
102 East 1st St.	6,000	15,000	29:71
104 East 1st St.	5,000	12,000	29:71
106 East 1st St.	5,000	12,000	29:71
118 East 1st St.	1,000	15,000	6:94
105 East 2nd St.	5,000	13,000	28:72
107 East 2nd St.	10,000	18,000	36:64
109 East 2nd St.	10,000	18,000	36:64
111 East 2nd St.	8,000	18,000	25:75
113 East 2nd St.	10,000	18,000	36:64
115 East 2nd St.	16,000	13,000	32:68
104 East 3rd St.	5,000	9,000	36:64
106 East 3rd St.	6,000	13,000	32:68
108 East 3rd St.	6,000	16,000	24:76
110 East 3rd St.	5,000	16,000	24:76
112 East 3rd St.	5,000	16,000	24:76
114 East 3rd St.	5,000	16,000	24:76
116 East 3rd St.	5,000	16,000	24:76
118 East 3rd St.	5,000	16,000	24:76
120 East 3rd St.	5,000	16,000	24:76
122 East 3rd St.	5,000	16,000	24:76

HOUSTON STREET SECTION—*Continued*

GROUP A: PARCELS WHOSE TAXES WOULD BE INCREASED

Address	Assessed Values		Ratio
	Improvements	Land	
124 East 3rd St.	$5,000	$16,000	24:76
126 East 3rd St.	5,000	16,000	24:76
128 East 3rd St.	5,000	16,000	24:76
130 East 3rd St.	5,000	18,000	22:78
132 East 3rd St.	5,000	18,000	22:78
134 East 3rd St.	5,000	18,000	22:78
136 East 3rd St.	5,000	18,000	22:78
138 East 3rd St.	5,000	18,000	22:78
140 East 3rd St.	2,000	12,000	14:86
	$463,803	$1,151,700	

GROUP B: PARCELS WHOSE TAXES WOULD BE DECREASED

Address	Assessed Values		Ratio
	Improvements	Land	
8-10 First Ave.	$37,000	$53,000	41:59
18 First Ave.	30,000	40,000	43:57
26 First Ave.	37,000	44,000	46:54
180-84 E. Houston St.	45,000	50,000	47:53
196 E. Houston St.	5,000	8,000	38.46:61.54
198 E. Houston St.	12,000	19,000	41:59
200 E. Houston St.	12,000	18,500	40:60
202 E. Houston St.	12,000	18,000	40:60
206 E. Houston St.	11,500	17,500	40:60
214-18 E. Houston St.	2,500	32,000	44:56
220 E. Houston St.	10,000	15,000	40:60
80-2 E. First St.	33,000	32,000	51:49
90 E. First St.	32,000	33,000	49:51
94 E. First St.	32,000	33,000	49:51
98 E. First St.	32,000	33,000	49:51
110-12 E. First St.	33,000	29,000	53:47
114-16 E. First St.	31,000	29,000	52:48
103 East 2nd St.	11,000	16,000	41:59
104-6 East 2nd St.	35,000	50,000	41:59
110 East 2nd St.	35,000	36,000	49:51
112 East 2nd St.	25,000	21,000	54:46
114 East 2nd St.	25,000	21,000	54:46
116 East 2nd St.	25,000	21,000	54:46
117-19 East 2nd St.	30,000	30,000	50:50
120 East 2nd St.	25,000	21,000	54:46
122 East 2nd St.	25,000	21,000	54:46
124 East 2d St.	25,000	21,000	54:46
126 East 2nd St.	25,000	21,000	54:46
128 East 2nd St.	25,000	21,000	54:46
132 East 2nd St.	31,500	31,500	50:50
136 East 2nd St.	31,000	31,000	50:50
	$780,500	$866,500	

ELEVATOR APARTMENT SECTION

(Standard Composite Ratio: 38.34:61.66)

GROUP A: PARCELS WHOSE TAXES WOULD BE INCREASED

None.

GROUP B: PARCELS WHOSE TAXES WOULD BE DECREASED

Address	Assessed Values		Ratio
	Improvements	Land	
4185 Broadway	$185,000	$95,000	66:34
4197 Broadway	200,000	105,000	66:34
4221 Broadway	175,000	100,000	64:36
4233-39 Broadway	149,000	96,000	71:29
4241 Broadway	170,000	100,000	63:37
717 West 177th St	119,000	41,000	74:26
701 West 178th St	150,000	80,000	65:35
718 West 178th St	114,000	41,000	74:26
825 West 178th St	118,500	31,500	79:21
830 West 179th St	118,500	31,500	79:21
725 West 180th St	194,000	39,000	71:29
804 West 180th St	125,000	45,000	74:26
720 West 181st St	125,000	60,000	68:32
728 West 181st St	135,000	60,000	69:31
736 West 181st St	142,000	63,000	69:31
S.W.C. 181st St., bet. Pinehurst & Northern Ave. (Comfort Realty Co.)	155,000	60,000	70:30
S.E.C. 181st St., bet. Pinehurst & Northern Ave. (Ft. View Const. Co.)	143,000	52,000	73:27
S.E.C. Ft. Washington Av. & 180th St	135,000	65,000	67:33
454 Ft. Washingtton Ave	305,000	135,000	69:31
N.E.C. Ft. Washington Ave. & 180th St	175,000	80,000	69:31
N.W.C. Ft. Washington Ave. & 177th St	153,000	67,000	70:30
S.W.C. Ft. Washington Ave. & 178th St	153,000	67,000	70:30
S.W.C. Ft. Washington Ave. & 179th St	130,000	60,000	68:32
N.W.C. Ft. Washington Ave. & 179th St	143,000	65,000	61:31
S.W.C. Ft. Washington Ave. & 180th St	141,000	64,000	68:32
447 Ft. Washington Ave	134,000	66,000	67:33
— Ft. Washington Ave	91,000	49,000	65:35
— Ft. Washington Ave	135,000	72,000	65:35
N.W.C. Pinehurst Ave. & 177th St	147,000	48,000	75:25
S.W.C. Pinehurst Ave. & 178th St	147,000	48,000	75:25
S.E.C. Pinehurst Ave. & 179th St	122,000	43,000	74:26
N.E.C. Pinehurst Ave. & 179th St	125,000	45,000	74:26
S.E.C. Pinehurst Ave. & 181st St	163,000	67,000	71:29
S.E.C. Pinehurst Ave. & 180th St	124,000	36,000	75:25
N.E.C. Pinehurst Ave. & 179th St	124,000	36,000	75:25
	$5,165,000	$2,213,000	

WALK-UP APARTMENT SECTION

(Standard Composite Ratio: 38.34:61.66)

GROUP A: PARCELS WHOSE TAXES WOULD BE INCREASED

None.

GROUP B: PARCELS WHOSE TAXES WOULD BE DECREASED

Address	Assessed Values		Ratio
	Improvements	Land	
— Audubon Ave.	$48,000	$27,000	64:36
185 Audubon Ave.	53,500	33,500	62:38
189 Audubon Ave.	21,000	14,000	60:40
199-209 Audubon Ave.	43,000	33,000	56:44
247-51 Audubon Ave.	128,000	62,000	67:33
255 Audubon Ave.	17,500	21,500	56:44
503-5 West 174th St.	29,000	14,000	67:33
509 West 174th St.	43,000	21,000	67:33
557-61 West 174th St.	60,000	32,000	65:35
503-5 West 175th St.	28,000	17,000	62:38
507-9 West 175th St.	28,000	17,000	62:38
511-13 West 175th St.	28,000	17,000	62:38
515-17 West 175th St.	28,000	17,000	62:38
516-18 West 175th St.	25,000	14,000	64:36
520 West 175th St.	25,000	14,000	64:36
521 West 175th St.	31,000	19,000	62:38
502 West 176th St.	27,000	14,000	66:34
503 West 176th St.	26,500	13,500	67:33
505-7 West 176th St.	26,500	13,500	67:33
506 West 176th St.	27,000	14,000	66:34
509-11 West 176th St.	26,500	13,500	67:33
510 West 176th St.	27,000	14,000	66:34
513-15 West 176th St.	26,500	13,500	67:33
514 West 176th St.	27,000	14,000	66:34
574-80 West 176th St.	84,000	42,000	67:33
502-4 West 177th St.	26,500	13,500	67:33
503-17 West 177th St.	106,000	54,000	66:34
506-8 West 177th St.	26,500	13,500	67:33
510-12 West 177th St.	26,500	13,500	67:33
514-16 West 177th St.	26,500	13,500	67:33
575-87 West 177th St.	86,000	56,000	63:37
510-12 West 178th St.	25,000	19,000	57:43
534-36 West 178th St.	38,000	30,000	56:44
586-90 West 178th St.	48,000	32,000	60:40
592-96 West 178th St.	48,000	32,000	60:40
2300 Amsterdam Ave.	36,000	31,000	55:45
2304-6 Amsterdam Ave.	29,000	24,000	55:45
2364 Amsterdam Ave.	23,000	20,000	53:47
2366 Amsterdam Ave.	23,000	20,000	53:47
1340-2 St. Nicholas Ave.	29,000	31,000	48:52
1344-6 St. Nicholas Ave.	24,000	24,000	50:50
1348-50 St. Nicholas Ave.	24,000	24,000	50:50
1352-4 St. Nicholas Ave.	24,000	24,000	50:50
1356 St. Nicholas Ave.	29,000	34,000	46:54
	$1,632,000	$1,034,000	

RIVERSIDE DRIVE SECTION

(Standard Composite Ratio: 38.34:61.66)

Group A: Parcels Whose Taxes Would Be Increased

Address	Owner or Occupant	Assessed Values — Improvements	Assessed Values — Land	Ratio
	C. M. Schwab	$650,000	$1,050,000	38.2:61.8
60	A. R. Barbery	21,000	35,000	37.5:62.5
64	J. L. Miller	16,000	27,000	37.2:62.8
71	Edgar Lehman	15,000	25,000	37.5:62.5
73	Est. L. Lewisohn	15,000	25,000	37.5:62.5
77	M. L. Williams	14,000	24,000	36.9:63.1
95	T. Simon	14,000	24,000	36.9:63.1
96	Jas. Richards	12,000	20,000	37.5:62.5
97	Wm. H. Gentzlinger	12,000	20,000	37.5:62.5
		$769,000	$1,250,000	

Group B: Parcels Whose Taxes Would Be Decreased

Address	Owner or Occupant	Assessed Values — Improvements	Assessed Values — Land	Ratio
1	L. S. F. Prentiss	$53,000	$57,000	48:52
3	Wm. Guggenheim	42,000	53,000	44:56
4	Angir M. Booth	47,000	53,000	47:53
23	S. J. Hull	28,000	30,000	48:52
24	Geo. C. Nickerson	28,000	30,000	48:52
31	J. Harvey and Chas. S. Neel	36,000	42,000	46.2:53.8
32	Sarah L. Shanley	32,000	28,000	53.3:46.7
33	T. C. Flynn	32,000	29,000	52.5:47.5
34	F. F. White	34,000	30,000	53.1:46.9
35	Wesley Thorn	24,000	20,000	54.5:45.5
36	Elsie Boyd	25,000	22,000	53.2:46.8
37	H. Blatchford	23,000	22,000	51.1:48.9
38	Mary Ehrmann	25,000	20,000	55.5:44.5
39	H. Fisk	33,000	45,000	42.3:57.7
40	M. D. Brill	33,000	37,000	47.1:52.9
41	F. and F. L. Humphreys	25,000	24,000	51:49
42	W. L. Brown	40,000	40,000	50:50
43	Clarence True	22,000	20,000	52.4:47.6
45	A. E. Pelham	18,000	24,000	42.9:57.1
51	Alice R. Hall	35,000	35,000	50:50
61	S. E. Miller	13,500	17,500	44:56
62	D. Purcell, et al	14,000	18,000	44:56
63	Nora E. P. Bergman	15,000	21,000	42:58
72	Jno. L. Scannell	11,000	17,000	39:61
74	H. G. Atwater	16,000	24,000	40:60
75	Louis Newman	23,000	27,000	46:54
76	Sophie M. Edwards	17,000	27,000	39:61
78	Julie W. Leach	24,000	28,000	46:54
80	Frieda Armond	25,000	33,000	43:57
81	John B. Manning	19,000	21,000	48:52
82	Isabel de F. Collron	20,000	23,000	46:54
83	Harrison B. Moore	20,000	23,000	46:54
84	Delos McCurdy, Trustee	21,000	22,000	49:51
85	Hester J. Morton	20,000	21,000	49:51
86	Grace Carroll	28,000	35,000	44:56
90	Josephine L. Biedler	22,000	33,000	40:60
91	Sarah E. Knapp	21,000	22,000	49:51
92	Met. Imp. Co.	19,500	27,000	42:58
93	C. M. Higgins	20,500	24,000	46:54
94	Eliza M. Pelgram	19,500	25,000	44:56
98	Jane A. Goodman	17,000	23,000	43:57
99	Anna A. Pollack	20,000	30,000	40:60
		$1,061,000	$1,202,500	

FIFTH AVENUE SECTION

(Standard Composite Ratio: 38.34:61.66)

GROUP A: PARCELS WHOSE TAXES WOULD BE INCREASED

Address	Owner or Occupant	Assessed Values Improvements	Assessed Values Land	Ratio
...	Louisa M. Gerry	$200,000	$1,200,000	14:86
800	Helen C. Bostwick	65,000	335,000	16:84
801	A. C. Bostwick	25,000	175,000	12:88
802	A. C. Bostwick	25,000	175,000	12:88
803	George R. Fearing	55,000	200,000	22:78
804	W. E. Roosevelt	20,000	220,000	8:92
805-7	E. L. Winthrop	60,000	720,000	8:92
810	Geo. Amsinck	70,000	295,000	19:81
811	W. F. Loring	20,000	180,000	14:86
812	Clara L. McMurtry	38,000	202,000	16:84
813	Hugh J. Chisholm	85,000	160,000	35:65
814	Thos. Rutter	35,000	175,000	17:83
815	G. G. Lake	35,000	175,000	17:83
816	A. L. Gerry	70,000	155,000	31:69
817	Pen Alpha Realty Co.	90,000	300,000	23:77
820	J. B. Haggin	40,000	800,000	5.95
824	Cath. L. Kernochan	65,000	195,000	25:75
825	I. V. Brokaw	50,000	170,000	23:77
826	Josephine Brooks	65,000	170,000	28:72
827	E. J. Berwind	115,000	335,000	26:74
830	Jas. B. Haggin	180,000	350,000	34:66
833	Wm. Guggenheim	170,000	280,000	37.8:62.2
834	Three States Realty Co.	170,000	280,000	37.8:62.2
835	J. W. Herbert	90,000	200,000	31:69
836	Isadore Wormser, Jr.	20,000	175,000	10:90
837	Sophie A. Sherman	120,000	455,000	21:79
842-3	John J. Astor	600,000	1,300,000	32:68
844	J. J. Astor	100,000	175,000	36:64
845	Elizabeth B. Schley	110,000	475,000	18:82
850-2	H. O. Havemeyer Est.	200,000	775,000	21:79
855	Cecelia Borg	55,000	320,000	15:85
...	Geo. Gould	250,000	525,000	32:68
858	Thos. F. Ryan	325,000	1,200,000	21:79
864	5th Av. & 68th St. Co.	75,000	610,000	11:89
871	H. P. Whitney	425,000	875,000	33:67
874	Wm. Mitchell	130,000	395,000	25:75
875	Daniel G. Reed	85,000	165,000	34:66
876	Mary B. Harrison	95,000	205,000	32:68
...	Ogden Mills	115,000	585,000	16:84
880	E. H. Harriman	200,000	675,000	23:77
881	A. Lewisohn	65,000	485,000	12:88
883	John Sloan	80,000	320,000	20:80
900	Mrs. N. E. Bayliss	60,000	325,000	16:84
...	Mary I. Burden	100,000	400,000	20:80
912	John N. Sterling	70,000	175,000	29:71
914	Samuel Thorne	110,000	300,000	27:73
922	Geo. W. Quintard	65,000	310,000	17:83
926	J. W. Simpson	85,000	180,000	32:68
927	A. D. Pell	200,000	550,000	27:73
...	S. B. Chapin	45,000	240,000	16:84
931	J. D. Lynig	20,000	160,000	14:86
932	M. L. Schiff	40,000	210,000	16:84
933	L. V. Harkness	95,000	180,000	35:65
934	A. W. Hoyt	110,000	295,000	27:73
...	Five Boroughs Realty Co.	165,000	310,000	35:65
...	Martha M. Wysong	135,000	265,000	34:66
963	Sarah H. Dietrich	75,000	150,000	33:67
964	Dr. Geo. H. Butler	62,000	153,000	29:71
967	Theresa Schiff	150,000	310,000	33:67
969	Wm. V. Lawrence	75,000	245,000	23:77
972	Payne Whitney	230,000	455,000	34:66

FIFTH AVENUE SECTION—*Continued*

Group A: Parcels Whose Taxes Would Be Increased

Address	Owner or Occupant	Assessed Values Improvements	Assessed Values Land	Ratio
...	Isaac D. Fletcher	$125,000	$340,000	27:73
...	Isaac V. Brokaw	100,000	400,000	20:80
984	Isaac V. Brokaw	90,000	155,000	37:63
986	Wm. J. Curtis	60,000	150,000	29:71
987	W. Lewisohn	80,000	150,000	35:65
988	Pauline Murray	45,000	150,000	23:77
989	Nicholas F. Brady	70,000	230,000	23:77
990	Frank W. Woolworth	125,000	235,000	35:65
993	Edinee Reisinger	175,000	325,000	35:65
1006	Katherine F. Gilshenen	35,000	135,000	21:79
1007	Kate F. Timmerman	60,000	115,000	34:66
1008	Sallie J. A. Hall	95,000	155,000	38:62
1009	James B. Duke	140,000	225,000	30:70
1020	William Salomon	115,000	410,000	22:78
1028	Harriet V. S. Thorn	115,000	200,000	37:63
1031	James H. Hammersley	50,000	300,000	14:86
1032	Annie Leary	50,000	100,000	33:67
1033	George Smith	150,000	100,000	33:67
....	James B. Clews	65,000	160,000	29:71
1041	Lloyd Warren	30,000	190,000	14:86
1043	David Mayer	10,000	90,000	10:90
1044	Matthew H. Beers	35,000	90,000	28:72
1045	R. Hopkins	25,000	90,000	22:78
1046	Michael Dreicer	50,000	90,000	36:64
1048	Wm. S. Miller	125,000	275,000	31:69
1053	George Leary	40,000	80,000	33:67
1054	W. H. Erhort	60,000	170,000	26:74
1056	Keokee M. Perin	28,000	82,000	25:75
....	James Speyer	140,000	460,000	23:77
....	Henry Phipps	300,000	800,000	27:73
1071	Philip Livingston	105,000	170,000	38.2:61.8
1080	Percival Farquhar	105,000	175,000	37:63
....	Andrew Carnegie	475,000	1,875,000	20:80
1116	Jacob Ruppert	35,000	370,000	9:91
		$10,088,000	$31,417,000	

Group B: Parcels Whose Taxes Would Be Decreased

Address	Owner or Occupant	Assessed Values Improvements	Assessed Values Land	Ratio
854	Geo. F. Mason	$180,000	$245,000	42:58
856	E. H. Gary	285,000	375,000	43:57
923	Eliza Guggenheimer	110,000	170,000	39.3:60.7
924	Georgia W. Warren	125,000	200,000	38.5:61.5
925	M. W. Terrell	85,000	115,000	39.5:60.5
...	Caroline H. Bertron	120,000	180,000	40:60
...	E. S. Harkness	220,000	320,000	41:59
954	S. W. Bridgeham	155,000	185,000	46:54
956	J. H. Harding	180,000	200,000	47:53
962	W. A. Clark Realty Co.	3,000,000	1,000,000	75:25
...	J. B. Duke	600,000	850,000	41:59
973	Georgia D. Heredia	120,000	180,000	40:60
985	Isaac V. Brokaw	100,000	150,000	40:60
991	Zelma K. Clark	95,000	145,000	40:60
992	Rocklege Cons. Co.	95,000	144,000	40:60
1014	J. F. A. Clarke	95,000	130,000	42:58
1015	George J. Gould	95,000	130,000	42:58
1025	Lloyd S. Bryce	150,000	200,000	43:57
1026	Mary J. Kingsland	178,000	182,000	49:51
1027	Harriet S. Clark	185,000	200,000	48:52
1033	Helen C. Robbins	70,000	100,000	41:59

FIFTH AVENUE SECTION—*Concluded*
Group B: Parcels Whose Taxes Would Be Decreased

	Address	Assessed Values		Ratio
		Improvements	Land	
1068	Hamilton M. Weed	$145,000	$105,000	58:42
1069	Emily A. V. B. Reynolds	165,000	185,000	47:53
....	Louise M. Pollack	115,000	180,000	39:61
1072	W. W. Fuller	115,000	120,000	49:51
1073	John H. Hanan	115,000	120,000	49:51
....	Benj. N. Duke	220,000	245,000	47:53
1081	Eliza W. Van Ingen	100,000	110,000	48:52
1082	Eleonore Phillips	75,000	100,000	43:57
1083	Archer M. Huntington	105,000	120,000	47:53
....	I. Townsend Burden	200,000	245,000	45:55
1109	Frieda S. Warburg	275,000	215,000	56:44
		$7,873,000	$15,019,000	

SECTION OF SIDE STREETS EAST OF FIFTH AVENUE

(Standard Composite Ratio: 38.34:61.66)

Group A: Parcels Whose Taxes Would Be Increased

Address	Assessed Values Improvements	Land	Ratio
13 East 60th St.	$30,000	$85,000	26:74
15 East 60th St.	30,000	85,000	26:74
17 East 60th St.	30,000	85,000	26:74
19 East 60th St.	30,000	85,000	26:74
21 East 60th St.	10,000	62,000	13:87
23 East 60th St.	8,000	52,000	13:87
25 East 60th St.	31,000	160,000	16:84
5 East 61st St.	45,000	205,000	13:87
7 East 61st St.	8,000	96,000	8:92
8 East 61st St.	45,000	110,000	29:71
9 East 61st St.	8,000	95,000	8:92
15 East 61st St.	9,000	93,000	8:92
17 East 61st St.	53,000	92,000	37:63
19 East 61st St.	8,000	33,000	19:81
20 East 61st St.	8,000	92,000	8:92
21 East 61st St.	7,000	20,000	26:74
22 East 61st St.	8,000	75,000	10:90
23 East 61st St.	3,000	22,000	12:88
24 East 61st St.	6,000	60,000	9:91
25 East 61st St.	10,000	50,000	17:83
26 East 61st St.	8,000	70,000	10:90
28 East 61st St.	12,000	90,000	12:88
— East 61st St.	15,000	210,000	7:93
4 East 62nd St.	70,000	175,000	29:71
5 East 62nd St.	10,000	98,000	9:91
7 East 62nd St.	9,000	97,000	8:92
9 East 62nd St.	8,000	96,000	8:92
12 East 62nd St.	11,000	95,000	10:90
14 East 62nd St.	10,000	94,000	9:91
15 East 62nd St.	35,000	70,000	33:67
16 East 62nd St.	10,000	80,000	11:89
17 East 62nd St.	9,000	69,000	11:89
18 East 62nd St.	22,000	78,000	22:78
19 East 62nd St.	8,000	68,000	13:87
20 East 62nd St.	7,000	54,000	11:89
21 East 62nd St.	7,000	60,000	10:90
22 East 62nd St.	9,000	73,000	11:89
24 East 62nd St.	35,000	58,000	38:62
26 East 62nd St.	7,000	58,000	11:89
28 East 62nd St.	45,000	110,000	29:71
2 East 63rd St.	2,000	63,000	2:98
4 East 63rd St.	2,000	62,000	3:97
6 East 63rd St.	2,000	61,000	3:97
8 East 63rd St.	27,000	96,000	22:78
10 East 63rd St.	8,000	94,000	8:92
12 East 63rd St.	15,000	92,000	14:86
14 East 63rd St.	20,000	90,000	18:82
16 East 63rd St.	7,000	64,000	10:90
18 East 63rd St.	7,000	64,000	10:90
20 East 63rd St.	7,000	64,000	10:90
28 East 63rd St.	27,000	64,000	30:70
1 East 63rd St.	12,000	100,000	11:89
3 East 63rd St.	10,000	98,000	9:91
7 East 63rd St.	14,000	94,000	13:87
9 East 63rd St.	11,000	92,000	11:89
11 East 63rd St.	10,000	90,000	10:90
13 East 63rd St.	9,000	71,000	11:89
21 East 63rd St.	36,000	74,000	33:67
8 East 64th St.	5,000	76,000	6:94
9 East 64th St.	37,000	173,000	18:82
10 East 64th St.	5,000	75,000	6:94

SECTION OF SIDE STREETS EAST OF FIFTH AVENUE—*Continued*
GROUP A: PARCELS WHOSE TAXES WOULD BE INCREASED

Address	Assessed Values		Ratio
	Improvements	Land	
12 East 64th St.	$5,000	$74,000	6:94
14 East 64th St.	5,000	73,000	6:94
15 East 64th St.	8,000	106,000	7:93
16 East 64th St.	33,000	72,000	31:69
17 East 64th St.	21,000	67,000	24:76
18 East 64th St.	50,000	90,000	36:64
19 East 64th St.	5,000	71,000	7:93
20 East 64th St.	20,000	88,000	19:81
21 East 64th St.	5,000	60,000	8:92
22 East 64th St.	39,000	86,000	31:69
23 East 64th St.	20,000	53,000	27:73
24 East 64th St.	7,000	71,000	9:91
25 East 64th St.	5,000	53,000	7:93
26 East 64th St.	9,000	71,000	11:89
27 East 64th St.	25,000	95,000	21:79
30 East 64th St.	25,000	125,000	17:83
2 East 65th St.	10,000	85,000	11:89
4 East 65th St.	13,000	99,000	12:88
5 East 65th St.	42,000	98,000	30:70
9 East 65th St.	10,000	96,000	9:91
11 East 65th St.	13,000	107,000	12:88
13 East 65th St.	15,000	80,000	11:89
14 East 65th St.	15,000	75,000	17:83
15 East 65th St.	30,000	110,000	21:79
16 East 65th St.	9,000	68,000	12:88
17 East 65th St.	13,000	90,000	13:87
18 East 65th St.	7,000	62,000	10:90
19 East 65th St.	13,000	90,000	13:87
20 East 65th St.	45,000	90,000	33:67
21 East 65th St.	10,000	70,000	12:88
23 East 65th St.	9,000	60,000	13:87
25 East 65th St.	10,000	100,000	9:91
1-3 East 66th St.	25,000	135,000	16:84
2 East 66th St.	8,000	80,000	9:91
4 East 66th St.	8,000	79,000	9:91
6 East 66th St.	18,000	78,000	19:81
8 East 66th St.	18,000	77,000	19:81
10 East 66th St.	8,000	76,000	10:90
11 East 66th St.	37,000	95,000	28:72
12 East 66th St.	16,000	96,000	14:86
13 East 66th St.	11,000	80,000	12:88
14 East 66th St.	15,000	95,000	14:86
15 East 66th St.	11,000	67,000	14:86
16 East 66th St.	14,000	94,000	13:87
17 East 66th St.	14,000	70,000	17:83
18 East 66th St.	10,000	93,000	10:90
19 East 66th St.	16,000	70,000	19:81
20 East 66th St.	15,000	70,000	15:85
22 East 66th St.	8,000	70,000	10:90
4 East 67th St.	20,000	110,000	15:85
6 East 67th St.	15,000	80,000	16:84
7 East 67th St.	57,000	103,000	36:64
8 East 67th St.	57,000	108,000	35:65
9 East 67th St.	38,000	102,000	27:73
11 East 67th St.	10,000	90,000	10:90
12 East 67th St.	12,000	108,000	10:90
13 East 67th St.	10,000	90,000	10:90
14 East 67th St.	10,000	90,000	10:90
17 East 67th St.	15,000	100,000	13:87
18 East 67th St.	15,000	100,000	13:87
19 East 67th St.	20,000	80,000	20:80
20 East 67th St.	17,000	108,000	14:84
21 East 67th St.	12,000	80,000	13:87

SECTION OF SIDE STREETS EAST OF FIFTH AVENUE—*Continued*
GROUP A: PARCELS WHOSE TAXES WOULD BE INCREASED

Address	Assessed Values		Ratio
	Improvements	Land	
22 East 67th St.	$45,000	$95,000	32:68
23 East 67th St.	12,000	70,000	15:85
24 East 67th St.	70,000	220,000	20:80
——— (Madison Ave.)	20,000	160,000	11:89
5 East 68th St.	125,000	225,000	36:64
6 East 68th St.	10,000	85,000	11:91
8 East 68th St.	61,000	99,000	38.1:61.9
10 East 68th St.	17,000	98,000	15:85
12 East 68th St.	7,000	75,000	9:91
14 East 68th St.	8,000	77,000	9:91
22 East 68th St.	6,000	61,000	9:91
24 East 68th St.	6,000	61,000	9:91
26 East 68th St.	6,000	61,000	9:91
28 East 68th St.	8,000	70,000	10:90
——— (Madison Ave.)	25,000	110,000	19:81
3 East 69th St.	66,000	104,000	38.82:61.18
4 East 69th St.	40,000	150,000	21:79
5 East 69th St.	35,000	135,000	21:79
6 East 69th St.	30,000	100,000	23:77
7 East 69th St.	27,000	118,000	19:81
8 East 69th St.	125,000	250,000	33:67
9 East 69th St.	32,000	108,000	23:77
11 East 69th St.	28,000	122,000	19:81
12 East 69th St.	40,000	160,000	20:80
13 East 69th St.	55,000	125,000	31:69
14 East 69th St.	22,000	108,000	17:83
15 East 69th St.	35,000	100,000	26:74
16 East 69th St.	35,000	120,000	21:79
17 East 69th St.	30,000	170,000	15:85
18 East 69th St.	13,000	67,000	37:63
4 East 70th St.	70,000	140,000	33:67
6 East 70th St.	35,000	90,000	28:72
8 East 70th St.	10,000	65,000	13:87
10 East 70th St.	7,000	80,000	8:92
12 East 70th St.	15,000	105,000	12:88
14 East 70th St.	30,000	65,000	32:88
16 East 70th St.	20,000	65,000	24:76
18 East 70th St.	10,000	75,000	12:88
20 East 70th St.	10,000	75,000	12:88
22-24 East 70th St.	10,000	50,000	17:83
——— (Madison Ave.)	25,000	155,000	14:86
3-5 East 71st St.	125,000	325,000	28:72
9 East 71st St.	85,000	360,000	19:81
11 East 71st St.	55,000	130,000	30:70
13 East 71st St.	25,000	80,000	24:76
15 East 71st St.	20,000	100,000	17:83
17 East 71st St.	15,000	75,000	17:83
19 East 71st St.	20,000	95,000	17:83
21 East 71st St.	50,000	120,000	29:71
4 East 72nd St.	50,000	105,000	32:68
6 East 72nd St.	50,000	100,000	33:67
8 East 72nd St.	35,000	85,000	29:71
9 East 72nd St.	120,000	230,000	34:66
10 East 72nd St.	40,000	85,000	32:68
12 East 72nd St.	35,000	85,000	29:71
14 East 72nd St.	60,000	110,000	35:65
15 East 72nd St.	33,000	77,000	30:70
16 East 72nd St.	60,000	105,000	36:63
17 East 72nd St.	15,000	75,000	17:83
18 East 72nd St.	55,000	100,000	35:65
19 East 72nd St.	25,000	75,000	25:75
20 East 72nd St.	55,000	105,000	34:66
22 East 72nd St.	50,000	100,000	33:67

SECTION OF SIDE STREETS EAST OF FIFTH AVENUE—*Continued*
GROUP A: PARCELS WHOSE TAXES WOULD BE INCREASED

Address	Assessed Values		Ratio
	Improvements	Land	
24 East 72nd St.	$110,000	$250,000	31:69
——— (Madison Ave.)	275,000	475,000	36.7:63.3
1 East 73rd St.	40,000	100,000	29:71
3 East 73rd St.	10,000	95,000	10:90
5 East 73rd St.	45,000	75,000	37.5:62.5
7 East 73rd St.	225,000	375,000	37.5:62.5
8 East 73rd St.	15,000	70,000	18:82
10 East 73rd St.	14,000	67,000	17:83
12 East 73rd St.	10,000	65,000	13:87
17 East 73rd St.	40,000	70,000	36:64
18 East 73rd St.	10,000	65,000	13:87
21 East 73rd St.	20,000	45,000	31:69
24 East 73rd St.	30,000	52,000	37:63
25 East 73rd St.	20,000	50,000	29:71
26 East 73rd St.	30,000	55,000	35:65
27 East 73rd St.	8,000	50,000	14:86
29 East 73rd St.	3,000	32,000	9:91
——— (Madison Ave.)	15,000	60,000	20:80
3 East 74th St.	3,000	70,000	4:96
4 East 74th St.	40,000	85,000	32:68
5 East 74th St.	15,000	85,000	15:85
6 East 74th St.	10,000	70,000	12:88
7 East 74th St.	15,000	85,000	15:85
8 East 74th St.	9,000	69,000	12:88
10 East 74th St.	7,000	68,000	9:91
11 East 74th St.	8,000	64,000	11:89
12 East 74th St.	7,000	67,000	10:90
13 East 74th St.	6,000	64,000	9:91
14 East 74th St.	24,000	66,000	27:73
15 East 74th St.	13,000	62,000	17:83
16 East 74th St.	19,000	66,000	22:78
17 East 74th St.	6,000	62,000	9:91
18 East 74th St.	6,000	62,000	9:91
19 East 74th St.	6,000	60,000	9:91
20 East 74th St.	7,000	65,000	10:90
21 East 74th St.	15,000	60,000	20:80
22 East 74th St.	7,000	60,000	10:90
23 East 74th St.	9,000	73,000	11:89
24 East 74th St.	5,000	50,000	9:91
25 East 74th St.	15,000	71,000	17:83
26 East 74th St.	6,000	49,000	11:89
27 East 74th St.	10,000	70,000	12:88
28 East 74th St.	5,000	40,000	11:89
29 East 74th St.	18,000	105,000	15:85
——— (Madison Ave.)	15,000	60,000	20:80
2 East 75th St.	45,000	110,000	29:71
3 East 75th St.	70,000	110,000	26:74
5 East 75th St.	70,000	110,000	26:74
6 East 75th St.	70,000	160,000	30:70
8 East 75th St.	45,000	75,000	37.5:62.5
9 East 75th St.	10,000	80,000	11:89
10 East 75th St.	15,000	55,000	21·79
11 East 75th St.	6,000	60,000	9:91
11-A East 75th St.	28,000	46,000	38:62
12 East 75th St.	9,000	71,000	11:89
14 East 75th St.	7,000	73,000	9:91
15 East 75th St.	19,000	46,000	29:71
16 East 75th St.	7,000	71,000	9:91
17 East 75th St.	12,000	55,000	17:83
18 East 75th St.	29,000	71,000	29:71
19 East 75th St.	5,000	25,000	17:83
20 East 75th St.	9,000	69,000	12:888
21 East 75th St.	5,000	27,000	16:84

SECTION OF SIDE STREETS EAST OF FIFTH AVENUE—*Continued*
GROUP A: PARCELS WHOSE TAXES WOULD BE INCREASED

Address	Assessed Values Improvements	Assessed Values Land	Ratio
22 East 75th St.	$14,000	$70,000	17:83
23 East 75th St.	8,000	42,000	16:84
3 East 76th St.	60,000	105,000	36:67
8 East 76th St.	50,000	75,000	40:60
9 East 76th St.	40,000	65,000	38.1:61.9
12 East 76th St.	9,000	58,000	13:87
14 East 76th St.	35,000	60,000	36.8:63.2
15 East 76th St.	30,000	52,000	37:63
16 East 76th St.	33,000	57,000	36.6:63.4
17 East 76th St.	30,000	55,000	35:65
18 East 76th St.	35,000	65,000	35:65
19 East 76th St.	33,000	62,000	35:65
20 East 76th St.	9,000	56,000	14:86
21 East 76th St.	27,000	53,000	33:67
22 East 76th St.	6,000	52,000	11:89
23 East 76th St.	8,000	52,000	13:87
24 East 76th St.	8,000	54,000	13:87
25 East 76th St.	8,000	52,000	13:87
26 East 76th St.	24,000	52,000	31:69
27 East 76th St.	8,000	45,000	15:85
28 East 76th St.	10,000	55,000	15:85
29 East 76th St.	10,000	65,000	13:87
30 East 76th St.	15,000	85,000	15:85
6 East 77th St.	42,000	80,000	34:66
8 East 77th St.	40,000	80,000	33:67
9 East 77th St.	9,000	48,000	16:84
10 East 77th St.	35,000	78,000	31:69
11 East 77th St.	7,000	45,000	13:87
12 East 77th St.	27,000	76,000	26:74
13 East 77th St.	18,000	45,000	29:71
14 East 77th St.	25,000	75,000	25:75
15 East 77th St.	15,000	45,000	25:75
16 East 77th St.	25,000	75,000	25:75
17 East 77th St.	7,000	45,000	13:87
18 East 77th St.	35,000	75,000	32:68
19 East 77th St.	15,000	45,000	25:75
21 East 77th St.	4,500	33,000	12:88
23 East 77th St.	4,500	33,000	12:88
25 East 77th St.	4,500	33,000	12:88
27 East 77th St.	4,500	33,000	12:88
29 East 77th St.	6,000	66,000	8:92
31 East 77th St.	5,000	35,000	12:88
33 East 77th St.	5,000	35,000	12:88
35 East 77th St.	15,000	53,000	22:78
2 East 78th St.	35,000	100,000	26:74
4 East 78th St.	24,000	66,000	27:23
8 East 78th St.	20,000	95,000	17:83
9 East 78th St.	85,000	140,000	37.7:62.3
10 East 78th St.	20,000	85,000	19:81
11 East 78th St.	50,000	100,000	33:67
12 East 78th St.	10,000	60,000	14:86
14 East 78th St.	10,000	60,000	14:86
15 East 78th St.	60,000	100,000	37:63
16 East 78th St.	12,000	48,000	20:80
18 East 78th St.	12,000	48,000	20:80
20 East 78th St.	10,000	75,000	12:88
22 East 78th St.	5,000	43,000	10:90
24 East 78th St.	5,000	42,000	11:89
26 East 78th St.	8,000	36,000	18:82
— East 79th St.	18,000	62,000	22:78
9 East 79th St.	25,000	60,000	29:71
11 East 79th St.	7,000	70,000	9:91
13 East 79th St.	7,000	70,000	9:91

SECTION OF SIDE STREETS EAST OF FIFTH AVENUE—*Continued*
GROUP A: PARCELS WHOSE TAXES WOULD BE INCREASED

Address	Assessed Values — Improvements	Assessed Values — Land	Ratio
15 East 79th St.	$8,000	$60,000	12:88
17 East 79th St.	30,000	60,000	33:67
19 East 79th St.	10,000	70,000	12:88
21 East 79th St.	15,000	60,000	20:80
23 East 79th St.	15,000	60,000	20:80
25 East 79th St.	20,000	85,000	19:81
27 East 79th St.	19,000	81,000	19:81
29 East 79th St.	11,000	74,000	13:87
31 East 79th St.	30,000	170,000	15:85
4 East 80th St.	15,000	45,000	25:75
5 East 80th St.	30,000	60,000	33:67
6 East 80th St.	15,000	45,000	25:75
7 East 80th St.	30,000	50,000	37:63
8 East 80th St.	15,000	45,000	25:75
10 East 80th St.	15,000	45,000	25:75
12 East 80th St.	15,000	45,000	25:75
13 East 80th St.	29,000	47,000	38.5:61.5
14 East 80th St.	23,000	55,000	29:71
18 East 80th St.	20,000	55,000	27:73
19 East 80th St.	30,000	55,000	35:65
20 East 80th St.	32,000	55,000	37:63
21 East 80th St.	30,000	55,000	35:65
22 East 80th St.	15,000	48,000	24:76
24 East 80th St.	15,500	47,000	25:75
26 East 80th St.	12,000	44,000	21:79
28 East 80th St.	20,000	65,000	24:76
2 East 81st St.	5,000	48,000	9:91
4 East 81st St.	17,000	48,000	26:74
5 East 81st St.	17,000	48,000	26:14
6 East 81st St.	15,000	48,000	24:76
7 East 81st St.	11,000	48,000	19:81
8 East 81st St.	12,000	48,000	20:80
9 East 81st St.	10,000	48,000	17:83
10 East 81st St.	10,000	45,000	18:82
11 East 81st St.	10,000	45,000	18:82
12 East 81st St.	10,000	45,000	18:82
14 East 81st St.	10,000	45,000	18:82
15 East 81st St.	10,000	45,000	18:82
17 East 81st St.	10,000	45,000	18:82
19 East 81st St.	10,000	45,000	18:82
20 East 81st St.	11,000	44,000	20:80
22 East 81st St.	11,000	44,000	20:80
25 East 81st St.	5,000	30,000	35:65
2 East 82nd St.	32,000	68,000	32:68
6 East 82nd St.	10,000	46,000	18:82
8 East 82nd St.	8,000	43,000	16:84
10 East 82nd St.	10,000	43,000	19:81
12 East 82nd St.	11,000	46,000	16:84
16 East 82nd St.	15,000	55,000	21:79
19 East 82nd St.	25,000	55,000	31:69
3 East 83rd St.	1,000	128,000	2:99
7 East 83rd St.	35,000	100,000	26:74
9 East 83rd St.	35,000	100,000	26:74
11 East 83rd St.	23,000	47,000	33:67
13 East 83rd St.	20,000	45,000	31:69
14 East 83rd St.	10,000	44,000	19:81
15 East 83th St.	13,000	39,000	25:75
17 East 83rd St.	12,000	39,000	24:76
19 East 83rd St.	9,000	39,500	19:81
20 East 83rd St.	10,000	44,000	19:81
21 East 83rd St.	10,000	35,000	22:78
22 East 83rd St.	21,000	44,000	32:68
23 East 83rd St.	9,000	33,000	21:79

SECTION OF SIDE STREETS EAST OF FIFTH AVENUE—*Continued*
Group A: Parcels Whose Taxes Would Be Increased

Address	Assessed Values Improvements	Assessed Values Land	Ratio
24 East 83rd St.	$10,000	$44,000	19:81
25 East 83rd St.	9,000	33,000	21:79
26-28 East 83rd St.	28,000	99,000	22:78
27 East 83rd St.	9,000	33,000	21:79
29 East 83rd St.	17,000	53,000	24:76
2 East 84th St.	2,000	55,000	4:96
3 East 84th St.	12,000	55,000	18:82
4-6-8 East 84th St.	15,000	205,000	7:93
5 East 84th St.	7,000	55,000	18:82
14 East 84th St.	10,000	130,000	7:93
16 East 84th St.	34,000	57,000	37:63
18 East 84th St.	33,000	57,000	37:63
20 East 84th St.	33,000	57,000	37:63
22 East 84th St.	3,000	21,000	12:88
24 East 84th St.	4,000	28,000	12:88
26 East 84th St.	4,000	28,000	12:88
28 East 84th St.	7,000	46,000	13:87
2 East 85th St.	10,000	30,000	25:75
4 East 85th St.	8,000	21,000	18:82
6 East 85th St.	7,500	22,500	25:75
8 East 85th St.	8,000	22,000	27:73
9 East 85th St.	10,000	30,000	25:75
10 East 85th St.	8,000	22,000	27:73
12 East 85th St.	7,500	22,500	25:75
14 East 85th St.	3,000	27,000	10:90
22-24 East 85th St.	9,000	55,000	14:86
26 East 85th St.	1,000	27,000	4:96
28 East 85th St.	8,000	27,000	23:77
1 East 86th St.	22,000	48,000	31:69
2 East 86th St.	10,000	40,000	20:80
3 East 86th St.	4,000	35,000	10:90
4 East 86th St.	10,000	40,000	20:80
5 East 86th St.	6,000	40,000	13:87
6 East 86th St.	10,000	40,000	20:80
8 East 86th St.	6,000	40,000	13:87
10 East 86th St.	6,000	40,000	13:87
19 East 86th St.	25,000	55,000	31:69
19 East 88th St.	12,000	68,000	15:85
15 East 90th St.	10,000	55,000	15:85
— East 90th St.	3,000	30,000	9:91
22 East 91st St.	10,000	121,000	8:92
24 East 91st St.	10,000	55,000	15:85
2 East 92nd St.	10,000	40,000	20:80
3 East 92nd St.	11,000	42,000	21:79
4 East 92nd St.	10,000	40,000	20:80
5 East 92nd St.	11,000	42,000	21:79
6 East 92nd St.	7,000	36,000	16:84
7 East 92nd St.	10,000	40,000	20:80
8 East 92nd St.	8,000	38,000	17:83
9 East 92nd St.	10,000	40,000	20:80
10 East 92nd St.	8,000	40,000	17:83
11 East 92nd St.	10,000	40,000	20:80
12 East 92nd St.	10,500	42,000	20:80
13 East 92nd St.	11,000	50,000	18:82
14 East 92nd St.	15,000	40,000	27:73
15 East 92nd St.	13,000	39,000	25:75
16 East 92nd St.	9,000	35,000	20:80
17 East 92nd St.	10,000	38,000	21:79
18 East 92nd St.	11,000	46,000	19:81
19 East 92nd St.	10,000	38,000	21:79
20 East 92nd St.	11,000	44,000	20:80
21 East 92nd St.	10,000	39,000	20:80
22 East 92nd St.	10,000	40,000	20:80

SECTION OF SIDE STREETS EAST OF FIFTH AVENUE—*Continued*

GROUP A: PARCELS WHOSE TAXES WOULD BE INCREASED

Address	Assessed Values		Ratio
	Improvements	Land	
23 East 92nd St.	$11,000	$41,000	21:79
24 East 92nd St.	22,000	44,000	33:67
25 East 92nd St.	11,000	39,000	22:78
26 East 92nd St.	9,000	40,000	18:82
28 East 92nd St.	16,000	40,000	29:71
1 East 93rd St.	12,000	45,000	21:79
3 East 93rd St.	11,000	44,000	20:80
4 East 93rd St.	7,000	140,000	5:95
5 East 93rd St.	10,500	43,000	20:80
6 East 93rd St.	7,000	40,000	15:85
7 East 93rd St.	10,500	42,000	20:80
8 East 93rd St.	7,000	39,000	15:85
9 East 93rd St.	10,000	41,000	20:80
10 East 93rd St.	8,500	43,500	16:84
11 East 93rd St.	10,000	39,000	20:80
12 East 93rd St.	7,500	43,000	15:85
14 East 93rd St.	7,000	40,000	15:85
15 East 93rd St.	10,000	40,000	20:80
16 East 93rd St.	7,000	40,000	15:85
17 East 93rd St.	9,500	38,000	20:80
18 East 93rd St.	7,000	40,000	15:85
19 East 93rd St.	9,500	38,000	20:80
20 East 93rd St.	7,000	40,000	15:85
21 East 93rd St.	9,000	39,000	19:81
22 East 93rd St.	7,000	40,000	15:85
23 East 93rd St.	10,000	50,000	17:83
24 East 93rd St.	9,000	40,000	18:82
25 East 93rd St.	5,000	27,000	16:84
27 East 93rd St.	5,000	27,000	16:84
29 East 93rd St.	6,000	27,000	18:82
31 East 93rd St.	5,000	27,000	16:84
33 East 93rd St.	8,000	27,000	15:85
	$9,430,500	$34,575,000	

GROUP B: PARCELS WHOSE TAXES WOULD BE DECREASED

Address	Assessed Values		Ratio
	Improvements	Land	
4 East 61st St.	$155,000	$205,000	43:57
6 East 61st St.	125,000	180,000	41:59
11 East 61st St.	66,000	94,000	41:59
1 East 62nd St.	125,000	180,000	41:59
6 East 62nd St.	79,000	106,000	43:57
8 East 62nd St.	73,000	97,000	43:57
10 East 62nd St.	89,000	96,000	48:52
11 East 62nd St.	115,000	175,000	40:60
5 East 63rd St.	66,000	96,000	41:59
15 East 63rd St.	69,000	86,000	45:55
17 East 63rd St.	95,000	105,000	47:53
3 East 64th St.	215,000	285,000	43:57
4 East 64th St.	90,000	120,000	43:57
28 East 64th St.	61,000	84,000	42:58
6 East 65th St.	102,000	98,000	51:49
7 East 65th St.	68,000	97,000	41:59
8-10 East 65th St.	175,000	175,000	50:50
12 East 65th St.	50,000	75,000	40:60
5 East 66th St.	102,000	108,000	48:52
9 East 66th St.	155,000	185,000	46:54
2 East 67th St.	115,000	135,000	46:54
5 East 67th St.	76,000	180,000	42:58

SECTION OF SIDE STREETS EAST OF FIFTH AVENUE—*Continued*
GROUP B: PARCELS WHOSE TAXES WOULD BE DECREASED

Address	Assessed Values		Ratio
	Improvements	Land	
15 East 67th St.	$90,000	$125,000	42:58
16 East 67th St.	80,000	100,000	44:56
9 East 68th St.	245,000	180,000	58:42
18-20 East 68th St.	100,000	130,000	43:57
3 East 69th St.	66,000	104,000	38.82:61.18
3 East 70th St.	85,000	125,000	40:60
11 East 70th St.	115,000	135,000	46:54
12 East 70th St.	87,000	113,000	44:56
13 East 70th St.	90,000	110,000	45:55
14 East 70th St.	91,000	109,000	45:55
15 East 70th St.	80,000	105,000	43:57
16 East 70th St.	90,000	105,000	46:54
17 East 70th St.	80,000	100,000	44:56
18 East 70th St.	85,000	100,000	46:54
19 East 70th St.	105,000	120,000	48:52
870 Madison Ave.	87,000	78,000	53:47
7 East 72nd St.	85,000	105,000	45:55
14 East 73rd St.	50,000	65,000	43:57
16 East 73rd St.	50,000	65,000	43:57
19 East 73rd St.	40,000	60,000	40:60
20 East 73rd St.	50,000	65,000	43:57
22 East 73rd St.	50,000	65,000	43:57
23 East 73rd St.	60,000	50,000	55:45
1 East 75th St.	155,000	185,000	54:46
5 East 76th St.	40,000	60,000	40:60
6 East 76th St.	52,000	80,000	39.3:60.7
7 East 76th St.	51,000	74,000	41:59
10 East 76th St.	54,000	66,000	45:55
11 East 76th St.	37,000	58,000	38.9:61.1
11½ East 76th St.	46,000	64,000	42:58
4 East 77th St.	60,000	85,000	41:59
3 East 78th St.	140,000	145,000	49:51
4 East 78th St.	95,000	145,000	40:60
5 East 78th St.	75,000	100,000	43:57
6 East 78th St.	65,000	100,000	39:61
7 East 78th St.	75,000	100,000	43:57
8 East 78th St.	120,000	125,000	49:51
10 East 78th St.	110,000	105,000	51:49
12 East 78th St.	75,000	100,000	43:57
14 East 78th St.	75,000	95,000	40:60
16 East 78th St.	100,000	125,000	44:56
18 East 78th St.	100,000	100,000	50:50
— East 78th St.	87,000	93,000	48:52
2 East 80th St.	60,000	60,000	50:50
3 East 80th St.	65,000	100,000	39:61
9 East 80th St.	30,000	45,000	40:60
11 East 80th St.	47,000	45,000	49:51
15-17 East 80th St.	100,000	100,000	56:44
16 East 80th St.	40,000	55,000	42:58
3 East 81st St.	45,000	50,000	47:53
16 East 81st St.	45,000	45,000	50:50
18 East 81st St.	50,000	45,000	53:47
21 East 81st St.	50,000	45,000	53:47
23 East 81st St.	51,000	46,000	53:47
24-26 East 81st St.	99,500	70,500	66:44
3 East 82nd St.	70,000	60,000	54:46
4 East 82nd St.	38,000	52,000	42:58
5 East 82nd St.	72,000	58,000	55:45
7 East 82nd St.	45,000	55,000	45:55
9 East 82nd St.	40,000	55,000	42:58
11 East 82nd St.	40,000	55,000	42:58
14 East 82nd St.	47,000	48,000	49:51
15 East 82nd St.	40,000	55,000	42:58

SECTION OF SIDE STREETS EAST OF FIFTH AVENUE—*Concluded*
Group B: Parcels Whose Taxes Would Be Decreased

Address	Assessed Values		Ratio
	Improvements	Land	
17 East 82nd St.	$40,000	$55,000	42:58
18 East 82nd St.	68,000	57,000	54:46
20 East 82nd St.	66,000	59,000	53:47
22 East 82nd St.	70,000	65,000	52:48
24 East 82nd St.	68,000	59,000	54:46
6 East 83rd St.	85,000	70,000	55:45
8 East 83rd St.	80,000	65,000	55:45
10 East 83rd St.	75,000	55,000	58:42
7 East 84th St.	45,000	55,000	45:55
9 East 84th St.	85,000	55,000	61:39
11 East 84th St.	88,000	57,000	61:39
13-15 East 84th St.	75,000	100,000	43:57
7 East 86th St.	45,000	65,000	61:59
13 East 86th St.	47,000	58,000	45:55
15 East 86th St.	47,000	53,000	47:53
17 East 86th St.	52,000	58,000	47:53
4 East 87th St.	130,000	90,000	59:41
6 East 87th St.	150,000	155,000	49:51
5 East 88th St.	65,000	60,000	52:48
7 East 88th St.	57,000	53,000	52:48
9 East 88th St.	58,000	57,000	50:50
4 East 89th St.	134,000	66,000	66:33
5 East 89th St.	70,000	80,000	47:53
9 East 89th St.	68,000	62,000	52:48
11 East 89th St.	58,000	47,000	55:45
— East 89th St.	69,000	51,000	57:43
9 East 90th St.	85,000	60,000	59:41
11 East 90th St.	85,000	55,000	61:39
	$8,902,500	$10,067,500	

SECTION OF SIDE STREETS OFF RIVERSIDE DRIVE

(Standard Composite Ratio: 38.34:61.66)

Group A: Parcels Whose Taxes Would Be Increased

Address	Assessed Values Improvements	Assessed Values Land	Ratio
327 West 82nd St.	$7,000	$21,000	25:75
331 West 82nd St.	12,000	25,000	33:67
300 West 83rd St.	4,000	44,000	8:92
302 West 83rd St.	3,000	31,000	9:91
304 West 83rd St.	3,000	25,000	11:89
306 West 83rd St.	3,000	18,000	14:86
308 West 83rd St.	6,000	14,000	29:71
309 West 83rd St.	4,500	12,500	26:74
310 West 83rd St.	5,500	14,500	27:73
311 West 83rd St.	4,500	12,500	26:74
312 West 83rd St.	4,000	14,000	26:74
313 West 83rd St.	4,500	12,500	26:74
314 West 83rd St.	4,000	14,000	26:74
315 West 83rd St.	4,500	12,500	26:74
316 West 83rd St.	3,300	14,500	19:81
301 West 84th St.	8,000	20,000	29:71
328 West 84th St.	5,000	12,500	29:71
330 West 84th St.	7,500	15,000	33:67
332 West 84th St.	7,500	15,000	33:67
334 West 84th St.	6,500	13,500	33:67
338 West 84th St.	9,000	15,000	37:63
340 West 84th St.	6,500	13,500	33:67
342 West 84th St.	6,500	13,500	33:67
344 West 84th St.	8,000	15,000	35:65
347 West 84th St.	6,500	13,500	33:67
300 West 85th St.	7,000	15,000	32:68
302 West 85th St.	5,000	15,000	25:75
304 West 85th St.	8,000	13,500	37:63
314 West 85th St.	35,000	65,000	35:65
316 West 85th St.	7,000	13,000	35:65
318 West 85th St.	7,000	13,000	35:65
320 West 85th St.	7,000	13,000	35:65
322 West 85th St.	7,000	13,000	35:65
323 West 85th St.	1,000	21,000	5:95
324 West 85th St.	7,000	13,000	35:65
326 West 85th St.	7,000	13,000	35:65
329 West 85th St.	6,500	16,500	28:72
331 West 85th St.	6,500	16,500	28:72
333 West 85th St.	6,500	16,500	28:72
335 West 85th St.	6,500	16,500	28:72
337 West 85th St.	6,500	16,500	28:72
339-41 West 85th St.	11,000	21,000	33:67
303 West 86th St.	11,500	20,500	36:64
304 West 86th St.	12,500	21,000	37:63
306 West 86th St.	12,500	21,000	37:63
308 West 86th St.	12,000	20,000	38:62
310 West 86th St.	12,000	20,000	37:63
312 West 86th St.	11,000	18,500	37:63
314 West 86th St.	13,000	21,500	38:62
316 West 86th St.	12,500	21,000	37:63
318 West 86th St.	12,500	21,000	37:63
320 West 86th St.	12,500	21,000	37:63
322 West 86th St.	12,500	21,000	37:63
328 West 86th St.	1,000	55,000	2:98
332 West 86th St.	11,000	20,000	35:65
334 West 86th St.	11,000	20,000	35:65
336 West 86th St.	11,000	20,000	35:65
337 West 86th St.	11,000	20,000	35:65
338 West 86th St.	12,000	20,000	37:63
339 West 86th St.	11,000	20,000	35:65
341 West 86th St.	11,000	20,000	35:65

SECTION OF SIDE STREETS OFF RIVERSIDE DRIVE—*Continued*

GROUP A: PARCELS WHOSE TAXES WOULD BE INCREASED

Address	Assessed Values		Ratio
	Improvements	Land	
343 West 86th St.	$11,000	$20,000	35:65
307 West 87th St.	8,000	13,000	38:62
313 West 87th St.	7,500	13,500	36:64
317 West 87th St.	9,000	15,000	37:63
319 West 87th St.	9,000	15,000	37:63
321 West 87th St.	9,000	15,000	37:63
322 West 87th St.	9,000	15,000	37:63
323 West 87th St.	9,000	15,000	37:63
325 West 87th St.	9,000	15,000	37:63
— West 87th St.	1,000	58,000	2:98
	$578,800	$1,350,000	

GROUP B: PARCELS WHOSE TAXES WOULD BE DECREASED

Address	Assessed Values		Ratio
	Improvements	Land	
307 West 82nd St.	$10,000	$15,000	40:60
309 West 82nd St.	10,000	15,000	40:60
310 West 82nd St.	13,000	13,000	50:50
311 West 82nd St.	10,000	15,000	40:60
312 West 82nd St.	12,000	12,500	49:51
313 West 82nd St.	10,000	15,000	40:60
314 West 82nd St.	13,000	13,000	50:50
315 West 82nd St.	10,000	15,000	40:60
317 West 82nd St.	14,000	15,000	48:52
318 West 82nd St.	12,000	13,000	48:52
319 West 82nd St.	14,000	15,000	48:52
320 West 82nd St.	12,000	11,000	52:48
321 West 82nd St.	14,000	15,000	48:52
323 West 82nd St.	14,000	15,000	48:52
324 West 82nd St.	12,000	11,000	52:48
325 West 82nd St.	15,000	15,000	50:50
326 West 82nd St.	14,000	18,000	44:56
329 West 82nd St.	31,000	24,000	56:44
307 West 83rd St.	10,000	14,000	42:58
332 West 83rd St.	17,500	17,500	50:50
303 West 84th St.	11,000	14,000	44:56
305 West 84th St.	14,500	13,000	53:47
307 West 84th St.	14,500	13,000	53:47
309 West 84th St.	14,000	12,500	53:47
311 West 84th St.	15,000	13,000	54:46
313 West 84th St.	14,000	12,500	53:47
317 West 84th St.	14,500	13,000	53:47
319 West 84th St.	9,500	14,500	40:60
321 West 84th St.	10,000	13,500	41:59
323 West 84th St.	10,000	13,500	41:59
325 West 84th St.	10,000	13,500	41:59
327 West 84th St.	10,000	13,500	41:59
329 West 84th St.	10,000	13,500	41:59
331 West 84th St.	10,000	13,500	41:59
333 West 84th St.	10,000	13,500	41:59
335 West 84th St.	11,000	13,500	45:55
336 West 84th St.	6,500	13,500	44:66
337 West 84th St.	11,000	13,500	45:55
339 West 84th St.	11,000	14,500	43:57
341 West 84th St.	15,000	13,000	54:46
343 West 84th St.	13,000	12,500	52:48
345 West 84th St.	15,000	13,000	54:46
346 West 84th St.	12,000	17,000	41:59
349 West 84th St.	14,000	13,000	52:48

SECTION OF SIDE STREETS OFF RIVERSIDE DRIVE—*Continued*
GROUP B: PARCELS WHOSE TAXES WOULD BE DECREASED

Address	Assessed Values		Ratio
	Improvements	Land	
351 West 84th St.	$12,500	$12,500	50:50
353 West 84th St.	12,500	12,500	50:50
355 West 84th St.	12,500	12,500	50:50
357 West 84th St.	15,000	13,000	54:46
309 West 85th St.	15,000	14,000	52:48
311 West 85th St.	14,500	13,500	52:48
313 West 85th St.	15,000	14,000	52:48
327 West 85th St.	15,000	14,000	52:48
332 West 85th St.	20,000	20,000	50:50
334 West 85th St.	20,000	20,000	50:50
302 West 86th St.	12,000	19,000	38.7:61.3
305 West 86th St.	11,000	20,000	45:65
307 West 86th St.	11,000	20,000	45:65
309 West 86th St.	11,000	20,000	45:65
311 West 86th St.	14,000	20,000	41:59
313 West 86th St.	15,000	17,000	47:53
315 West 86th St.	14,000	18,000	44:56
317 West 86th St.	14,000	17,000	45:55
319 West 86th St.	14,000	18,000	44:56
321 West 86th St.	14,000	17,000	45:55
323 West 86th St.	17,500	18,500	49:51
324 West 86th St.	17,500	19,500	42:58
325 West 86th St.	17,500	19,500	47:53
327 West 86th St.	15,000	18,000	45:55
329 West 86th St.	16,000	20,000	43:57
330 West 86th St.	11,000	15,000	42:58
331 West 86th St.	16,000	18,000	47:53
333 West 86th St.	16,000	20,000	43:57
335 West 86th St.	13,000	20,000	39.4:60.6
345 West 86th St.	20,000	24,000	45:55
347 West 86th St.	21,000	24,000	47:53
349 West 86th St.	23,000	25,000	57:43
381 West 86th St.	23,000	25,000	57:43
302 West 87th St.	8,500	12,500	40:60
303 West 87th St.	9,000	14,000	39.1:60.9
304 West 87th St.	8,500	12,500	40:60
305 West 87th St.	8,500	13,500	38.6:61.4
306 West 87th St.	8,500	12,500	40:60
308 West 87th St.	8,500	12,500	40:60
309 West 87th St.	8,500	13,500	38.6:61.4
310 West 87th St.	8,000	12,000	40:60
311 West 87th St.	8,500	13,500	38.6:61.4
312 West 87th St.	8,500	12,500	40:60
315 West 87th St.	8,500	13,500	38.6:61.4
324 West 87th St.	11,000	15,000	42:58
326 West 87th St.	11,000	15,000	42:58
327 West 87th St.	14,000	12,000	54:46
328 West 87th St.	11,000	15,000	42:58
329 West 87th St.	13,000	11,500	53:47
330 West 87th St.	11,000	15,000	42:58
331 West 87th St.	13,000	11,500	53:47
332 West 87th St.	11,000	15,000	42:58
333 West 87th St.	14,000	12,000	54:46
334 West 87th St.	11,000	15,000	42:58
335 West 87th St.	14,000	14,000	50:50
336 West 87th St.	11,000	15,000	42:58
337 West 87th St.	14,000	14,000	50:50
338 West 87th St.	11,000	15,000	42:58
339 West 87th St.	18,000	13,500	57:43
340 West 87th St.	11,000	15,000	42:58
341 West 87th St.	19,000	15,000	56:44
342 West 87th St.	11,000	15,000	42:58
343 West 87th St.	19,000	15,000	56:44

SECTION OF SIDE STREETS OFF RIVERSIDE DRIVE—*Concluded*
GROUP B: PARCELS WHOSE TAXES WOULD BE DECREASED

Address	Assessed Values		Ratio
	Improvements	Land	
344 West 87th St.	$20,000	$15,000	57:43
345 West 87th St.	19,000	15,000	56:44
346 West 87th St.	21,000	15,000	58:42
347 West 87th St.	19,000	15,000	56:44
348 West 87th St.	20,000	15,000	57:43
349 West 87th St.	19,000	15,000	56:44
350 West 87th St.	20,000	15,000	57:43
351 West 87th St.	19,000	15,000	56:44
352 West 87th St.	20,000	15,000	57:43
353 West 87th St.	19,000	15,000	56:44
355 West 87th St.	19,000	15,000	56:44
302 West 88th St.	14,000	15,000	48:52
303 West 88th St.	11,000	14,000	40:54
304 West 88th St.	15,000	15,500	49:51
305 West 88th St.	12,000	13,000	48:52
306 West 88th St.	15,000	15,500	48:52
307 West 88th St.	12,000	14,000	46:54
308 West 88th St.	15,000	15,500	48:52
309 West 88th St.	11,000	14,000	44:56
310 West 88th St.	15,000	15,000	50:50
311 West 88th St.	17,500	13,500	56:44
312 West 88th St.	15,000	15,500	48:52
313 West 88th St.	12,000	14,000	46:54
314 West 88th St.	15,000	15,500	48:52
315 West 88th St.	20,000	15,000	57:43
316 West 88th St.	12,000	15,000	44:56
317 West 88th St.	20,000	15,000	57:43
318 West 88th St.	12,000	15,000	44:56
319 West 88th St.	17,000	15,000	53:47
320 West 88th St.	12,000	15,000	44:56
321 West 88th St.	17,000	15,000	53:47
322 West 88th St.	12,000	15,000	44:56
323 West 88th St.	17,000	15,000	56:44
324 West 88th St.	12,000	15,000	44:56
325 West 88th St.	19,000	15,000	56:44
326 West 88th St.	15,000	14,000	52:48
327 West 88th St.	19,000	15,000	56:44
328 West 88th St.	14,500	13,500	52:48
329 West 88th St.	19,000	15,000	56:44
330 West 88th St.	14,500	13,500	52:48
331 West 88th St.	19,000	15,000	56:44
332 West 88th St.	18,000	15,000	55:45
333 West 88th St.	19,000	15,000	56:44
334 West 88th St.	18,000	15,000	55:45
335 West 88th St.	19,000	15,000	56:44
336 West 88th St.	18,500	15,500	54:46
337 West 88th St.	19,000	15,000	56:44
338 West 88th St.	18,500	15,500	54:46
339 West 88th St.	19,000	15,000	56:44
340 West 88th St.	18,500	15,500	54:46
341 West 88th St.	19,000	15,000	56:44
342 West 88th St.	18,500	15,500	54:46
344 West 88th St.	16,500	15,500	52:48
	$2,289,500	$2,419,500	

SECTION OF SIDE STREETS WEST OF CENTRAL PARK

(Standard Composite Ratio: 38.34:61.66)

GROUP A: PARCELS WHOSE TAXES WOULD BE INCREASED

Address	Assessed Values		Ratio
	Improvements	Land	
5 West 90th St.	$9,000	$15,000	38:62
7 West 90th St.	9,000	15,000	38:62
9 West 90th St.	9,000	15,000	38:62
1 West 90th St.	9,000	15,000	38:62
3 West 90th St.	9,000	15,000	38:62
5 West 90th St.	9,000	15,000	38:62
7 West 90th St.	7,500	14,000	35:65
9 West 90th St.	7,500	13,500	36:64
0 West 90th St.	8,500	14,000	38:62
1 West 90th St.	7,500	13,500	36:64
8 West 90th St.	8,000	15,000	35:65
0 West 90th St.	7,000	15,000	32:68
2 West 90th St.	8,000	15,000	35:65
4 West 90th St.	7,000	15,000	32:68
8 West 90th St.	7,000	15,000	32:68
0 West 90th St.	8,000	15,000	35:65
3 West 90th St.	8,000	14,000	36:64
4 West 90th St.	8,000	14,000	36:64
5 West 90th St.	8,000	14,000	36:64
6 West 90th St.	8,000	14,000	36:64
7 West 90th St.	8,000	14,000	36:64
8 West 90th St.	8,000	14,000	36:64
9 West 90th St.	8,000	14,000	36:64
0 West 90th St.	8,000	14,000	36:64
1 West 90th St.	6,000	14,000	30:70
3 West 90th St.	6,000	14,000	30:70
5 West 90th St.	6,000	14,000	30:70
8 West 91st St.	7,500	13,500	36:64
0 West 91st St.	7,500	13,500	36:64
2 West 91st St.	7,500	13,500	36:64
4 West 91st St.	9,500	13,500	38:62
6 West 91st St.	9,500	13,500	38:62
8 West 91st St.	9,500	13,500	38:62
0 West 91st St.	9,500	13,500	38:62
2 West 91st St.	7,500	13,500	36:64
4 West 91st St.	7,500	13,500	36:64
5 West 91st St.	7,000	15,000	32:68
6 West 91st St.	7,500	13,500	36:64
7 West 91st St.	5,500	13,000	30:70
9 West 91st St.	9,000	15,000	38:62
3 West 91st St.	9,000	15,000	37:63
5 West 91st St.	8,000	13,000	38:62
7 West 91st St.	8,000	15,000	35:65
9 West 91st St.	6,000	13,500	31:69
0 West 91st St.	5,500	16,000	25:75
2 West 91st St.	5,500	16,000	25:75
4 West 91st St.	5,000	16,000	24:76
1 West 92nd St.	3,000	11,000	21:79
3 West 92nd St.	4,000	14,000	22:78
5 West 92nd St.	4,000	14,000	22:78
7 West 92nd St.	4,000	14,000	22:78
9 West 92nd St.	4,000	14,000	22:78
1 West 92nd St.	4,000	14,000	22:78
3 West 92nd St.	4,000	14,000	22:78
5 West 92nd St.	4,000	14,000	22:78
7 West 92nd St.	4,000	14,000	22:78
9 West 92nd St.	4,000	14,000	22:78
1 West 92nd St.	4,000	14,000	22:78
3 West 92nd St.	4,000	14,000	22:78
5 West 92nd St.	4,000	14,000	22:78
7 West 92nd St.	4,000	14,000	22:78

SECTION OF SIDE STREETS WEST OF CENTRAL PARK—*Continued*
GROUP A: PARCELS WHOSE TAXES WOULD BE INCREASED

Address	Assessed Values		Ratio
	Improvements	Land	
59 West 92nd St.	$4,000	$14,000	22:78
61 West 92nd St.	4,000	14,000	22:78
62 West 92nd St.	9,500	16,500	37:63
63 West 92nd St.	4,000	14,000	22:78
64 West 92nd St.	6,000	15,000	29:71
65 West 92nd St.	4,000	14,000	22:78
66 West 92nd St.	6,000	15,000	29:71
67 West 92nd St.	4,000	14,000	22:78
68 West 92nd St.	6,000	15,000	29:71
69 West 92nd St.	4,000	14,000	22:78
70 West 92nd St.	6,000	15,000	29:71
71 West 92nd St.	4,000	14,000	22:78
72 West 92nd St.	4,500	14,500	24:76
8 West 93rd St.	3,000	18,000	14:86
19 West 93rd St.	2,000	13,500	16:84
21 West 93rd St.	2,500	14,000	15:85
23 West 93rd St.	2,500	14,000	15:85
25 West 93rd St.	2,500	14,000	15:85
27 West 93rd St.	2,500	14,000	15:85
29 West 93rd St.	2,500	14,000	15:85
31 West 93rd St.	2,500	13,000	16:84
33 West 93rd St.	2,500	13,000	16:84
35 West 93rd St.	2,500	13,000	16:84
45 West 93rd St.	1,500	9,000	14:86
47 West 93rd St.	1,500	13,000	10:90
49 West 93rd St.	1,500	9,000	14:86
57 West 93rd St.	2,000	10,000	17:83
58 West 93rd St.	2,000	10,000	17:83
61 West 93rd St.	2,000	10,000	17:83
63 West 93rd St.	2,000	10,000	17:83
65 West 93rd St.	2,000	10,000	17:83
67 West 93rd St.	2,000	10,000	17:83
19 West 94th St.	6,000	10,500	36:64
21 West 94th St.	7,000	12,000	37:63
22 West 94th St.	6,000	12,500	32:68
23 West 94th St.	5,500	11,000	33:67
24 West 94th St.	5,500	11,000	33:67
25 West 94th St.	6,500	11,500	36:64
26 West 94th St.	5,500	11,500	32:68
27 West 94th St.	6,000	10,500	36:64
28 West 94th St.	6,500	11,000	37:63
29 West 94th St.	6,000	10,500	36:64
30 West 94th St.	6,000	11,000	35:65
32 West 94th St.	7,500	12,500	37:63
37 West 94th St.	6,000	12,000	33:67
38 West 94th St.	7,500	12,500	37:63
39 West 94th St.	6,000	12,000	33:67
40 West 94th St.	6,000	12,500	32:68
41 West 94th St.	6,000	12,000	33:67
42 West 94th St.	5,500	11,000	33:67
43 West 94th St.	6,000	12,000	33:67
44 West 94th St.	5,500	11,000	33:67
45 West 94th St.	6,500	13,500	32:68
46 West 94th St.	4,500	9,500	32:68
47 West 94th St.	4,000	9,500	30:70
55 West 94th St.	7,000	13,500	34:66
57 West 94th St.	7,000	13,500	34:66
59 West 94th St.	7,000	13,500	34:66
61 West 94th St.	6,000	13,000	32:68
62 West 94th St.	6,500	12,000	35:65
63 West 94th St.	6,000	12,000	33:67
64 West 94th St.	6,500	12,000	35:65
65 West 94th St.	6,000	12,000	33:67

SECTION OF SIDE STREETS WEST OF CENTRAL PARK—*Continued*

GROUP A: PARCELS WHOSE TAXES WOULD BE INCREASED

Address	Assessed Values Improvements	Assessed Values Land	Ratio
66 West 94th St.	$6,500	$12,000	35:65
67 West 94th St.	6,500	13,500	32:68
68 West 94th St.	6,500	12,000	35:65
69 West 94th St.	6,500	13,500	32:68
70 West 94th St.	6,500	12,000	35:65
71 West 94th St.	6,500	13,500	32:68
72 West 94th St.	6,500	12,000	35:65
76 West 94th St.	6,000	11,000	35:65
5 West 95th St.	9,000	17,000	35:65
25 West 95th St.	6,500	11,000	37:63
27 West 95th St.	6,500	11,000	37:63
29 West 95th St.	6,500	11,000	37:63
33 West 95th St.	5,500	11,000	33:67
35 West 95th St.	5,500	10,000	35:65
37 West 95th St.	5,500	10,000	35:65
39 West 95th St.	5,500	10,500	34:66
40 West 95th St.	5,000	12,500	29:71
42 West 95th St.	4,500	12,000	27:73
43 West 95th St.	6,500	11,000	37:63
44 West 95th St.	5,000	13,000	28:72
45 West 95th St.	7,000	11,500	38:62
46 West 95th St.	4,500	12,500	26:74
47 West 95th St.	7,000	11,500	38:62
48 West 95th St.	4,500	12,000	27:73
49 West 95th St.	7,000	11,500	38:62
50 West 95th St.	4,500	12,000	27:73
51 West 95th St.	7,000	11,500	38:62
52 West 95th St.	6,000	11,000	35:65
54 West 95th St.	4,500	12,000	27:73
56 West 95th St.	4,500	12,500	26:74
58 West 95th St.	4,000	11,000	27:73
60 West 95th St.	6,000	12,000	33:67
62 West 95th St.	6,500	12,500	34:66
64 West 95th St.	4,000	11,000	27:73
66 West 95th St.	4,500	12,500	26:74
67 West 95th St.	5,500	11,000	33:67
68 West 95th St.	4,000	12,000	25:75
69 West 95th St.	5,500	11,000	33:67
71 West 95th St.	6,500	12,000	35:65
73 West 95th St.	6,000	11,500	34:66
75 West 95th St.	5,000	10,000	33:67
	$950,500	$2,133,500	

GROUP B: PARCELS WHOSE TAXES WOULD BE DECREASED

Address	Assessed Values Improvements	Assessed Values Land	Ratio
2 West 90th St.	$2,500	$19,000	57:43
4 West 90th St.	11,000	14,000	44:56
6 West 90th St.	11,000	14,000	44:56
8 West 90th St.	11,000	13,500	45:55
10 West 90th St.	11,000	14,000	44:56
12 West 90th St.	11,500	15,500	43:57
14 West 90th St.	11,500	15,500	43:57
16 West 90th St.	11,500	15,500	43:57
18 West 90th St.	14,000	15,500	47:53
20 West 90th St.	14,000	15,500	43:57
22 West 90th St.	11,000	15,000	42:58
23 West 90th St.	12,500	12,500	50:50

SECTION OF SIDE STREETS WEST OF CENTRAL PARK—*Continued*
GROUP B: PARCELS WHOSE TAXES WOULD BE DECREASED

Address	Assessed Values — Improvements	Assessed Values — Land	Ratio
24 West 90th St.	$11,000	$15,000	42:58
25 West 90th St.	13,000	13,000	50:50
26 West 90th St.	11,000	15,000	42:58
27 West 90th St.	13,000	13,000	50:50
29 West 90th St.	9,500	14,500	40:60
31 West 90th St.	10,000	15,000	40:60
33 West 90th St.	9,500	14,500	40:60
35 West 90th St.	10,000	15,000	40:60
36 West 90th St.	10,000	15,000	40:60
37 West 90th St.	9,500	14,500	40:60
39 West 90th St.	10,000	15,000	40:60
41 West 90th St.	9,500	14,500	40:60
42 West 90th St.	7,000	15,000	40:60
43 West 90th St.	10,000	15,000	40:60
44 West 90th St.	18,000	15,000	55:45
45 West 90th St.	9,000	14,000	39:61
46 West 90th St.	18,000	15,000	55:45
47 West 90th St.	9,500	12,500	43:57
48 West 90th St.	19,000	15,000	56:44
49 West 90th St.	9,500	12,500	43:57
50 West 90th St.	19,000	15,000	56:44
51 West 90th St.	9,500	13,000	42:58
52 West 90th St.	19,000	15,000	56:44
17 West 91st St.	8,500	13,500	38.64:61.36
19 West 91st St.	9,500	13,500	41:59
21 West 91st St.	9,500	13,500	41:59
22 West 91st St.	9,500	13,500	41:59
23 West 91st St.	9,500	13,500	41:59
24 West 91st St.	9,500	13,500	41:59
25 West 91st St.	9,000	13,000	41:59
26 West 91st St.	9,500	13,500	41:59
27 West 91st St.	10,000	13,500	43:57
29 West 91st St.	11,000	14,000	44:56
31 West 91st St.	9,000	14,000	39:61
33 West 91st St.	11,000	14,000	44:56
35 West 91st St.	8,500	13,500	38.64:61.36
37 West 91st St.	11,000	14,000	39:61
39 West 91st St.	11,000	14,000	44:56
41 West 91st St.	9,000	14,000	39:61
43 West 91st St.	9,000	14,000	39:61
48 West 91st St.	9,500	13,500	41:59
50 West 91st St.	9,500	13,500	41:59
51 West 91st St.	8,500	13,500	38.64:61.36
52 West 91st St.	9,500	13,500	41:59
54 West 91st St.	9,500	13,500	41:59
56 West 91st St.	11,000	15,000	42:58
58 West 91st St.	11,000	14,000	44:56
60 West 91st St.	11,000	15,000	42:58
62 West 91st St.	11,000	14,000	44:56
64 West 91st St.	11,000	15,000	42:58
66 West 91st St.	11,000	14,000	44:56
68 West 91st St.	11,000	15,000	42:58
30 West 92nd St.	8,500	12,500	40:60
32 West 92nd St.	9,500	12,500	43:57
34 West 92nd St.	9,500	12,500	43:57
36 West 92nd St.	9,500	12,500	43:57
38 West 92nd St.	9,500	12,500	43:57
40 West 92nd St.	9,500	12,500	43:57
42 West 92nd St.	8,000	12,500	42:58
44 West 92nd St.	10,500	12,500	46:54
46 West 92nd St.	9,000	13,000	41:51
48 West 92nd St.	9,500	13,000	42:58
50 West 92nd St.	9,500	13,000	42:58

SECTION OF SIDE STREETS WEST OF CENTRAL PARK—*Concluded*
GROUP B: PARCELS WHOSE TAXES WOULD BE DECREASED

Address	Assessed Values — Improvements	Assessed Values — Land	Ratio
52 West 92nd St.	$9,500	$13,000	42:58
54 West 92nd St.	9,500	13,000	42:58
56 West 92nd St.	9,500	12,500	43:57
58 West 92nd St.	8,500	12,500	40:60
60 West 92nd St.	20,500	21,500	49:51
11 West 94th St.	8,500	13,500	38.64:61.36
13 West 94th St.	9,000	13,000	41:59
14 West 94th St.	8,500	12,500	40:60
15 West 94th St.	9,000	12,000	43:57
16 West 94th St.	8,500	12,500	40:60
17 West 94th St.	9,000	12,000	43:57
18 West 94th St.	8,500	12,500	40:60
20 West 94th St.	8,500	12,500	40:60
31 West 94th St.	7,500	8,500	47:53
33 West 94th St.	7,500	8,500	47:53
34 West 94th St.	7,500	11,500	39:61
35 West 94th St.	9,000	13,000	41:59
36 West 94th St.	7,500	11,500	39:61
49 West 94th St.	9,500	13,500	41:59
51 West 94th St.	9,500	13,500	41:59
53 West 94th St.	9,500	13,500	41:59
60 West 94th St.	12,000	16,500	42:58
73 West 94th St.	9,000	13,000	41:59
74 West 94th St.	11,000	13,000	46:54
75 West 94th St.	9,000	14,000	39:61
4 West 95th St.	9,000	11,000	45:55
6 West 95th St.	9,000	11,000	45:55
7 West 95th St.	13,000	13,000	50:50
8 West 95th St.	9,000	11,000	45:55
9 West 95th St.	14,000	12,000	54:46
10 West 95th St.	11,000	12,000	48:52
11 West 95th St.	12,000	12,000	50:50
12 West 95th St.	11,500	12,500	48:52
13 West 95th St.	12,500	12,500	50:50
14 West 95th St.	11,500	12,000	48:52
16 West 95th St.	11,500	13,000	47:53
17 West 95th St.	9,500	12,000	44:56
18 West 95th St.	8,000	12,000	40:60
19 West 95th St.	9,500	12,500	43:57
20 West 95th St.	8,500	12,500	40:60
21 West 95th St.	10,500	12,500	46:54
22 West 95th St.	8,500	12,500	40:60
23 West 95th St.	11,000	13,000	46:54
24 West 95th St.	9,500	12,000	44:56
26 West 95th St.	9,500	12,000	44:56
28 West 95th St.	9,500	12,000	44:56
30 West 95th St.	9,500	12,000	44:56
31 West 95th St.	7,500	11,000	40:60
32 West 95th St.	9,500	12,000	44:56
34 West 95th St.	9,500	12,000	44:56
36 West 95th St.	9,500	12,000	44:56
38 West 95th St.	9,500	12,000	44:56
63 West 95th St.	9,000	13,000	41:59
65 West 95th St.	9,000	13,000	41:59
	$1,322,500	$1,726,500	

SECTION OF SIDE STREETS EAST OF LEXINGTON AVE.

(Standard Composite Ratio: 38.34:61.66)

Group A: Parcels Whose Taxes Would Be Increased

Address	Assessed Values		Ratio
	Improvements	Land	
157 East 70th St.	$ 8,000	$33,000	19:81
174 East 70th St.	3,500	15,500	18:82
175 East 70th St.	6,000	15,000	29:71
177 East 70th St.	3,000	11,000	21:79
179 East 70th St.	3,000	11,000	21:79
181 East 70th St.	3,000	14,000	18:82
146 East 71st St.	4,000	11,500	26:74
148 East 71st St.	4,000	12,000	25:75
150 East 71st St.	4,500	14,000	22:78
151 East 71st St.	3,500	12,000	23:77
152 East 71st St.	5,000	14,500	26:74
153 East 71st St.	3,500	11,000	24:76
154 East 71st St.	6,000	18,000	25:75
155 East 71st St.	14,000	18,000	36:64
156 East 71st St.	6,000	18,000	25:75
158 East 71st St.	9,000	18,000	33:67
159 East 71st St.	7,000	18,000	28:72
160 East 71st St.	5,500	14,500	27:73
164 East 71st St.	7,000	11,000	38.33:61.67
166 East 71st St.	7,000	11,000	38.33:61.67
168 East 71st St.	8,000	15,000	35:65
169 East 71st St.	4,500	15,000	23:77
170 East 71st St.	8,000	15,000	35:65
171 East 71st St.	4,000	13,500	23:77
172 East 71st St.	5,000	15,000	25:75
181 East 71st St.	4,500	15,000	23:77
183 East 71st St.	4,500	15,000	23:77
185 East 71st St.	5,000	15,000	25:75
187 East 71st St.	4,500	13,500	25:75
145 East 72nd St.	5,000	18,000	22:78
152 East 72nd St.	10,000	20,000	33:67
154 East 72nd St.	6,000	17,000	26:74
156 East 72nd St.	6,000	16,000	27:73
158 East 72nd St.	6,000	18,500	24:76
160 East 72nd St.	6,000	18,500	24:76
162 East 72nd St.	6,000	18,000	25:75
164 East 72nd St.	6,000	18,000	25:75
166 East 72nd St.	6,000	18,000	25:75
168 East 72nd St.	6,000	16,000	27:73
170 East 72nd St.	6,000	16,000	27:73
172 East 72nd St.	6,000	16,000	27:73
174 East 72nd St.	6,000	16,000	27:73
176 East 72nd St.	6,000	16,000	27:73
178 East 72nd St.	6,000	16,000	27:73
149 East 73rd St.	42,000	70,000	37:63
153 East 73rd St.	1,000	12,000	7:93
155 East 73rd St.	1,000	12,000	7:93
157 East 73rd St.	1,500	14,000	7:93
170 East 73rd St.	9,500	17,500	35:65
171 East 73rd St.	2,000	12,500	14:86
172 East 73rd St.	9,500	17,500	35:65
175 East 73rd St.	2,500	12,500	14:86
180 East 73rd St.	9,500	17,500	35:65
181 East 73rd St.	2,000	12,500	14:86
183 East 73rd St.	2,500	12,500	17:83
184-6 East 73rd St.	7,000	28,000	20:80
144 East 74th St.	5,000	20,000	20:80
146 East 74th St.	4,000	13,000	24:76
148 East 74th St.	4,000	12,000	26:74
150 East 74th St.	4,000	11,000	27:73
153 East 74th St.	5,000	13,000	28:72

SECTION OF SIDE STREETS EAST OF LEXINGTON AVENUE—*Continued*

GROUP A: PARCELS WHOSE TAXES WOULD BE INCREASED

Address	Assessed Values — Improvements	Assessed Values — Land	Ratio
154 East 74th St.	$4,500	$12,500	28:72
155 East 74th St.	4,000	12,000	25:75
156 East 74th St.	4,500	12,500	28:72
157 East 74th St.	5,000	12,000	29:71
158 East 74th St.	4,500	12,500	28:72
159 East 74th St.	4,000	12,000	25:75
168 East 74th St.	9,000	19,000	34:66
170 East 74th St.	9,000	19,000	32:68
172 East 74th St.	9,000	19,000	32:68
148 East 78th St.	3,500	9,500	27:73
149 East 78th St.	3,000	9,500	24:76
150 East 78th St.	4,000	11,000	27:73
151 East 78th St.	3,500	9,500	27:73
152 East 78th St.	4,000	11,000	27:73
153 East 78th St.	2,500	7,000	26:74
154 East 78th St.	4,000	11,000	27:73
155 East 78th St.	2,500	7,000	26:74
156 East 78th St.	4,000	11,000	27:73
157 East 78th St.	3,000	11,000	21:79
158 East 78th St.	4,000	11,000	27:73
159 East 78th St.	2,500	11,000	18:82
160 East 78th St.	4,000	11,000	27:73
161 East 78th St.	2,500	11,000	18:82
163-5 East 78th St.	6,000	22,000	21:79
167 East 78th St.	3,000	11,000	21:79
169 East 78th St.	3,000	11,000	21:79
171 East 78th St.	3,000	11,000	21:79
173 East 78th St.	3,000	11,000	21:79
175 East 78th St.	3,000	11,000	21:79
177 East 78th St.	3,000	11,000	21:79
150 East 79th St.	3,500	11,500	23:77
152 East 79th St.	3,500	10,500	25:75
154 East 79th St.	4,000	12,000	25:75
158 East 79th St.	8,000	14,000	36:64
160 East 79th St.	8,000	14,000	36:64
162 East 79th St.	8,000	14,000	36:64
164 East 79th St.	8,000	14,000	36:64
168 East 79th St.	10,500	17,500	37:63
170 East 79th St.	4,000	13,000	23:77
172 East 79th St.	4,000	13,000	23:77
174 East 79th St.	4,000	13,000	23:77
176 East 79th St.	4,000	13,000	23:77
178 East 79th St.	8,500	17,500	33:67
180 East 79th St.	3,500	11,500	23:77
182 East 79th St.	3,500	11,500	23:77
184 East 79th St.	3,500	11,500	23:77
	$578,500	$1,570,000	

GROUP B: PARCELS WHOSE TAXES WOULD BE DECREASED

Address	Assessed Values — Improvements	Assessed Values — Land	Ratio
154 East 70th St.	$57,000	$38,000	59:41
155 East 70th St.	12,000	17,000	41:59
158 East 70th St.	17,500	17,500	50:50
159 East 70th St.	12,000	17,000	41:59
160 East 70th St.	16,500	17,500	49:51
161 East 70th St.	14,000	18,000	44:56
162 East 70th St.	16,500	17,500	49:51
163 East 70th St.	19,000	23,000	45:55

SECTION OF SIDE STREETS EAST OF LEXINGTON AVENUE—*Concluded*
GROUP B: PARCELS WHOSE TAXES WOULD BE DECREASED

Address	Assessed Values		Ratio
	Improvements	Land	
164 East 70th St.	$14,500	$17,500	45:55
165 East 70th St.	25,000	30,000	45:55
168-72 East 70th St.	65,000	55,000	54:46
169 East 70th St.	13,000	15,000	46:54
171 East 70th St.	11,000	15,000	42:58
176 East 70th St.	16,000	16,000	50:50
157 East 71st St.	19,000	18,000	51:49
161 East 71st St.	9,000	13,500	40:60
162 East 71st St.	17,500	14,500	55:45
163 East 71st St.	9,000	13,500	40:60
165 East 71st St.	14,000	15,000	48:52
167 East 71st St.	13,000	15,000	46:54
173-75 East 71st St.	33,000	27,000	55:45
177 East 71st St.	16,000	18,000	47:53
179 East 71st St.	26,000	18,000	59:41
147 East 72nd St.	12,000	18,000	40:60
149 East 72nd St.	15,000	18,000	45:55
151 East 72nd St.	15,000	18,000	45:55
180 East 72nd St.	18,000	22,000	45:55
160-2 East 73rd St.	45,000	46,000	49:51
164 East 73rd St.	35,000	30,000	54:46
168 East 73rd St.	15,500	17,500	47:53
173 East 73rd St.	8,500	12,500	40:60
178 East 73rd St.	15,500	17,500	47:53
182 East 73rd St.	13,500	17,500	44:56
151 East 74th St.	9,000	13,000	41:59
152 East 74th St.	23,000	11,000	68:32
160 East 74th St.	18,500	12,500	60:40
161 East 74th St.	15,500	13,500	53:47
162 East 74th St.	17,500	12,500	58:42
163 East 74th St.	14,500	13,500	52:48
164 East 74th St.	17,500	12,500	58:42
165 East 74th St.	14,500	13,500	52:48
166 East 74th St.	17,500	12,500	58:42
167 East 74th St.	14,500	13,500	52:48
169 East 74th St.	14,500	13,500	52:48
162 East 78th St.	11,000	11,000	50:50
164 East 78th St.	13,000	15,000	46:54
166 East 78th St.	13,000	15,000	46:54
	$872,000	$866,000	

SECTION IN WASHINGTON SQUARE DISTRICT
(Standard Composite Ratio: 38.34:61.66)

GROUP A: PARCELS WHOSE TAXES WOULD BE INCREASED

Address	Assessed Values		Ratio
	Improvements	Land	
5-7-9 W. 9th St.	$10,000	$109,000	8:92
6 West 9th St.	2,000	22,000	8:92
8 West 9th St.	2,500	28,500	8:92
10 West 9th St.	1,500	22,000	6:94
11 West 9th St.	2,000	15,500	11:89
12 West 9th St.	3,000	27,000	10:90
13 West 9th St.	2,000	15,500	11:89
14 West 9th St.	1,500	20,500	7:93
15 West 9th St.	2,000	15,500	11:89
16 West 9th St.	1,500	19,500	7:93
17 West 9th St.	7,000	24,500	22:78
18 West 9th St.	3,000	20,000	13:87
24 West 9th St.	2,500	20,000	11:89
25 West 9th St.	2,500	16,000	13:87
26 West 9th St.	2,500	20,000	11:89
27 West 9th St.	3,500	14,000	20:80
28 West 9th St.	2,500	20,000	11:89
29 West 9th St.	2,500	14,000	15:85
30 West 9th St.	2,500	20,000	11:89
31 West 9th St.	2,500	14,500	15:85
32 West 9th St.	2,000	20,000	9:91
33 West 9th St.	2,500	14,500	15:85
34 West 9th St.	2,000	20,000	9:91
35 West 9th St.	2,500	14,500	15:85
36 West 9th St.	2,000	20,000	9:91
37 West 9th St.	2,500	14,500	15:85
39 West 9th St.	2,500	14,500	15:85
41 West 9th St.	2,500	14,500	15:85
43 West 9th St.	6,000	24,000	20:80
45 West 9th St.	2,500	13,500	16:84
47 West 9th St.	8,500	22,500	27:73
51 West 9th St.	2,500	13,500	16:84
52 West 9th St.	2,500	20,000	11:89
53 West 9th St.	2,500	13,500	16:84
54 West 9th St.	2,500	13,500	16:84
55 West 9th St.	2,000	17,000	11:89
56 West 9th St.	2,500	13,500	16:84
57 West 9th St.	2,000	17,000	11:89
58 West 9th St.	2,500	13,500	16:84
59 West 9th St.	2,000	17,000	11:89
60 West 9th St.	3,000	20,000	13:87
61 West 9th St.	500	17,000	3:97
63 West 9th St.	500	17,000	3:97
65 West 9th St.	500	17,000	3:97
67 West 9th St.	1,000	17,000	6:94
7 West 10th St.	2,700	24,300	10:90
8 West 10th St.	10,000	28,000	26:74
9 West 10th St.	3,000	25,500	11:89
10 West 10th St.	10,000	28,000	26:74
11-13 West 10th St.	20,000	55,000	27:73
12 West 10th St.	18,000	34,000	35:65
14 West 10th St.	17,500	36,500	33:67
15 West 10th St.	8,000	26,000	24:76
16 West 10th St.	18,000	37,000	33:67
17 West 10th St.	9,500	25,500	27:73
18 West 10th St.	15,000	28,000	35:65
19 West 10th St.	9,600	25,500	26:74
20 West 10th St.	5,000	18,000	22:78
21 West 10th St.	10,000	26,000	28:72
22 West 10th St.	5,000	17,500	22:78
23 West 10th St.	9,500	28,500	25:75
24 West 10th St.	5,000	17,500	22:78
25 West 10th St.	5,500	22,000	20:80

SECTION OF WASHINGTON SQUARE DISTRICT—*Continued*
GROUP A: PARCELS WHOSE TAXES WOULD BE INCREASED

Address	Assessed Values		Ratio
	Improvements	Land	
26 West 10th St.	$4,000	$16,000	20:80
27 West 10th St.	5,500	22,000	20:80
28 West 10th St.	4,000	16,000	20:80
29 West 10th St.	5,000	22,000	19:81
30 West 10th St.	4,000	16,000	20:80
32 West 10th St.	4,000	16,000	20:80
33 West 10th St.	3,500	21,500	14:86
34 West 10th St.	6,000	16,000	27:73
35 West 10th St.	3,000	17,500	15:85
36 West 10th St.	5,000	17,500	22:78
37 West 10th St.	6,500	20,500	24:76
39 West 10th St.	3,500	20,500	15:85
40 West 10th St.	4,000	19,000	17:83
41 West 10th St.	5,500	20,500	21:79
43 West 10th St.	3,500	20,500	15:85
44 West 10th St.	4,500	17,500	20:80
46 West 10th St.	4,500	17,500	20:80
48 West 10th St.	2,000	17,500	10:90
56 West 10th St.	2,500	17,500	12:88
58 West 10th St.	4,000	17,500	19:81
59-67 West 10th St.	12,000	88,000	10:90
69 West 10th St.	2,000	12,000	14:86
10 West 11th St.	3,000	26,000	10:90
11 West 11th St.	3,000	22,000	12:88
13 West 11th St.	1,500	16,500	5:95
14 West 11th St.	3,500	19,000	16:84
15 West 11th St.	1,000	18,500	5:95
16 West 11th St.	3,500	19,000	16:84
17 West 11th St.	1,000	19,000	5:95
18 West 11th St.	3,500	19,000	16:84
19 West 11th St.	1,000	19,000	5:95
20 West 11th St.	3,500	19,000	16:84
21 West 11th St.	2,000	19,000	10:90
22 West 11th St.	3,500	19,000	16:84
23 West 11th St.	2,000	19,000	10:90
24 West 11th St.	3,500	19,000	16:84
25 West 11th St.	2,000	19,000	10:90
26 West 11th St.	3,500	19,000	16:84
28 West 11th St.	5,000	21,000	19:81
30 West 11th St.	5,000	19,000	17:83
32 West 11th St.	5,000	18,500	18:82
34 West 11th St.	5,000	18,500	18:82
35 West 11th St.	2,500	21,500	10:90
37 West 11th St.	2,500	20,500	11:89
39 West 11th St.	3,000	20,000	13:87
40 West 11th St.	3,500	17,500	17:83
41 West 11th St.	3,500	21,000	11:89
42 West 11th St.	3,500	17,500	17:83
43 West 11th St.	3,000	21,000	13:87
44 West 11th St.	3,500	17,500	17:83
46 West 11th St.	4,000	17,500	19:81
48 West 11th St.	4,000	17,500	15:85
49 West 11th St.	1,000	22,000	4:96
50 West 11th St.	3,000	17,500	15:85
51 West 11th St.	1,000	22,000	4:96
52 West 11th St.	2,000	18,500	10:90
54 West 11th St.	2,000	18,500	10:90
60 West 11th St.	2,000	18,500	10:90
62 West 11th St.	2,000	19,000	10:90
64 West 11th St.	2,500	18,500	12:88
66 West 11th St.	2,500	18,500	12:88
68 West 11th St.	2,500	18,500	12:88
71 West 11th St.	3,000	21,000	13:87
	$518,300	$2,660,800	

MOUNT MORRIS PARK SECTION

(Standard Composite Ratio: 38.34:61.66)

Group A: Parcels Whose Taxes Would Be Increased

Address	Assessed Values		Ratio
	Improvements	Land	
104 West 119th St.	$4,700	$9,300	33:67
106 West 119th St.	5,700	9,300	38:62
108 West 119th St.	5,700	9,300	38:62
110 West 119th St.	5,700	9,300	38:62
112 West 119th St.	5,700	9,300	38:62
114 West 119th St.	6,600	10,400	38.82:61.18
116 West 119th St.	5,700	9,300	38:62
118 West 119th St.	5,700	9,300	38:62
120 West 119th St.	5,700	9,300	38:62
122 West 119th St.	5,700	9,300	38:62
146 West 119th St.	4,700	9,300	33:67
147 West 119th St.	5,600	10,400	35:65
148 West 119th St.	4,700	9,300	33:67
149 West 119th St.	5,600	10,400	35:65
150 West 119th St.	4,700	9,300	33:67
151 West 119th St.	5,600	10,400	35:65
152 West 119th St.	4,700	9,300	33:67
153 West 119th St.	5,600	10,400	35:65
154 West 119th St.	4,700	9,300	33:67
155 West 119th St.	4,600	10,400	31:69
156 West 119th St.	4,700	9,300	33:67
158 West 119th St.	4,200	8,800	32:68
3 West 120th St.	7,000	15,000	32:68
5 West 120th St.	7,000	13,000	31.1:61.9
7 West 120th St.	6,500	13,500	32:68
9 West 120th St.	5,000	11,500	30:70
11 West 120th St.	5,000	11,500	30:70
13 West 120th St.	5,500	11,500	32:68
15 West 120th St.	6,000	13,000	32:68
17 West 120th St.	5,500	13,000	30:70
19 West 120th St.	6,000	13,000	32:68
21 West 120th St.	5,500	13,000	30:70
23 West 120th St.	6,000	13,000	32:68
25 West 120th St.	6,000	13,000	32:68
102 West 120th St.	5,700	9,300	38:62
104 West 120th St.	5,700	9,300	38:62
106 West 120th St.	5,700	9,300	38:62
108 West 120th St.	5,700	9,300	38:62
110 West 120th St.	5,700	9,300	38:62
127 West 120th St.	6,600	10,900	38:62
129 West 120th St.	6,600	10,900	38:62
131 West 120th St.	6,100	10,100	36:64
134 West 120th St.	3,700	9,300	28:72
136 West 120th St.	3,700	9,300	28:72
138 West 120th St.	3,700	9,300	28:72
140 West 120th St.	3,200	8,800	27:73
142 West 120th St.	3,700	9,300	28:72
144 West 120th St.	3,700	9,300	28:72
146 West 120th St.	3,700	9,300	28:72
148 West 120th St.	3,400	8,600	28:72
150 West 120th St.	3,400	8,600	28:72
152 West 120th St.	3,400	8,600	28:72
155 West 120th St.	3,500	8,500	29:71
157 West 120th St.	3,500	8,500	29:71
159 West 120th St.	2,500	9,000	28:72
14 West 121st St.	5,500	12,500	31:69
16 West 121st St.	6,500	12,500	34:66
18 West 121st St.	6,500	12,500	34:66
20 West 121st St.	5,500	12,500	31:69
22 West 121st St.	6,500	12,500	34:66
26 West 121st St.	7,500	12,500	37:63

MOUNT MORRIS PARK SECTION—*Continued*
GROUP A: PARCELS WHOSE TAXES WOULD BE INCREASED

Address	Assessed Values		Ratio
	Improvements	Land	
101 West 121st St.	$6,500	$10,500	38.24:61.76
105 West 121st St.	4,200	7,800	35:65
111 West 121st St.	4,200	7,800	35:65
135 West 121st St.	6,200	10,800	36:64
137 West 121st St.	6,200	10,800	36:64
139 West 121st St.	6,200	10,800	36:64
141 West 121st St.	6,200	10,800	36:64
143 West 121st St.	6,800	10,800	38.28:61.72
145 West 121st St.	6,800	10,800	38.28:61.72
147 West 121st St.	6,100	10,400	37:63
149 West 121st St.	6,100	10,400	37:63
159 West 121st St.	5,700	9,300	38:62
164 West 121st St.	4,200	7,800	35:65
4 West 122nd St.	9,000	16,000	36:64
6 West 122nd St.	6,500	12,500	34:66
7 West 122nd St.	7,500	12,500	37:63
8 West 122nd St.	7,000	13,000	35:65
9 West 122nd St.	6,000	12,000	33:67
11 West 122nd St.	6,000	12,000	33:67
12 West 122nd St.	7,000	13,000	35:65
13 West 122nd St.	6,000	12,000	33:67
14 West 122nd St.	7,000	13,000	35:65
15 West 122nd St.	6,000	12,000	33:67
16 West 122nd St.	7,500	12,500	37:63
17 West 122nd St.	6,000	12,000	33:67
19 West 122nd St.	6,000	12,000	33:67
21 West 122nd St.	7,500	12,500	37:63
104 West 122nd St.	3,500	11,000	29:71
106 West 122nd St.	5,200	8,800	37:63
108 West 122nd St.	4,700	9,300	38:62
110 West 122nd St.	4,700	9,300	38:62
112 West 122nd St.	4,700	9,300	38:62
114 West 122nd St.	4,700	9,300	38:62
116 West 122nd St.	4,700	9,300	38:62
118 West 122nd St.	4,700	9,300	38:62
120 West 122nd St.	5,700	9,800	37:63
122 West 122nd St.	5,700	9,300	38:62
124 West 122nd St.	5,700	9,800	37:63
126 West 122nd St.	5,700	9,800	37:63
128 West 122nd St.	5,700	9,800	37:63
130 West 122nd St.	5,700	9,800	37:63
138 West 122nd St.	5,000	9,000	36:64
140 West 122nd St.	5,000	9,000	36:64
142 West 122nd St.	6,100	10,900	36:64
144 West 122nd St.	5,000	9,000	36:64
146 West 122nd St.	5,000	9,000	36:64
148 West 122nd St.	5,000	9,000	36:64
2 West 123rd St.	6,000	13,000	32:68
3 West 123rd St.	5,000	12,500	29:71
4 West 123rd St.	4,000	10,500	28:72
5 West 123rd St.	4,000	12,000	25:75
6 West 123rd St.	4,000	10,500	28:72
7 West 123rd St.	5,000	12,000	29:71
8 West 123rd St.	4,000	10,500	28:72
9 West 123rd St.	3,000	12,000	20:80
10 West 123rd St.	4,000	10,500	28:72
11 West 123rd St.	1,500	7,500	17:83
12 West 123rd St.	4,000	10,500	28:72
13 West 123rd St.	1,500	7,500	17:83
14 West 123rd St.	4,000	10,500	28:72
16 West 123rd St.	3,500	11,000	24:76
17 West 123rd St.	2,500	10,500	19:81
18 West 123rd St.	4,000	10,500	28:72

MOUNT MORRIS PARK SECTION—*Continued*

Group A: Parcels Whose Taxes Would Be Increased

Address	Assessed Values — Improvements	Assessed Values — Land	Ratio
19 West 123rd St.	$3,500	$10,500	25:75
20 West 123rd St.	4,000	10,500	28:72
21 West 123rd St.	2,500	10,500	19:81
22 West 123rd St.	4,000	10,500	28:72
24 West 123rd St.	4,000	10,500	28:72
26 West 123rd St.	4,000	11,500	26:74
102 West 123rd St.	5,000	11,000	31:69
103 West 123rd St.	5,500	10,500	34:66
104 West 123rd St.	5,600	10,400	35:65
106 West 123rd St.	1,600	10,400	13:87
108 West 123rd St.	5,600	10,400	35:65
110 West 123rd St.	5,600	10,400	35:65
112 West 123rd St.	5,600	10,400	35:65
113 West 123rd St.	6,100	10,400	37:63
114 West 123rd St.	5,600	10,400	35:65
116 West 123rd St.	5,600	10,400	35:65
117 West 123rd St.	6,100	10,400	37:63
118 West 123rd St.	5,600	10,400	35:65
119 West 123rd St.	6,100	10,400	37:63
120 West 123rd St.	5,600	10,400	35:65
121 West 123rd St.	5,900	10,100	37:63
122 West 123rd St.	5,600	10,400	35:65
123 West 123rd St.	5,300	9,700	35:65
124 West 123rd St.	900	8,600	10:90
125 West 123rd St.	5,500	10,000	35:65
126 West 123rd St.	900	8,600	10:90
127 West 123rd St.	5,300	9,700	35:65
128 West 123rd St.	$900	8,600	10:90
129 West 123rd St.	5,800	9,700	37:63
130 West 123rd St.	5,000	14,000	26:74
132 West 123rd St.	3,700	8,800	30:70
134 West 123rd St.	3,700	8,300	31:69
136 West 123rd St.	3,400	9,100	27:73
138 West 123rd St.	1,600	8,400	16:84
140 West 123rd St.	1,400	8,600	14:86
142 West 123rd St.	1,400	8,600	14:86
144 West 123rd St.	3,400	9,100	27:73
145 West 123rd St.	6,100	10,400	37:63
146 West 123rd St.	3,700	8,800	30:70
148 West 123rd St.	3,700	8,800	30:70
149 West 123rd St.	5,600	10,400	35:65
150 West 123rd St.	3,700	8,800	30:70
152 West 123rd St.	3,700	8,300	31:69
153 West 123rd St.	4,700	8,800	35:65
154 West 123rd St.	3,800	8,200	32:68
155 West 123rd St.	4,700	8,800	35:65
156 West 123rd St.	4,500	7,500	37:63
157 West 123rd St.	4,700	8,800	35:65
158 West 123rd St.	3,300	7,200	31:69
159 West 123rd St.	4,700	9,800	32:68
160 West 123rd St.	3,300	7,200	31:69
161 West 123rd St.	3,400	8,100	30:70
162 West 123rd St.	3,300	7,200	31:69
163 West 123rd St.	4,000	10,000	29:71
164 West 123rd St.	3,300	7,200	31:69
166 West 123rd St.	3,300	7,200	31:69
168 West 123rd St.	3,500	8,000	30:70
54 West 124th St.	2,000	12,000	14:86
56 West 124th St.	2,500	12,000	17:83
58 West 124th St.	2,500	12,000	17:83
60 West 124th St.	2,000	12,000	14:86
78 West 124th St.	3,000	15,000	17:83

MOUNT MORRIS PARK SECTION—*Continued*

GROUP A: PARCELS WHOSE TAXES WOULD BE INCREASED

Address	Assessed Values		Ratio
	Improvements	Land	
1 Mt. Morris Ave., W.	$9,000	$24,000	27:73
2 Mt. Morris Ave., W.	7,000	15,000	32:68
3 Mt. Morris Ave., W.	7,000	15,000	32:68
4 Mt. Morris Ave., W.	7,000	15,000	32:68
5 Mt. Morris Ave., W.	7,000	15,000	32:68
10 Mt. Morris Ave., W.	11,000	26,000	30:70
11 Mt. Morris Ave., W.	9,000	28,000	24:76
12 Mt. Morris Ave., W.	8,000	18,000	31:69
13 Mt. Morris Ave., W.	8,000	18,000	31:69
14 Mt. Morris Ave., W.	10,000	20,000	33:67
26 Mt. Morris Ave., W.	1,500	14,500	9:91
27 Mt. Morris Ave., W.	3,000	14,000	28:82
28 Mt. Morris Ave., W.	3,000	14,000	28:82
29 Mt. Morris Ave., W.	3,000	14,000	28:82
30 Mt. Morris Ave., W.	3,000	22,000	12:88
32 Mt. Morris Ave., W.	10,000	20,000	33:67
33 Mt. Morris Ave., W.	10,000	20,000	33:67
34 Mt. Morris Ave., W.	10,000	20,000	33:67
	$1,015,200	$2,237,200	

GROUP B: PARCELS WHOSE TAXES WOULD BE DECREASED

Address	Assessed Values		Ratio
	Improvements	Land	
105 West 118th St.	$9,600	$10,400	48:52
107 West 118th St.	10,600	10,400	50:50
109 West 118th St.	10,600	10,400	50:50
111 West 118th St.	10,600	10,400	50:50
113 West 118th St.	10,600	10,400	50:50
115 West 118th St.	10,600	10,400	50:50
117 West 118th St.	10,600	10,400	50:50
119 West 118th St.	10,600	10,400	50:50
121 West 118th St.	10,600	10,400	50:50
123 West 118th St.	10,600	10,400	50:50
125 West 118th St.	10,600	10,400	50:50
127 West 118th St.	10,600	10,400	50:50
129 West 118th St.	10,600	10,400	50:50
131 West 118th St.	10,600	10,400	50:50
133 West 118th St.	10,600	10,400	50:50
135 West 118th St.	10,600	10,400	50:50
137 West 118th St.	10,600	10,400	50:50
145 West 118th St.	8,700	9,300	48:52
147 West 118th St.	8,700	9,300	48:52
149 West 118th St.	9,700	9,300	51:49
151 West 118th St.	9,200	8,800	51:49
153 West 118th St.	8,700	9,300	48:52
155 West 118th St.	8,700	9,300	48:52
157 West 118th St.	8,700	9,300	48:52
103 West 119th St.	6,400	8,600	43:57
105 West 119th St.	7,400	8,600	47:54
107 West 119th St.	6,400	8,600	43:57
109 West 119th St.	8,200	9,800	46:54
111 West 119th St.	8,200	9,800	46:54
113 West 119th St.	8,200	9,800	46:54
115 West 119th St.	7,700	9,300	45:55
117 West 119th St.	10,600	10,400	50:50
119 West 119th St.	10,600	10,400	50:50
121 West 119th St.	10,600	10,400	50:50
123 West 119th St.	10,600	10,400	50:50
124 West 119th St.	6,600	9,300	42:58

MOUNT MORRIS PARK SECTION—*Continued*

GROUP B: PARCELS WHOSE TAXES WOULD BE DECREASED

Address	Assessed Values Improvements	Assessed Values Land	Ratio
125 West 119th St.	$10,600	$10,400	50:50
126 West 119th St.	10,600	10,400	50:50
127 West 119th St.	10,600	10,400	50:50
128 West 119th St.	10,600	10,400	50:50
129 West 119th St.	10,600	10,400	50:50
130 West 119th St.	10,600	10,400	50:50
131 West 119th St.	10,600	10,400	50:50
132 West 119th St.	10,600	10,400	50:50
133 West 119th St.	10,600	10,400	50:50
134 West 119th St.	10,600	10,400	50:50
135 West 119th St.	10,600	10,400	50:50
136 West 119th St.	10,600	10,400	50:50
137 West 119th St.	10,600	10,400	50:50
138 West 119th St.	10,600	10,400	50:50
139 West 119th St.	10,600	10,400	50:50
140 West 119th St.	10,600	10,400	50:50
141 West 119th St.	10,600	10,400	50:50
142 West 119th St.	10,600	10,400	50:50
143 West 119th St.	10,600	10,400	50:50
144 West 119th St.	10,600	10,400	50:50
145 West 119th St.	10,600	10,400	50:50
107 West 120th St.	6,600	10,400	38.82:61.18
109 West 120th St.	7,100	10,400	42:58
111 West 120th St.	7,100	10,400	42:58
112 West 120th St.	7,600	10,400	42:58
113 West 120th St.	7,100	10,400	42:58
114 West 120th St.	7,600	10,400	42:58
115 West 120th St.	7,100	10,400	42:58
116 West 120th St.	7,600	10,400	42:58
117 West 120th St.	8,100	10,400	44:56
118 West 120th St.	7,200	9,800	42:58
119 West 120th St.	7,100	10,400	41:59
120 West 120th St.	7,200	9,800	42:58
121 West 120th St.	7,600	10,400	42:58
122 West 120th St.	7,600	10,400	42:58
123 West 120th St.	8,100	10,400	44:56
124 West 120th St.	7,200	9,800	42:58
125 West 120th St.	8,100	10,400	44:56
126 West 120th St.	7,200	9,800	42:58
128 West 120th St.	7,200	9,800	42:58
133 West 120th St.	6,600	10,400	38.82:61.18
135 West 120th St.	6,600	10,400	38.82:61.18
137 West 120th St.	6,600	10,400	38.82:61.18
139 West 120th St.	6,600	10,400	38.82:61.18
141 West 120th St.	6,600	10,400	38.82:61.18
143 West 120th St.	6,700	9,800	41:59
145 West 120th St.	6,700	9,800	41:59
147 West 120th St.	6,700	9,800	41:59
149 West 120th St.	6,700	9,800	41:59
151 West 120th St.	6,700	9,300	42:58
153 West 120th St.	6,700	9,300	42:58
154 West 120th St.	6,400	8,600	43:57
156 West 120th St.	6,400	8,600	43:57
158 West 120th St.	6,400	8,600	43:57
160 West 120th St.	6,400	8,600	43:57
162 West 120th St.	6,400	8,600	43:57
164 West 120th St.	6,400	8,600	43:57
1 West 121st St.	10,000	13,000	43:57
3 West 121st St.	9,500	12,500	43:57
4 West 121st St.	9,500	12,500	43:57
5 West 121st St.	8,500	12,500	40:60
6 West 121st St.	9,500	12,500	43:57
7 West 121st St.	9,000	13,000	41:59

MOUNT MORRIS PARK SECTION—*Continued*
GROUP B: PARCELS WHOSE TAXES WOULD BE DECREASED.

Address	Assessed Values		Ratio
	Improvements	Land	
8 West 121st St.	$9,500	$12,500	43:57
9 West 121st St.	8,000	12,000	40:60
10 West 121st St.	9,500	12,500	43:57
11 West 121st St.	8,500	12,500	40:60
12 West 121st St.	9,500	12,500	43:57
13 West 121st St.	8,000	12,000	40:60
15 West 121st St.	8,500	12,500	40:60
17 West 121st St.	8,500	12,500	40:60
19 West 121st St.	8,500	12,500	40:60
21 West 121st St.	9,000	13,000	41:59
102 West 121st St.	8,500	11,500	42:58
103 West 121st St.	5,900	9,100	39:61
104 West 121st St.	7,600	10,400	42:58
106 West 121st St.	8,100	10,900	43:57
107 West 121st St.	5,900	9,100	39:61
108 West 121st St.	8,100	10,900	43:57
109 West 121st St.	5,900	9,100	39:61
110 West 121st St.	7,600	10,400	42:58
112 West 121st St.	11,600	11,400	50:50
113 West 121st St.	5,900	9,100	38.83:61.17
115 West 121st St.	6,600	10,400	38.83:61.17
116 West 121st St.	9,600	10,400	48:52
117 West 121st St.	6,600	10,400	38.83:61.17
118 West 121st St.	10,100	10,400	49:51
119 West 121st St.	6,600	10,400	38.83:61.17
120 West 121st St.	9,600	10,400	48:52
121 West 121st St.	6,600	10,400	38.83:61.17
122 West 121st St.	10,600	10,400	50:50
123 West 121st St.	6,600	10,400	38.83:61.17
124 West 121st St.	10,600	10,400	50:50
125 West 121st St.	6,600	10,400	38.83:61.17
126 West 121st St.	9,600	10,400	49:51
127 West 121st St.	6,600	10,400	38.83:61.17
128 West 121st St.	10,600	10,400	50:50
129 West 121st St.	6,600	10,400	38.83:61.17
130 West 121st St.	10,600	10,400	50:50
131 West 121st St.	6,600	10,400	38.83:61.17
132 West 121st St.	10,100	10,400	49:51
133 West 121st St.	6,600	10,400	38.83:61.17
134 West 121st St.	9,100	10,400	47:53
136 West 121st St.	6,600	10,400	38.82:61.18
138 West 121st St.	6,600	10,400	38.82:61.18
140 West 121st St.	6,600	10,400	38.82:61.18
142 West 121st St.	6,600	10,400	38.82:61.18
144 West 121st St.	6,600	10,400	38.82:61.18
146 West 121st St.	7,700	9,300	45:55
148 West 121st St.	7,700	9,300	45:55
150 West 121st St.	7,700	9,300	45:55
151 West 121st St.	6,200	9,800	38.75:61.25
152 West 121st St.	7,700	9,300	45:55
153 West 121st St.	6,200	9,800	38.75:61.25
154 West 121st St.	7,700	9,300	45:55
155 West 121st St.	6,200	9,800	38.75:61.25
156 West 121st St.	6,700	9,300	42:58
157 West 121st St.	6,200	9,300	40:60
158 West 121st St.	6,700	9,300	42:58
160 West 121st St.	6,200	8,800	41:59
162 West 121st St.	6,200	8,800	41:59
10 West 122nd St.	9,500	13,500	41:59
18 West 122nd St.	8,600	5,400	61.4:38.6
105 West 122nd St.	6,200	9,800	38.75:62.25
107 West 122nd St.	6,200	9,800	38.75:62.25
109 West 122nd St.	6,200	9,800	38.75:62.25

MOUNT MORRIS PARK SECTION—*Concluded*
GROUP B: PARCELS WHOSE TAXES WOULD BE DECREASED

Address	Assessed Values		Ratio
	Improvements	Land	
111 West 122nd St.	$6,200	$9,800	38.75:62.25
115 West 122nd St.	8,600	10,400	45:55
131 West 122nd St.	9,000	14,000	44:56
132 West 122nd St.	6,400	9,600	40:60
133 West 122nd St.	6,400	8,600	43:57
134 West 122nd St.	7,500	9,300	44:56
135 West 122nd St.	6,400	8,600	43:57
136 West 122nd St.	6,300	9,200	40:60
137 West 122nd St.	6,400	8,600	43:57
139 West 122nd St.	6,400	8,600	43:57
141 West 122nd St.	6,400	8,600	43:57
143 West 122nd St.	6,400	8,600	43:57
147 West 122nd St.	7,600	10,400	42:58
150 West 122nd St.	7,200	9,800	42:58
151 West 122nd St.	6,600	10,400	38.78:61.22
152 West 122nd St.	9,200	9,800	48:52
154 West 122nd St.	7,200	9,800	42:58
156 West 122nd St.	6,700	9,300	41:59
158 West 122nd St.	6,700	9,300	41:59
160 West 122nd St.	7,200	9,800	42:58
162 West 122nd St.	7,200	9,800	42:58
164 West 122nd St.	7,200	9,800	42:58
165 West 122nd St.	7,500	9,500	44:56
28 West 123rd St.	5,500	7,500	42:56
30 West 123rd St.	5,500	7,500	42:56
6 Mt. Morris Ave., W.	11,000	16,000	41:59
7 Mt. Morris Ave., W.	11,000	16,000	41:59
8 Mt. Morris Ave., W.	11,000	16,000	41:59
9 Mt. Morris Ave., W.	11,000	16,000	41:59
	$1,579,300	$1,963,900	

II. THE BRONX

SAMPLE DISTRICT FROM ASSESSMENT SECTION NINE, BOROUGH OF THE BRONX

(Standard Composite Ratio: 38.71:61.29)

GROUP A: PARCELS WHOSE TAXES WOULD BE INCREASED

Address	Assessed Values		Ratio
	Improvements	Land	
286 Willis Ave	$5,000	$10,000	33:67
288 Willis Ave	6,000	10,000	37:63
290 Willis Ave	3,500	10,000	26:74
292 Willis Ave	3,500	10,000	26:74
294 Willis Ave	2,700	6,000	31:69
296 Willis Ave	2,500	6,000	29:71
298 Willis Ave	4,000	9,000	31:69
340 Willis Ave	4,000	7,000	36:64
342 Willis Ave	4,000	7,000	36:64
352 Willis Ave	5,000	9,000	36:64
409 East 141st St	1,500	4,500	25:75
	$41,700	$88,500	

GROUP B: PARCELS WHOSE TAXES WOULD BE DECREASED

Address	Assessed Values		Ratio
	Improvements	Land	
403 East 139th St	$4,500	$3,000	60:40
405 East 139th St	3,000	3,000	50:50
407 East 139th St	3,000	3,000	50:50
409 East 139th St	3,000	3,000	50:50
411 East 139th St	3,000	3,000	50:50
413 East 139th St	3,000	3,000	50:50
415 East 139th St	3,000	3,000	50:50
417 East 139th St	3,000	3,000	50:50
419 East 139th St	3,000	3,000	50:50
421 East 139th St	3,000	3,000	50:50
423 East 139th St	3,000	3,000	50:50
425 East 139th St	3,000	3,000	50:50
427 East 139th St	3,000	3,000	50:50
429 East 139th St	3,000	3,000	50:50
431 East 139th St	3,000	3,000	50:50
433 East 139th St	3,000	3,000	50:50
435 East 139th St	3,000	3,000	50:50
437 East 139th St	3,000	3,000	50:50
439 East 139th St	3,000	3,000	50:50
441 East 139th St	3,000	3,000	50:50
443 East 139th St	3,000	3,000	50:50
445 East 139th St	3,000	3,000	50:50
447 East 139th St	3,000	3,000	50:50
449 East 139th St	3,000	3,000	50:50
451 East 139th St	3,000	3,000	50:50
453 East 139th St	3,000	3,000	50:50
455 East 139th St	3,000	3,000	50:50
457 East 139th St	3,000	3,000	50:50
459 East 139th St	3,000	3,000	50:50
461 East 139th St	3,000	3,000	50:50
463 East 139th St	3,000	3,000	50:50
465 East 139th St	3,000	3,000	50:50
467 East 139th St	3,000	3,000	50:50
469 East 139th St	3,000	3,000	50:50
471 East 139th St	3,000	3,000	50:50
473 East 139th St	3,000	3,000	50:50
475 East 139th St	3,000	3,000	50:50

Group B: Parcels Whose Taxes Would Be Decreased

Address	Assessed Values		Ratio
	Improvements	Land	
477 East 139th St.	$3,000	$3,000	50:50
479 East 139th St.	3,000	3,000	50:50
481 East 139th St.	3,000	3,000	50:50
483 East 139th St.	3,000	3,000	50:50
485 East 139th St.	3,000	3,000	50:50
487 East 139th St.	3,000	3,000	50:50
489 East 139th St.	3,000	3,000	50:50
491 East 139th St.	3,000	3,000	50:50
493 East 139th St.	3,000	3,000	50:50
495 East 139th St.	3,000	3,000	50:50
497 East 139th St.	3,000	3,000	50:50
499 East 139th St.	3,000	3,000	50:50
501 East 139th St.	4,500	3,000	60:40
404 East 140th St.	3,500	2,000	64:36
406 East 140th St.	4,500	3,000	60:40
408 East 140th St.	3,000	3,000	50:50
410 East 140th St.	3,000	3,000	50:50
412 East 140th St.	3,000	3,000	50:50
414 East 140th St.	3,000	3,000	50:50
416 East 140th St.	3,000	3,000	50:50
418 East 140th St.	3,000	3,000	50:50
420 East 140th St.	3,000	3,000	50:50
422 East 140th St.	3,000	3,000	50:50
424 East 140th St.	3,000	3,000	50:50
426 East 140th St.	3,000	3,000	50:50
428 East 140th St.	3,000	3,000	50:50
430 East 140th St.	3,000	3,000	50:50
432 East 140th St.	3,000	3,000	50:50
434 East 140th St.	3,000	3,000	50:50
436 East 140th St.	3,000	3,000	50:50
438 East 140th St.	3,000	3,000	50:50
440 East 140th St.	3,000	3,000	50:50
442 East 140th St.	3,000	3,000	50:50
444 East 140th St.	3,000	3,000	50:50
446 East 140th St.	3,000	3,000	50:50
448 East 140th St.	3,000	3,000	50:50
450 East 140th St.	3,000	3,000	50:50
452 East 140th St.	3,000	3,000	50:50
454 East 140th St.	3,000	3,000	50:50
456 East 140th St.	3,000	3,000	50:50
458 East 140th St.	3,000	3,000	50:50
460 East 140th St.	3,000	3,000	50:50
462 East 140th St.	3,000	3,000	50:50
464 East 140th St.	3,000	3,000	50:50
466 East 140th St.	3,000	3,000	50:50
468 East 140th St.	3,000	3,000	50:50
470 East 140th St.	3,000	3,000	50:50
472 East 140th St.	3,000	3,000	50:50
474 East 140th St.	3,000	3,000	50:50
476 East 140th St.	3,000	3,000	50:50
478 East 140th St.	3,000	3,000	50:50
480 East 140th St.	3,000	3,000	50:50
482 East 140th St.	3,000	3,000	50:50
484 East 140th St.	3,000	3,000	50:50
486 East 140th St.	3,000	3,000	50:50
488 East 140th St.	3,000	3,000	50:50
490 East 140th St.	3,000	3,000	50:50
492 East 140th St.	3,000	3,000	50:50
494 East 140th St.	3,000	3,000	50:50
496 East 140th St.	3,000	3,000	50:50
498 East 140th St.	3,000	3,000	50:50
500 East 140th St.	3,000	3,000	50:50
502 East 140th St.	3,000	3,000	50:50
504 East 140th St.	4,500	3,000	60:40

GROUP B: PARCELS WHOSE TAXES WOULD BE DECREASED

Address	Assessed Values		Ratio
	Improvements	Land	
344 Willis Ave.	$4,000	$6,000	40:60
346 Willis Ave.	4,000	6,000	40:60
348 Willis Ave.	4,000	6,000	40:60
350 Willis Ave.	4,000	6,000	40:60
405 East 141st St.	1,400	2,200	39:61
407 East 141st St.	1,400	2,200	39:61
411 East 141st St.	3,800	3,000	56:44
413 East 141st St.	2,500	3,000	45:55
415 East 141st St.	2,500	3,000	45:55
417 East 141st St.	2,500	3,000	45:55
419 East 141st St.	2,500	3,000	45:55
421 East 141st St.	2,500	3,000	45:55
423 East 141st St.	2,700	3,300	45:55
425 East 141st St.	2,700	3,300	45:55
427 East 141st St.	2,700	3,300	45:55
429 East 141st St.	2,700	3,300	45:55
431 East 141st St.	2,700	3,300	45:55
433 East 141st St.	2,700	3,300	45:55
435 East 141st St.	2,700	3,300	45:55
437 East 141st St.	2,700	3,300	45:55
439 East 141st St.	2,700	3,300	45:55
441 East 141st St.	2,700	3,300	45:55
443 East 141st St.	2,700	3,300	45:55
445 East 141st St.	2,700	3,300	45:55
447 East 141st St.	2,700	3,300	45:55
449 East 141st St.	2,700	3,300	45:55
451 East 141st St.	2,700	3,300	45:55
453 East 141st St.	2,700	3,300	45:55
455 East 141st St.	2,700	3,300	45:55
457 East 141st St.	2,700	3,300	45:55
459 East 141st St.	2,700	3,300	45:55
461 East 141st St.	2,700	3,300	45:55
463 East 141st St.	2,700	3,400	44:56
465 East 141st St.	2,700	3,300	45:55
467 East 141st St.	2,700	3,300	45:55
469 East 141st St.	2,700	3,300	45:55
471 East 141st St.	2,700	3,300	45:55
473 East 141st St.	2,700	3,300	45:55
475 East 141st St.	2,700	3,300	45:55
477 East 141st St.	2,700	3,300	45:55
479 East 141st St.	2,700	3,300	45:55
481 East 141st St.	2,700	3,300	45:55
483 East 141st St.	2,700	3,300	45:55
485 East 141st St.	2,700	3,300	45:55
487 East 141st St.	2,700	3,300	45:55
489 East 141st St.	2,700	3,300	45:55
404 East 142nd St.	2,850	2,850	50:50
406 East 142nd St.	2,750	2,950	48:52
408 East 142nd St.	2,700	3,000	47:53
410 East 142nd St.	2,700	3,000	47:53
412 East 142nd St.	2,700	3,000	47:53
414 East 142nd St.	2,700	3,000	47:53
416 East 142nd St.	2,700	3,000	47:53
418 East 142nd St.	2,700	3,000	47:53
420 East 142nd St.	2,700	3,000	47:53
422 East 142nd St.	2,200	3,000	42:58
424 East 142nd St.	2,200	3,000	42:58
426 East 142nd St.	2,200	3,000	42:58
428 East 142nd St.	2,600	2,700	49:51
430 East 142nd St.	3,000	2,700	53:47
432 East 142nd St.	2,600	2,700	49:51
434 East 142nd St.	2,600	2,700	49:51
436 East 142nd St.	2,600	2,700	49:51
438 East 142nd St.	2,700	3,000	47:53

GROUP B: PARCELS WHOSE TAXES WOULD BE DECREASED

Address	Assessed Values		Ratio
	Improvements	Land	
440 East 142nd St.	$2,700	$3,000	47:53
442 East 142nd St.	2,700	3,000	47:53
444 East 142nd St.	2,700	3,000	47:53
446 East 142nd St.	2,700	3,000	47:53
448 East 142nd St.	2,700	3,000	47:53
450 East 142nd St.	2,700	3,000	47:53
452 East 142nd St.	2,700	3,000	47:53
454 East 142nd St.	2,700	3,000	47:53
456 East 142nd St.	2,600	3,100	46:54
458 East 142nd St.	2,600	3,100	46:54
460 East 142nd St.	2,600	3,100	46:54
462 East 142nd St.	2,600	3,100	46:54
464 East 142nd St.	2,600	3,100	46:54
468 East 142nd St.	2,600	3,100	46:54
470 East 142nd St.	2,600	3,100	46:54
472 East 142nd St.	2,600	3,100	46:54
474 East 142nd St.	2,600	3,100	46:54
476 East 142nd St.	2,500	3,200	44:56
478 East 142nd St.	2,500	3,200	44:56
480 East 142nd St.	2,500	3,200	44:56
482 East 142nd St.	2,500	3,200	44:56
484 East 142nd St.	2,500	3,200	44:56
486 East 142nd St.	2,500	3,200	44:56
488 East 142nd St.	2,500	3,200	44:56
490 East 142nd St.	2,500	3,200	44:56
492 East 142nd St.	2,500	3,200	44:56
494 East 142nd St.	2,500	3,200	44:56
496 East 142nd St.	2,500	3,200	44:56
498 East 142nd St.	2,500	3,100	45:55
— East 142nd St.	2,500	3,100	45:55
500 East 142nd St.	2,500	3,200	44:56
	$563,600	$609,500	

SAMPLE DISTRICT FROM ASSESSMENT SECTION TEN, BOROUGH OF THE BRONX

(Standard Composite Ratio: 38.71:61.29)

GROUP A: PARCELS WHOSE TAXES WOULD BE INCREASED

Address	Assessed Values		Ratio
	Improvements	Land	
1224 Union Ave.	$2,500	$5,000	33:67
1226 Union Ave.	2,500	5,000	33:67
1228 Union Ave.	2,500	5,000	33:67
1230 Union Ave.	2,500	5,000	33:67
1232 Union Ave.	2,500	5,000	33:67
1333 Prospect Ave.	3,300	6,700	33:67
—— East 156th St (S.S., bet. Kelly and Beck)	3,500	6,000	37:63
818 East 169th St.	2,200	3,500	38.6:61.4
822 East 169th St.	2,200	3,700	37:63
824 East 169th St.	2,200	3,600	38:62
826 East 169th St.	2,200	3,600	38:62
828 East 169th St.	2,200	3,500	38.6:61.4
	$30,300	$55,600	

GROUP B: PARCELS WHOSE TAXES WOULD BE DECREASED

Address	Assessed Values		Ratio
	Improvements	Land	
1234 Union Ave.	$2,200	$2,800	44:56
1236 Union Ave.	2,200	2,800	44:56
952 East 156th St.	5,000	4,000	56:44
953 East 156th St.	5,000	4,000	56:44
956 East 156th St.	5,000	4,000	56:44
957 East 156th St.	5,000	4,000	56:44
958 East 156th St.	5,000	4,000	56:44
959 East 156th St.	5,000	4,000	56:44
960 East 156th St.	5,000	4,000	56:44
961 East 156th St.	5,000	4,000	56:44
962 East 156th St.	5,000	4,000	56:44
963 East 156th St.	5,000	4,000	56:44
966 East 156th St.	5,000	4,000	56:44
967 East 156th St.	5,000	4,000	56:44
969 East 156th St.	7,500	6,000	56:44
811 East 168th St.	4,400	3,200	58:42
813 East 168th St.	4,400	3,200	58:42
815 East 168th St.	4,400	3,200	58:42
817 East 168th St.	4,400	3,200	58:42
819 East 168th St.	4,400	3,200	58:42
821 East 168th St.	4,400	3,200	58:42
802 East 169th St.	2,900	2,700	52:48
804 East 169th St.	2,900	2,600	53:47
806 East 169th St.	2,800	2,400	54:46
808 East 169th St.	2,800	3,300	46:54
810 East 169th St.	2,800	3,100	47:53
812 East 169th St.	2,800	2,900	49:51
814 East 169th St.	2,800	2,800	50:50
816 East 169th St.	2,800	3,000	48:52
820 East 169th St.	2,300	3,600	38.98:61.02
830 East 169th St.	2,200	3,300	40:60
— East 169th St.	7,000	6,500	52:48
1240 East 169th St.	4,100	5,900	41:59
712 Beck St.	5,000	3,200	58:42
714 Beck St.	5,000	3,200	58:42
716 Beck St.	5,000	3,200	58:42
718 Beck St.	5,000	3,200	58:42
719 Beck St.	5,000	3,500	59:41
720 Beck St.	5,000	3,200	58:42

GROUP B: PARCELS WHOSE TAXES WOULD BE DECREASED

Address	Assessed Values		Ratio
	Improvements	Land	
721 Beck St.	$5,000	$3,500	59:41
722 Beck St.	5,000	3,200	58:42
723 Beck St.	5,000	3,500	59:41
724 Beck St.	5,000	3,200	58:42
725 Beck St.	5,000	3,500	59:41
726 Beck St.	5,000	3,200	58:42
751 Beck St.	5,000	4,000	56:44
752 Beck St.	5,500	4,000	58:42
753 Beck St.	5,000	4,000	56:44
754 Beck St.	5,500	4,000	58:42
755 Beck St.	5,000	4,000	56:44
756 Beck St.	5,000	4,000	56:44
757 Beck St.	5,000	4,000	56:44
758 Beck St.	5,000	4,000	56:44
759 Beck St.	5,000	4,000	56:44
760 Beck St.	5,500	4,000	58:42
761 Beck St.	5,000	4,000	56:44
762 Beck St.	5,500	4,000	58:42
763 Beck St.	5,000	4,000	56:44
764 Beck St.	5,000	4,000	56:44
765 Beck St.	5,000	4,000	56:44
766 Beck St.	5,000	4,000	56:44
767 Beck St.	5,000	4,000	56:44
768 Beck St.	5,500	4,000	58:42
769 Beck St.	5,000	4,000	56:44
770 Beck St.	5,500	4,000	58:42
771 Beck St.	5,500	4,000	58:42
772 Beck St.	5,000	4,000	56:44
773 Beck St.	5,500	4,000	58:42
774 Beck St.	5,000	4,000	56:44
775 Beck St.	5,500	4,000	58:42
776 Beck St.	5,500	4,000	58:42
777 Beck St.	5,500	4,000	58:42
778 Beck St.	5,500	4,000	58:42
730 Kelly St.	8,000	4,500	64:36
732 Kelly St.	8,000	4,500	64:36
734 Kelly St.	6,000	4,500	57:43
736 Kelly St.	6,000	4,500	57:43
738 Kelly St.	5,500	4,500	55:45
740 Kelly St.	6,000	4,500	57:43
742 Kelly St.	4,500	4,500	50:50
744 Kelly St.	4,500	4,500	50:50
746 Kelly St.	4,500	4,500	50:50
748 Kelly St.	4,500	4,500	50:50
750 Kelly St.	5,000	4,500	53:47
752 Kelly St.	5,000	4,500	53:47
754 Kelly St.	8,000	4,500	64:36
756 Kelly St.	8,000	4,500	64:36
	$426,000	$395,500	

SAMPLE DISTRICT FROM ASSESSMENT SECTION ELEVEN, BOROUGH OF THE BRONX

(Standard Composite Ratio: 38.71:61.29)

GROUP A: PARCELS WHOSE TAXES WOULD BE INCREASED

Address	Assessed Values — Improvements	Assessed Values — Land	Ratio
1335 Findlay Ave.	$2,400	$5,600	30:70
1348 Teller Ave.	2,200	4,800	31:69
— Washington Ave. (E.S., 181-182d Sts.)	5,000	11,000	31:69
1234 Washington Ave.	1,700	2,800	38:62
2136 Washington Ave.	1,700	2,800	38:62
2138 Washington Ave.	1,700	2,800	38:62
2140 Washington Ave.	1,500	4,500	25:75
2146 Washington Ave.	1,900	4,600	29:71
2148-48½ Washington Ave.	1,600	6,900	19:81
2152 Washington Ave.	2,300	5,200	31:69
2156 Washington Ave.	2,700	4,800	36:64
2164 Washington Ave.	2,500	4,000	36:64
2166 Washington Ave.	2,500	4,000	38.46:61.54
2168 Washington Ave.	2,000	4,000	38.46:61.54
2172-74 Washington Ave.	3,000	8,000	27:73
2179 Washington Ave.	1,700	3,100	35:65
2181 Washington Ave.	1,700	3,300	34·66
2163 Bathgate Ave.	2,700	4,300	38.5:61.5
2165 Bathgate Ave.	2,700	4,300	38.5:61.5
2167 Bathgate Ave.	2,700	4,300	38.5:61.5
	$46,200	$95,100	

GROUP B: PARCELS WHOSE TAXES WOULD BE DECREASED

Address	Assessed Values — Improvements	Assessed Values — Land	Ratio
1300 Findlay Ave.	$4,900	$2,100	70:30
1302 Findlay Ave.	5,000	2,000	71:29
1304 Findlay Ave.	3,600	2,400	60:40
1306 Findlay Ave.	3,200	2,000	60:40
1308 Findlay Ave.	3,200	2,000	60:40
1310 Findlay Ave.	3,200	2,000	60:40
1312 Findlay Ave.	3,200	2,000	60:40
1314 Findlay Ave.	3,500	2,500	58:42
1316 Findlay Ave.	3,500	2,500	58:42
1318 Findlay Ave.	3,000	2,000	60:40
1320 Findlay Ave.	3,000	2,000	60:40
1322 Findlay Ave.	3,000	2,000	60:40
1324 Findlay Ave.	3,000	2,000	60:40
1326 Findlay Ave.	3,500	2,500	60:40
1304 Teller Ave.	2,400	1,600	60:40
1306 Teller Ave.	2,400	1,600	60:40
1308 Teller Ave.	2,400	1,600	60:40
1310 Teller Ave.	2,400	1,600	60:40
1312 Teller Ave.	2,400	1,600	60:40
1314 Teller Ave.	2,400	1,600	60:40
1315 Teller Ave.	3,300	2,200	60:40
1316 Teller Ave.	2,400	1,600	60:40
1317 Teller Ave.	3,300	2,200	60:40
1318 Teller Ave.	2,400	1,600	60:40
1319 Teller Ave.	4,300	2,700	61:39
1320 Teller Ave.	2,400	1,600	60:40
1322 Teller Ave.	3,600	2,400	66:34
1323-25 Teller Ave.	9,900	6,100	62:38
1324 Teller Ave.	3,400	2,400	60:40
1326 Teller Ave.	3,400	1,600	60:40

Group B: Parcels Whose Taxes Would Be Decreased

Address	Assessed Values Improvements	Assessed Values Land	Ratio
1327 Teller Ave.	$4,200	$2,800	60:40
1328 Teller Ave.	3,400	1,600	60:40
1329 Teller Ave.	4,200	2,800	60:40
1330 Teller Ave.	3,400	1,600	60:40
—— Teller Ave.	5,700	2,800	67:33
1332 Teller Ave.	3,600	2,400	60:40
—— Teller Ave.	5,700	2,800	67:33
1334 Teller Ave.	2,400	1,600	60:40
—— Teller Ave.	5,700	2,800	67:33
1336 Teller Ave.	2,400	1,600	60:40
—— Teller Ave.	4,700	2,800	63:37
1338 Teller Ave.	2,400	1,600	60:40
1340 Teller Ave.	2,100	2,400	47:53
1342 Teller Ave.	4,100	2,400	63:37
1346 Teller Ave.	4,600	2,400	66:34
1354 Teller Ave.	6,100	2,400	72:28
1356 Teller Ave.	6,100	2,400	72:28
1358 Teller Ave.	3,300	2,400	58:42
1360 Teller Ave.	6,600	2,400	73:27
1364 Teller Ave.	3,100	2,400	56:44
1366 Teller Ave.	2,400	1,600	60:40
1368 Teller Ave.	2,400	1,600	60:40
1369 Teller Ave.	3,000	3,000	50:50
1370 Teller Ave.	2,400	1,600	60:40
1371 Teller Ave.	3,000	3,000	50:50
1372 Teller Ave.	2,800	2,400	54:46
1373 Teller Ave.	3,000	3,000	50:50
1374 Teller Ave.	2,100	2,400	47:53
1379 Teller Ave.	5,500	2,500	69:31
—— Teller Ave.	5,800	7,200	45:55
1386 Teller Ave.	2,600	1,400	65:35
1388 Teller Ave.	4,800	2,700	64:36
351 East 169th St.	6,200	3,300	65:35
353 East 169th St.	3,300	2,200	60:40
355 East 169th St.	3,300	2,200	60:40
357 East 169th St.	3,300	2,200	60:40
359 East 169th St.	3,300	2,200	60:40
361 East 169th St.	3,300	2,200	60:40
363 East 169th St.	3,300	2,200	60:40
365 East 169th St.	3,300	2,200	60:40
367 East 169th St.	3,300	2,200	60:40
392 East 170th St.	4,700	1,300	78:22
394 East 170th St.	4,700	1,300	78:22
396 East 170th St.	4,800	2,700	64:36
1291-95 Clay Ave.	9,000	9,000	50:50
1297 Clay Ave.	3,000	3,000	50:50
1299 Clay Ave.	3,300	2,200	60:40
1301 Clay Ave.	3,200	2,300	58:42
1303 Clay Ave.	3,200	2,300	58:42
1305 Clay Ave.	4,200	2,300	65:35
1307 Clay Ave.	4,300	2,200	66:34
1309 Clay Ave.	4,200	2,300	65:35
1311 Clay Ave.	3,000	3,000	50:50
1315 Clay Ave.	2,500	3,000	45:55
1317 Clay Ave.	2,100	1,900	53:47
1319 Clay Ave.	2,100	1,900	53:47
1321 Clay Ave.	2,100	1,900	53:47
1323 Clay Ave.	2,500	2,800	47:53
1325 Clay Ave.	2,700	2,800	49:51
1327 Clay Ave.	2,300	1,900	55:45
1329 Clay Ave.	2,100	1,900	52:48
1331 Clay Ave.	2,100	1,900	52:48
1337 Clay Ave.	3,200	2,800	53:47
1339 Clay Ave.	3,200	2,800	53:47

GROUP B: PARCELS WHOSE TAXES WOULD BE DECREASED

Address	Assessed Values		Ratio
	Improvements	Land	
1341 Clay Ave.	$2,100	$1,900	53:47
1343 Clay Ave.	2,100	1,900	53:47
1345 Clay Ave.	2,100	1,900	53:47
1347 Clay Ave.	2,100	1,900	53:47
1349-51 Clay Ave.	4,400	3,600	55:45
1353 Clay Ave.	3,200	2,700	54:46
1355 Clay Ave.	3,200	2,700	54:46
1357 Clay Ave.	2,800	2,700	51:49
1359 Clay Ave.	2,800	2,700	51:49
1361 Clay Ave.	2,800	2,700	46:54
1363 Clay Ave.	2,200	1,800	55:45
1365 Clay Ave.	2,200	1,800	55:45
1367 Clay Ave.	2,200	1,800	55:45
1369 Clay Ave.	4,700	2,800	63:37
1371 Clay Ave.	4,700	2,800	60:40
1377 Clay Ave.	4,500	2,000	69:31
1379 Clay Ave.	4,500	2,000	69:31
1381 Clay Ave.	4,500	2,000	69:31
1383 Clay Ave.	5,200	1,800	74:26
1385 Clay Ave.	4,000	2,000	67:33
1387 Clay Ave.	4,000	2,000	67:33
182nd St. (S.S., Washington to Bathgate).	4,700	2,000	70:30
	4,500	2,000	69:31
	4,200	2,000	68:32
	4,200	1,800	70:30
2132 Washington Ave.	3,700	3,800	49:51
2150 Washington Ave.	3,500	5,000	41:59
2158 Washington Ave.	2,700	3,800	42:58
2160 Washington Ave.	2,700	3,800	42:58
2162 Washington Ave.	2,600	3,900	40:60
2176 Washington Ave.	4,100	2,900	59:41
2178 Washington Ave.	4,100	2,900	57:43
2180 Washington Ave.	4,000	3,000	56:44
2182 Washington Ave.	4,000	3,200	51:49
2153 Bathgate Ave.	6,000	6,000	50:50
2155 Bathgate Ave.	2,000	3,000	40:60
2157 Bathgate Ave.	2,000	3,000	40:60
2159 Bathgate Ave.	2,000	3,000	40:60
2161 Bathgate Ave.	2,000	3,000	40:60
2169 Bathgate Ave.	5,200	4,300	55:45
2171 Bathgate Ave.	3,200	4,300	43:57
2173 Bathgate Ave.	3,200	4,300	43:57
2175 Bathgate Ave.	4,000	5,000	44:56
2177 Bathgate Ave.	4,000	6,000	40:60
	$486,000	$370,700	

SAMPLE DISTRICT FROM ASSESSMENT SECTION TWELVE, BOROUGH OF THE BRONX

(The district consists of parts of assessments blocks:
    3294—between Bainbridge and Briggs avenues and between East 194th and East 196th streets—;
    3298—between Bainbridge and Briggs avenues and between Bedford Park Boulevard and East 201st Street—; and
    3299—between Perry and Briggs avenues and between Mosholu Parkway South and East 201st Street.)

(Standard Composite Ratio: 38.71:61.29)

GROUP A: PARCELS WHOSE TAXES WOULD BE INCREASED

Address	Assessed Values		Ratio
	Improvements	Land	
265 Bedford Park Boulevard	$5,500	$11,500	32:68
Briggs Ave. E.S., bet. Bedford Park Blvd. and E. 201st St.			
G. Goldberg	3,200	6,600	33:67
James Wilson	3,400	6,600	34:66
Bainbridge Ave. (W.S., bet. Bedford Park Blvd. and E. 201st St.)			
Cath. McCormack	3,200	3,200	32:68
	$15,300	$27,900	

GROUP B: PARCELS WHOSE TAXES WOULD BE DECREASED

Address	Assessed Values		Ratio
	Improvements	Land	
2654 Briggs Ave.	$3,500	$2,500	58:42
—— Briggs Ave.	3,500	2,300	60:40
—— Briggs Ave.	3,500	2,300	60:40
—— Briggs Ave.	3,500	2,300	60:40
—— Briggs Ave.	3,500	2,300	60:40
—— Briggs Ave.	3,500	2,300	60:40
—— Briggs Ave.	3,500	2,300	60:40
—— Briggs Ave.	5,800	2,300	72:28
—— Briggs Ave.	5,800	2,300	72:28
—— Briggs Ave.	5,800	2,300	72:28
—— Briggs Ave.	5,800	2,300	72:28
—— Briggs Ave.	5,800	2,300	72:28
—— Briggs Ave.	5,800	2,300	72:28
—— Briggs Ave.	5,800	2,300	72:28
—— Briggs Ave.	5,800	2,300	72:29
—— Briggs Ave.	5,800	2,300	72:28
2686 Briggs Ave.	5,800	2,400	71:29
2958 Briggs Ave.	3,300	3,000	55:45
—— Briggs Ave.	3,300	3,000	55:45
2962 Briggs Ave.	4,400	6,600	40:60
—— Briggs Ave.	4,200	3,300	56:44
2972 Briggs Ave.	5,500	3,300	62:38
—— Briggs Ave.	4,200	3,300	56:44
2976 Briggs Ave.	5,400	6,600	40:60
2984 Briggs Ave.	4,000	3,300	55:45
2655 Bainbridge Ave.	3,700	2,700	58:42
—— Bainbridge Ave.	3,700	2,700	58:42
—— Bainbridge Ave.	3,700	2,700	58:42
—— Bainbridge Ave.	3,700	2,700	58:42
—— Bainbridge Ave.	3,700	2,700	58:42
—— Bainbridge Ave.	3,700	2,700	58:42
—— Bainbridge Ave.	3,700	2,700	58:42
—— Bainbridge Ave.	3,700	2,700	58:42
—— Bainbridge Ave.	5,000	2,700	64:36
2671 Bainbridge Ave.	6,100	2,700	69:31
2673 Bainbridge Ave.	5,600	2,700	67:33
2677 Bainbridge Ave.	5,000	2,700	65:35

GROUP B: PARCELS WHOSE TAXES WOULD BE DECREASED

Address	Assessed Values		Ratio
	Improvements	Land	
2679 Bainbridge Ave.	$5,000	$2,800	64:36
2681 Bainbridge Ave.	5,000	2,800	64:36
—— Bainbridge Ave.	3,500	2,800	56:44
—— Bainbridge Ave.	5,800	3,600	62:38
—— Bainbridge Ave.	5,800	3,600	62:38
—— Bainbridge Ave.	7,500	7,200	51:49
2951 Bainbridge Ave.	6,400	3,600	64:36
—— Bainbridge Ave.	8,000	3,600	69:31
—— Bainbridge Ave.	6,300	7,200	47:53
—— Bainbridge Ave.	3,500	3,300	51:49
—— Bainbridge Ave.	3,600	3,200	53:47
—— Bainbridge Ave.	6,700	4,800	58:42
—— Bainbridge Ave.	6,700	4,800	58:42
—— Bainbridge Ave.	6,700	4,800	58:42
—— Bainbridge Ave.	4,800	3,200	60:40
—— Bainbridge Ave.	4,800	3,200	60:40
267 Bedford Park Boulevard	9,000	9,000	50:50
—— East 201st St.	7,500	6,000	56:44
—— East 201st St.	4,000	2,700	60:40
—— East 201st St.	4,800	2,700	64:36
—— East 201st St.	3,500	2,700	56:44
—— East 201st St.	3,500	2,700	56:44
—— East 201st St.	3,500	2,700	56:44
—— East 201st St.	4,500	7,000	39:61
—— East 201st St.	4,400	3,600	55:45
311 East 201st St.	5,000	3,100	62:38
—— East 201st St.	5,000	3,000	63:37
—— East 201st St.	5,000	3,100	62:38
317 East 201st St.	6,500	6,000	52:48
—— East 201st St.	3,400	2,600	57:43
—— East 201st St.	3,400	2,200	61:39
—— East 201st St.	3,400	2,200	61:39
—— East 201st St.	3,200	3,600	47:53
—— East 201st St.	3,700	3,600	51:49
—— East 201st St.	3,000	2,700	53:47
—— East 201st St.	5,000	6,000	45:55
302 Mosholu Parkway	7,000	6,000	54:46
—— Mosholu Parkway	6,000	8,500	41:59
—— Mosholu Parkway	7,000	6,500	52:48
314 Mosholu Parkway	7,000	6,200	53:47
—— Mosholu Parkway	11,000	10,000	52:48
2999 Perry Ave.	7,300	4,200	63:37
3003 Perry Ave.	8,200	8,800	48:52
	$403,000	$296,100	

SAMPLE DISTRICT FROM ASSESSMENT SECTION FIFTEEN, BOROUGH OF THE BRONX

(The district consists of parts of assessment blocks:
4048—between Rhinelander and Morris Park avenues and between Unionport Road, Victor and Amethyst streets—;
4051—between Rhinelander and Morris Park avenues and between Cruger and Holland avenues.)

(Standard Composite Ratio: 38.71:61.29)

GROUP A: PARCELS WHOSE TAXES WOULD BE INCREASED

None

GROUP B: PARCELS WHOSE TAXES WOULD BE DECREASED

Address	Assessed Values Improvements	Land	Ratio
Mead St.	$1,900	$1,800	51:49
Mead St.	3,300	1,200	73:27
Mead St.	1,700	1,450	54:46
Mead St.	2,500	1,200	68:32
Mead St.	4,000	1,200	77:23
Mead St.	4,000	1,200	77:23
Mead St.	4,000	1,200	77:23
Mead St.	3,300	1,200	73:27
Mead St.	3,300	1,200	71:29
Mead St.	3,300	1,200	71:29
Mead St.	1,600	1,200	57:43
Mead St.	2,200	1,200	73:27
Mead St.	2,200	1,200	73:27
Unionport Road	2,800	1,600	64:36
Unionport Road	2,700	1,600	63:37
Unionport Road	1,500	1,600	48:52
Unionport Road	3,000	2,500	55:45
Unionport Road	2,600	1,200	68:32
Baker Ave.	3,000	1,200	71:29
Baker Ave.	3,400	1,200	74:26
Baker Ave.	3,400	1,200	74:26
Baker Ave.	1,400	1,200	54:46
Baker Ave.	4,200	1,200	78:22
Baker Ave.	4,200	1,200	78:22
Baker Ave.	2,000	1,200	62:38
Baker Ave.	3,200	1,200	73:27
Baker Ave.	2,800	1,200	70:30
Baker Ave.	2,800	1,200	70:30
Baker Ave.	2,800	1,200	70:30
Baker Ave.	2,800	1,200	70:30
Baker Ave.	2,800	1,200	70:30
Baker Ave.	7,000	1,800	80:20
Morris Park Ave.	4,800	5,200	50:50
Morris Park Ave.	3,500	3,500	50:50
Morris Park Ave.	5,100	2,900	64:36
Morris Park Ave.	1,500	1,900	44:56
Morris Park Ave.	1,500	1,900	44:56
Morris Park Ave.	1,500	1,900	44:56
Morris Park Ave.	4,000	2,900	58:42
Morris Park Ave.	4,900	4,300	53:47
Morris Park Ave.	6,500	2,500	72:28
Morris Park Ave.	11,000	3,500	76:24
Amethyst St.	2,500	1,000	65:35
Amethyst St.	3,200	1,100	74:26
Amethyst St.	3,200	1,100	74:26
Amethyst St.	3,200	1,100	74:26
Amethyst St.	3,800	1,200	76:24
Amethyst St.	3,200	1,200	73:27
Amethyst St.	3,000	1,200	71:29
Amethyst St.	3,800	1,200	76:24
Amethyst St.	4,000	1,200	77:23
Amethyst St.	3,200	1,200	73:27
Amethyst St.	3,200	1,200	73:27

Group B: Parcels Whose Taxes Would Be Decreased

Address	Assessed Values — Improvements	Assessed Values — Land	Ratio
Amethyst St.	$3,200	$1,200	73:27
Amethyst St.	3,200	1,200	73:27
Amethyst St.	3,200	1,800	64:36
Rhinelander Ave.	3,200	1,000	76:24
Rhinelander Ave.	3,200	1,000	76:24
Rhinelander Ave.	3,000	1,000	75:25
Rhinelander Ave.	3,700	1,000	73:27
Rhinelander Ave.	1,300	1,200	52:48
Victor St.	2,700	1,700	61:39
Victor St.	2,200	1,200	73:27
Victor St.	2,200	1,200	73:27
Victor St.	2,200	1,200	73:27
Victor St.	2,200	1,200	73:27
Victor St.	2,200	1,200	73:27
Victor St.	2,800	1,200	70:30
Victor St.	3,200	1,200	73:27
Victor St.	3,200	1,200	73:27
Victor St.	3,200	1,200	73:27
Victor St.	3,200	1,200	73:27
Victor St.	3,500	1,400	71:29
Victor St.	2,000	1,500	57:43
Cruger Ave.	3,000	1,200	71:29
Cruger Ave.	1,800	1,200	60:40
Cruger Ave.	3,000	1,200	71:29
Cruger Ave.	2,800	1,200	70:30
Cruger Ave.	3,200	1,200	73:27
Cruger Ave.	3,200	1,200	73:27
Cruger Ave.	3,300	1,200	73:27
Cruger Ave.	3,300	1,200	73:27
Cruger Ave.	3,300	1,200	73:27
Cruger Ave.	3,300	1,200	73:27
Cruger Ave.	3,300	1,200	73:27
Cruger Ave.	3,300	1,200	73:27
Cruger Ave.	3,300	1,200	73:27
Cruger Ave.	3,300	1,200	73:27
Cruger Ave.	3,200	1,200	73:27
Cruger Ave.	3,200	1,200	73:27
Cruger Ave.	3,200	1,200	73:27
Cruger Ave.	3,200	1,150	74:26
Cruger Ave.	3,200	1,150	74:26
Cruger Ave.	3,200	1,000	76:24
Cruger Ave.	3,200	900	78:22
Holland Ave.	3,200	1,200	73:27
Holland Ave.	3,200	1,200	73:27
Holland Ave.	3,200	1,200	73:27
Holland Ave.	3,200	1,200	73:27
Holland Ave.	3,200	1,200	73:27
Holland Ave.	3,400	1,200	74:26
Holland Ave.	3,400	1,200	74:26
Holland Ave.	3,400	1,200	74:26
Holland Ave.	3,200	1,200	73:27
Holland Ave.	3,200	1,200	73:27
Holland Ave.	3,000	1,200	71:29
Holland Ave.	3,000	1,200	71:29
Holland Ave.	3,000	1,200	71:29
Holland Ave.	3,000	1,200	71:29
Holland Ave.	1,800	1,200	60:40
Holland Ave.	2,900	1,200	71:29
Holland Ave.	3,100	1,200	72:28
Holland Ave.	3,000	1,200	71:29
Holland Ave.	3,100	1,200	72:28
Holland Ave.	3,300	1,200	66:34
Holland Ave.	3,500	1,200	74:26
Holland Ave.	3,500	1,200	74:26
	$369,100	$162,550	

SAMPLE DISTRICT FROM ASSESSMENT SECTION SEVENTEEN, BOROUGH OF THE BRONX

(The district consists of parts of assessment blocks:
- 4837—between White Plains Road and Barnes Avenue and between East 223rd and East 224th streets—;
- 4838—between White Plains Road and Barnes Avenue and between East 224th and East 225th streets—;
- 4847—between Barnes and Bronxwood avenues and between East 222d and East 223rd streets—; and
- 4848—between Barnes and Bronxwood avenues and between East 223rd and 224th streets.)

(*Standard Composite Ratio: 38.71:61.29*)

GROUP A: PARCELS WHOSE TAXES WOULD BE INCREASED

Address	Assessed Values		Ratio
	Improvements	Land	
East 224th St.	$1,400	$5,100	22:78
East 224th St.	1,400	4,800	23:77
White Plains Road	2,900	7,500	28:72
White Plains Road	2,900	5,500	35:65
East 222d St.	1,300	2,200	37:63
Barnes Ave.	1,800	2,900	38.298:61.702
East 223d St.	1,000	1,800	36:64
East 223d St.	800	1,800	31:69
	$13,500	$31,600	

GROUP B: PARCELS WHOSE TAXES WOULD BE DECREASED

Address	Assessed Values		Ratio
	Improvements	Land	
Barnes Ave.	$5,200	$1,600	76·24
Barnes Ave.	10,000	3,500	74:26
East 223d St.	4,350	1,050	81:19
East 223d St.	4,400	1,000	81:19
East 223d St.	4,350	1,050	81:19
East 223d St.	4,350	1,050	81:19
East 223d St.	4,350	1,050	81:19
East 223d St.	4,350	1,050	81:19
East 223d St.	3,600	1,100	77:23
East 223d St.	4,100	2,200	65:35
East 223d St.	4,000	1,200	77:23
East 223d St.	3,700	1,200	76:24
East 223d St.	3,800	2,700	58:42
East 223d St.	2,200	2,000	52:48
East 223d St.	2,200	1,000	69:31
East 223d St.	2,600	1,000	72:28
East 223d St.	900	1,000	47:53
East 223d St.	800	900	47:53
East 223d St.	3,600	900	80:20
East 223d St.	1,600	900	64:36
East 223d St.	2,700	900	75·25
East 223d St.	1,800	900	67:33
East 223d St.	1,800	1,800	50:50
East 223d St.	1,800	2,700	40:60
East 223d St.	2,500	900	74:26
East 223d St.	3,000	2,700	53:47
East 223d St.	3,400	1,000	77:23
East 223d St.	3,400	1,000	77:23
East 223d St.	3,400	1,000	77:23
East 223d St.	3,400	1,000	77:23
East 223d St.	3,600	1,000	78:22
East 223d St.	3,600	1,000	78:22
East 223d St.	3,400	1,000	77:23

GROUP B: PARCELS WHOSE TAXES WOULD BE DECREASED

Address	Assessed Values		Ratio
	Improvements	Land	
East 224th St.	$4,500	$1,200	79:21
East 224th St.	2,100	1,200	64:36
East 224th St.	2,100	2,400	47:53
East 224th St.	2,600	1,100	70:30
East 224th St.	2,100	1,100	66:34
East 224th St.	2,500	1,100	69:31
East 224th St.	3,700	1,100	77:23
East 224th St.	3,700	1,100	77:23
East 224th St.	3,700	1,100	77:23
East 224th St.	3,700	1,100	77:23
East 224th St.	2,100	800	72:28
East 224th St.	2,100	800	72:28
East 224th St.	2,100	800	72:28
East 224th St.	2,100	800	72:28
East 224th St.	3,600	1,200	75:25
East 224th St.	2,200	1,200	65:35
East 224th St.	2,200	1,200	65:35
East 224th St.	2,200	1,200	65:35
East 224th St.	4,200	5,100	45:55
East 224th St.	1,800	1,000	64:36
East 224th St.	4,000	1,000	80:20
East 224th St.	3,000	1,800	62:38
East 224th St.	3,300	1,200	73:27
East 224th St.	2,200	1,200	65:35
East 224th St.	2,200	1,200	65:35
East 224th St.	2,800	1,200	70:30
East 224th St.	2,800	1,200	70:30
East 224th St.	2,700	1,700	61:39
White Plains Road	2,700	2,700	50:50
East 225th St.	1,600	2,400	40:60
East 225th St.	3,000	1,200	71:29
East 225th St.	3,000	1,200	71:29
East 225th St.	3,550	1,250	67:33
East 225th St.	4,200	1,100	79:21
East 225th St.	4,200	1,100	79:21
East 225th St.	4,200	1,100	79:21
East 225th St.	4,200	1,100	79:21
East 225th St.	4,400	1,100	80:20
East 222nd St.	5,400	1,700	76:24
East 222nd St.	3,600	1,000	78:22
East 222nd St.	3,600	1,000	78:22
East 222nd St.	7,100	2,200	76:24
East 222nd St.	2,100	1,100	66:34
East 222nd St.	1,800	2,200	45:55
East 222nd St.	10,800	3,600	75:25
East 222nd St.	3,600	1,200	75:25
	$263,600	$109,700	

III. BROOKLYN

SAMPLE DISTRICT FROM ASSESSMENT SECTION FIVE, BOROUGH OF BROOKLYN

(Standard Composite Ratio: 39.44 : 60.56)

GROUP A: PARCELS WHOSE TAXES WOULD BE INCREASED

Address	Assessed Values		Ratio
	Improvements	Land	
01 Troy Ave.	$1,250	$2,850	30:70
03 Troy Ave.	525	1,875	22:78
05 Troy Ave.	1,100	2,100	36:64
13 Troy Ave.	500	1,800	22:78
	$3,375	$8,625	

GROUP B: PARCELS WHOSE TAXES WOULD BE DECREASED

Address	Assessed Values		Ratio
	Improvements	Land	
27 Albany Ave.	$7,800	$3,200	71:29
29 Albany Ave.	3,650	1,650	69:31
31 Albany Ave.	3,350	1,650	67:33
33 Albany Ave.	3,350	1,650	67:33
35 Albany Ave.	3,350	1,650	67:33
37 Albany Ave.	3,350	1,650	67:33
39 Albany Ave.	3,350	1,650	67:33
41 Albany Ave.	3,350	1,650	67:33
43 Albany Ave.	3,350	1,650	67:33
45 Albany Ave.	3,350	1,650	67:33
47 Albany Ave.	3,350	1,650	67:33
49 Albany Ave.	3,350	1,650	67:33
51 Albany Ave.	3,350	1,650	67:33
53 Albany Ave.	6,100	3,200	66:34
00 Park Place	4,400	2,500	64:36
02 Park Place	3,800	1,500	72:28
04 Park Place	3,800	1,500	72:28
08 Park Place	3,800	1,500	72:28
10-12 Park Place	6,000	2,300	72:28
12 Park Place	5,800	1,500	79:21
14 Park Place	5,700	1,600	78:22
16 Park Place	5,700	1,500	79:21
18 Park Place	5,700	1,500	79:21
20 Park Place	5,700	1,500	79:21
22 Park Place	5,700	1,500	79:21
174 Park Place	3,150	2,050	61:39
176 Park Place	3,150	2,050	61:39
178 Park Place	3,150	2,050	61:39
190 Park Place	3,900	2,100	71:29
192 Park Place	3,900	2,100	71:29
196 Park Place	3,900	2,100	71:29
198 Park Place	3,900	2,100	71:29
200 Park Place	3,900	2,100	71:29
202 Park Place	2,500	2,000	56:44
204 Park Place	2,500	2,000	56:44
206 Park Place	2,500	2,000	56:44
208 Park Place	2,500	2,000	56:44
210 Park Place	2,500	2,000	56:44
212 Park Place	2,500	2,000	56:44
214 Park Place	2,500	2,000	56:44
216 Park Place	2,500	2,000	56:44
218 Park Place	2,500	2,000	56:44
220 Park Place	2,500	2,000	56:44
222 Park Place	2,500	2,000	56:44

Group B: Parcels Whose Taxes Would Be Decreased

Address	Assessed Values		Ratio
	Improvements	Land	
1224 Park Place	$2,500	$2,000	56:44
1226 Park Place	2,500	2,000	56:44
1228 Park Place	2,500	2,000	56:44
1230 Park Place	2,500	2,000	56:44
1232 Park Place	2,500	2,000	56:44
1254 Park Place	3,850	1,950	66:34
1256 Park Place	3,850	1,950	66:34
1258 Park Place	3,850	1,950	66:34
1262 Park Place	3,850	1,950	66:34
1264 Park Place	3,850	1,950	66:34
1266 Park Place	3,850	1,950	66:34
1268 Park Place	3,850	1,950	66:34
1270 Park Place	3,850	1,950	66:34
1272 Park Place	3,850	1,950	66:34
1274 Park Place	3,850	1,950	66:34
1278 Park Place	3,850	1,950	66:34
1280 Park Place	4,050	1,950	67:33
1282 Park Place	3,050	1,750	70:30
1282* Park Place	3,950	1,850	68:32
1288 Park Place	3,850	1,750	68:32
1290 Park Place	3,700	1,800	67:33
1292 Park Place	3,650	1,950	65:35
1294 Park Place	3,650	1,950	65:35
1296 Park Place	3,650	1,950	65:35
1298 Park Place	3,650	1,950	65:35
1300 Park Place	3,700	1,900	66:34
1302 Park Place	3,750	1,850	67:33
1304 Park Place	3,750	1,850	67:33
1308 Park Place	3,800	1,800	68:32
1310 Park Place	3,850	1,750	69:31
1312 Park Place	3,900	1,700	70:30
1203 Sterling Place	1,950	1,450	57:43
1205 Sterling Place	1,800	1,700	51:49
1207 Sterling Place	1,950	1,450	57:43
1209 Sterling Place	1,950	1,450	57:43
1211 Sterling Place	1,950	1,450	57:43
1215 Sterling Place	2,550	2,050	55:45
1217 Sterling Place	2,550	2,050	55:45
1219 Sterling Place	2,550	2,050	55:45
1221 Sterling Place	2,550	2,050	55:45
1223 Sterling Place	2,550	2,050	55:45
1225 Sterling Place	2,550	2,050	55:45
1227 Sterling Place	1,480	1,150	56:44
1229 Sterling Place	2,550	2,050	55:45
1231 Sterling Place	2,550	2,050	55:45
1233 Sterling Place	2,550	2,050	55:45
1235 Sterling Place	2,350	1,950	55:45
1237 Sterling Place	2,350	1,950	55:45
1239 Sterling Place	2,350	1,950	55:45
1241 Sterling Place	2,350	1,950	55:45
1243 Sterling Place	2,350	1,950	55:45
1245 Sterling Place	2,350	1,950	55:45
1247 Sterling Place	2,350	1,950	55:45
1249 Sterling Place	2,350	1,950	55:45
1251 Sterling Place	2,350	1,950	55:45
1253 Sterling Place	2,350	1,950	55:45
1255 Sterling Place	2,350	1,950	55:45
1257 Sterling Place	2,350	1,950	55:45
1259 Sterling Place	2,350	1,950	55:45
1261 Sterling Place	2,350	1,950	55:45
1263 Sterling Place	2,350	1,950	55:45
1289 Sterling Place	3,800	1,800	68:32

* Thus in record.

GROUP B: PARCELS WHOSE TAXES WOULD BE DECREASED

Address	Assessed Values		Ratio
	Improvements	Land	
1291 Sterling Place	$3,800	$1,800	68:32
1293 Sterling Place	3,800	1,800	68:32
1295 Sterling Place	3,800	1,800	68:32
1297 Sterling Place	3,800	1,800	68:32
1299 Sterling Place	3,800	1,800	68:32
1301 Sterling Place	3,800	1,800	68:32
1303 Sterling Place	3,800	1,800	68:32
1307 Sterling Place	3,800	1,800	68:32
1309 Sterling Place	3,800	1,800	68:32
1311 Sterling Place	3,800	1,800	68:32
1313 Sterling Place	4,000	1,600	71:29
1315 Sterling Place	4,000	1,600	71:29
1319 Sterling Place	4,000	1,800	69:31
1321 Sterling Place	4,050	1,750	70:30
1323 Sterling Place	4,050	1,750	70:30
1325 Sterling Place	4,000	1,800	69:31
1327 Sterling Place	4,000	1,800	69:31
1329 Sterling Place	4,000	1,800	69:31
1331 Sterling Place	3,975	1,825	69:31
1333 Sterling Place	3,950	1,850	68:32
1335 Sterling Place	3,925	1,875	68:32
1337 Sterling Place	4,200	2,900	59:41
1343 Sterling Place	3,950	1,950	67:33
1345 Sterling Place	3,950	1,850	68:32
1347 Sterling Place	3,950	1,850	68:32
204 Troy Ave	2,400	2,500	49:51
206 Troy Ave	2,500	1,200	62.5:37.5
206a Troy Ave	2,300	1,200	66:34
207 Troy Ave	6,025	1,875	76:24
208 Troy Ave	2,300	1,200	66:34
210 Troy Ave	2,300	1,200	66:34
211 Troy Ave	2,550	1,950	57:43
212 Troy Ave	2,300	1,200	66:34
214 Troy Ave	2,300	1,200	66:34
216 Troy Ave	2,300	1,200	66:34
218 Troy Ave	2,300	1,200	66:34
220 Troy Ave	2,300	1,200	66:34
222 Troy Ave	2,300	1,200	66:34
224 Troy Ave	2,300	1,200	66:34
226 Troy Ave	2,300	1,200	66:34
228 Troy Ave	2,500	1,200	62.5:37.5
230 Troy Ave	3,500	2,500	58:42
	$471,555	$271,025	

SAMPLE DISTRICT FROM ASSESSMENT SECTION SIX, BOROUGH OF BROOKLYN

(Standard Composite Ratio: 39.44:60.56)

GROUP A: PARCELS WHOSE TAXES WOULD BE INCREASED

Address	Assessed Values		Ratio
	Improvements	Land	
336 McDonough St.	$1,900	$8,100	19:81
338 McDonough St.	3,200	8,100	28:72
406-10 McDonough St.	2,850	6,250	31:69
333 Decatur St.	1,675	3,125	35:65
339 Decatur St.	1,500	2,500	37.5:62.5
343 Decatur St.	1,500	2,500	37.5:62.5
345 Decatur St.	1,500	2,500	37.5:62.5
	$14,125	$33,075	

GROUP B: PARCELS WHOSE TAXES WOULD BE DECREASED

Address	Assessed Values		Ratio
	Improvements	Land	
298 McDonough St.	$10,750	$6,750	61:39
300 McDonough St.	7,125	2,575	74:26
302 McDonough St.	7,125	2,575	74:26
304 McDonough St.	7,500	2,700	74:26
306 McDonough St.	6,025	2,175	74:26
308 McDonough St.	7,125	2,575	73:27
310 McDonough St.	7,125	2,575	73:27
312 McDonough St.	7,125	2,575	73:27
314 McDonough St.	7,125	2,575	73:27
316 McDonough St.	7,300	2,700	73:27
318 McDonough St.	6,825	2,575	73:27
320 McDonough St.	6,825	2,575	73:27
322 McDonough St.	6,825	2,575	73:27
324 McDonough St.	6,825	2,575	73:27
326 McDonough St.	6,825	2,575	73:27
328 McDonough St.	6,825	2,575	73:27
330 McDonough St.	6,825	2,575	73:27
332 McDonough St.	6,825	2,575	72:28
344 McDonough St.	5,300	2,700	66:34
346 McDonough St.	5,300	2,700	66:34
348 McDonough St.	5,300	2,700	66:34
350 McDonough St.	5,400	2,700	67:33
362 McDonough St.	7,375	2,625	74:26
364 McDonough St.	7,375	2,625	74:26
366 McDonough St.	7,375	2,625	74:26
368 McDonough St.	7,375	2,625	74:26
370 McDonough St.	7,375	2,625	74:26
372 McDonough St.	14,800	5,200	74:26
374 McDonough St.	5,350	2,250	70:30
376 McDonough St.	5,350	2,250	70:30
378 McDonough St.	5,350	2,250	70:30
380 McDonough St.	5,475	2,325	70:30
382 McDonough St.	5,475	2,325	70:30
384 McDonough St.	5,475	2,325	70:30
386 McDonough St.	5,675	2,375	70:30
400 McDonough St.	3,825	2,075	65:35
400a McDonough St.	3,825	2,075	65:35
402 McDonough St.	3,825	2,075	65:35
404 McDonough St.	2,975	3,125	49:51
412 McDonough St.	7,825	3,125	72:28
414 McDonough St.	6,200	2,500	71:29
416 McDonough St.	6,200	2,500	71:29
418 McDonough St.	6,200	2,500	71:29
420 McDonough St.	6,200	2,500	71:29
422 McDonough St.	6,200	2,500	71:29

GROUP B: PARCELS WHOSE TAXES WOULD BE DECREASED

Address	Assessed Values		Ratio
	Improvements	Land	
424 McDonough St.	$6,200	$2,500	71:29
426 McDonough St.	6,200	2,500	71:29
428 McDonough St.	6,200	2,500	71:29
430 McDonough St.	6,200	2,500	71:29
432 McDonough St.	6,200	2,500	71:29
434 McDonough St.	6,200	2,500	71:29
225 Decatur St.	17,000	6,000	74:26
227 Decatur St.	7,125	2,375	75:25
229 Decatur St.	7,125	2,375	75:25
231 Decatur St.	7,125	2,375	75:25
233 Decatur St.	7,125	2,375	75:25
235 Decatur St.	3,675	2,325	61:39
237 Decatur St.	3,675	2,325	61:39
237a Decatur St.	3,675	2,325	61:39
239 Decatur St.	3,675	2,325	61:39
241 Decatur St.	3,675	2,325	61:39
243 Decatur St.	3,675	2,325	61:39
245 Decatur St.	4,700	2,800	63:37
247 Decatur St.	4,700	2,800	63:37
249 Decatur St.	4,700	2,800	63:37
251 Decatur St.	4,700	2,800	63:37
253 Decatur St.	4,100	2,800	59:41
255 Decatur St.	4,100	2,800	59:41
257 Decatur St.	4,100	2,800	59:41
259 Decatur St.	9,000	2,800	76:24
271 Decatur St.	6,075	2,625	70:30
273 Decatur St.	5,950	2,550	70:30
275 Decatur St.	5,950	2,550	70:30
277 Decatur St.	5,950	2,550	70:30
279 Decatur St.	5,950	2,550	70:30
281 Decatur St.	6,375	2,625	71:29
283 Decatur St.	6,375	2,625	71:29
285 Decatur St.	6,375	2,625	71:29
287 Decatur St.	6,375	2,625	71:29
289 Decatur St.	6,375	2,625	71:29
291 Decatur St.	4,875	2,625	65:35
293 Decatur St.	4,875	2,625	65:35
295 Decatur St.	4,875	2,625	65:35
297 Decatur St.	4,875	2,625	65:35
299 Decatur St.	4,950	2,550	66:34
301 Decatur St.	11,400	5,100	69:31
307 Decatur St.	4,400	2,500	64:36
309 Decatur St.	4,200	2,500	63:37
311 Decatur St.	4,200	2,500	63:37
313 Decatur St.	4,200	2,500	63:37
315 Decatur St.	4,400	2,500	64:36
317 Decatur St.	4,550	2,250	67:33
319 Decatur St.	4,550	2,250	67:33
321 Decatur St.	4,550	2,250	67:33
323 Decatur St.	4,650	2,250	67:33
325 Decatur St.	3,650	2,450	60:40
327 Decatur St.	3,575	2,325	61:39
329 Decatur St.	3,575	2,325	61:39
331 Decatur St.	3,575	2,325	61:39
335 Decatur St.	3,025	2,075	59:41
335a Decatur St.	3,025	2,075	59:41
337 Decatur St.	3,025	2,075	59:41
341 Decatur St.	2,500	2,500	50:50
347 Decatur St.	2,500	1,900	43:57
349 Decatur St.	2,500	1,900	43:57
351 Decatur St.	2,500	1,900	43:57
353 Decatur St.	2,125	2,975	58:42
355 Decatur St.	2,125	2,975	58:42
357 Decatur St.	2,125	3,175	60:40

GROUP B: PARCELS WHOSE TAXES WOULD BE DECREASED

Address	Assessed Values		Ratio
	Improvements	Land	
359 Decatur St.	$2,125	$3,175	60:40
361 Decatur St.	3,175	2,125	60:40
363 Decatur St.	2,525	2,075	55:45
365 Decatur St.	2,525	2,075	55:45
367 Decatur St.	2,525	2,075	55:45
369 Decatur St.	2,525	2,075	55:45
371 Decatur St.	2,325	2,075	53:47
373 Decatur St.	7,500	5,000	60:40
300 Reid Ave.	13,900	5,100	73:27
302 Reid Ave.	4,800	2,300	68:32
302* Reid Ave.	4,800	2,300	68:32
304a Reid Ave.	4,800	2,300	68:32
306 Reid Ave.	4,800	2,300	68:32
308 Reid Ave.	4,800	2,300	68:32
	$677,415	$323,275	

* Thus in record.

SAMPLE DISTRICT FROM ASSESSMENT SECTION EIGHT, BOROUGH OF BROOKLYN

(Standard Composite Ratio: 39.44:60.56)

GROUP A: PARCELS WHOSE TAXES WOULD BE INCREASED

Address	Assessed Values		Ratio
	Improvements	Land	
599 Bedford Ave.	$2,900	$7,600	29:71
	$2,900	$7,600	

GROUP B: PARCELS WHOSE TAXES WOULD BE DECREASED

Address	Assessed Values		Ratio
	Improvements	Land	
583 Bedford Ave.	$8,300	$8,700	49:51
585 Bedford Ave.	4,300	4,700	48:52
587 Bedford Ave.	4,300	4,700	48:52
589 Bedford Ave.	4,300	4,700	48:52
591 Bedford Ave.	4,300	4,700	48:52
593 Bedford Ave.	3,600	4,900	42:58
595 Bedford Ave.	3,600	4,900	42:58
597 Bedford Ave.	3,600	4,900	42:58
134 Keap St.	4,850	3,850	56:44
136 Keap St.	3,600	3,700	49:51
138 Keap St.	3,600	3,700	49:51
140 Keap St.	3,600	3,700	49:51
142 Keap St.	3,600	3,700	49:51
144 Keap St.	3,600	3,700	49:51
146 Keap St.	3,600	3,700	49:51
148 Keap St.	3,600	3,700	49:51
150 Keap St.	5,300	3,700	59:41
152 Keap St.	3,600	3,700	49:51
154 Keap St.	3,400	3,300	51:49
156 Keap St.	3,400	3,400	50:50
158 Keap St.	3,400	3,400	50:50
160 Keap St.	3,200	3,300	56·44
162 Keap St.	3,200	3,300	56·44
164 Keap St.	3,200	3,300	56·44
166 Keap St.	3,200	3,300	56·44
168 Keap St.	3,750	2,650	59:41
170 Keap St.	3,750	2,650	59:41
— Keap St.	3,750	2,650	59:41
— Keap St.	3,750	2,650	59:41
188 Keap St.	3,800	3,800	50:50
190 Keap St.	3,700	3,600	51:49
192 Keap St.	3,700	3,600	51:49
194 Keap St.	3,650	3,650	50:50
196 Keap St.	3,650	3,650	50:50
198 Keap St.	3,650	3,650	50:50
200 Keap St.	5,350	3,650	59:41
202 Keap St.	8,850	3,650	71:29
204 Keap St.	8,850	3,650	71:29
206 Keap St.	4,850	3,650	57:43
208 Keap St.	2,550	3,250	44:56
210 Keap St.	2,550	3,250	44:56
212 Keap St.	2,550	3,250	44:56
214 Keap St.	2,950	3,250	48:52
216 Keap St.	2,550	3,250	44:56
218 Keap St.	4,050	3,450	54:46
220 Keap St.	4,050	3,250	55:45
222 Keap St.	4,050	3,250	55:45
224 Keap St.	4,050	3,250	55:45
226 Keap St.	4,050	3,250	55·45
228 Keap St.	4,750	3,050	61:39
230 Keap St.	4,750	3,050	61:39

Group B: Parcels Whose Taxes Would Be Decreased

Address	Assessed Values		Ratio
	Improvements	Land	
232 Keap St.	$4,750	$3,050	61:39
238 Keap St.	4,150	4,350	49:51
240 Keap St.	3,900	2,900	57:43
242 Keap St.	3,900	2,900	57:43
244 Keap St.	3,900	2,900	57:43
246 Keap St.	4,250	2,950	59:41
248 Keap St.	4,200	3,000	58:42
252 Keap St.	4,600	2,900	61:39
254 Keap St.	4,600	2,900	61:39
256 Keap St.	4,900	3,300	60:40
258 Keap St.	4,800	3,200	60:40
260 Keap St.	4,600	2,900	61:39
262 Keap St.	3,450	3,050	53:47
264 Keap St.	2,950	3,050	49:51
266 Keap St.	2,950	3,050	49:51
268 Keap St.	2,950	3,050	49:51
270 Keap St.	3,750	3,050	55:45
272 Keap St.	3,750	3,050	55:45
280 Keap St.	2,850	2,850	50:50
282 Keap St.	2,850	2,850	50:50
284 Keap St.	2,850	2,850	50:50
286 Keap St.	2,850	2,850	50:50
117 Hooper St.	3,800	3,300	53:47
119 Hooper St.	4,800	3,700	56:44
121 Hooper St.	3,900	3,300	54:46
123 Hooper St.	3,850	3,350	53:47
125 Hooper St.	3,900	3,400	53:47
127 Hooper St.	3,850	3,350	53:47
129 Hooper St.	3,850	3,350	53:47
131 Hooper St.	3,900	3,600	52:48
133 Hooper St.	3,900	3,600	52:48
135 Hooper St.	3,900	3,600	52:48
137 Hooper St.	3,800	3,000	56:44
139 Hooper St.	3,800	2,900	57:43
141 Hooper St.	3,900	2,900	57:43
143 Hooper St.	3,500	2,900	55:45
145 Hooper St.	3,500	2,900	55:45
147 Hooper St.	3,500	3,000	54:46
167 Hooper St.	3,650	2,550	59:41
169 Hooper St.	4,700	3,100	60:40
171 Hooper St.	4,700	3,100	60:40
173 Hooper St.	4,700	3,100	60:40
175 Hooper St.	4,700	3,100	60:40
177 Hooper St.	3,900	3,100	56:44
179 Hooper St.	3,850	3,150	55:45
181 Hooper St.	3,800	3,200	54:46
183 Hooper St.	4,550	3,150	59:41
185 Hooper St.	3,650	2,650	58:42
185* Hooper St.	3,350	2,650	56:44
189 Hooper St.	3,350	2,650	56:44
191 Hooper St.	3,300	2,700	55:45
193 Hooper St.	4,600	3,200	59:41
195 Hooper St.	4,600	3,200	59:41
197 Hooper St.	4,600	3,200	59:41
199 Hooper St.	4,600	3,200	59:41
201 Hooper St.	4,600	3,200	59:41
203 Hooper St.	4,500	3,300	58:42
205 Hooper St.	4,700	3,100	60:40
207 Hooper St.	4,600	3,200	59:41
209 Hooper St.	3,600	3,200	53:47
211 Hooper St.	2,700	3,400	44:56
213 Hooper St.	3,750	2,550	60:40

* Thus in record.

GROUP B: PARCELS WHOSE TAXES WOULD BE DECREASED

Address	Assessed Values		Ratio
	Improvements	Land	
215 Hooper St.	$3,750	$2,550	60:40
217 Hooper St.	3,750	2,550	60:40
219 Hooper St.	3,750	2,550	60:40
221 Hooper St.	4,000	3,800	42:58
233 Hooper St.	3,100	3,100	50:50
235 Hooper St.	2,900	3,000	49:51
237 Hooper St.	2,900	2,950	50:50
239 Hooper St.	3,350	2,900	54:46
241 Hooper St.	3,400	2,850	55:45
243 Hooper St.	3,450	2,800	57:43
245 Hooper St.	3,450	2,850	52:48
247 Hooper St.	3,300	3,000	52:48
249 Hooper St.	3,300	3,000	52:48
251 Hooper St.	3,300	3,000	52:48
253 Hooper St.	3,700	3,000	55:45
255 Hooper St.	3,700	3,000	55:45
257 Hooper St.	2,700	3,000	47:53
259 Hooper St.	2,700	3,000	47:53
261 Hooper St.	2,700	3,000	47:53
263 Hooper St.	2,700	3,000	47:53
265 Hooper St.	2,700	3,000	47:53
267 Hooper St.	2,150	2,850	43:57
269 Hooper St.	2,150	2,850	43:57
271 Hooper St.	2,150	2,850	43:57
273 Hooper St.	2,150	2,850	43:57
275 Hooper St.	2,600	2,900	47:53
277 Hooper St.	3,100	2,600	54:46
279 Hooper St.	3,400	2,300	60:40
113 Lee Ave.	4,700	3,600	57:43
115 Lee Ave.	4,800	3,200	60:40
117 Lee Ave.	3,800	3,200	54:46
119 Lee Ave.	7,800	5,200	60:40
243 Marcy Ave.	3,050	2,950	51:49
245 Marcy Ave.	3,050	2,950	51:49
247 Marcy Ave.	3,050	2,950	51:49
249 Marcy Ave.	3,050	2,950	51:49
251 Marcy Ave.	3,050	2,950	51:49
253 Marcy Ave.	3,100	4,400	41:59
258 Marcy Ave.	2,500	3,500	42:58
260 Marcy Ave.	2,500	3,500	42:58
272 Division Ave.	2,400	2,900	45:55
274 Division Ave.	2,350	2,950	44:56
276 Division Ave.	2,650	2,950	47:53
280 Division Ave.	2,400	2,800	46:54
282 Division Ave.	3,800	4,000	49:51
6 Harrison Ave.	2,600	3,900	60:40
8 Harrison Ave.	2,600	3,900	60:40
8* Harrison Ave.	2,600	3,400	57:43
	$584,800	$526,650	

* Thus in record.

SAMPLE DISTRICT FROM ASSESSMENT SECTION TWELVE, BOROUGH OF BROOKLYN

(Standard Composite Ratio: 39.44:60.56)

GROUP A: PARCELS WHOSE TAXES WOULD BE INCREASED

None.

GROUP B: PARCELS WHOSE TAXES WOULD BE DECREASED

Address	Assessed Values		Ratio
	Improvements	Land	
365 New Jersey Ave.	$11,000	$3,000	79:21
373 New Jersey Ave.	3,800	1,000	79:21
375 New Jersey Ave.	3,400	1,100	76:24
377 New Jersey Ave.	3,400	1,100	76:24
403 New Jersey Ave.	3,000	1,000	75:25
405 New Jersey Ave.	3,000	1,000	75:25
407 New Jersey Ave.	3,000	1,000	75:25
411 New Jersey Ave.	3,000	1,000	75:25
413 New Jersey Ave.	3,000	1,000	75:25
415 New Jersey Ave.	3,000	1,000	75:25
417 New Jersey Ave.	3,000	1,000	75:25
419 New Jersey Ave.	3,000	1,000	75:25
423 New Jersey Ave.	3,000	1,000	75:25
426 New Jersey Ave.	5,500	2,000	73:27
366 Belmont Ave.	1,500	1,200	56:44
372 Belmont Ave.	1,000	1,100	48:52
374 Belmont Ave.	900	1,100	45:55
376 Belmont Ave.	1,000	1,000	50:50
378 Belmont Ave.	1,500	1,500	50:50
363 Vermont St.	3,850	950	79:21
365 Vermont St.	3,850	950	80:20
367 Vermont St.	3,800	1,000	80:20
368 Vermont St.	2,000	1,000	71:29
369 Vermont St.	3,850	950	80:20
370 Vermont St.	2,000	1,000	71:29
371 Vermont St.	3,850	950	80:20
372 Vermont St.	2,000	1,000	71:29
375 Vermont St.	3,850	950	80:20
377 Vermont St.	3,850	950	80:20
379 Vermont St.	4,300	1,000	81:19
381 Vermont St.	4,300	1,000	81:19
385 Vermont St.	4,300	1,000	81:19
387 Vermont St.	4,300	1,000	81:19
388 Vermont St.	4,000	1,000	80:20
389 Vermont St.	4,300	1,000	81:19
390 Vermont St.	4,000	1,000	80:20
391 Vermont St.	4,300	1,000	81:19
392 Vermont St.	4,000	1,000	80:20
393 Vermont St.	4,300	1,000	81:19
394 Vermont St.	4,000	1,000	80:20
395 Vermont St.	4,300	1,000	81:19
396 Vermont St.	4,000	1,000	80:20
399 Vermont St.	4,300	1,000	81:19
400 Vermont St.	4,000	1,000	80:20
401 Vermont St.	7,000	2,000	78:22
402 Vermont St.	7,500	2,000	79:21
	$170,100	$51,800	

GROUP B: PARCELS WHOSE TAXES WOULD BE DECREASED

Address	Assessed Values		Ratio
	Improvements	Land	
321 Wyona St.	$3,500	$1,500	70:30
323 Wyona St.	2,600	900	74:26
325 Wyona St.	2,600	900	74:26

GROUP B: PARCELS WHOSE TAXES WOULD BE DECREASED

Address	Assessed Values		Ratio
	Improvements	Land	
326 Wyona St.	$2,500	$1,000	72:28
327 Wyona St.	2,600	900	74:26
328 Wyona St.	2,500	1,000	72:28
329 Wyona St.	2,600	900	74:26
330 Wyona St.	2,500	1,000	72:28
331 Wyona St.	2,600	900	74:26
333 Wyona St.	2,600	900	74:26
334 Wyona St.	3,000	1,000	75:25
335 Wyona St.	2,600	900	74:26
336 Wyona St.	3,000	1,000	75:25
337 Wyona St.	2,600	900	74:26
338 Wyona St.	3,000	1,000	75:25
339 Wyona St.	2,600	900	74:26
340 Wyona St.	3,000	1,000	75:25
341 Wyona St.	2,600	900	74:26
342 Wyona St.	3,000	1,000	75:25
343 Wyona St.	2,600	900	74:26
344 Wyona St.	3,000	1,000	75:25
345 Wyona St.	2,600	900	74:26
346 Wyona St.	3,000	1,000	75:25
347 Wyona St.	2,600	900	74:26
348 Wyona St.	3,000	1,000	75:25
349 Wyona St.	2,600	900	74:26
350 Wyona St.	3,000	1,000	75:25
351 Wyona St.	2,600	900	74:26
352 Wyona St.	3,000	1,000	75:25
353 Wyona St.	2,600	900	74:26
354 Wyona St.	3,000	1,000	60:40
355 Wyona St.	2,600	900	74:26
357 Wyona St.	2,600	900	74:26
359 Wyona St.	2,600	900	74:26
361 Wyona St.	2,600	900	74:26
363 Wyona St.	3,100	1,900	62:38
332 Bradford St.	2,500	1,500	63:37
334 Bradford St.	2,500	1,500	63:37
338 Bradford St.	2,500	1,500	63:37
340 Bradford St.	3,000	1,500	67:33
344 Bradford St.	2,500	1,500	63:37
346 Bradford St.	3,050	950	76:24
348 Bradford St.	3,050	950	76:24
350 Bradford St.	3,050	950	76:24
352 Bradford St.	3,050	950	76:24
354 Bradford St.	2,850	950	75:25
356 Bradford St.	3,050	950	76:24
358 Bradford St.	3,050	950	76:24
360 Bradford St.	3,050	950	76:24
362-66* Bradford St.	3,050	950	76:24
364 Bradford St.	3,050	950	76:24
366 Bradford St.	6,100	1,900	76:24
	$318,600	$106,100	

* Thus in record.

SAMPLE DISTRICT FROM ASSESSMENT SECTION SIXTEEN, BOROUGH OF BROOKLYN

(Standard Composite Ratio: 39.44:60.56)

GROUP A: PARCELS WHOSE TAXES WOULD BE INCREASED

Address	Assessed Values		Ratio
	Improvements	Land	
1135 Ditmas Ave.	$3,200	$5,100	39:61
1720 Ditmas Ave.	6,500	10,500	38:62
584 Newkirk Ave.	6,500	10,000	39:61
1715 Newkirk Ave.	17,500	30,000	37:67
	$33,700	$55,600	

GROUP B: PARCELS WHOSE TAXES WOULD BE DECREASED

Address	Assessed Values		Ratio
	Improvements	Land	
407 Dorchester Road	$5,300	$5,700	48:52
445 Dorchester Road	5,400	5,100	51:49
445* Dorchester Road	4,700	5,300	47:53
446 Dorchester Road	7,200	4,600	61:39
447 Dorchester Road	5,700	6,100	48:52
448 Dorchester Road	6,400	4,900	57:43
450 Dorchester Road	5,000	5,000	50:50
456 Dorchester Road	4,700	3,500	57:43
1106 Dorchester Road	4,700	3,500	57:43
451 Westminster Road	5,300	3,200	62:38
455 Westminster Road	4,800	3,200	60:40
456 Westminster Road	5,000	3,200	61:39
461 Westminster Road	4,900	3,200	60:40
462 Westminster Road	4,800	3,200	60:40
465 Westminster Road	5,500	3,200	63:37
466 Westminster Road	4,800	3,200	60:40
470 Westminster Road	4,800	3,200	60:40
471 Westminster Road	5,100	3,200	61:39
473 Westminster Road	5,800	3,200	64:36
476 Westminster Road	5,000	3,200	61:39
480 Westminster Road	5,500	3,200	63:37
481 Westminster Road	5,100	3,200	61:39
485 Westminster Road	5,300	4,000	57:43
486 Westminster Road	5,000	3,200	61:39
491 Westminster Road	4,600	3,600	56:44
492 Westminster Road	4,800	3,600	57:43
497 Westminster Road	4,200	3,200	57:43
498 Westminster Road	4,800	3,200	60:40
501 Westminster Road	4,800	3,200	60:40
502 Westminster Road	4,800	3,200	60:40
506 Westminster Road	4,800	3,200	60:40
507 Westminster Road	5,400	3,200	63:37
512 Westminster Road	5,200	4,000	57:43
515 Westminster Road	6,200	3,400	65:35
518 Westminster Road	4,700	4,800	49:51
— Ditmas Ave.	4,400	4,600	49:51
1115 Ditmas Ave.	5,000	4,000	56:44
1121 Ditmas Ave.	4,600	4,000	53:47
1207 Ditmas Ave.	6,600	6,400	51:49
1211 Ditmas Ave.	5,500	4,500	55:45
1217 Ditmas Ave.	5,200	4,500	54:46
1221 Ditmas Ave.	6,000	7,000	46:54
— Ditmas Ave.	10,000	11,000	48:52
1690 Ditmas Ave.	12,000	10,500	53:47
1700 Ditmas Ave.	12,700	10,800	54:46
1712 Ditmas Ave.	8,400	8,100	51:49
— Ditmas Ave.	10,400	8,300	56:44

* Thus in record.

GROUP B: PARCELS WHOSE TAXES WOULD BE DECREASED

Address	Assessed Values		Ratio
	Improvements	Land	
1890 Ditmas Ave.	$12,500	$11,300	53:47
453 Stratford Road	6,300	3,200	66:34
457 Stratford Road	5,600	3,200	64:36
461 Stratford Road	6,000	3,200	65:35
467 Stratford Road	6,000	3,200	65:35
471 Stratford Road	5,000	3,200	61:39
— Stratford Road	5,200	3,200	62:38
481 Stratford Road	5,000	3,200	61:39
— Stratford Road	5,200	3,200	62:38
493 Stratford Road	5,100	3,200	62:38
501 Stratford Road	5,100	3,200	62:38
505 Stratford Road	5,100	3,200	62:38
— Stratford Road	5,400	3,200	63:37
449 Argyle Road	6,100	3,600	63:37
455 Argyle Road	6,100	3,200	61:39
456 Argyle Road	3,800	3,200	54:46
459 Argyle Road	5,000	3,200	61:39
460 Argyle Road	3,800	3,200	54:46
465 Argyle Road	5,300	3,200	62:38
466 Argyle Road	4,000	3,200	56:44
469 Argyle Road	5,300	3,200	62:38
472 Argyle Road	7,400	7,600	49:51
475 Argyle Road	5,300	3,200	62:38
481 Argyle Road	5,300	3,200	62:38
483 Argyle Road	5,300	3,200	62:38
484 Argyle Road	4,200	4,000	51:49
490 Argyle Road	6,000	4,000	60:40
491 Argyle Road	5,300	3,200	62:38
495 Argyle Road	5,300	3,200	62:38
496 Argyle Road	4,600	3,600	56:44
501 Argyle Road	5,800	3,200	64:36
505 Argyle Road	5,300	3,200	62:38
508 Argyle Road	4,900	3,600	58:42
511 Argyle Road	5,800	3,200	64:36
512 Argyle Road	4,200	3,600	54:46
515 Argyle Road	5,800	3,200	64:36
520 Argyle Road	4,700	4,800	49:51
521 Argyle Road	5,800	3,200	64:36
1303 Argyle Road	5,800	4,700	55:45
449 Rugby Road	6,500	3,400	66:34
454 Rugby Road	6,000	4,000	60:40
457 Rugby Road	5,800	3,400	63:37
458 Rugby Road	6,200	3,400	65:35
459 Rugby Road	6,200	3,400	65:35
462 Rugby Road	4,800	3,400	59:41
467 Rugby Road	4,800	3,400	59:41
469 Rugby Road	6,200	3,400	65:35
470 Rugby Road	6,400	3,400	65:35
474 Rugby Road	5,900	3,400	63:37
477 Rubgy Road	5,400	3,400	61:39
479 Rugby Road	6,100	3,400	64:36
480 Rugby Road	6,600	5,100	56:44
484 Rugby Road	6,750	4,250	61:39
485 Rugby Road	5,800	3,400	63:37
489 Rugby Road	6,200	3,400	65:35
494 Rugby Road	6,450	4,250	60:40
495 Rugby Road	6,100	3,400	64:36
498 Rugby Road	6,200	3,400	65:35
501 Rugby Road	5,800	3,400	63:37
502 Rugby Road	6,200	3,400	65:35
503 Rugby Road	6,200	3,400	65:35
506 Rugby Road	5,900	3,400	63:37
509 Rugby Road	7,600	3,400	69:31
512 Rugby Road	6,200	3,400	65:35

GROUP B: PARCELS WHOSE TAXES WOULD BE DECREASED

Address	Assessed Values		Ratio
	Improvements	Land	
513 Rugby Road	$6,500	$3,400	66:34
516 Rugby Road	7,300	3,400	68:32
517 Rugby Road	6,600	3,400	66:34
522 Rugby Road	5,900	3,400	63:37
523 Rugby Road	9,000	5,000	64:36
526 Rugby Road	7,200	5,800	55:45
452 Marlborough Road	5,700	3,200	64:36
456 Marlborough Road	5,000	3,200	61:39
458 Marlborough Road	4,700	3,200	59:41
462 Marlborough Road	5,700	3,200	64:36
466 Marlborough Road	5,600	3,200	64:36
470 Marlborough Road	6,200	3,200	66:34
474 Marlborough Road	4,700	3,200	59:41
476 Marlborough Road	4,700	3,200	59:41
480 Marlborough Road	6,200	3,200	66:34
484 Marlborough Road	5,900	3,200	65:35
488 Marlborough Road	4,700	3,200	60:40
492 Marlborough Road	6,200	3,200	66:34
496 Marlborough Road	4,700	3,200	60:40
500 Marlborough Road	4,700	3,200	60:40
504 Marlborough Road	4,700	3,200	60:40
508 Marlborough Road	6,400	5,400	54:46
537 East 17th St.	6,200	6,000	51:49
543 East 17th St.	6,200	6,000	51:49
546 East 17th St.	7,300	6,500	53:47
549 East 17th St.	6,200	6,000	51:49
552 East 17th St.	6,200	6,000	51:49
555 East 17th St.	6,200	6,000	51:49
560 East 17th St.	6,200	6,000	51:49
561 East 17th St.	7,000	6,000	54:46
564 East 17th St.	6,200	6,000	51:49
572 East 17th St.	7,700	7,900	49:51
— East 17th St.	5,800	4,700	55:45
— East 17th St.	6,200	3,600	63:37
653 East 17th St.	5,500	5,000	52:48
659 East 17th St.	5,700	5,000	53:47
665 East 17th St.	6,500	5,000	57:43
671 East 17th St.	5,500	5,000	52:48
677 East 17th St.	7,000	5,000	58:42
689 East 17th St.	6,000	5,000	55:45
701 East 17th St.	7,000	5,000	58:42
707 East 17th St.	5,500	5,000	52:48
713 East 17th St.	5,500	5,000	52:48
719 East 17th St.	5,500	5,000	52:48
725 East 17th St.	5,750	5,000	54:46
578 Newkirk Ave.	6,500	6,300	51:49
1603 Newkirk Ave.	3,700	5,000	53:47
1609 Newkirk Ave.	3,300	4,000	45:55
1615 Newkirk Ave.	7,800	4,700	62:38
1815 Newkirk Ave.	5,800	4,700	55:45
1819 Newkirk Ave.	6,000	4,700	56:44
511 East 16th St.	5,500	4,750	54:46
513 East 16th St.	5,750	4,750	55:45
519 East 16th St.	5,500	4,750	54:46
523 East 16th St.	5,500	4,750	54:46
549 East 16th St.	5,500	5,500	50:50
525 East 18th St.	5,500	6,000	48:53
531 East 18th St.	5,750	5,750	50:50
532 East 18th St.	6,300	5,400	54:46
535 East 18th St.	5,500	5,750	49:51
539 East 18th St.	6,000	5,750	51:49
543 East 18th St.	5,500	5,750	49:51
544 East 18th St.	6,250	5,750	52:48
548 East 18th St.	6,250	5,750	52:48

GROUP B: PARCELS WHOSE TAXES WOULD BE DECREASED

Address	Assessed Values		Ratio
	Improvements	Land	
554 East 18th St.	$5,600	$6,900	45:55
635 East 18th St.	5,300	5,200	51:49
639 East 18th St.	5,400	3,800	59:41
642 East 18th St.	6,200	3,800	62:38
643 East 18th St.	6,000	4,500	57:43
646 East 18th St.	6,300	3,200	66:34
649 East 18th St.	7,200	4,500	62:38
652 East 18th St.	7,000	4,500	61:39
655 East 18th St.	4,500	4,500	50:50
658 East 18th St.	4,500	4,500	50:50
661 East 18th St.	7,200	4,500	62:38
664 East 18th St.	6,000	4,500	57:43
667 East 18st St.	4,500	4,500	50:50
670 East 18th St.	6,700	4,500	60:40
673 East 18th St.	5,500	4,500	55:45
674 East 18th St.	4,500	4,500	50:50
679 East 18th St.	7,000	4,500	61:39
682 East 18th St.	5,300	4,500	54:46
685 East 18th St.	7,900	4,500	64:36
690 East 18th St.	6,250	4,500	58:42
693 East 18th St.	4,500	4,500	50:50
699 East 18th St.	7,700	4,500	63:37
700 East 18th St.	7,700	4,500	63:37
705 East 18th St.	8,000	4,500	64:36
706 East 18th St.	7,500	4,500	63:37
711 East 18th St.	5,300	4,500	54:46
712 East 18th St.	8,000	4,500	64:36
717 East 18th St.	4,500	4,500	50:50
718 East 18th St.	4,500	4,500	50:50
723 East 18th St.	6,700	4,500	60:40
724 East 18th St.	5,300	4,500	54:46
729 East 18th St.	7,000	4,500	61:39
730 East 18th St.	4,500	4,500	50:50
520 East 19th St.	6,650	6,850	49:51
526 East 19th St.	6,800	6,000	53:47
530 East 19th St.	6,800	6,000	53:47
536 East 19th St.	6,800	6,000	53:47
540 East 19th St.	7,000	6,300	53:47
616 East 19th St.	5,700	4,300	52:48
624 East 19th St.	4,450	4,050	52:48
630 East 19th St.	4,500	4,500	50:50
636 East 19th St.	6,300	4,500	58:42
642 East 19th St.	6,500	4,500	59:41
648 East 19th St.	4,900	4,500	52:48
654 East 19th St.	5,300	4,500	54:46
660 East 19th St.	4,700	4,500	51:49
666 East 19th St.	6,000	4,500	57:43
672 East 19th St.	4,700	4,500	51:49
678 East 19th St.	4,600	4,500	51:49
684 East 19th St.	4,700	4,500	51:49
690 East 19th St.	5,650	4,500	56:44
696 East 19th St.	6,350	4,500	59:41
702 East 19th St.	5,450	4,500	55:45
708 East 19th St.	6,350	4,500	59:41
714 East 19th St.	5,450	4,500	55:45
720 East 19th St.	6,500	4,500	59:41
1703 Avenue G.	6,400	7,600	46:54
1709 Avenue G.	7,000	4,750	60:40
1721 Avenue G.	7,400	7,600	49:51
1803 Avenue G.	6,900	5,250	57:43
1809 Avenue G.	5,000	4,750	51:49
1815 Avenue G.	7,500	4,750	61:39
1821 Avenue G.	8,250	5,250	61:39
	$1,396,600	$1,050,550	

SAMPLE DISTRICT FROM ASSESSMENT SECTION NINETEEN, BOROUGH OF BROOKLYN

(The district consists of assessment blocks:
    6172—between 18th and 19th avenues and between 70th and 71st streets—;
    6178—between 13th and 14th avenues and between 71st and 72nd streets—;
    6200—between 13th and 14th avenues and between 73rd and 74th streets—;
    6222—between 13th and 14th avenues and between 75th and 76th streets—; and
    6233—between 13th and 14th avenues and between 76th and 77th streets.)

(Standard Composite Ratio: 39.44:60.56)

GROUP A: PARCELS WHOSE TAXES WOULD BE INCREASED

Address	Assessed Values Improvements	Land	Ratio
7308 14th Ave.	$2,500	$4,500	36:64
	$2,500	$4,500	

GROUP B: PARCELS WHOSE TAXES WOULD BE DECREASED

Address	Assessed Values Improvements	Land	Ratio
7001 18th Ave.	$7,000	$1,500	82:18
7003 18th Ave.	5,000	1,000	83:17
7007 18th Ave.	5,000	1,000	83:17
7011 18th Ave.	5,000	1,000	83:17
7015 18th Ave.	5,000	1,000	83:17
7017 18th Ave.	10,000	2,000	83:17
7021 18th Ave.	5,000	1,000	83:17
—— 18th Ave.	5,000	1,000	83:17
7023 18th Ave.	7,000	1,500	82:18
—— 70th St.	4,000	4,700	85:15
—— 70th St.	4,000	4,700	85:15
—— 70th St.	4,000	4,700	85:15
—— 70th St.	4,000	4,700	85:15
—— 70th St.	4,000	4,700	85:15
—— 70th St.	4,000	4,700	85:15
—— 70th St.	4,000	4,700	85:15
—— 70th St.	4,000	4,700	85:15
—— 70th St.	3,000	700	81:19
—— 70th St.	3,000	700	81:19
—— 70th St.	3,000	700	81:19
—— 70th St.	3,000	700	81:19
—— 70th St.	3,000	700	81:19
—— 70th St.	3,000	700	81:19
—— 70th St.	3,000	700	81:19
—— 70th St.	3,000	700	81:19
—— 70th St.	3,000	700	81:19
—— 70th St.	3,000	700	81:19
—— 70th St.	3,000	700	81:19
—— 70th St.	3,000	700	81:19
—— 70th St.	3,000	700	81:19
—— 70th St.	3,000	700	81:19
—— 70th St.	3,400	1,200	74:26
—— 71st St.	3,000	700	81:19
—— 71st St.	3,000	700	81:19
—— 71st St.	3,000	700	81:19
—— 71st St.	3,000	700	81:19

GROUP B: PARCELS WHOSE TAXES WOULD BE DECREASED

Address	Assessed Values Improvements	Land	Ratio
—— 71st St.	$3,000	$700	81:19
—— 71st St.	3,000	700	81:19
—— 71st St.	3,000	700	81:19
—— 71st St.	3,000	700	81:19
—— 71st St.	3,000	700	81:19
1835 71st St.	3,000	700	81:19
—— 71st St.	3,000	700	81:19
—— 71st St.	3,000	700	81:19
—— 71st St.	3,000	700	81:19
—— 71st St.	3,000	700	81:19
—— 71st St.	3,000	700	81:19
1855 71st St.	3,000	700	81:19
—— 71st St.	3,000	700	81:19
—— 71st St.	3,000	700	81:19
—— 71st St.	3,000	700	81:19
—— 71st St.	3,000	700	81:19
—— 71st St.	3,000	700	81:19
—— 71st St.	3,000	700	81:19
—— 71st St.	3,000	700	81:19
—— 71st St.	3,000	700	81:19
—— 71st St.	3,000	700	81:19
—— 71st St.	3,000	700	81:19
—— 71st St.	3,000	700	81:19
—— 71st St.	3,000	700	81:19
—— 71st St.	3,400	1,100	76:24
—— 71st St.	2,100	800	72:29
—— 71st St.	1,900	1,800	51:49
—— 71st St.	2,100	1,800	54:46
—— 71st St.	2,100	1,800	54:46
—— 71st St.	2,100	800	72:28
—— 71st St.	2,100	800	72:28
—— 71st St.	2,100	800	72:28
—— 71st St.	2,100	800	72:28
—— 71st St.	2,100	800	72:28
—— 71st St.	2,100	800	72:28
—— 71st St.	2,100	800	72:28
—— 71st St.	2,100	800	72:28
—— 71st St.	2,100	800	72:28
—— 71st St.	2,100	800	72:28
7104 14th Ave.	3,500	2,900	55:45
7108 14th Ave.	3,000	2,600	54:46
7115 14th Ave.	3,600	3,900	48:52
—— 14th Ave.	2,100	1,800	54:46
7316 14th Ave.	3,400	2,800	55:45
7320 14th Ave.	3,500	4,500	44:56
—— 14th Ave.	4,800	4,200	53:47
—— 14th Ave.	4,300	2,600	62:38
—— 14th Ave.	4,300	2,600	62:38
—— 14th Ave.	3,100	2,900	52:48
—— 14th Ave.	3,100	2,600	54:46
—— 14th Ave.	3,100	2,600	54:46
—— 14th Ave.	3,100	2,600	54:46
—— 14th Ave.	3,300	2,900	53:47
—— 72nd St.	2,800	1,800	55:45
—— 72nd St.	4,000	1,800	69:31
—— 72nd St.	4,000	1,800	69:31
—— 72nd St.	4,000	1,800	69:31
—— 72nd St.	4,000	1,800	69:31
—— 72nd St.	4,000	1,800	69:31
—— 72nd St.	3,700	1,800	67:33
—— 72nd St.	3,500	900	80:20
—— 72nd St.	3,500	900	80:20
—— 72nd St.	3,500	900	80:20
—— 72nd St.	3,500	900	80:20

GROUP B: PARCELS WHOSE TAXES WOULD BE DECREASED

Address	Assessed Values		Ratio
	Improvements	Land	
—— 72nd St.	$3,500	$900	80:20
—— 72rd St.	3,500	900	80:20
—— 72nd St.	3,500	900	80:20
—— 72nd St.	3,500	900	80:20
—— 72nd St.	3,500	900	80:20
—— 13th Ave.	7,700	2,300	77:23
—— 13th Ave.	5,200	1,500	78:22
—— 13th Ave.	5,200	1,500	78:22
—— 13th Ave.	5,200	1,500	78:22
—— 13th Ave.	5,200	1,500	78:22
—— 13th Ave.	5,200	1,500	78:22
—— 13th Ave.	5,200	1,500	78:22
—— 13th Ave.	5,200	1,500	78:22
—— 13th Ave.	5,200	1,500	78:22
—— 13th Ave.	7,700	2,300	77:23
—— 13th Ave.	4,500	1,200	79:21
—— 13th Ave.	4,500	1,200	79:21
—— 13th Ave.	4,500	1,200	79:21
—— 13th Ave.	4,500	1,200	79:21
—— 13th Ave.	4,500	1,200	79:21
—— 13th Ave.	4,500	1,200	79:21
—— 13th Ave.	4,500	1,200	79:21
—— 13th Ave.	4,500	1,200	79:21
—— 13th Ave.	4,500	1,200	79:21
—— 13th Ave.	4,500	1,200	79:21
—— 13th Ave.	7,500	1,500	83:17
—— 73rd St.	4,200	1,800	70:30
—— 73rd St.	4,200	1,800	70:30
—— 73rd St.	4,200	1,800	70:30
—— 73rd St.	4,200	1,800	70:30
—— 73rd St.	4,200	1,800	70:30
—— 73rd St.	3,900	1,800	68:32
—— 73rd St.	4,500	900	83:17
—— 73rd St.	2,400	1,800	57:43
—— 73rd St.	2,400	1,800	57:43
—— 73rd St.	2,400	1,800	57:43
—— 73rd St.	2,400	1,800	57:43
—— 73rd St.	3,800	1,800	68:32
—— 73rd St.	2,400	1,800	57:43
—— 73rd St.	2,700	1,800	60:40
—— 74th St.	2,800	1,800	61:39
—— 74th St.	2,800	1,800	61:39
—— 74th St.	2,500	1,800	58:42
—— 74th St.	2,500	1,800	58:42
—— 74th St.	2,800	1,800	61:39
—— 74th St.	2,500	1,800	58:42
—— 74th St.	2,800	1,800	61:39
—— 74th St.	4,450	1,800	66:34
—— 74th St.	4,700	1,800	72:28
—— 74th St.	4,700	1,800	72:28
—— 74th St.	4,700	1,800	72:28
—— 74th St.	4,700	1,800	72:28
—— 75th St.	2,500	1,700	60:40
—— 75th St.	2,450	1,550	62:38
—— 75th St.	2,450	1,550	62:38
—— 75th St.	2,450	1,550	62:38
—— 75th St.	2,450	1,550	62:38
—— 75th St.	2,450	1,550	62:38
—— 75th St.	2,750	1,550	64:36
—— 75th St.	4,300	2,000	68:32
—— 75th St.	4,300	2,000	68:32
—— 75th St.	4,300	2,000	68:32
—— 75th St.	4,300	2,600	62:38
—— 76th St.	3,200	1,000	76:24

GROUP B: PARCELS WHOSE TAXES WOULD BE DECREASED

Address	Assessed Values		Ratio
	Improvements	Land	
—— 76th St.	$3,000	$1,000	75:25
—— 76th St.	3,000	1,000	75:25
—— 76th St.	3,000	1,000	75:25
—— 76th St.	3,000	1,000	75:25
—— 76th St.	3,000	1,000	75:25
—— 76th St.	3,000	1,000	75:25
—— 76th St.	3,000	1,000	75:25
—— 76th St.	3,000	1,000	75:25
—— 76th St.	3,000	1,000	75:25
—— 76th St.	3,000	1,000	75:25
—— 76th St.	3,000	1,000	75:25
—— 76th St.	3,000	1,000	75:25
—— 76th St.	3,000	1,000	75:25
—— 76th St.	3,000	1,000	75:25
—— 76th St.	4,000	900	82:18
—— 77th St.	3,000	1,000	75:25
—— 77th St.	3,000	1,000	75:25
—— 77th St.	3,000	1,000	75:25
—— 77th St.	3,000	1,000	75:25
—— 77th St.	3,000	1,000	75:25
—— 77th St.	3,000	1,000	75:25
—— 77th St.	3,000	1,000	75:25
—— 77th St.	3,000	1,000	75:25
—— 77th St.	3,000	1,000	75:25
—— 77th St.	3,000	1,000	75:25
—— 77th St.	3,000	1,000	75:25
—— 77th St.	3,000	1,000	75:25
—— 77th St.	3,000	1,000	75:25
—— 77th St.	3,000	1,000	75:25
—— 77th St.	3,600	900	80:20
—— 77th St.	3,600	900	80:20
—— 77th St.	3,600	900	80:20
—— 77th St.	3,600	900	80:20
—— 77th St.	3,600	900	80:20
—— 77th St.	3,600	900	80:20
—— 77th St.	3,600	900	80:20
—— 77th St.	3,600	900	80:20
	$728,550	$297,600	

SAMPLE DISTRICT FROM ASSESSMENT SECTION TWENTY, BOROUGH OF BROOKLYN

(The district consists of assessment blocks:
    6687—between avenues G and H and between Westminster and Argyle roads—;
    6688—between avenues G and H and between Argyle and Rugby roads—;
    6689—between Avenue G and Waldorf Court and between Rugby Road and E. 17th Street—; and
    6690—between Waldorf and Wellington courts and between Rugby Road and E. 17th Street.)

(Standard Composite Ratio: 39.44:60.56)

Group A: Parcels Whose Taxes Would Be Increased

Address	Assessed Values — Improvements	Assessed Values — Land	Ratio
788 East 17th St.	$6,400	$12,600	34:66
	$6,400	$12,600	

Group B: Parcels Whose Taxes Would Be Decreased

Address	Assessed Values — Improvements	Assessed Values — Land	Ratio
1202 Avenue G	$8,700	$5,700	60:40
1212 Avenue G	6,300	3,400	65:35
1304 Avenue G	4,950	4,850	51:49
1312 Avenue G	6,450	4,250	60:40
1316 Avenue G	5,000	3,400	60:40
1320 Avenue G	5,300	5,700	48:52
1404 Avenue G	5,150	4,850	52:48
1410 Avenue G	6,750	4,250	60:40
1416 Avenue G	6,200	4,400	59:41
1422 Avenue G	6,200	4,400	59:41
1426 Avenue G	6,000	4,400	58:42
1430 Avenue G	6,000	4,100	59:41
1434 Avenue G	4,500	2,700	63:37
1444 Avenue G	4,400	2,800	61:39
1448 Avenue G	6,000	4,200	59:41
*1554 Avenue G	5,400	4,400	55:45
1462 Avenue G	5,000	4,400	53:47
1466 Avenue G	5,000	4,400	53:47
1470 Avenue G	6,000	4,300	58:42
1476 Avenue G	7,200	7,300	50:50
715 Argyle Road	4,550	4,250	52:48
716 Argyle Road	5,050	4,250	54:46
*716 Argyle Road	5,700	3,400	63:37
720 Argyle Road	5,500	3,400	62:38
721 Argyle Road	4,750	4,250	53:47
722 Argyle Road	4,750	4,250	53:47
725 Argyle Road	4,500	3,400	57:43
726 Argyle Road	4,400	3,400	56:44
*726 Argyle Road	5,800	3,400	63:37
730 Argyle Road	5,900	3,400	63:37
731 Argyle Road	4,400	3,400	56:44
732 Argyle Road	4,900	3,400	59:41
735 Argyle Road	5,000	3,400	60:40
736 Argyle Road	4,400	3,400	56:44
739 Argyle Road	4,800	3,400	59:41
740 Argyle Road	4,600	3,400	58:42
*740 Argyle Road	5,500	3,400	62:38
744 Argyle Road	5,900	3,400	63:37
745 Argyle Road	4,400	3,400	56:44
746 Argyle Road	4,500	3,400	57:43
750 Argyle Road	5,000	3,400	60:40

* Thus in record.

GROUP B: PARCELS WHOSE TAXES WOULD BE DECREASED

Address	Assessed Values		Ratio
	Improvements	Land	
751 Argyle Road	$4,600	$3,400	58:42
752 Argyle Road	4,900	3,400	59:41
752 Argyle Road	4,900	3,400	59:41
754 Argyle Road	6,000	3,400	64:36
755 Argyle Road	4,400	3,400	56:44
756 Argyle Road	5,000	3,400	60:40
759 Argyle Road	4,800	3,400	59:41
760 Argyle Road	4,400	3,400	56:44
*760 Argyle Road	4,900	3,400	59:41
764 Argyle Road	4,800	3,400	59:41
765 Argyle Road	4,700	3,400	58:42
766 Argyle Road	4,600	3,400	58:42
769 Argyle Road	4,400	3,400	56:44
770 Argyle Road	4,800	3,400	59:41
*770 Argyle Road	6,100	3,400	64:36
775 Argyle Road	5,000	3,400	60:40
776 Argyle Road	4,400	3,400	56:44
779 Argyle Road	4,800	3,400	59:41
780 Argyle Road	4,900	3,400	59:41
*780 Argyle Road	4,900	3,400	59:41
783 Argyle Road	4,600	3,400	58:42
784 Argyle Road	4,700	3,400	58:42
*784 Argyle Road	4,575	3,825	54:46
790 Argyle Road	4,900	3,400	59:41
*790 Argyle Road	4,875	3,825	56:44
793 Argyle Road	4,500	3,400	57:43
794 Argyle Road	5,000	4,300	54:46
*794 Argyle Road	5,000	4,000	56:44
719 Westminster Road	5,950	4,250	58:42
725 Westminster Road	5,750	4,250	57:43
729 Westminster Road	5,800	3,400	63:37
733 Westminster Road	6,300	3,400	65:35
737 Westminster Road	5,800	3,400	63:37
741 Westminster Road	5,800	3,400	63:37
745 Westminster Road	5,800	3,400	63:37
751 Westminster Road	5,800	3,400	63:37
755 Westminster Road	5,800	3,400	63:37
761 Westminster Road	5,800	3,400	63:37
765 Westminster Road	5,800	3,400	63:37
771 Westminster Road	5,800	3,400	63:37
775 Westminster Road	5,800	3,400	63:37
781 Westminster Road	5,800	3,400	63:37
785 Westminster Road	5,800	3,400	63:37
789 Westminster Road	5,800	3,400	63:37
793 Westminster Road	5,800	4,000	59:41
715 Rugby Road	6,100	3,400	64:36
721 Rugby Road	4,400	3,400	56:44
725 Rugby Road	4,800	4,400	52:48
741 Rugby Road	4,500	3,800	54:46
745 Rugby Road	4,600	3,800	55:45
751 Rugby Road	4,400	3,400	56:44
755 Rugby Road	5,600	4,800	54:46
12 Waldorf Court	4,800	3,200	60:40
15 Waldorf Court	4,400	3,200	58:42
16 Waldorf Court	3,400	3,200	58:42
19 Waldorf Court	6,300	3,200	66:34
20 Waldorf Court	5,220	3,280	61:39
23 Waldorf Court	5,000	3,200	61:39
26 Waldorf Court	4,380	3,120	58:42
27 Waldorf Court	6,100	3,200	66:34
28 Waldorf Court	5,400	3,000	64:36
31 Waldorf Court	4,400	3,000	59:41

* Thus in record.

GROUP B: PARCELS WHOSE TAXES WOULD BE DECREASED

Address	Assessed Values		Ratio
	Improvements	Land	
34 Waldorf Court	$4,500	$2,500	64:36
35 Waldorf Court	4,500	2,500	64:36
43 Waldorf Court	4,500	2,500	64:36
44 Waldorf Court	4,500	3,200	69:31
47 Waldorf Court	6,000	3,200	65:35
51 Waldorf Court	4,500	3,600	56:44
52 Waldorf Court	7,500	3,600	68:32
55 Waldorf Court	5,000	3,600	58:42
56 Waldorf Court	6,240	3,960	61:39
61 Waldorf Court	5,000	3,600	58:42
62 Waldorf Court	6,050	4,050	60:40
65 Waldorf Court	5,000	3,600	58:42
66 Waldorf Court	6,850	4,950	58:42
*735 Waldorf Court	5,300	4,800	52:48
744 East 17th St	6,000	4,000	60:40
758 East 17th St	6,500	4,500	55:45
762 East 17th St	6,200	5,700	52:48
776 East 17th St	8,400	6,100	58:42
782 East 17th St	8,000	5,500	59:41
15 Wellington Court	4,400	3,200	58:42
19 Wellington Court	4,400	3,200	58:42
23 Wellington Court	4,600	3,200	59:41
27 Wellington Court	5,000	3,200	61:39
33 Wellington Court	5,000	3,000	63:37
35 Wellington Court	4,500	2,500	64:36
43 Wellington Court	6,900	3,900	64:36
49 Wellington Court	5,200	3,200	62:38
53 Wellington Court	6,100	3,600	63:37
57 Wellington Court	5,250	4,050	56:44
65 Wellington Court	7,150	4,950	59:41
	$707,930	$492,710	

* Thus in record.

SAMPLE DISTRICT FROM ASSESSMENT SECTION TWENTY-THREE, BOROUGH OF BROOKLYN

(The district consists of assessment blocks:
 7560—between avenues G and H and between E. 32nd Street and New York Avenue—;
 7561—between avenues G and H and between New York Avenue and E. 34th Street—;
 7562—between avenues G and H and between E. 34th and E. 35th streets.)

(*Standard Composite Ratio: 39.44:60.56*)

GROUP A: PARCELS WHOSE TAXES WOULD BE INCREASED

None.

GROUP B: PARCELS WHOSE TAXES WOULD BE DECREASED

Address	Assessed Values		Ratio
	Improvements	Land	
6 East 32nd St.	$4,100	$4,000	51:49
9 East 32nd St.	4,000	2,000	65:35
11 East 32nd St.	3,900	2,000	64:36
13 East 32nd St.	3,400	2,000	61:39
15 East 32nd St.	3,200	2,000	59:41
17 East 32nd St.	3,600	2,000	62:38
19 East 32nd St.	3,500	2,000	67:33
21 East 32nd St.	3,900	2,000	64:36
23 East 32nd St.	3,600	2,000	62:38
25 East 32nd St.	2,700	2,000	55:45
27 East 32nd St.	4,400	3,300	57:43
30 East 32nd St.	3,700	2,200	63:37
32 East 32nd St.	3,450	2,250	61:39
34 East 32nd St.	5,050	2,750	65:35
37 East 32nd St.	4,050	2,750	60:40
3204 Glenwood Road	4,450	2,950	60:40
3208 Glenwood Road	2,000	2,600	51:49
3212 Glenwood Road	3,000	2,600	54:46
3216 Glenwood Road	3,500	2,600	57:43
3220 Glenwood Road	5,000	3,300	60:40
3304 Glenwood Road	4,150	2,950	58:42
3308 Glenwood Road	3,300	2,600	56:44
3312 Glenwood Road	3,300	2,600	56:44
3316 Glenwood Road	4,200	2,600	62:38
3320 Glenwood Road	4,150	2,950	58:42
3404 Glenwood Road	3,800	2,700	58:42
3408 Glenwood Road	3,200	2,400	57:43
3412 Glenwood Road	3,200	2,400	57:43
3418 Glenwood Road	3,800	2,400	61:39
3422 Glenwood Road	3,800	2,400	58:42
1595 New York Ave.	3,100	2,200	59:41
1598 New York Ave.	4,300	2,200	66:34
1599 New York Ave.	2,500	2,200	53:47
1605 New York Ave.	3,300	2,200	60:40
1606 New York Ave.	2,900	2,200	57:43
1609 New York Ave.	3,700	2,200	63:37
1610 New York Ave.	3,000	2,200	58:42
1613 New York Ave.	3,600	2,200	62:38
1619 New York Ave.	3,500	2,200	61:39
1620 New York Ave.	3,500	2,200	61:39
1624 New York Ave.	2,900	2,200	57:43
1626 New York Ave.	2,500	2,200	61:39
1630 New York Ave.	2,500	2,200	61:39
1634 New York Ave.	2,600	2,200	62:38
1635 New York Ave.	4,300	2,200	66:34
1639 New York Ave.	3,700	1,100	77:23
1641 New York Ave.	3,700	1,100	77:23
1644 New York Ave.	4,100	2,200	65:35

GROUP B: PARCELS WHOSE TAXES WOULD BE DECREASED

Address	Assessed Values		Ratio
	Improvements	Land	
1645 New York Ave.	$2,900	$2,200	57:43
1647 New York Ave.	2,200	3,200	59:41
1648 New York Ave.	3,100	2,200	59:41
1651 New York Ave.	2,900	2,200	57:43
1652 New York Ave.	2,800	2,200	56:44
1653 New York Ave.	2,500	2,200	53:47
1656 New York Ave.	3,600	2,200	62:38
1660 New York Ave.	3,100	2,200	59:41
1664 New York Ave.	3,950	2,050	66:34
925 East 34th St.	4,500	2,000	69:31
929 East 34th St.	3,700	2,000	65:35
933 East 34th St.	3,200	2,000	62:38
934 East 34th St.	5,000	2,000	71:29
937 East 34th St.	3,000	2,000	60:40
938 East 34th St.	2,800	2,000	58:42
941 East 34th St.	4,200	2,000	68:32
942 East 34th St.	2,700	2,000	57:43
945 East 34th St.	3,900	2,000	66:34
947 East 34th St.	4,100	2,000	67:33
949 East 34th St.	4,100	2,000	67:33
950 East 34th St.	3,800	2,000	66:34
954 East 34th St.	3,800	2,000	66:34
955 East 34th St.	4,000	2,000	67:33
958 East 34th St.	3,100	2,000	61:39
962 East 34th St.	3,200	2,000	62:38
966 East 34th St.	3,200	2,000	62:38
967 East 34th St.	3,100	2,000	61:39
969 East 34th St.	3,800	2,000	66:34
974 East 34th St.	4,000	2,000	67:33
979 East 34th St.	3,500	2,000	64:36
987 East 34th St.	5,200	2,000	72:28
988 East 34th St.	3,600	2,000	64:36
—— Avenue H.	5,000	5,300	49:51
856 Avenue H.	4,600	1,800	72:28
860 Avenue H.	3,600	1,800	67:33
864 Avenue H.	3,700	1,800	67:33
868 Avenue H.	4,300	1,800	70:30
872 Avenue H.	3,500	1,800	66:34
876 Avenue H.	2,500	1,800	58:42
880 Avenue H.	6,000	1,800	77:23
890 Avenue H.	3,100	1,800	63:37
894 Avenue H.	2,600	1,800	59:41
908-10 Avenue H.	4,000	900	82:18
912 Avenue H.	4,000	900	82:18
914 Avenue H.	4,000	900	82:18
3413 Avenue H.	4,000	1,600	71:29
3419 Avenue H.	3,000	2,400	56:44
	$345,550	$208,450	

IV. QUEENS

SAMPLE DISTRICT FROM WARD ONE, BOROUGH OF QUEENS

(The district consists of assessment blocks:
  79—between Crescent and Ely avenues and between Jamaica Avenue and Elm Street—; and
  174—between Trowbridge Street and Hoyt Avenue and between Woolsey and Willow streets.)

(*Standard Composite Ratio: 38.49 : 61.51*)

GROUP A: PARCELS WHOSE TAXES WOULD BE INCREASED

Ward, Lot or Map No.	Assessed Values Improvements	Land	Ratio

(Between Crescent and Ely Avenues and between Jamaica Avenue and Elm Street.)

Ward, Lot or Map No.	Improvements	Land	Ratio
9	$2,200	$4,800	20:80
11	3,200	4,800	31:69
30	800	1,600	33:67
31	800	1,600	33:67
34	800	1,600	33:67
35	800	1,600	33:67
45	1,100	2,800	38:62
56	1,000	2,000	33:67
	$10,700	$20,800	

GROUP B: PARCELS WHOSE TAXES WOULD BE DECREASED

(Between Crescent and Ely Avenues and between Jamaica Avenue and Elm Street.)

Ward, Lot or Map No.	Improvements	Land	Ratio
1	$1,600	$1,900	46:54
3	1,600	1,900	46:54
4	1,500	1,900	44:56
5	1,300	1,900	41:59
6	1,300	1,900	41:59
7	2,100	2,400	47:53
8	2,100	2,400	47:53
15	1,800	2,400	47:53
20	1,700	2,700	38.64:61.36
21	1,000	800	56:44
22	1,000	800	56:44
23	1,000	800	56:44
24	1,100	1,400	44:56
25	1,100	1,400	44:56
26	3,100	1,900	62:38
27	2,900	1,500	66:34
28	1,200	1,500	44:56
29	1,200	1,500	44:56
33	1,400	1,600	47:53
36	1,500	1,600	48:52
37	1,500	1,600	48:52
41	1,500	1,300	54:46
42	1,500	1,300	54:46
43	2,500	2,000	56:44
45	2,300	2,300	50:50
47	1,400	1,800	44:56
48	1,000	1,300	43:57
49	1,000	1,300	43:57
50	1,000	1,300	43:57
51	1,000	1,300	43:57
52	950	1,350	41:59
53	950	1,350	41:59
54	950	1,350	41:59
55	1,400	2,100	40:60
56	1,400	1,400	50:50
59	2,700	2,500	52:48

GROUP B: PARCELS WHOSE TAXES WOULD BE DECREASED

Ward, Lot or Map No.	Assessed Values		Ratio
	Improvements	Land	

(Between Trowbridge Street and Hoyt Avenue and between Woolsey and Willow streets.)

Ward, Lot or Map No.	Improvements	Land	Ratio
2	$3,500	$1,000	78:22
3	3,500	1,000	78:22
4	3,500	1,000	78:22
5	3,450	850	80:20
6	3,450	850	80:20
7	3,450	850	80:20
9	3,450	850	80:20
12	3,500	1,000	78:22
13	3,500	1,000	78:22
14	3,500	1,000	78:22
15	1,600	1,900	49:51
16	1,700	1,600	52:48
17	2,700	1,600	63:37
18	2,100	1,600	57:43
42	3,900	1,400	74:26
43	2,000	1,400	59:41
44	900	1,400	39:61
50	1,500	1,400	52:48
51	3,100	1,400	69:31
52	2,400	2,800	46:54
54	1,100	1,400	44:56
75	5,000	1,000	83:17
76	5,000	1,000	83:17
77	5,000	1,000	83:17
78	5,000	1,000	83:17
	$143,050	$111,850	

SAMPLE DISTRICT FROM WARD TWO, BOROUGH OF QUEENS

(The district consists of parts of assessment blocks:
 175—between Centre and De Bevoise avenues and between Midwood and Washington avenues;
 176—between De Bevoise and Harmon avenues and between Midwood and Cooper avenues;
 55—between Railroad and Ludlow Avenue and between 5th Street and Whitney Avenue; and
 65—between Elmhurst and Whitney avenues and between 3d and 4th streets.)

(Standard Composite Ratio: 38.49 : 61.51)

GROUP A: PARCELS WHOSE TAXES WOULD BE INCREASED

None.

GROUP B: PARCELS WHOSE TAXES WOULD BE DECREASED

Ward, Lot or Map No.	Assessed Values Improvements	Land	Ratio
(Between Centre and De Bevoise avenues and between Midwood and Washington avenues.)			
6	$6,800	$1,200	85:15
7	3,300	800	81:19
8	3,000	800	79:21
9	3,000	800	79:21
10	3,300	800	81:19
11	3,300	800	81:19
12	3,300	800	81:19
13	3,300	800	81:19
14	3,300	800	81:19
15	3,300	800	81:19
16	3,300	800	81:19
17	3,300	800	81:19
18	3,300	800	81:19
19	3,300	800	81:19
20	3,300	800	81:19
21	3,300	800	81:19
22	3,300	800	81:19
23	3,300	800	81:19
24	3,300	800	81:19
25	3,300	800	81:19
26	3,400	800	81:19
27	3,400	800	81:19
28	3,400	800	81:19
29	3,400	800	81:19
30	3,400	1,200	74:26
(Between De Bevoise and Harmon avenues and between Midwood and Cooper avenues.)			
1	$6,300	$1,200	84:16
2	3,300	800	81:19
3	3,300	800	81:19
4	3,300	800	81:19
5	3,300	800	81:19
8	3,300	800	81:19
9	3,300	800	81:19
10	3,300	800	81:19
11	3,300	800	81:19
12	3,300	800	81:19
13	3,300	800	81:19
14	3,300	800	81:19
15	3,300	800	81:19
16	3,300	800	81:19
18	3,300	800	81:19
19	3,300	800	81:19
20	3,300	800	81:19
21	3,300	800	81:19

GROUP B: PARCELS WHOSE TAXES WOULD BE DECREASED—Continued

Ward, Lot or Map No.	Assessed Values Improvements	Land	Ratio

(Between De Bevoise and Harmon avenues and between Midwood and Cooper avenues.)

Ward, Lot or Map No.	Improvements	Land	Ratio
17	$3,300	$800	81:19
22	3,300	600	85:15
27	6,200	800	89:11
28	5,000	800	86:14
29	3,300	800	81:19
30	3,300	800	81:19
31	3,300	800	81:19
32	3,300	800	81:19
33	3,300	800	81:19
34	3,300	800	81:19
35	3,300	800	81:19
36	3,300	800	81:19
37	3,300	800	81:19
38	3,300	800	81:19
39	3,300	800	81:19
40	3,300	800	81:19
41	3,300	800	81:19
42	3,300	800	81:19
43	3,300	800	81:19
44	3,300	800	81:19
45	3,300	800	81:19
46	3,300	800	81:19

(Between Railroad and Ludlow avenues and between 5th Street and Whitney Avenue.)

Ward, Lot or Map No.	Improvements	Land	Ratio
1	$6,500	$4,000	62:38
6	3,000	1,200	71:29
7	3,000	1,200	71:29
8	2,800	1,200	70:30
9	2,800	1,200	70:30
10	2,800	1,200	70:30
11	2,800	1,200	70:30
12	2,800	1,200	70:30
13	2,800	1,200	70:30
14	2,800	1,200	70:30
15	2,800	1,200	70:30
16	3,000	1,200	71:29
27	2,250	2,250	50:50
29	2,000	3,000	40:60
31	2,000	1,500	57:43
33	2,000	1,500	57:43
35	2,200	1,500	60:40
39	3,400	1,200	74:26
40	3,300	1,200	73:27
41	3,300	1,200	73:27
42	3,300	1,200	73:27
43	3,400	1,200	74:26

(Between Elmhurst and Whitney avenues and between 3d and 4th streets.)

Ward, Lot or Map No.	Improvements	Land	Ratio
5	$3,000	$1,300	70:30
6	2,900	1,300	69:31
6½	2,900	1,300	69:31
7	2,900	1,300	69:31
8	2,900	1,300	69:31
9	2,900	1,300	69:31
10	2,900	1,300	69:31
10½	2,900	1,300	69:31
11	2,900	1,300	69:31
12	3,000	1,300	70:30
17	2,800	1,500	65:35
18	2,100	1,200	64:35
19	2,100	1,200	64:36
20	2,100	1,200	64:36
21	2,800	1,500	65:35
23	2,200	1,600	58:42

GROUP B: PARCELS WHOSE TAXES WOULD BE DECREASED

Ward, Lot or Map No.	Assessed Values		Ratio
	Improvements	Land	
(Between Elmhurst and Whitney avenues and between 3d and 4th streets.)—*Cont'd.*			
24	$2,200	$1,600	58:42
25	2,200	1,600	58:42
26	2,200	1,600	58:42
29	2,200	1,600	58:42
30	2,200	1,600	58:42
31	2,200	1,600	58:42
32	2,200	1,600	58:42
	$349,250	$118,350	

SAMPLE DISTRICT FROM WARD THREE, BOROUGH OF QUEENS

(The district consists of assessment blocks:

    75—between Percy Street and Parsons Avenue and between Lincoln and Amity streets—;

    75—between Bowne and Parsons avenues and between Amity Street and Madison Avenue—;

    77—between Parsons Avenue and Percy Street and between Madison Avenue and Amity Street—; and

    78—between Bowne and Parsons avenues and between Madison Avenue and Barclay Street.)

(Standard Composite Ratio: 39.51 : 60.49)

GROUP A: PARCELS WHOSE TAXES WOULD BE INCREASED

Ward, Lot or Map No.	Assessed Values Improvements	Land	Ratio
(Between Percy Street and Parsons Avenue and between Lincoln and Amity streets.)			
7	$2,300	$3,700	38.33:61.67
(Between Bowne and Parsons avenues and between Amity Street and Madison Avenue.)			
7	$3,600	$8,200	31:69
39	3,100	8,100	28:72
47	2,800	5,400	34:66
	$11,800	$25,400	

GROUP B: PARCELS WHOSE TAXES WOULD BE DECREASED

Ward, Lot or Map No.	Assessed Values Improvements	Land	Ratio
(Between Percy Street and Parsons Avenue and between Lincoln and Amity streets.)			
1	$6,550	$6,650	50:50
4	4,500	6,150	40:60
8	11,400	13,100	47:53
14	3,700	3,700	50:50
18	2,700	2,500	52:48
19	3,750	5,650	40:60
22	3,050	3,150	49:51
33	2,800	2,800	50:50
35	2,200	2,500	47:53
37	2,100	2,500	46:54
39	2,100	2,500	46:54
41	2,200	2,500	47:53
43	2,100	2,800	43:57
49	2,600	3,100	46:54
51	3,050	2,150	59:41
52	2,300	2,700	46:54
54	4,700	3,300	59:41
56	2,350	1,950	55:45
58	2,350	1,950	55:45
59	2,650	1,950	58:42
60	2,050	1,650	55:45
61	3,500	2,800	56:44
63	2,000	2,800	42:58
65	2,100	2,800	43:57
67	1,750	1,550	53:47
69	2,750	1,550	53:47
80	3,950	3,850	51:49
82	4,900	3,700	57:43
85	4,000	3,700	52:48

GROUP B: PARCELS WHOSE TAXES WOULD BE DECREASED

Ward, Lot or Map No.	Assessed Values		Ratio
	Improvements	Land	

(Between Bowne and Parsons avenues and between Amity Street and Madison Avenue.)

Ward, Lot or Map No.	Improvements	Land	Ratio
1	$8,300	$6,200	57:43
14	2,400	2,800	46:54
16	2,700	2,800	49:51
18	4,200	2,800	53:47
20	2,900	2,800	51:49
22	3,950	5,550	42:58
26	3,500	3,300	68:49
28	3,700	5,500	40:60
35	4,300	6,700	39:61
45	2,900	2,700	52:48
51	2,350	2,650	47:53
53	2,600	2,600	50:50

(Between Parsons Avenue and Percy Street and between Madison Avenue and Amity Street.)

Ward, Lot or Map No.	Improvements	Land	Ratio
3	$2,800	$2,700	51:49
8	13,100	12,900	50:50
20	2,225	1,775	56:44
21	2,425	1,775	58:42
22	2,800	3,600	44·56
24	2,800	1,800	61:39
25	2,400	1,800	57:43
34	3,100	2,900	52:48
36	2,550	2,150	54:46
37	2,650	2,150	55:45
39	2,650	2,150	55:45
40	2,700	2,400	53:47
42	3,600	3,200	53:47
44	3,900	4,500	46:54
50	3,700	4,000	48:52
53	2,450	2,150	53:47
54	2,500	2,700	48:52
56	2,300	2,700	46:54
58	2,500	2,700	48:52
60	2,500	2,700	48:52
62	2,500	2,700	48:52
64	2,950	4,050	42:58
66	2,950	4,050	42:58
68	3,000	2,700	53:47
70	2,950	4,050	42:58
73	3,450	4,050	46:54
76	2,300	2,700	46:54
78	2,300	2,700	46:54
80	2,300	2,700	46:54

(Between Bowne and Parsons avenues and between Madison Avenue and Barclay Street.)

Ward, Lot or Map No.	Improvements	Land	Ratio
13	$3,000	$2,800	52:48
15	3,500	2,800	56:44
17	2,450	2,250	52:48
19	2,650	2,250	54:46
21	2,850	5,050	36:64
25	2,750	5,050	35:65
34	5,700	5,300	52:48
37	3,650	3,350	52:48
39	3,250	3,350	49:51
42	2,650	3,350	44:56
	$274,100	$297,800	

SAMPLE DISTRICT FROM WARD FOUR, BOROUGH OF QUEENS

(The district consists of assessment blocks:

    279—between Ridgewood Avenue and Fulton Street and between Lefferts Avenue and Church Street—;

    280—between Fulton Street and Park Place and between Birch Street and Lefferts Avenue—;

    281—between Ridgewood Avenue and Fulton Street and between Birch Street and Lefferts Avenue—;

    282—between Fulton Street and Atlantic Avenue and between Spruce and Birch streets—;

    784—between Myrtle Avenue and Alsop Street and between Shelton Avenue and Willett Street—;

    785—between Myrtle Avenue and Alsop Street and between Willett Street and Hillside Avenue—;

    786—between Alsop and Roy streets and between Shelton Avenue and Willett Street;—and

    787—between Alsop and Roy avenues and between Willett and Hillside avenues.)

(Standard Composite Ratio: 38.49:61.51)

Group A: Parcels Whose Taxes Would Be Increased

Ward, Lot or Map No.	Assessed Values Improvements	Land	Ratio
(Between Ridgewood Avenue and Fulton Street and between Lefferts Avenue and Church Street.)			
48	$1,250	$2,750	31:69
(Between Fulton Street and Park Place and between Birch Street and Lefferts Avenue.)			
39	$350	$950	27:73
54	3,000	7,500	29:71
(Between Ridgewood Avenue and Fulton Street and between Birch Street and Lefferts Avenue.)			
31	$3,200	$7,800	29:71
63	3,000	2,300	37:43
(Between Myrtle Avenue and Alsop Street and between Shelton Avenue and Willett Street.)			
29	$1,800	$3,200	36:64
49	2,100	3,400	38:62
60	2,700	5,000	35:65
(Between Myrtle Avenue and Alsop Street and between Willett Street and Hillside Avenue.)			
1	$1,500	$3,100	33:67
21	1,700	3,800	31:69
23	1,500	3,800	27:73
47	2,000	3,200	38:62
52	1,800	3,200	36:64
54	1,800	3,200	36:64
(Between Alsop and Roy streets and between Shelton Avenue and Willett Street.)			
1	$3,000	$8,000	27:73
44	2,500	4,500	36:64
60	2,500	4,000	38:62
62	2,500	4,500	36:64
64	1,900	3,600	35:65
66	4,200	6,800	38:62
70	6,000	10,000	38:62
	$50,300	$94,600	

GROUP B: PARCELS WHOSE TAXES WOULD BE DECREASED

Ward, Lot or Map No.	Assessed Values		Ratio
	Improvements	Land	

(Between Ridgewood Avenue and Fulton Street and between Lefferts Avenue and Church Street.)

1	$3,200	$3,000	52:48
7	4,100	3,900	51:49
10	5,000	2,700	65:35
12	3,500	2,700	56:44
14	4,000	3,000	57:43
16	5,000	6,000	45:55
21	2,800	3,000	48:52
23	3,600	3,000	55:45
25	3,000	3,000	50:50
27	5,500	3,300	62:38
31	6,000	3,500	63:37
34	3,200	2,300	58:42
36	3,300	2,200	60:40
38	3,300	2,200	60:40
40	4,100	2,200	65:35
42	3,600	2,200	62:38
44	2,600	2,200	54:46
46	2,750	2,750	50:50
50	2,950	2,750	52:48

(Between Fulton Street and Park Place and between Birch Street and Lefferts Avenue.)

1	$6,800	$5,700	54:46
8	2,500	2,000	56:44
10	4,500	2,300	66:34
12	4,000	2,000	67:33
14	4,000	2,000	67:33
16	2,850	1,750	62:38
19	2,450	1,550	61:39
21	2,450	1,550	61:39
22	3,050	1,750	64:36
24	3,050	1,750	64:36
26	3,050	1,750	64:36
28	3,050	1,750	64:36
30	9,000	3,000	75:25
37	3,100	1,900	62:38
40	14,000	6,000	70:30
47	3,100	2,400	57:43
49	3,100	2,400	57:43
52	3,000	3,000	50:50
61	3,900	3,600	52:48

(Between Ridgewood Avenue and Fulton Street and between Birch Street and Lefferts Avenue.)

1	$3,000	$2,000	60:40
8	2,750	3,750	42:58
12	2,750	3,750	42:58
16	2,750	3,750	42:58
20	2,550	1,750	59:41
22	2,550	1,750	59:41
24	4,500	6,500	41:59
37	3,800	2,200	63:37
39	2,250	2,250	50:50
41	3,000	3,000	50:50
43	2,600	3,000	46:54
45	4,800	2,700	64:36
47	3,100	3,300	48:52
49	3,400	2,700	56:44
51	3,400	3,600	49:51

(Between Fulton Street and Atlantic Avenue and between Spruce and Birch streets.)

1	$3,500	$900	80:20
2	3,500	900	80:20
3	5,700	1,800	76:24
5	4,300	2,100	67:33

237

GROUP B: PARCELS WHOSE TAXES WOULD BE DECREASED

Ward, Lot or Map No.	Assessed Values		Ratio
	Improvements	Land	

(Between Fulton Street and Atlantic Avenue and between Spruce and Birch streets)—*Con.*

7	$4,500	$1,200	79:21
9	4,500	1,200	79:21
10	4,500	1,200	79:21
12	4,500	1,200	79:21
13	2,600	1,400	65:35
15	2,800	2,600	52:48
26	4,000	1,400	74:26
28	1,000	1,800	64:36
37	3,250	1,050	76:24
38	3,500	1,500	70:30
39	2,700	3,000	47:53
42	2,700	2,000	57:43
44	2,800	2,000	58:42
46	2,000	1,000	67:33
47	3,800	2,000	71:29
51	4,550	3,750	55:45
55	5,250	2,250	70:30
57	2,500	2,000	56:44
59	3,050	1,750	64:36
61	3,050	1,750	64:36

(Between Myrtle Avenue and Alsop Street and between Shelton Avenue and Willett Street.)

1	$11,000	$9,000	55:45
7	3,200	4,800	40:60
11	1,500	2,000	43:57
13	2,900	4,000	42:58
16	2,300	3,600	39:61
19	3,400	4,100	45:55
22	4,300	3,200	57:43
24	2,600	3,200	45:55
27	3,800	3,200	54:46
32	4,700	5,300	47:53
36	2,200	3,300	60:40
42	3,000	4,500	60:40
46	3,000	3,300	48:52
51	3,000	3,500	46:54
54	4,800	5,200	48:52
58	2,300	3,500	40:60

(Between Myrtle Avenue and Alsop Street and between Willett Street and Hillside Avenue.)

26	$3,850	$1,650	70:30
27	3,850	1,650	70:30
28	3,850	1,650	70:30
29	3,850	1,650	70:30
30	3,850	1,650	70:30
44	2,300	3,000	43:57
49	3,000	3,200	48:52
57	2,500	3,200	44:56
59	2,300	3,200	42:58
62	2,500	3,400	42:58

(Between Myrtle Avenue and Alsop Street and between Willett Street and Hillside Avenue.)

31	$3,850	$1,650	70:30
32	4,000	2,000	67:33
33	3,835	1,465	72:28
34	3,835	1,465	72:28
35	3,825	1,375	74:26
36	7,000	1,000	41:59

GROUP B: PARCELS WHOSE TAXES WOULD BE DECREASED

Ward, Lot or Map No.	Assessed Values		Ratio
	Improvements	Land	

(Between Alsop and Roy streets and between Shelton Avenue and Willett Street.)

Ward, Lot or Map No.	Improvements	Land	Ratio
6	$2,500	$4,700	35:65
10	2,500	2,400	51:49
12	1,900	2,400	44:56
15	2,300	3,100	43:57
17	3,100	3,100	50:50
20	2,600	3,100	46:54
24	3,700	5,300	41:59
28	4,200	3,300	56:44
30	2,100	2,300	48:52
46	2,800	4,000	41:59
50	2,700	1,800	60:40
52	2,700	1,800	60:40
54	2,700	1,800	60:40
56	2,700	1,800	60:40

(Between Alsop and Roy avenues and between Willett and Hillside avenues.)

Ward, Lot or Map No.	Improvements	Land	Ratio
26	$3,200	$3,800	46:54
28	3,200	3,800	40:54
31	2,700	3,800	42:58
34	4,000	3,600	53:47
37	2,600	2,400	52:48
39	2,600	2,400	52:48
41	2,600	2,400	52:48
43	2,600	2,400	52:48
45	2,600	2,400	52:48
47	2,300	2,700	55:45
50	2,600	2,300	53:47
52	2,600	2,300	53:47
54	2,600	2,300	53:47
56	2,600	2,300	53:47
	$477,755	$370,505	

SAMPLE DISTRICT FROM WARD FIVE, BOROUGH OF QUEENS

(The district consists of assessment blocks:
  10—between Washington and Newport avenues and between Seventh and Eighth avenues—;
  19—between Central and State avenues and between Cleveland, Nostrand and Roanoke avenues—;
  33—between Jerome and Stratton avenues and between Boulevard and Atlantic Ocean—; and
  42—between Grove and Hammels avenues and between Atlantic Ocean and Boulevard.)

(*Standard Composite Ratio: 38.49 : 61.51*)

GROUP A: PARCELS WHOSE TAXES WOULD BE INCREASED

Ward, Lot or Map No.	Assessed Values Improvements	Land	Ratio
(Between Central and State avenues and between Cleveland, Nostrand and Roanoke avenues.)			
9	$1,900	$3,100	38:62
11	1,900	3,100	38:62
17	3,600	6,000	38:62
19	1,000	7,500	12:88
22	2,000	7,500	21:79
24	3,100	6,400	33:67
30	400	4,800	8:92
33	1,700	4,800	26:74
36	2,200	4,800	31:69
39	2,500	5,000	33:67
42	1,500	8,500	15:85
56	1,500	3,200	32:68
60	1,500	7,000	18:82
62	1,500	5,700	21:79
78	3,000	6,500	32:68
(Between Jerome and Stratton avenues and between Boulevard and Atlantic Ocean.)			
3	$1,000	$5,000	17:83
13	3,200	5,800	36:64
67	3,000	5,000	38:62
(Between Grove and Hammels avenues and between Atlantic Ocean and Boulevard.)			
32½	$1,100	$1,800	38:62
	$37,600	$101,500	

GROUP B: PARCELS WHOSE TAXES WOULD BE DECREASED

Ward, Lot or Map No.	Assessed Values Improvements	Land	Ratio
(Between Washington and Newport avenues and between Seventh and Eighth avenues.)			
1	$7,200	$3,800	65:35
3	5,200	3,300	61:39
5	4,000	5,000	44:56
7	4,000	2,000	67:33
8	4,100	2,000	67:33
10	4,400	2,000	69:31
12	4,400	2,000	69:31
12½	3,800	2,000	66:34
19	3,000	2,000	60:40
20	3,000	2,000	60:40
24	4,000	2,000	67:33
27	3,000	2,000	60:40
28	4,000	2,000	67:33
29	5,500	2,000	73:27
33	4,500	2,000	69:31
34	5,000	2,500	67:33
36	3,000	3,000	50:50
45	3,700	2,000	65:35
47	6,400	5,100	57:33
52	3,200	1,800	64:36
54	2,800	1,800	61:39
66	5,650	2,850	66:34

GROUP B: PARCELS WHOSE TAXES WOULD BE DECREASED

Ward, Lot or Map No.	Assessed Values Improvements	Land	Ratio

(Between Central and State avenues and between Cleveland, Nostrand and Roanoke avenues.)

1	$2,000	$2,000	50:50
1½	2,200	2,300	49:51
	$98,050	$59,450	

(Between Central and State avenues and between Cleveland, Nostrand and Roanoke avenues.)

2	$2,200	$3,000	42:58
4	2,700	3,800	42:58
7	2,900	3,100	48:52
12	2,300	3,100	43:57
13	10,500	7,500	58:42
50	4,500	3,200	44:56
52	3,000	3,200	48:52
54	2,200	3,200	41:59
75	5,500	6,000	48:52

(Between Jerome and Stratton avenues and between Boulevard and Atlantic Ocean.)

1	$6,000	$4,000	60:40
25	9,200	5,800	61:39
28	4,700	5,800	45:55
32	4,400	5,100	46:54
35	7,000	5,000	58:42
38	12,700	7,300	68:32
41	2,300	3,200	42:58
45	2,300	3,200	42:58
52	9,000	9,500	49:51
58	4,100	3,900	51:49
61	4,500	3,900	54:46
64	4,600	3,900	54:46
72	4,500	5,000	47:53
78	4,800	4,500	52:48
81	8,750	6,750	56:44
91	11,000	9,000	55:45

(Between Grove and Hammels avenues and between Atlantic Ocean and Boulevard.)

1	$9,000	$5,000	64:36
15	1,600	900	64:36
16	1,600	900	64:36
17	1,600	900	64:36
18	2,100	900	67:33
19	2,100	900	67:33
20	2,500	1,800	58:42
21	2,500	1,800	58:42
21½	1,900	900	68:32
22	1,900	900	68:32
22½	1,650	950	63:27
23	2,000	1,000	67:33
23½	1,925	975	66:34
27	1,600	900	64:36
28	4,600	3,400	58:42
32	4,400	1,800	71:29
37	2,400	3,100	44:56
45	1,700	900	65:35
57	1,700	700	71:29
56	1,700	900	65:35
58	1,400	1,000	58:42
60	1,400	1,000	58:42
61	1,800	900	67:33
62	5,500	4,500	55:45
68	2,200	900	71:29
69	2,200	900	71:29
70	2,200	900	71:29

GROUP B: PARCELS WHOSE TAXES WOULD BE DECREASED

Ward, Lot or Map No.	Assessed Values		Ratio
	Improvements	Land	

(Between Grove and Hammels avenues and between Atlantic Ocean and Boulevard.)—*Con.*

71	$1,600	$700	70:30
72	1,600	700	70:30
73	4,600	1,600	74:26
75	1,700	700	71:29
76	1,700	1,000	63:37
77	1,700	900	65:35
	$313,775	$226,625	

V. RICHMOND

SAMPLE DISTRICT FROM WARD ONE, BOROUGH OF RICHMOND

(The district consists of assessment blocks:
7—between Sherman and Madison avenues and between First and Fourth avenues—;
1—between Westervelt Avenue, Jersey Street and Seventh Avenue.—;
9A—between Castleton Avenue, Richmond Turnpike and Jersey Street—; and
4—between Dongan and Bodine streets and between Richmond Terrace and Cedar Street.)

(Standard Composite Ratio: 39.51:60.49)

Group A: Parcels Whose Taxes Would Be Increased

Ward, Lot or Map No.	Improvements	Land	Ratio
(Between Sherman and Madison avenues and between First and Fourth avenues.)			
65	$1,000	$1,600	38:62
55	600	2,000	23:77
(Between Westervelt Avenue and Jersey Street and Seventh Avenue.)			
310	$350	$550	38.88:61.11
	$1,950	$4,150	

Group B: Parcels Whose Taxes Would Be Decreased

Ward, Lot or Map No.	Improvements	Land	Ratio
(Between Sherman and Madison avenues and between First and Fourth avenues.)			
54	$6,500	$2,000	76:24
58	2,000	800	71:29
60	1,400	800	64:36
61	1,400	800	64:36
62	2,200	800	73:27
63	900	800	53:47
64	2,200	800	73:27
66	1,600	800	67:33
69	3,200	800	80:20
70	1,400	800	64:36
71	2,800	800	78:22
72	2,000	800	71:29
73	2,400	800	75:25
74	6,800	1,600	79:21
75	1,900	800	70:30
77	2,400	2,000	55:45
78	1,600	1,600	50:50
82	3,400	1,600	68:32
83	2,600	1,200	68:32
85	2,200	1,600	58:42
86	3,500	1,600	69:31
89	2,500	1,600	61:39
90	3,000	1,600	65:35
93	3,000	1,600	65:35
94	5,500	1,600	77:23
97	2,000	1,100	65:35
98	2,125	1,075	66:34
99	2,000	1,100	65:35
100	2,125	1,075	66:34
101	2,100	1,400	60:40
102	2,200	1,500	59:41

Group B: Parcels Whose Taxes Would Be Decreased

Ward, Lot or Map No.	Assessed Values Improvements	Land	Ratio
(Between Westervelt Avenue, Jersey Street and Seventh Avenue.)			
1	$1,900	$900	68:32
2	500	600	45:55
3	2,800	1,600	64:36
5	2,500	800	76:24
7	475	425	53:47
8	1,575	425	79:21
9	1,575	425	79:21
10	1,950	450	81:19
12	1,350	450	75:25
13	650	450	59:41
15	950	450	68:32
16	1,200	900	57:43
18	1,225	475	72:28
19	1,225	475	72:28
20	1,425	475	75:25
21	1,525	475	76:24
298	850	950	47:53
299	1,550	950	62:38
301	5,800	2,700	68:32
307	1,800	500	78:22
308	900	500	64:36
309	1,800	1,200	60:40
312	700	800	47:53
313	1,100	1,000	52:48
314	700	1,100	44:56
(Between Castleton Avenue, Richmond Turnpike and Jersey Street.)			
1	$1,800	$1,400	56:44
3	2,000	600	77:23
5	1,800	600	75:25
6	1,600	600	73:27
7	1,000	600	63:37
8	1,100	1,200	48:52
10	500	600	45:55
11	1,300	600	68:32
12	1,500	600	71:29
13	1,000	1,400	42:58
15	5,200	1,500	78:22
17	2,000	600	77:23
18	3,000	600	83:17
19	2,200	600	79:21
20	4,400	1,200	79:21
22	3,000	900	77:23
24	4,000	1,200	77:23
26	4,150	1,050	80:20
28	1,050	550	66:34
29	2,000	600	77:23
32	1,150	750	61:39
(Between Dongan and Bodine streets and between Richmond Terrace and Cedar Street.)			
1	$3,100	$1,400	69:31
3	2,800	800	78:22
5	3,300	800	81:19
7	3,200	800	80:20
9	3,000	1,500	67:33
10	2,100	500	81:19
11	2,300	500	82:18
12	2,000	1,000	67:33
14	3,000	600	83:17
16	3,100	900	78:22
17	2,600	1,000	72:28
19	2,100	500	81:19

GROUP B: PARCELS WHOSE TAXES WOULD BE DECREASED

Ward, Lot or Map No.	Assessed Values		Ratio
	Improvements	Land	

(Between Dongan and Bodine streets and between Richmond Terrace and Cedar Street—*Continued*.)

20	$2,400	$500	83:17
21	3,150	750	81:19
23	3,150	750	81:19
24	3,000	1,000	75:25
26	1,900	500	79:21
27	2,800	500	85:15
28	1,625	475	77:23
37	3,500	700	83:17
38	3,300	1,200	73:27
39	5,500	1,500	79:21
42	2,300	500	82:18
43	2,300	500	82:18
44	2,000	500	80:20
45	1,820	480	79:21
46	1,980	520	79:21
47	3,000	1,000	75:25
49	1,800	500	78:22
50	1,800	500	78:22
51	1,600	500	77:23
52	3,200	1,000	76:24
54	1,800	500	78:22
55	1,800	500	78:22
56	1,800	500	78:22
	$254,850	$100,145	

SAMPLE DISTRICT FROM WARD TWO, BOROUGH OF RICHMOND

(The district consists of blocks between
 Broad and McKeon streets and between Brownell and Quinn streets;
 Richmond Road and Targee Street and between Broad and Chestnut streets;
 Richmond Road and Cebra Avenue and between Stone and Beach streets; and
 Bertha Place and Duncan Avenue and between Eddy and Theresa streets.)

(Standard Composite Ratio: 39.51:60.49)

GROUP A: PARCELS WHOSE TAXES WOULD BE INCREASED

Ward, Lot or Map No.	Assessed Values Improvements	Land	Ratio
(Between Richmond Road and Targee Street and between Broad and Chestnut streets.)			
144	$1,800	$3,200	36:64
(Between Richmond Road and Cebra Avenue and between Stone and Beach streets.)			
191	$3,500	$7,500	32:68
	$5,300	$10,700	

GROUP B: PARCELS WHOSE TAXES WOULD BE DECREASED

Ward, Lot or Map No.	Assessed Values Improvements	Land	Ratio
(Between Broad and McKeon streets and between Brownell and Quinn streets.)			
124	$1,900	$600	76:24
211	2,100	900	67:33
211A	1,000	500	67:33
212	1,700	800	68:32
213	1,700	800	68:32
214	2,000	800	71:29
215	2,600	800	77:23
216	1,800	800	69:31
217	1,000	800	56:44
218	1,700	800	68:32
219	2,000	800	71:29
220	2,200	800	73:27
221	1,200	800	60:40
224	1,900	900	68:32
225	800	900	47:53
226	1,900	900	68:32
227	900	900	50:50
228	1,700	900	65:35
229	900	900	50:50
230	2,800	900	76:24
231	4,200	1,800	67:33
233	2,500	2,800	47:53
235	2,300	1,200	66:34
236	3,600	1,200	75:25
237	1,600	1,200	57:43
238	1,800	1,200	60:40
239	1,600	1,200	57:43
242	2,600	1,200	68:32
243	4,300	1,200	78:22
244	1,100	1,200	48:52
245	1,300	1,200	45:55
246	1,300	1,200	52:48
247	1,300	1,200	52:48
248	4,000	1,200	77:23
249	3,100	1,200	72:28
250	1,400	1,400	50:50
251	4,100	2,400	63:37
253	800	1,200	40:60
254	800	1,200	40:60
255	1,000	1,200	45:55
256	6,100	2,400	72:28
258	1,600	1,200	57:43
259	4,200	1,300	76:24

GROUP B: PARCELS WHOSE TAXES WOULD BE DECREASED

Ward, Lot or Map No.	Assessed Values Improvements	Land	Ratio
(Between Richmond Road and Targee Street and between Broad and Chestnut streets.)			
134	$3,200	$900	78:22
136	1,700	1,100	61:39
142	1,300	900	59:41
228	1,200	600	67:33
229	3,000	1,200	71:29
231	1,200	600	67:33
232	700	600	54:46
233	1,300	600	68:32
234	1,300	600	68:32
235	1,100	900	55:45
236	1,900	1,200	40:60
236A	1,000	300	85:15
236B	800	400	67:33
238	....	500	67:33
239	....	500	79:21
240	1,400	600	67:33
241	900	600	60:40
242	800	700	53:47
243	3,300	1,500	69:31
(Between Richmond Road and Cebra Avenue and between Stone and Beach streets.)			
115	$2,300	$2,200	51:49
117	3,100	1,400	69:31
118	2,900	1,600	64:36
119	2,900	1,600	64:36
120	6,200	3,800	62:38
122	9,200	4,800	66:34
126	19,000	8,000	70:30
130	3,500	3,000	54:46
132	6,000	3,000	67:33
137	3,900	4,700	45:55
138	2,500	2,500	50:50
190	8,100	1,900	81:19
190A	17,000	5,000	77:23
192	5,000	3,500	59:41
193	5,500	4,000	58:42
194	1,800	1,400	56:44
195	1,800	1,000	64:36
196	2,500	2,000	56:44
198	8,000	3,000	73:27
201	2,100	2,100	50:50
203	3,700	1,800	67:33
205A	1,850	350	84:16
205B	6,100	900	87:13
206	5,500	4,000	58:42
209	2,800	3,000	48:52
211	5,500	3,000	65:35
274	1,700	500	77:23
275	2,000	600	77:23
276	2,200	600	78:22
277	2,000	500	80:20
278	2,100	500	81:19
(Between Bertha Place and Duncan Avenue and between Eddy and Theresa streets)			
16	$1,800	$800	69:31
17	1,800	800	69:31
19	1,700	800	68:32
104	3,200	1,800	64:36
107	4,500	1,000	82:18
112	3,800	1,200	76:24
129	2,200	600	79:21
131	2,400	600	80:20
133	2,300	300	88:12
134	2,600	600	81:19
	$296,850	$155,550	

SAMPLE DISTRICT FROM WARD THREE, BOROUGH OF RICHMOND

(The district consists of assessment blocks:

    23—between Simonson Place and Heberton Avenue and between Anderson Avenue and Grace Church Place—;

    24—between Simonson and Washington places and between Post and Anderson avenues—;

    25—between Heberton Avenue and Washington Place and between Anderson Avenue and Albion Place—;

    47—between Nicholas and Lafayette avenues and between Harrison Avenue and Slaight Street—; and

    159—between Sherman Street and LaFarge Avenue and between LaFarge Place and Richmond Avenue.)

(Standard Composite Ratio: 39.51 : 60.49)

Group A: Parcels Whose Taxes Would Be Increased

Ward, Lot or Map No.	Assessed Values Improvements	Land	Ratio
(Between Simonson Place and Heberton Avenue and between Anderson Avenue and Grace Church Place.)			
787	$1,000	$3,000	25:75
805	2,000	4,000	33:67
827	800	1,400	36:64
	$3,800	$8,400	

Group B: Parcels Whose Taxes Would Be Decreased

Ward, Lot or Map No.	Assessed Values Improvements	Land	Ratio
(Between Simonson Place and Heberton Avenue and between Anderson Avenue and Grace Church Place.)			
791	$1,400	$2,800	46:54
795	2,650	350	88:12
796	2,200	800	73:27
797	2,200	800	73:27
798	1,400	1,400	50:50
800	2,500	800	76:24
802	2,500	800	76:24
803	3,700	800	82:18
807	4,000	2,500	62:38
809	3,100	2,400	56:44
811	3,200	1,800	64:36
813	5,000	2,500	67:33
814	2,600	1,400	65:35
816	4,550	1,950	70:30
819	2,525	875	74:26
820	3,300	700	83:17
824	2,050	1,050	66:34
826	1,675	925	64:36
829	2,500	1,200	56:44
830	1,600	1,600	50:50
832	6,600	1,400	83:17
834	1,000	800	56:44
836	3,200	1,000	76:24
838	1,200	500	71:29
839	1,500	500	75:25
840	2,500	500	83:17
841	3,100	800	73:27

GROUP B: PARCELS WHOSE TAXES WOULD BE DECREASED

Ward, Lot or Map No.	Assessed Values		Ratio
	Improvements	Land	

(Between Simonson and Washington places and between Post and Anderson avenues.)

844	$1,500	$1,000	60:40
846	1,800	1,000	44:56
848	900	500	64:36
849	1,200	500	71:29
851	500	1,000	33:67
853	650	850	43:57
854	700	500	58:42
861	4,000	2,500	62:38
867	2,800	500	85:15
868	2,800	500	85:15
869	2,000	2,000	50:50
874	1,400	800	64:36
876	2,550	850	75:25
877	1,800	1,200	60:40

(Between Heberton Avenue and Washington Place and between Anderson Avenue and Albion Place.)

879	$3,000	$1,400	68:32
881	3,000	1,000	75:25
882	2,950	1,050	74:26
885	2,000	1,000	67:33
887	1,950	1,050	65:35
888	1,950	1,150	63:37
890	2,000	1,400	59:41
891	1,800	1,200	60:40
893	1,650	1,050	61:39
894	3,300	3,500	49:51
899	3,025	1,175	72:28
901	2,925	1,075	73:27
903	3,950	1,050	79:21
904	3,800	3,200	54:46
907	3,625	2,875	56:44
909	3,100	2,400	56:44
911	3,500	4,500	44:56

(Between Nicholas and Lafayette avenues and between Harrison Avenue and Slaight Street.)

594	$2,500	$1,000	71:29
595	3,000	800	79:21
596	2,000	800	71:29
598	2,000	600	77:23
599	2,800	1,200	70:30
601	1,900	600	76:24
602	2,200	600	79:21
603	2,200	600	79:21
604	1,900	600	76:24
605	2,000	600	77:23
606	2,300	700	77:23
610	2,500	1,000	71:29
612	1,400	800	64:36
614	6,900	1,400	83:17
616	1,500	600	71:29
617	1,400	400	78:22
619	1,600	400	80:20
620	1,400	400	78:22
621	1,400	400	78:22
622	1,000	800	56:44
624	2,400	1,100	69:31
626	1,200	800	60:40

GROUP B: PARCELS WHOSE TAXES WOULD BE DECREASED

Ward, Lot or Map No.	Assessed Values		Ratio
	Improvements	Land	

(Between Sherman Street and LaFarge Avenue and between LaFarge Place and Richmond Avenue.)

Ward, Lot or Map No.	Improvements	Land	Ratio
1	$2,400	$600	80:20
3	1,100	300	79:21
4	1,200	300	80:20
5	1,250	250	83:17
6	1,200	400	75:25
9	1,325	475	74:26
10	1,350	250	84:16
11	1,350	250	84:16
12	1,300	500	72:28
14	1,150	250	82:18
15	950	250	79:21
16	4,100	400	89:11
17	1,400	300	82:18
18	1,400	600	70:30
20	1,400	600	70:30
22	1,400	300	82:18
23	2,600	400	87:13
24	1,200	500	71:29
26	3,000	1,500	67:33
31	1,050	450	70:30
33	950	250	79:21
34	1,650	350	83:17
	$231,855	$110,800	

SAMPLE DISTRICT FROM WARD FOUR, BOROUGH OF RICHMOND

(The district consists of blocks
Between Townsend and Norwood avenues and between Bay and Centre Streets; and Between Staten Island Rapid Transit Railroad and Ormond Place and between Butler Place and Chestnut Avenue.)

(*Standard Composite Ratio: 39.51:60.49*)

Group A: Parcels Whose Taxes Would Be Increased

Ward, Lot or Map No.	Assessed Values — Improvements	Land	Ratio
(Between Townsend and Norwood avenues and between Bay and Centre streets.)			
100	$3,100	$5,400	36:64
(Between Staten Island Rapid Transit Railroad and Ormond Place and between Butler Place and Chestnut Avenue.)			
114	$900	$2,100	30:70
	$4,000	$7,500	

Group B: Parcels Whose Taxes Would Be Decreased

Ward, Lot or Map No.	Assessed Values — Improvements	Land	Ratio
(Between Townsend and Norwood avenues and between Bay and Centre streets.)			
79	$3,800	$2,600	59:41
82	3,050	1,250	71:29
84	2,550	1,250	67:33
89	900	900	50:50
90	900	900	50:50
91	3,600	2,400	60:40
104	4,100	2,400	63:37
108	3,200	2,400	57:43
110	3,200	1,200	65:35
112	2,550	1,150	69:31
113	2,700	1,100	71:29
115	1,625	1,375	54:46
116	2,850	1,650	63:37
118	1,400	900	61:39
120	2,300	950	71:29
121	4,500	2,000	69:31
127	1,800	600	75:25
128	1,900	600	76:24
129	3,800	1,200	76:24
129a	1,300	300	81:19
(Between Staten Island Rapid Transit Railroad and Ormond Place and between Butler Place and Chestnut Avenue.)			
126	$5,500	$1,500	79:21
131	1,500	500	75:25
395	5,250	1,750	75:25
406	1,200	600	67:33
418	1,275	225	85:15
424	5,100	900	85:15
430	900	200	82:18
440	1,250	250	83:17
442	1,150	250	82:18
444	1,150	250	82:18
446	2,300	500	82:18
450	1,250	250	83:17
452	1,150	250	82:18
454	1,150	250	82:18
456	1,250	250	83:17
458	1,250	250	83:17
460	1,050	450	70:30
464	5,550	450	93:7
471	8,750	2,250	80:20
	$100,000	$38,450	

SAMPLE DISTRICT FROM WARD FIVE, BOROUGH OF RICHMOND

(The district consists of assessment blocks:
   14—between Amboy Road and Eureka Place and between Butler Avenue and Bentley Street—;
   21—between E. Broadway and Amboy Road and between Johnson Avenue and William Street—; and
   25—between Wood and Fisher avenues and between E. Broadway and Amboy Road.)

(Standard Composite Ratio: 39.51:60.49)

GROUP A: PARCELS WHOSE TAXES WOULD BE INCREASED

Ward, Lot or Map No.	Assessed Values Improvements	Land	Ratio
(Between Amboy Road and Eureka Place and between Butler Avenue and Bentley Street)			
4	$1,025	$1,575	39:61
(Between E. Broadway and Amboy Road and between Johnson Avenue and William Street.)			
3	$450	$850	35:65
38	700	1,100	39:61
	$2,175	$3,525	

GROUP B: PARCELS WHOSE TAXES WOULD BE DECREASED

Ward, Lot or Map No.	Assessed Values Improvements	Land	Ratio
(Between Amboy Road and Eureka Place and between Butler Avenue and Bentley Street.)			
1	$1,900	$1,400	58:42
7	2,450	950	72:28
9	1,000	1,100	48:52
12	3,150	550	85:15
13	1,800	500	78:22
16	1,650	550	74:26
18	1,600	550	74:26
20	1,150	550	68:32
22	1,500	700	68:32
24	1,200	700	63:37
26	1,300	700	65:35
34	1,950	850	70:30
36	1,725	1,275	58:42
39	1,875	1,125	62:38
42	1,625	1,275	56:44
45	1,600	1,000	62:38
(Between E. Broadway and Amboy Road and between Johnson Avenue and William Street.)			
6	2,400	1,600	60:40
9	1,900	1,200	61:39
11	2,500	1,700	60:40
14	1,500	1,100	58:42
16	7,550	2,150	78:22
20	2,025	675	75:25
22	1,700	800	68:32
24	1,300	500	72:28
25	1,500	600	71:29
27	1,725	875	66:34
30	1,825	875	68:32
33	600	875	41:59
36	950	750	56:44
41	5,600	1,200	82:18
47	900	900	50:50
51	775	1,125	41:59
55	2,000	600	77:23

GROUP B: PARCELS WHOSE TAXES WOULD BE DECREASED

Ward, Lot or Map No.	Assessed Values Improvements	Land	Ratio

(Between E. Broadway and Amboy Road and between Johnson Avenue and William Street.)—*Continued.*

57	$1,100	$700	56:44
59	1,300	700	65:35
61	1,800	700	72:28
63	900	600	60:40
65	1,300	600	68:32
67	1,000	600	63:37
69	1,450	675	69:31
71	1,525	1,075	59:41
74	1,075	425	72:28
76	1,125	775	59:41
79	700	300	70:30
81	3,100	1,700	65:35
85	2,075	2,125	49:51
90	12,925	5,175	79:21
102	1,300	1,100	54:46
105	2,000	1,100	65:35
108	1,700	1,100	61:39
111	2,300	1,100	68:32
114	2,500	1,100	69:31
117	2,600	1,100	70:30
120	1,675	825	67:33
122	2,400	1,000	71:29
124	2,575	825	76:24
126	1,900	2,900	40:60
135	2,950	950	76:24
137	1,600	1,200	57:43
140	2,000	1,200	63:37
143	1,500	1,200	56:44
146	1,500	1,200	56:44
149	1,300	1,800	42:58
170	5,600	800	87:13
185	1,200	300	80:20

(Between Wood and Fisher Avenues and between E. Broadway and Amboy Road.)

1	$2,200	$1,200	65:35
5	2,175	725	75:25
7	3,450	1,350	72:28
10	1,525	675	69:31
12	1,175	1,225	49:51
15	1,100	700	61:39
17	1,500	1,000	60:40
20	2,700	1,000	73:27
22	3,850	1,150	77:23
26	1,400	600	70:30
28	1,700	600	74:26
29	1,400	600	70:30
30	1,400	600	70:30
32	1,700	600	74:26
33	1,900	600	76:24
36	2,350	1,150	67:33
38	1,400	600	70:30
39	3,425	475	88:12
41	1,625	475	77:23
42	2,550	1,150	69:31
45	1,425	675	68:32
54	2,075	1,225	63:37
56	1,400	600	70:30
58	1,400	600	70:30
60	2,075	725	74:26
62	1,900	700	73:27
64	1,900	700	73:27
66	1,600	700	70:30

GROUP B: PARCELS WHOSE TAXES WOULD BE DECREASED

Ward, Lot or Map No.	Assessed Values		Ratio
	Improvements	Land	

(Between Wood and Fisher avenues and between E. Broadway and Amboy Road—*Continued*)

73	$1,900	$600	76:24
75	2,400	600	80:20
85	1,200	1,800	40:60
87	1,550	750	67:33
89	2,275	825	73:27
94	1,725	775	69:31
96	1,725	575	75:25
98	2,150	650	77:23
100	1,825	975	65:35
103	1,725	1,675	51:49
108	1,325	775	63:37
110	1,050	650	62:38
112	1,925	675	64:36
114	1,150	650	64:36
116	2,425	675	78:22
118	1,850	1,050	64:36
121	2,700	1,000	63:37
125	2,075	925	69:31
126	3,425	675	84:16
130	4,525	675	87:13
132	2,750	650	81:19
134	1,475	725	67:33
138	1,625	675	71:29
142	2,525	675	79:21
144	2,150	650	77:23
146	1,650	650	72:28
	$241,600	$111,650	

HJ
9289
.N7
H2

Haig

Some probable effects of the exemption of improvements from taxation

287496

A.A. Twichell - 953
500 So Div

Printed in Dunstable, United Kingdom